Structural Fabrics in
Deep Sea Drilling Project Cores
from Forearcs

Micromelange: Fractured quartz grains coated with scaly clay from cataclastic shear zone, Barbados Ridge complex. See Lucas and Moore (this volume).

The Geological Society of America
Memoir 166

Structural Fabric in Deep Sea Drilling Project Cores From Forearcs

Edited by

J. Casey Moore
Department of Earth and Marine Sciences
University of California, Santa Cruz
Santa Cruz, California 95064

1986

Published by The Geological Society of America, Inc.
3300 Penrose Place, P.O. Box 9140, Boulder, Colorado 80301

Printed in U.S.A.

GSA Books Science Editor Campbell Craddock

Library of Congress Cataloging-in-Publication Data

Structural fabrics in Deep Sea Drilling Project cores
    from forearcs.

   (Memoir / The Geological Society of America ; 166)
   Includes bibliographies.
   1. Petrofabric analysis.   2. Marine sediments.
3. Rock deformation.   4. Diagenesis.   5. Metamorphism
(Geology)   6. Island arcs.   7. Deep Sea Drilling Project.
I. Moore, J. Casey, 1945–   . II. Series: Memoir
(Geological Society of America) ; 166.
QE440.S78   1986   551.8   86-22864
ISBN 0-8137-1166-5

Contents

v

Preface

Deep Sea Drilling Project cores from forearcs have a known tectonic setting and catch deformational and diagenetic-metamorphic processes while they are occurring. Analysis of the fabrics from these cores has great potential for furthering our understanding of initial structural processes in accretionary wedges, and for providing new insight into the evolution of ancient subduction complexes. Studies of these cores, conducted in the context of each drilling leg, have elucidated the structural development of forearcs but have understandably lacked consistency between legs in terminology, approach, and detail.

In order to bring this critical information to a broad geological audience in a uniform and condensed format, a group of geologists undertook the structural study of virtually all cores collected from forearcs during the Deep Sea Drilling Project. Neil Lundberg, at that time a post-doctoral researcher at the University of California at Santa Cruz, acted as a "common set of eyes" and re-examined DSDP cores from forearcs at the repositories in La Jolla, California, and Palisades, New York. Neil carefully described the fabrics in a consistent manner and logged their location at each site. The remainder of the structural synthesis group – Ed Beutner, Darrell Cowan, Rob Knipe, Steve Lucas, and Casey Moore – met during the springs of 1982 and 1983 in La Jolla where Neil reviewed his work, and the group sampled cores for analytical studies. Results of our structural synthesis were presented orally at the Penrose Conference on Structural Styles and Deformational Fabrics of Accretionary Complexes in the spring of 1984. This volume provides the principal written summary of our efforts.

The heart of this volume, Chapter 2, provides a comprehensive macroscopic and microscopic description of the cores. This catalogue of structural fabrics is complemented by Chapter 1, which includes tectonic overviews of the forearcs sampled by the cores, and Chapters 3 through 6 provide in-depth studies of especially significant structural features: faults, scaly fabrics, veins, and cataclastic fabrics. Chapters 7 and 8 present detailed analyses of core mineralogy and physical properties, respectively, which lead to fundamental insights into the incipient alteration of sediment in accretionary wedges. Experiments relevant to the interpretation of structural fabrics of DSDP cores constitute the subject of Chapter 9. The final chapter provides a theoretical overview of deformation mechanisms operative during deformation of material from DSDP cores, and the transition to deformation mechanisms that appear to be dominant in equivalent, more deeply buried rocks.

We gratefully acknowledge the Submarine Geology and Geophysics Program of the National Science Foundation (grants OCE8110394 and OCE8315836) for support of the synthesis and a generous publication subsidy that allowed reasonable pricing of this volume. The staff of the Deep Sea Drilling Project provided convenient access to the core repositories and graciously hosted our two meetings in La Jolla. We are also indebted to those who willingly reviewed the volume manuscripts, including Ken Aalto, Mariam Baltuck, Mark Brandon, Tim Byrne, Mark Cloos, Dan Davis, Grenville Draper, Jim Hein, Dave Larue, Alex Maltman, John Maxwell, Ric Sibson, Eli Silver, Carol Simpson, Bob Speed, Glenn Stockmal, Othmar Tobisch, Chi Wang, and Roland von Huene. We thank Cam Craddock, GSA Books Editor, for advice as well as his independent review of the entire manuscript.

This volume is dedicated to those of the international scientific community who have participated on the many cruises of the Deep Sea Drilling Project. These scientists willingly spent months at sea, receiving little financial remuneration but hopefully rich scientific satisfaction. To these people we owe the history of the oceans as we know it today, and the credit for collecting the materials synthesized here. This volume is also dedicated to the partners and families of the participating scientists who accepted their extended absences, and specifically to Susan, Allison, and Jay who have supported me during five drilling cruises.

Casey Moore
Santa Cruz
December, 1985

Geological Society of America
Memoir 166
1986

Tectonic overview of Deep Sea Drilling Project transects of forearcs

J. Casey Moore
Department of Earth and Marine Sciences
University of California, Santa Cruz
Santa Cruz, California 95064

Neil Lundberg
Department of Geological and Geophysical Sciences
Princeton University
Princeton, New Jersey 08544

ABSTRACT

Sediment-dominated forearcs of the northern Barbados Ridge, southern Mexico, and landward of the Nankai Trough show evidence of accretion of deep-sea and trench sediments in the style of fold-and-thrust belts; sediments are imbricately offscraped at the base of the trench slope and underplated at greater depths, perhaps locally via duplex accretion. Diminishing seismic coherence of accreted deposits during uplift suggests continuing structural evolution and dewatering, with the final result resembling the stratally disrupted accretionary complexes exposed on land. Fold-and-thrust style deformation is therefore a transient structural state in many accretionary wedges.

Sediment starved forearcs off Guatemala and the Marianas are underlain by igneous basement of either oceanic or volcanic-arc origin. Most of the oceanic sediment of the subducting plate is thrust beneath the base of the trench slope with little if any accretion. Underthrust sediment may be underplated or subducted. The seaward margin of the Mariana forearc has been tectonically truncated; Guatemala may have been either tectonically truncated or the site of prolonged subduction without accretion.

Forearc evolution off northern Japan involves superposition of differing tectonic regimes with tectonic erosion followed by accretion.

INTRODUCTION

From 1978 through 1982, the Deep Sea Drilling Project (DSDP), under sponsorship of the International Program of Ocean Drilling (IPOD), completed a series of transects across subduction zones that provide almost all the basic data for this tectonic overview and the volume that follows (Fig. 1). Prior DSDP penetrations at subduction zones had been at scattered localities, of which only one (Site 181, Leg 18 DSDP, Eastern Aleutian Trench) is discussed (see Lundberg & Moore, this volume). The sampling transects plus associated multichannel seismic reflection data indicated significant structural variation between individual convergent margins. Here we review the tectonic setting of each of these active margin transects in order to provide a context for the studies of small-scale fabrics that follow. Our overview is heavily dependent upon the Initial Reports from each of the cruises and perspectives obtained from previous summaries of active-margin drilling (e.g. von Huene, 1984; Uyeda, 1982) in addition to other insights developed since publication of the Initial Reports.

The following terminology is used here for the various forearcs described. *Accretionary wedge* refers to the mass of material in the forearc region that has been transferred from the underthrusting to overthrusting plate. Slope deposits, accumulated in situ, are considered distinct from the tectonically transferred accretionary wedge. *Offscraping* describes accretion at the base of the trench slope (Scholl and others, 1980). The *deformation front* is defined as the initial folding or thrusting of incoming material of the oceanic plate at the base of the trench slope or locally in an incipient state seaward of the base of the trench slope. *Underplating* refers to material transfer to the base of the accretionary wedge at depth (Watkins and others, 1981). The underplating

1

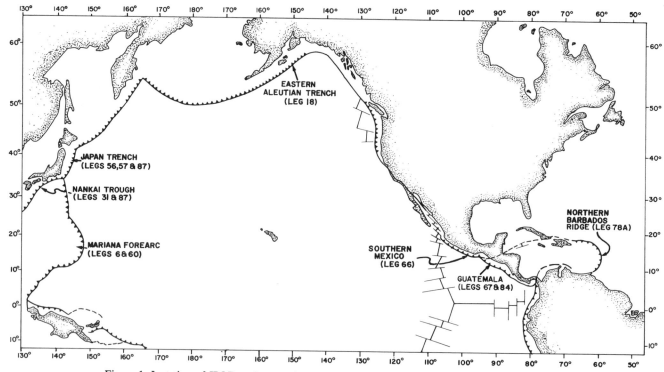

Figure 1. Location of IPOD active margin transects and Site 181, Leg 18, adjacent to the Eastern Aleutian Trench. Site 181 of Leg 18 does not lie on a transect but is discussed by Lundberg and Moore (this volume).

process may transfer material in the style of duplexes of fold-and-thrust belts (Silver and others, 1985). *Subduction* describes the descent of sediment or crust of the lower plate to mantle depths beneath the upper plate of a convergent plate boundary (Scholl and others, 1980). Accordingly sediment may be underthrust beneath the base of the trench slope and either underplated or truly subducted. *Subduction erosion* refers to the tectonic removal of material from the accretionary wedge during underthrusting (Scholl and others, 1980). *Tectonic erosion* or *tectonic truncation* refers to a non-specific type of crustal erosion that could be due either to subduction or strike-slip faulting (Karig, 1974). *Trench upper slope* and *trench lower slope* refer to those respective portions of the slope; they are commonly separated by either a *mid-slope terrace* or structural high (the *forearc outer ridge* of Dickinson and Seely [1979]). *Trench outer slope* describes the seaward slope of the trench.

Our review begins with clearly accretionary plate boundaries, continues with margins showing evidence for nonaccretion or tectonic erosion, and ends with a transect exhibiting a clearly defined composite history.

NORTHERN BARBADOS RIDGE, LEG 78A: ACCRETION, UNDERTHRUSTING, AND HIGH FLUID PRESSURES

The Barbados Ridge is one of the broadest accretionary

wedges in the world (Fig. 2). It is especially voluminous in the south where a thick abyssal fan sequence is being accreted. The southern Barbados Ridge is characterized by seismically defined folds and thrust faults in offscraped sediment with subjacent underthrusting of a thick, acoustically layered sequence beneath a prominent décollement (Westbrook and others, 1984; Biju-Duval and others, 1982). In the Leg 78A area of the northern Barbados Ridge the upper hemipelagic portion of the incoming sedimentary sequence is offscraped, whereas the lower pelagic portion is underthrust beneath a décollement (Fig. 3; Ngokwey, and others, 1984). Because the incoming sedimentary section in the Leg 78A area is thinner than that to the south, folds and thrust faults are not commonly seismically resolvable in the offscraped sequence.

In the Leg 78A area, drilling at Sites 541 and 542 penetrated the offscraped sedimentary sequence to the décollement, at which point unstable hole conditions prevented further deepening (Moore and Biju-Duval, 1984). Thrust faults that repeat the recovered section are documented biostratigraphically, lithologically, and structurally in cores (Fig. 3). Scaly mudstone and stratal disruption are developed along thrust faults and the décollement (Cowan and others, 1984; Moore and others, this volume). The additive displacements as well as volumetric balancing of the cross section (Fig. 3) indicate that only a small percentage of the total plate convergence is accounted for by thrusting at the deformation front of the northern Barbados Ridge (Moore and

TABLE 1. CHARACTERISTICS OF OCEANIC CRUST UNDERTHRUSTING FOREARCS AT DSDP TRANSECTS

Locality	Sediment Thickness (m)	Age Oceanic Crust	Convergence rate (km/m.y.)	Azimuth (degrees)	Azimuth ∧ Trench degrees[*]	Perpendicular rate (km/m.y.)	Reference
Barbados	1000	L. Cret.	19	282	65	17	Minster and Jordan (1978)
Barbados	1000	L. Cret.	37	245	78	36	Sykes and others (1982)
Nankai	1950	Miocene	26	313	75	25	Ranken and others (1984)
S. Mexico	700	Miocene	67	038	74	64	Minster and Jordan (1978)
Guatemala	500	Miocene	74	28	82	73	Minster and Jordan (1978)
Marianas	1125/225[**]	L. Jur.	71	323	32	38	Ranken and others (1984)
Japan	450?/380[**]	E. Cret.	104	290	80	102	Minster and Jordan (1978)

   * Azimuth ∧ Trench decribes angle between true azimuth and the azimuth of the trench axis and provides the basis for determining the perpendicular rate of convergence.

   ** Sediment thickness and age of oceanic crust were compiled from respective Initial Report Volumes that are referenced in text. Sediment thickness refers to total sediment at base of slope; thickness is measured from top of oceanic crust; in the case of the Marianas and Japan, asterisked value refers to thickness of sediment above high velocity cherty "basement" that characterizes much of the old oceanic crust of the Western Pacific. This thickness of lesser consolidated/lithified sediment would therefore be physically comparable to that overlying the oceanic crust at other localities and most likely to be offscraped.

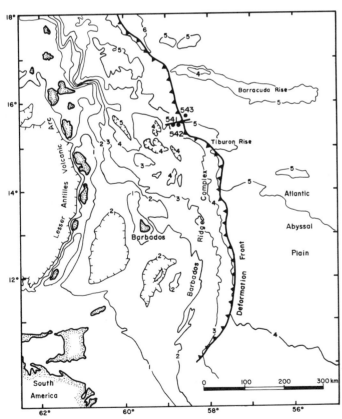

Figure 2. Location of Leg 78A drilling sites near deformation front of Barbados Ridge complex. Bathymetric contours in kilometers.

Biju-Duval, 1984). Substantial additional shortening must be taken up arcward across the accretionary wedge. Downhole temperature data (Davis and Hussong, 1984) as well as an inadvertent packer experiment (Moore and Biju-Duval, 1984) indicate that the décollement and associated active thrust faults harbor abnormal, nearly lithostatic, fluid pressures. The overpressured décollement, in turn, permits underthrusting of relatively weak sediment to at least 72 km arcward of the deformation front (Westbrook and others, 1982).

The Leg 78A cores consist entirely of hemipelagic and pelagic sediments offscraped from the Tiburon Rise, which is elevated above the terrigenous turbidite flows of the adjacent abyssal plain. Lithologically, the Leg 78A area may be a poor analog of the siliciclastic-dominated accretionary complexes common in the stratigraphic record.

NANKAI TROUGH, LEGS 31 AND 87 DSDP: FOLD AND THRUST STYLE DEFORMATION

The Nankai Trough marks the boundary between Eurasia and the Philippine Sea Plate along southwestern Japan. This subduction zone was the site of a single penetration during Leg 31 DSDP and a series of holes during Leg 87 DSDP (Fig. 4). Drilling and associated seismic data indicate that the initial deformation of the incoming sedimentary column occurs in the style of a classic fold-and-thrust belt (Fig. 5; Aoki and others, 1982; Karig, Kagami, and others, 1983; Karig, 1986). Here the upper 1300 m of sediments (trench fill and basinal sediments) form an

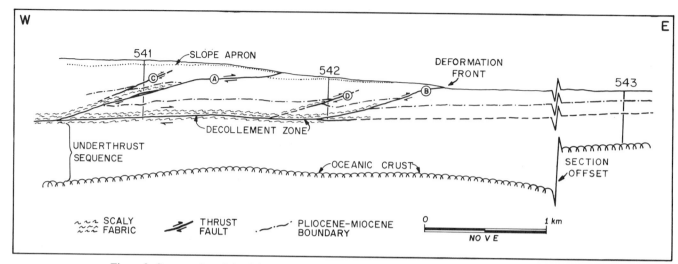

Figure 3. Cross-section of the deformation front of the northern Barbados Ridge in the Leg 78A area. Biostratigraphically defined faults A and B have greater than 70 m throw; faults C and D have less than 34 m throw. The cross section has no vertical exaggeration (VE).

imbricate stack at the deformation front, and the lower 600 m of sediment is underthrust beneath a décollement (Karig, 1986). Sediments in the Nankai Trough consist of hemipelagic muds, thin (less than 10 cm) sand and silt layers, and local coarse sand turbidites; subjacent sediments carried in from the adjacent Shikoku Basin are largely hemipelagic. Sedimentation rates in the trench range from about 900 m/m.y. to less than 300 m/m.y. (Kagami, Karig and others, 1986). The imbricate thrusts develop initially with a 30 degree landward dip, a horizontal spacing of about 3 km, and a maximum seismically definable displacement of 2.5 km (Karig, 1985).

Karig (1986) argued that two thirds of the 2 cm/yr convergence rate is taken up within 15 km landward of the deformation front with the remainder absorbed further landward across the accretionary wedge. This concentration of shortening near the base of the trench slope contrasts with the minor percentage of deformation taken up near the deformation front of the Barbados Ridge. Apparently the wide Barabados wedge provides a greater cross sectional area for strain distribution relative to the narrower Nankai accretionary wedge.

The Nankai accretionary wedge loses seismic coherence in a landward direction, presumably due to the continuing landward tilting of bedding surface, foliation development, and folding. This continuing deformation apparently results in the transformation of the aseismically defined imbricately thrust structural style to a stratally disrupted sequence characteristic of the accretionary complex exposed on Shikoku, northwest of the Nankai Trough (e.g. Taira and others, 1982).

MIDDLE AMERICA TRENCH OFF SOUTHERN MEXICO, LEG 66: PROGRESSIVE ACCRETION

The Middle America Trench off southern Mexico is bor-

dered on its landward side by a steep trench slope that lacks a forearc basin, a narrow continental shelf, and rugged coastal mountains (Fig. 6). Seismic reflection data indicate that the lower slope is underlain by landward-dipping reflectors; continental crust is the basement of the upper slope; the contact between the landward dipping reflectors and the continental crust is an acoustically diffuse "transition zone" (Fig. 7; Shipley, 1982).

The Middle America Trench in the Leg 66 area off southern Mexico is dominated by sand with an adjacent inner slope mantled by hemipelagic mud (Watkins, Moore and others, 1982). Drilling results confirm that landward-dipping reflectors beneath the inner slope consist of accreted sandy trench deposits that increase in age upslope to about 10 m.y. (Moore and others, 1982). Since the landward-dipping reflectors probably represent bedding surfaces, a gross stratigraphic inversion occurs, suggesting

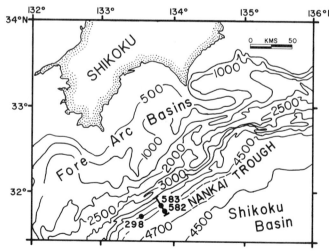

Figure 4. Location of Legs 31, 87 drilling sites and associated seismic data in Nankai Trough area, southwestern Japan.

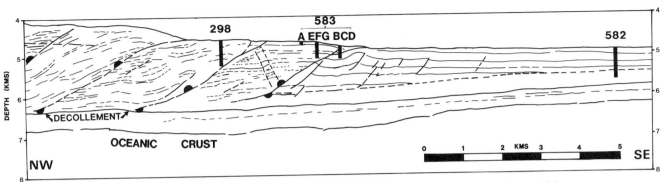

Figure 5. Depth section of the deformation front of the Nankai Trough subduction zone (Karig, 1986). Closed half circles show estimates of offset of thrust faults.

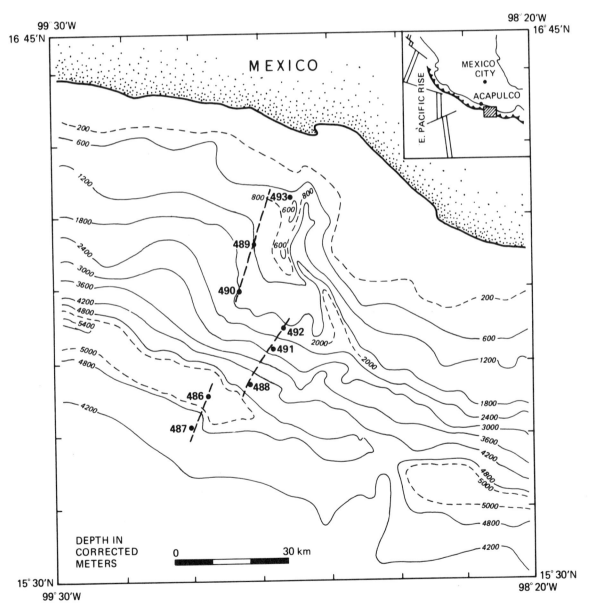

Figure 6. Location of Leg 66 drill sites spanning the Middle America Trench off southern Mexico. Cross section in Figure 7 extends along dashed line.

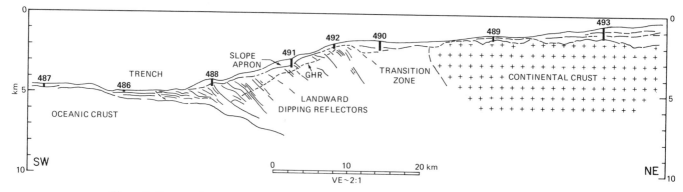

Figure 7. Cross section across the Middle America Trench off Southern Mexico in the Leg 66 drilling area (Moore and others, 1982). Vertical exaggeration (VE) is about 2:1.

imbricate thrusting. In contrast to the northern Barbados Ridge, none of the Leg 66 drill holes penetrated a biostratigraphically defined thrust fault, probably because high sedimentation rates present here result in thick fossil zones and therefore require a very deep hole to penetrate inverted zones. Paleobathymetry of drill cores landward of the zone of imbricate thrusting indicate continued uplift of the offscraped deposits (McMillen and Bachman, 1982), suggesting a subjacent process of basal accretion or underplating (Watkins and others, 1982).

The forearc off southern Mexico is characterized by a very young accretionary wedge that has grown by imbricate thrusting at the toe of the trench slope and by underplating at depth. A portion of the incoming sediment may also be subducted (Watkins and others, 1982). This young accretionary wedge lies in fault contact with older continental crust of sharply differing physical properties. Southern Mexico exemplifies a convergent plate boundary that has been tectonically truncated with subsequent accretion.

GUATEMALA FOREARC: LEGS 67 AND 84

Drilling in the Guatemala forearc (Fig. 8) was initiated with the expectation of penetrating an imbricately thrusted, offscraped sedimentary sequence (Seely and others, 1974); instead, drilling here provided the best example of a trench slope underlain by mafic rocks of principally ophiolitic affinity (Fig. 9; von Huene and Aubouin, 1982; Aubouin and von Huene, 1985). The discordance between ages of the incoming oceanic crust (Miocene) and the mafic basement at the toe of the slope (Cretaceous) indicates a lack of Neogene accretion and perhaps subduction erosion (Aubouin and von Huene, 1985). The mafic basement of the Guatemalan forearc consists of basalt, diabase, gabbro, and peridotite, and includes rocks metamorphosed to amphibolite facies. Although these rocks are principally of ophiolitic affinity, basaltic andesite occurs near the base of the slope (Aubouin and von Huene, 1985). The mafic basement yields Cretaceous radiometric ages and is overlain unconformably by Eocene sedimentary deposits (Aubouin and von Huene, 1985). According to

Seely (1977) and von Huene, Aubouin and others (1985), the Guatemalan shelf edge and trench slope underwent uplift in Paleogene time; a comparable history is inferred for similar rocks exposed on the Nicoya Peninsula of Costa Rica (Lundberg, 1982).

With the possible exception of Upper Cretaceous limestone at the toe of the trench slope all sediments cored from the Guatemalan slope were deposited during uplift (Aubouin and von Huene, 1985). The principal lithology of the Guatemalan slope deposits is hemipelagic and siliceous mud (mudstone) with subsidiary amounts of chalk (limestone) and sand (sandstone). Near the base of the slope, debris flows contain clasts of ophiolitic rock that are as much as 50 m in diameter. Along the IPOD transect, the trench fill is about 100 m thick and consists of hemipelagic mud and turbidites (von Huene, Aubouin and others, 1985). The absence of offscraped trench and Cocos-plate sediments beneath the inner slope indicates that all incoming deposits are being underthrust at the toe of the slope, and subsequently underplated at depth and/or subducted. Abnormally high fluid pressures beneath the slope probably facilitate underthrusting of the trench sediments (von Huene, 1985). The incoming oceanic plate is broken into horsts and grabens (Aubouin and von Huene, 1985) that are not filled by sediment in the trench axis. Thus, little sediment is available for accretion at the base of the trench slope. The horsts and grabens may also facilitate subduction erosion (Hilde, 1983).

MARIANA FOREARC: LEGS 6 AND 60

The Mariana forearc overlies a type-example intraoceanic subduction zone. Because this forearc region is isolated from any continental mass, sediment found in the forearc consists of pelagic deposits and detritus from the adjacent volcanic arc. The Mariana forearc is the most sediment-starved of any transected by DSDP. The following summary is based principally on an IPOD transect drilled during Leg 60 DSDP (Hussong, Uyeda, and others, 1982), although this forearc was penetrated by a single hole during Leg 6 DSDP (Fischer, Heezen, and others, 1971).

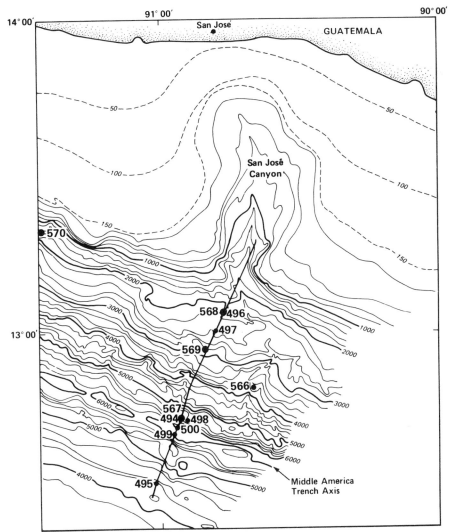

Figure 8. Location map for Guatemala forearc drilling, Legs 67 and 84. After von Huene, Aubouin and others (1985).

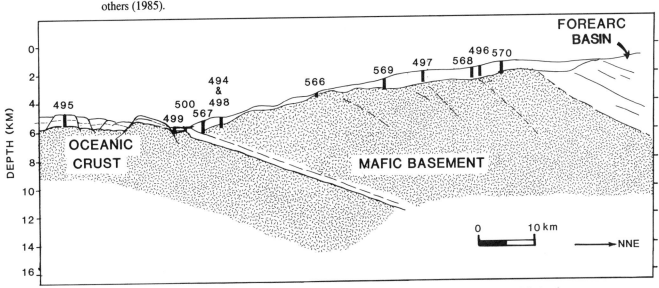

Figure 9. Cross section through Guatemala forearc after von Huene and Aubouin (1982) and Aubouin and von Huene (1985). Vertical exaggeration is about 2.5:1.

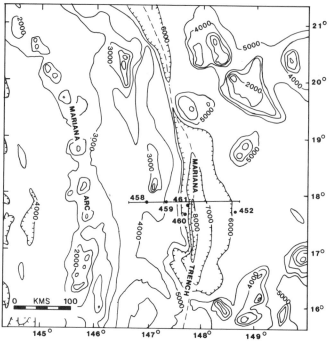

Figure 10. Location of Leg 60 drill sites in Mariana forearc as shown in Figure 11. Site 60 from Leg 6 lies off location map to the south near Guam.

song, 1980; Meijer and others, 1982). In addition, the forearc sediment apron is cut by numerous high-angle faults that may have both normal and strike-slip movement (Mrozowski and Hayes, 1980; Lundberg and Moore, this volume).

Sites 460 and 461 penetrated the shallow cover of the lower slope, revealing Quaternary radiolarian ooze and perhaps older (Eocene and Oligocene) pebbly mudstone with fragments of igneous and metamorphic rocks (Hussong, Uyeda, and others, 1982). The geochemistry of some of the basic fragments indicates that they are of arc origin (Wood and others, 1982), suggesting exposure of arc basement on the lower slope east of the outer high. Sediments at these lower slope sites contained reworked Mesozoic fossils, including Upper Cretaceous radiolarians and nannofossils, and Upper Jurassic *Calpionellids*. Site 452, located on the trench outer slope, penetrated a thin Quaternary sequence disconformably overlying an Upper Cretaceous cherty claystone; the resulting Paleogene hiatus is characteristic of this portion of the Western Pacific (Hussong, Uyeda and others, 1982). Oceanic basement was not reached at Site 452 but is inferred to be Late Jurassic, based on magnetic data (Hussong and Fryer, 1982).

Exposure of arc basement rock beyond the outer high and the dominance of pelagic and volcaniclastic deposits distinguishes the Mariana forearc from others transected by DSDP. The presence of reworked Mesozoic fossils on the lower trench slope suggests that some of the incoming Mesozoic oceanic crust has been accreted. Dredge hauls analyzed by Bloomer (1983) indicate a dominance of arc rocks seaward of the trench slope break with local examples of alkalic basalts, Mesozoic sedimentary rocks, and sheared sedimentary rocks; Bloomer believes the latter three rock types were derived from accreted seamounts. Accordingly the wedge of material labeled "Accretionary Wedge" on Figure 11 probably consists of offscraped seamounts and material reworked down-slope from the arc basement. Our interpretation of an accretionary wedge beneath the lowermost trench slope varies from the preferred view of Hussong and Uyeda (1982). Karig and Ranken (1983) also have argued for intermittent accretion of oceanic materials at the base of the Mariana trench slope at the latitude of Guam.

Along the Leg 60 transect a total of four DSDP sites transect the Mariana forearc (Fig. 10). Sites 458 and 459 lie in the upper-slope region of the forearc; drilling at these sites penetrated a sequence of radiolarian ooze, nannofossil ooze-chalk, and volcaniclastic sand turbidites, all with local ash layers, that overlays a basement of basalt and andesite. At Site 60 of Leg 6, located closer to the arc, drilling recovered a Miocene to Recent sequence of volcanic ash with interbedded nannofossil ooze-chalk. Drilling results studied in conjunction with seismic reflection and refraction data show (Fig. 11) that this upper-slope region consists of an ashy pelagic sediment apron underlain by volcanic basement of arc origin (Mrozowski and Hayes, 1980; LaTraille and Hus-

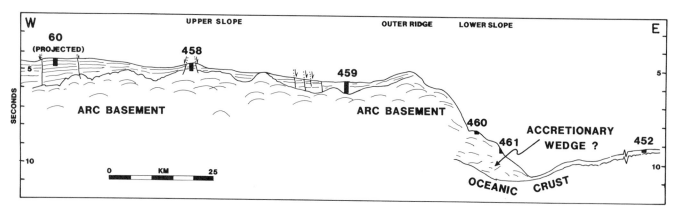

Figure 11. Cross section of Mariana Forearc. Line drawing from seismic reflection records of Mrozowski and Hayes (1982). Vertical scale in time; note "velocity pull-up" of oceanic crust beneath base of trench slope.

In summary, the Mariana forearc shows limited, if any, accretion, probably because of the sediment-starved nature of the trench and the well-lithified condition of most of the incoming oceanic sediment column. The presence of arc volcanic rocks anomalously close to the trench indicates removal of material from the forearc, perhaps by subduction erosion (Hussong and Uyeda, 1982; Bloomer, 1983) or strike-slip faulting (Lundberg and Moore, this volume).

JAPAN TRENCH: LEGS 56, 57, AND 87

The forearc of the Japan Trench was drilled during Legs 56, 57, and 87, providing a rather complete transect across this margin (Fig. 12). Our discussion of this classic trench system is largely summarized from von Huene and others (1982), Scientific Party (1980), and Kagami, Karig, and others (1986).

The deep sea terrace and upper slope landward of the Japan Trench are characterized at depth by landward-dipping reflectors, which are unconformably overlain by a shallowly dipping uppermost Paleogene to Neogene sedimentary cover more than 1 km thick (Fig. 13). Both IPOD and industry drilling results demonstrate that the landward-dipping reflectors represent Cretaceous sedimentary rocks, perhaps younging to early Paleogene age along their seaward extent. The unconformable contact between the sedimentary cover and subjacent landward-dipping reflectors generally cannot be traced beyond the mid-slope region. The landward-dipping reflectors apparently represent a Cretaceous to early Paleogene accretionary wedge (von Huene and others, 1982). Paleogene exposure of the wedge was followed by latest Paleogene and Neogene accumulation of initially shallow

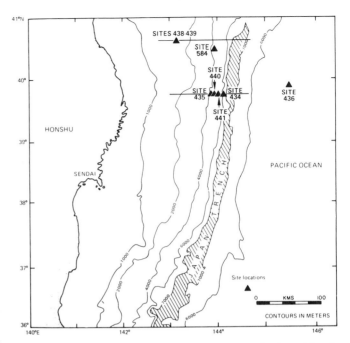

Figure 12. Location of Leg 56, 57, and 87 sites across the Japan Trench slope.

water deposits during the mid-Tertiary, producing the observed unconformity; subsidence has continued during most of the Tertiary. Langseth and others (1981) argue that subsidence was caused by mass removal (subduction erosion) at the base of the accretionary wedge coupled with a change in rate of subduction

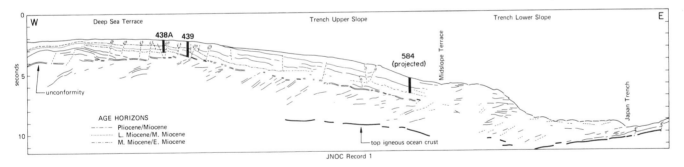

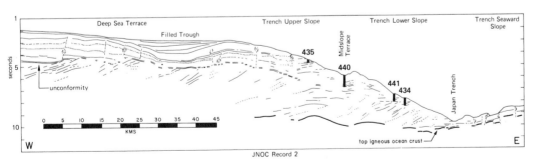

Figure 13. Line drawing of seismic reflection records across the Japan Trench slope in Leg 56-57 drilling area (von Huene and others, 1980). Vertical scale in time; note "velocity pull-up" of incoming oceanic crust.

or subduction of older (cooler) crust. Reflectors beneath the trench lower slope dip landward and are gradationally overlain by shallowly dipping slope sediments that were penetrated by drilling. The landward-dipping reflectors beneath the sampled slope deposits may represent accreted sediment. Part of the lowermost slope may also be a slump mass, as indicated by reprocessed seismic data and an extensive seabeam survey (Cadet, Kobayashi and others, 1986; von Huene, personal communication, 1985).

During the various drilling legs spanning the Japan trench slope, two sites (438 and 439) penetrated the deep sea terrace, two sites (434 and 441) cored the lower slope, and three sites (435, 440, and 584) lie in the transitional mid-slope region (Fig. 13). Drilling at sites 438 and 439 recovered a Pleistocene to lower Miocene sequence of interbedded mudstone, diatomaceous mudstone, and siltstone; an underlying sequence of sandy turbidites above massive Oligocene sandstone containing numerous articulated megafossils; volcanic breccia; and Cretaceous claystones that underlie an unconformity of about 40 m.y. Sites in the lower- and mid-slope regions are dominated by Quaternary to middle Miocene diatomaceous mudstone and mudstone. At least three slump horizons exist at Site 440. The lower and mid-slope sites apparently penetrated only slope sediments. The conspicuously diatomaceous character of the Japan Trench cores provides physical properties data and consolidation characteristics unique among the active margin transects (Carson and Bruns, 1980; Shepard and Bryant, 1980).

CONCLUSIONS

Structural and Lithologic Variety in Forearcs

Modern forearcs show variety in lithology and overall structural geology unanticipated a decade ago (von Huene, 1985). Accretionary margins transected by the DSDP (southern Mexico, Barbados, Nankai Trough) display a range of accretionary mechanisms and show a strong analogy to fold-and-thrust belts. Understanding this type of convergent margin has resulted from the integration of drilling results with excellent seismic reflection data. Conversely, the undoubtedly complex basement underlying nonaccretionary forearcs (e.g. Guatemala or Marianas) has not been well-imaged seismically; consequently, correlation and interpretation of drilling results has been difficult. Even though they are difficult to study, nonaccretionary forearcs must be an important and underappreciated component in the stratigraphic record.

Accretionary Wedges as Fold-and-Thrust Belts

Excellent seismic reflection profiles across the Nankai Trough (Leg 31, 87) show well-developed imbricate thrusts, fault-bend folds, and a distinct décollement, all features associated with classic fold-and-thrust belts (e.g. Bally and others, 1966; Price, 1981). In a similar setting, the northern Barbados Ridge area, drilling results reveal high fluid pressures along the décolle-

ment surface, which is also consistent with conditions required for long-distance transport along thrust surfaces (Hubbert and Rubey, 1959). In fact, high pore pressures are especially necessary for the development of fold-and-thrust structures in the partially consolidated sediment that lies on the underthrusting oceanic plates.

Structures characteristic of fold-and-thrust belts are most apparent in seismic reflection data, although drilling in the northern Barbados Ridge (Leg 78) area did penetrate biostratigraphically defined thrust faults and went into a décollement. The small-scale structures associated with the initial thrusting in the three accretionary margins differ from and are more complex than those developed during the initial deformation in well-studied on-land fold-and-thrust belts (e.g., Price, 1967). Therefore, the analogy between fold-and-thrust belts and the early deformation of accretionary wedges is best drawn at a macroscopic level.

Continuing Deformation of Accretionary Wedges

At accretionary convergent margins, seismic resolution commonly decreases arcward of the deformation front with the loss of acoustic evidence for the fold-and-thrust belt style of deformation (e.g., Karig, 1986). Moreover, since available estimates of convergence at the deformation front typically are less than the total plate convergence rate, distributed deformation must occur across the accretionary wedge (Moore and Biju-Duval, 1984; Karig, 1986). This continuing deformation of the accretionary wedge will lead to ever more complex structures. Early fold and thrust style structures may evolve to the more stratally disrupted structural style characteristic of subaerially exposed complexes exposed on land. Slope deposits accumulating over the deforming accretionary wedge will record the strain superimposed on the underlying offscraped deposits since their initial emplacement at the deformation front.

Mechanisms of Accretion

Seismic reflection data (e.g., Westbrook and others, 1984) and drilling results (Watkins and others, 1982) clearly require both offscraping of incoming sediment at the toe of the trench slope plus basal accretion or underplating; the latter is apparently accomplished by down-stepping of a décollement with the development of a thrust-bounded package or duplex (Boyer and Elliott, 1982; Silver and others, 1985; Sample and Fisher, 1986). Papers in this volume only report on offscraped deposits or superjacent slope blanket. Nevertheless, the deformational processes affecting offscraped and slope sediments may be similar to those superimposed on the underplated materials during their early structural history. The results of the detailed structural studies that follow therefore should have applicability not only to slope deposits and offscrapings, but also underplated materials of accretionary complexes exposed on land.

ACKNOWLEDGMENTS

The research reported here was supported by grants (OCE8110394 and OCE8315836) from the Submarine Geology and Geophysics Program of the National Science Foundation. Roland von Huene and Eli Silver provided thoughtful comments on the manuscript.

REFERENCES CITED

Aoki, Y., Tamano, T., and Kato, S., 1982, Detailed structure of the Nankai Trough from migrated seismic sections, *in* Watkins, J. S., and Drake, C. L., eds., Studies in continental margin geology: American Association of Petroleum Geologists Memoir No. 34, p. 309–322.

Aubouin, J., and von Huene, R., 1985, Summary: Leg 84, Middle America Trench transect off Guatemala and Costa Rica, *in* von Huene, R., Aubouin, J., and others, eds., Initial Reports of the Deep Sea Drilling Project: Washington, D.C, U.S. Government Printing Office, v. 84, p. 939–957.

Bally, A. W., Gordy, P. L., and Stewart, G. A., 1966, Structure, seismic data and orogenic evolution of the southern Canadian Rocky Mountains; Bulletin of Canadian Petroleum Geology, v. 14, p. 337–381.

Biju-Duval, B., Le Quellec, P., Mascle, A., Renard, V., and Valery, P., 1982, Multibeam bathymetric survey and high resolution seismic investigations of the Barbados Ridge complex (Eastern Caribbean): A key to the knowledge and interpretation of an accretionary wedge, *in* Le Pichon, X., Augustithis, S. S., and Mascle, J., eds., Geodynamics of the Hellenic Arc and Trench: Tectonophysics, v. 86, p. 275–304.

Bloomer, S. H., 1983, Distribution and origin of igneous rocks from the landward slopes of the Mariana Trench: Implications for its structure and evolution: Journal of Geophysical Research, v. 88, p. 7411–7428.

Boyer, S. E., and Elliott, D., 1982, Thrust systems: American Association of Petroleum Geologists Bulletin, v. 66, p. 1196–1230.

Cadet, J., Kobaayashi, K., and others, 1986, Japan Trench and its juncture with the Kuril Trench: Cruise results of the Kaiko Project: Leg 3: Tectonophysics (in press).

Carson, B., and Bruns, T. R., 1980, Physical properties of sediments from the Japan Trench Margin and outer trench slope: Results from Deep Sea Drilling Project Legs 56 and 57, *in* Scientific Party, Initial Reports of the Deep Sea Drilling Project: Washington, D.C., U.S. Government Printing Office, v. 56, 57, p. 1187–1199.

Cowan, D. S., Moore, J. C., Roeske, S. M., Lundberg, N., and Lucas, S. E., 1984, Structural features at the deformation front of the Barbados Ridge complex, Deep Sea Drilling Project Leg 78A, *in* Biju-Duval, B., Moore, J. C., and others, eds., Initial Reports of the Deep Sea Drilling Project: Washington, D.C., U.S. Government Printing Office, v. 78A, p. 535–548.

Davis, D. M., and Hussong, D. M., 1984, Geothermal observations during Deep Sea Drilling Project Leg 78A, *in* Biju-Duval, B., Moore, J. C., and others, eds., Initial Reports of the Deep Sea Drilling Project: Washington, D.C., U.S. Government Printing Office, v. 78A, p. 593–598.

Dickinson, W. R., and Seely, D. R., 1979, Structure and stratigraphy of forearc regions: American Association of Petroleum Geologists Bulletin, v. 63, p. 2–31.

Fischer, A. G., Heezen, B. C., and others, 1971, Initial Reports of the Deep Sea Drilling Project: Washington, D.C., U.S. Government Printing Office, v. 6, 1329 p.

Hilde, T.W.C., 1983, Sediment subduction versus accretion around the Pacific: Tectonophysics, v. 99, p. 381–397.

Hubbert, M. K., and Rubey, W. W., 1959, Role of fluid pressure in mechanics of overthrust faulting: Geological Society of America Bulletin, v. 70, p. 115–166.

Hussong, J., and Fryer, P., 1982, Structure and tectonics of the Mariana arc and fore-arc: Drill site selection surveys, *in* Hussong, D. M., Uyeda, S., and others, eds., Initial Reports of the Deep Sea Drilling Project: Washington, D.C., U.S. Government Printing Office, v. 60, p. 33–44.

Hussong, D. M., and Uyeda, S., 1982, Tectonic processes and the history of the Mariana Arc: A synthesis of the results of Deep Sea Drilling Project Leg 60, *in* Hussong, D. M., Uyeda, S., and others, eds., Initial Reports of the Deep Sea Drilling Project: Washington, D.C., U.S. Government Printing Office, v. 60, p. 909–929.

Hussong, D. M., Uyeda, S., and others, 1982, Initial Reports of the Deep Sea Drilling Project: Washington, D.C., U.S. Government Printing Office, v. 60, 929 p.

Kagami, H., Karig, D. E., and others, 1986, Initial Reports of the Deep Sea Drilling Project: Washington, D.C., U.S. Government Printing Office, v. 87 (in press).

Karig, D. E., 1974, Evolution of the western Pacific: Annual Review of Earth and Planetary Science, v. 2, p. 51–76.

—— , 1986, The framework of deformation in the Nankai Trough, *in* Karig, D. E., Kagami, H., and others, eds., Initial Reports of the Deep Sea Drilling Project: Washington, D.C., U.S. Government Printing Office, v. 87 (in press).

Karig, D. E., and Ranken, B., 1963, Marine geology of the fore-arc region, southern Mariana island arc, *in* Hayes, D. E., The Tectonic and Geologic Evolution of Southeast Asian Seas and Islands: American Geophysical Union, Geophysical monograph 27, pt. 2, p. 266–280.

Karig, D. E., Kagami, H., and others, 1983, Varied responses to subduction in Nankai Trough and Japan Trench forearcs: Nature, v. 304, p. 148–151.

Langseth, M. G., von Huene, R., Nasu, N., and Okada, H., 1981, Subsidence of the Japan Trench forearc region of Northern Honshu: Oceanologica Acta, v. 4. supplement, p. 173–179.

LaTraille, S. L., and Hussong, D. M., 1980, Crustal structure across the Mariana Island Arc, *in* Hays, D. E., ed., Tectonic and Geologic Evolution of Southeast Asian Seas and Islands: Washington, D.C., American Geophysical Union, Monograph 23, p. 209–221.

Lundberg, N., 1982, Evolution of the slope landward of the Middle America Trench, Nicoya Peninsula, Costa Rica, *in* Leggett, J. K., ed., Trench-Forearc Geology: Geological Society of London Special Publication no. 10, p. 131–147.

McMillen, K. J., Bachman, S. B., 1982, Paleobathymetry and tectonic evolution of the southern Mexico active margin, Deep Sea Drilling Project Leg 66, *in* Watkins, J. S., Moore, J. C., and others, Initial Reports of the Deep Sea Drilling Project: Washington, D.C., U.S. Government Printing Office, v. 66, p. 815–822.

Meijer, A., Anthony, E., and Regan, M., 1982, Petrology of volcanic rocks from the fore-arc sites, *in* Hussong, D., Uyeda, S., and others, eds., Initial Reports of the Deep Sea Drilling Project: Washington, D.C., U.S. Government Printing Office, v. 60, p. 709–733.

Moore, J. C., Watkins, J. S., and others, 1982, Geology and tectonic evolution of a juvenile accretionary terrane along a truncated convergent margin: Synthesis of results from Leg 66 of the Deep Sea Drilling Project, southern Mexico: Geological Society of America Bulletin, v. 93, p. 847–861.

Moore, J. C., and Biju-Duval, B., 1984, Tectonic synthesis Deep Sea Drilling Project Leg 78A: Structural evolution of offscraped and underthrust sediment, northern Barbados Ridge complex, *in* Biju-Duval, B., Moore, J. C., and others, eds., Initial Reports of the Deep Sea Drilling Project: Washington, D.C., U.S. Government Printing Office, v. 78A, p. 601–621.

Mrozowski, C., and Hayes, D., 1980, A seismic reflection study of faulting in the Mariana fore arc, *in* Hayes, D. E., The Tectonic and Geologic Evolution of Southeast Asian Seas and Islands: American Geophysical Union, Geophysical monograph 23, p. 223–234.

Ngokwey, K., Mascle, A., Biju-Duval, B., 1984, Geophysical setting of Deep Sea Drilling Project Sites 541, 542, *in* Biju-Duval, B., Moore, J. C., and others, eds., Initial Reports of the Deep Sea Drilling Project: Washington, D.C., U.S. Government Printing Office, v. 78A, p. 39–48.

Price, R. A., 1967, The tectonic significance of mesoscopic subfabrics in the southern Rocky Mountains of Alberta and British Columbia: Canadian

Journal of Earth Sciences, v. 4, p. 39–70.

——, 1981, The Cordilleran foreland thrust and fold belt in the southern Canadian Rocky Mountains, *in* McClay, K. R., and Price, N. J., eds., Thrust and Nappe Tectonics: Geological Society of London Special Publication No. 9, p. 427–448.

Sample, J. C., and Fisher, D. M., 1986, Duplex accretion and underplating in an ancient accretionary complex, Kodiak Islands, Alaska: Geology, v. 14, p. 160–163.

Scholl, D.W., von Huene, R., Vallier, T. L., and Howell, D. G., 1980, Sedimentary masses and concepts about tectonic processes at underthrust ocean margins: Geology, v. 8, p. 564–568.

Scientific Party, 1980, Initial Reports of the Deep Sea Drilling Project: Washington, D.C., U.S. Government Printing Office, v. 56–57, 1417 p.

Seely, D. R., 1977, The significance of landward vergence and oblique structural trends on trench inner slopes, *in* Talwani, M., and Pitmann, S. C., eds., Island Arcs, Deep Sea Trenches, and Back-Arc Basins: American Geophysical Union, Maurice Ewing Series 1, p. 187–198.

Seely, D. R., Vail, P. R., and Walton, G. G., 1974, Trench slope model, *in* Burk, G. A., and others, eds., The Geology of Continental Margins: New York, Springer-Verlag, p. 249–260.

Shepard, L. E., and Bryant, W. R., 1980, Consolidation characteristics of Japan Trench sediments, *in* Scientific Party, Initial Reports of the Deep Sea Drilling Project: Washington, D.C., U.S. Government Printing Office, v. 56–57, p. 1201–1205.

Shipley, T. H., 1982, Seismic facies and structural framework of the southern Mexico continental margin, *in* Watkins, J. S., Moore, J. C., and others, eds., Initial Reports of the Deep Sea Drilling Project: Washington, D.C., U.S. Government Printing Office, v. 66, p. 775–790.

Silver, E. A., Ellis, M. J., Breen, N. A., and Shipley, T. H., 1985, Comments on the growth of accretionary wedges: Geology, v. 13, p. 6–9.

Taira, A., Okada, H., Whitaker, J., and Smith, A., 1982, The Shimanto Belt of Japan: Cretaceous-lower Miocene active-margin sedimentation, *in* Leggett, J. K., ed., Trench-forearc geology: Sedimentation and tectonics on modern and ancient active plate margins: Geological Society of London Special Publication No., 10, p. 5–26.

Uyeda, S., 1982, Subduction zones: An introduction to comparative subductology: Tectonophysics, v. 81, p. 133–159.

von Huene, R., 1984, Tectonic processes along the front of modern convergent margins—research of the past decade: Annual Review of Earth and Planetary Sciences, v. 12, p. 359–381.

——, 1985, Direct measurement of pore fluid pressure, Leg. 84, Guatemala and Costa Rica, *in* von Huene, R., Aubouin, J., and others, eds., Initial Reports of the Deep Sea Drilling Project: Washington, D.C., U.S. Government Printing Office, v. 84, p. 767–772.

von Huene, R., and Aubouin, J., 1982, Summary—Leg 67, Middle American Trench transect off Guatemala, *in* Aubouin, J., von Huene, R., and others, eds., Initial Reports of the Deep Sea Drilling Project: Washington, D.C., U.S. Government Printing Office, v. 67, p. 775–793.

von Huene, R., Aubouin, J., and others, eds., 1985, Initial Reports of the Deep Sea Drilling Project: Washington, D.C., U.S. Government Printing Office, v. 84, 967 p.

von Huene, R., Langseth, M., Nasu, N., and Okada, H., 1980, Summary, Japan Trench Transect, *in* Lee, M., and Stout, L., eds., Initial Reports of the Deep Sea Drilling Project: Washington, D.C., U.S. Government Printing Office, v. 56, 57, pt. 1, p. 473–488.

——, 1982, A summary of Cenozoic tectonic history along IPOD Japan Transect: Geological Society of America Bulletin, v. 93, p. 829–846.

Watkins, J. S., and others, 1981, Accretion, underplating, and tectonic evolution, Middle America Trench, southern Mexico: Results from Leg 66 Deep Sea Drilling Project, *in* Blanchet, R., and Montadert, L., eds., Geology of continental margins, Colloque 3, 26th International Geological Congress: Paris, Oceanologica Acta, p. 213–224.

Watkins, J. S., and others, 1982, Tectonic synthesis, Leg 66 Deep Sea Drilling Project transect and vicinity, *in* Watkins, J. S., Moore, J. C., and others, eds., Initial Reports of the Deep Sea Drilling Project: Washington, D.C., U.S. Government Printing Office, v. 66, p. 837–849.

Watkins, J. S., Moore, J. C., and others, eds., 1982, Initial Reports of the Deep Sea Drilling Project: Washington, D.C., U.S. Government Printing Office, v. 66, 864 p.

Westbrook, G. K., Smith, M. J., Peacock, J. H., and Poulter, M. J., 1982, Extensive underthrusting of undeformed sediment beneath the accretionary complex of the Lesser Antilles subduction zone: Nature, v. 300, p. 625–628.

Westbrook, G., Mascle, A., and Biju-Duval, B., 1984, Geophysics and structure of the Lesser Antilles forearc, *in* Biju-Duval, B., Moore, J. C., and others, eds., Initial Reports of the Deep Sea Drilling Project: Washington, D.C., U.S. Government Printing Office, v. 78A, p. 23–38.

Wood, D. A., Marsh, N. G., and others, 1982, Geochemistry of igneous rocks recovered from a transect across the Mariana Trough, Arc, Forearc, and Trench, Sites 453 through 461, Deep Sea Drilling Project Leg 60, *in* Hussong, D., and Uyeda, S., and others, eds., Initial Reports of the Deep Sea Drilling Project: Washington, D.C., U.S. Government Printing Office, v. 60, p. 611–645.

Manuscript Accepted by the Society March 10, 1986

Geological Society of America
Memoir 166
1986

Macroscopic structural features in Deep Sea Drilling Project cores from forearc regions

Neil Lundberg
Department of Geological and Geophysical Sciences
Princeton University
Princeton, New Jersey 08544

J. Casey Moore
Department of Earth and Marine Sciences
University of California, Santa Cruz
Santa Cruz, California 95064

ABSTRACT

DSDP cores from active margins show a range of structural features, including bedding dips, semi-penetrative secondary fabrics, and faults. We have collected data on the distribution and orientation of structural features in all DSDP cores recovered to date in forearcs, and have carried out topical studies on selected fabrics. Graphic structural logs, compiled from a consistently acquired data set, show the distribution of structural features margin by margin, and allow comparisons to be drawn between margins. Most sediments cored in forearcs are in situ slope deposits, and bedding dips constitute a fundamental strain indicator. Histograms of bedding dips in slope deposits document a distinction between 1) actively deforming forearc regions underlain by Neogene and Quaternary accretionary wedges, and 2) less-deformed sedimentary sequences that overlie rigid basement terranes.

Structural fabrics in active-margin cores include stratal disruption and cataclastic fabrics, scaly foliation, spaced foliation, vein structure, kink bands, crenulation folds, web structure, and fissility. The distribution of structural fabrics in active-margin cores serves to distinguish between different structural regimes in forearc regions. Cores from upper-slope sites tend to be dominated by structures indicative of layer-parallel extension, which may have formed during postulated bedding-parallel shear in gravity-induced downslope movement of upper sediment layers. Cores from lower-slope sites tend to be dominated by compressional structures, presumably due to overall horizontal shortening resulting from plate convergence.

INTRODUCTION

Forearc terranes are among the most dynamic structural zones on earth. In this realm, the intricate deformation of accretionary complexes and their overlying slope sediments have provided an outstanding challenge for structural geologists. Here we present a synthesis of structural fabrics of Deep Sea Drilling Project cores recovered from this environment (Fig. 1). The observed structural fabrics probably represent the nascent stages of many features known from more complexly deformed orogenic belts and accordingly provide clues as to how the latter formed.

The structural study of cores is not a classical subdiscipline of marine geology; consequently, the description and analysis of structural fabrics of DSDP cores have been uneven. Inconsistencies have occurred in naming and interpreting structures, depending on the interests of scientists on the various legs. Moreover, significant confusion exists over what represents drilling deformation. The following synthesis of macroscopic fabrics is the result

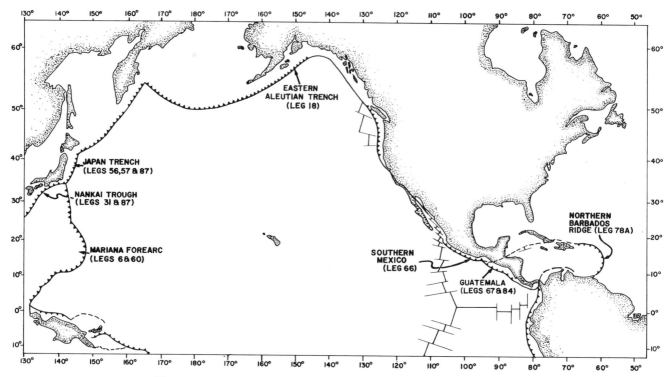

Figure 1. Location of Deep Sea Drilling Project transects across active margins.

of Lundberg's re-examination of DSDP cores from all forearc sites and our analysis of this consistently acquired data set. Our descriptions take the form of graphic structural logs of the drilling sites, macroscopic and microscopic representations of the fabrics, and various statistical summaries. We have made interpretations based on this level of investigation; selected structural fabrics are described and interpreted in detail in the papers that follow.

The synthesis is presented in two parts. The first part is essentially a catalog of structural features observed in DSDP cores from active margins: it includes definitions, descriptions, and interpretations of secondary fabrics and is illustrated by core photographs and photomicrographs. Graphic structural logs depict the distribution of structural features across each drilling transect. In the second part, these data are analyzed in a topical context. This latter part comprises three sections: an analysis of bedding dips, a summary of regional patterns of faulting, and an interpretation of the distribution of secondary fabrics.

PART 1: CATALOG OF CORE-SCALE STRUCTURAL FABRICS

We have worked out inconsistencies in naming the various structural fabrics through an examination of all active-margin cores by a "common set of eyes," while at the same time drawing on the experience of a variety of investigators who have been intimately involved in former structural studies of DSDP cores and in detailed fabric studies of ancient rocks. Fabrics studied include stratal disruption and related cataclastic fabrics, scaly

foliation, vein structure, spaced foliation, kinks, crenulation folds, web structure, stepped foliation, and fissility. Our microscopic studies have allowed us to describe these structural fabrics in detail. The studies were carried out with the ultimate goal of interpreting mechanisms of deformation and kinematic significance of the features.

The results of our macroscopic observations and microscopic studies follow, illustrated by photographs of the fabrics as viewed in the cores and in thin section. We also present core photographs of several additional features, including clastic dikes, breccias, and slump features. More detailed topical studies of selected features are included in related papers that follow.

Stratal Disruption and Cataclastic Fabrics

Definition. Stratal disruption refers to pervasive bedding discontinuities not attributed to primary deposition, bioturbation, or drilling deformation. These zones commonly show a foliation defined by preferentially oriented, elongate lenses of contrasting lithologies. Primary lithologic layering in these zones either is not resolvable macroscopically or is preserved only locally in cm-scale domains.

Description. Stratal disruption is characterized by dismemberment of cm- to mm-thick sand-rich bodies in a matrix of mudstone to siltstone (Figs. 2 and 3). Complex intermixing of sand and mud is well illustrated in a slabbed sample of Miocene sediment from the base of Site 492 off Mexico (Fig. 3c). A foliation is defined by a series of healed faults that crosscut relict

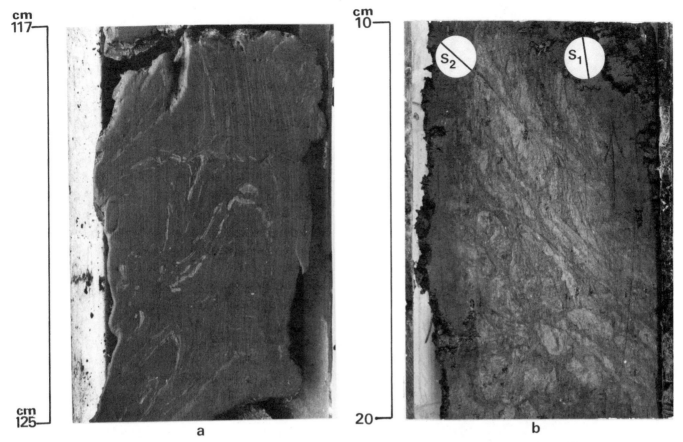

Figure 2. Stratal disruption. a) Deformed mudstone with sand and silt laminae at Interval 181-24-1, 113 to 130 cm (Aleutian Trench). [Note: designation of core intervals and samples follows DSDP convention, as follows: Site number (with Hole letter, if any)—Core number—Section number, followed by specific interval within the section (in cm) or by cc, denoting a sample taken from the core catcher. Each core represents a maximum drilled interval of 9.5 m, and is cut into 1.5-m-long sections.] Sand and silt laminae show early distension and tight to isoclinal folding. Folding is disharmonic and has been overprinted locally by drilling deformation defined by swirling of primary features in a pattern that is symmetric with respect to the core axis. Nearly vertical surficial striations are caused by scraping of core by a razor blade. b) Two superimposed, irregularly developed secondary foliations (S_1 and S_2) disrupt sand and scaly mudstone at Interval 492-30-2, 10 to 20 cm (southern Mexico). Bedding is not discernible macroscopically.

bedding at a high angle. Bedding has apparently been folded locally and apophyses or stringers of sand have been entrained along faults. Prior to impregnation, sand in this sample was uncemented and friable, whereas much of the fine-grained portion of the sample had become indurated and deformed into scaly mudstone.

Interpretation. The dispersed bodies of sand in stratally disrupted intervals have a high percentage of broken grains, which we believe cannot be explained by either compaction or drilling deformation, based on comparisons with control samples (see Lucas and Moore, this volume). Cataclastic stratal disruption in Leg 66 cores is found exclusively in lower-slope sites that display high and locally inconsistent bedding dips (Fig. 3; Sites 488, 491, and 492). Studies of samples of similar lithology buried at equivalent depths on the upper slope off Mexico show less

intense grain breakage (Lucas and Moore, this volume). Samples from the control site (Site 467, Leg 63) reveal essentially no grain destructive phenomena. Accordingly, broken grains in stratally disrupted zones probably are not the result of drilling deformation. Furthermore, comparison of the observed variation in grain-breakage frequency with dip histograms suggests that there is an increase in grain breakage concomitant with increasing bedding dip (Lucas and Moore, this volume).

Scaly Fabrics

Definition. Scaly foliation is defined by anastomosing polished and slickensided fracture surfaces, pervasive on a scale of millimeters. The overall orientation of the scaly foliation surfaces approximates a plane. Incipient scaly foliation is pervasive on a centimeter scale and does not show a distinct planar orientation

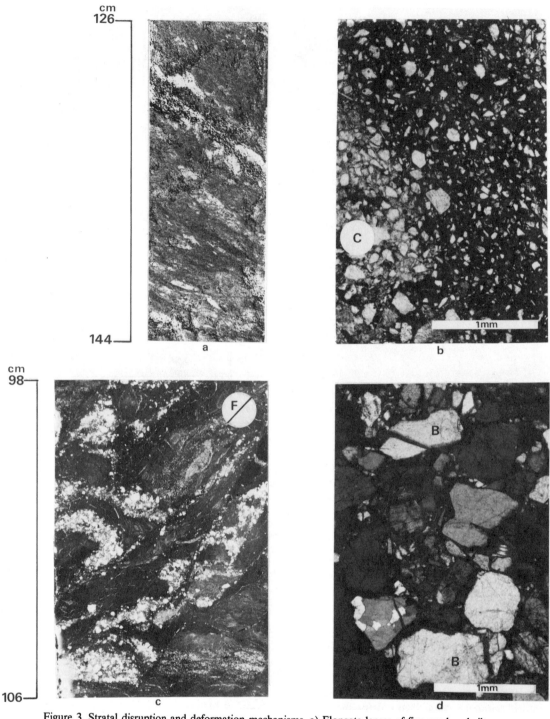

Figure 3. Stratal disruption and deformation mechanisms. a) Elongate lenses of fine sand and silt are bounded by dark, clay-rich zones at Interval 488-26-6, 126 to 144 cm (southern Mexico). b) Photomicrograph of impregnated thin section cut from interval shown in a. Coherent clusters of sand (lower left corner, marked with "C") have largely disaggregated by spalling off into bounding clay-rich zones; deformation is principally by disaggregative particulate flow. Plane polarized light, section cut normal to fabric. c) Complexly intermixed fine to coarse sand, silt, and scaly mudstone at Interval 492B-1-5, 98 to 106 cm (southern Mexico). Slab has been impregnated and polished. A crude planar fabric (F) is defined by anastomosing healed fracture surfaces; relict bedding is preserved locally, and appears folded at center left. d) Photomicrograph of thin section cut from sample shown in c. Broken grains of quartz (locally noted by "B") document cataclasis, which apparently occurred at depths comparable to that of recovery (287.5 m sub-bottom). Crossed nicols, section cut normal to core axis (i.e., horizontal in situ orientation).

as viewed in core sample. "Scaly fabric" refers inclusively to both scaly foliation and incipient scaly foliation. Intervals of scaly fabric typically exhibit stratal disruption if they contain lithologic contrasts.

Description. Scaly foliation is a classic fabric of onland accretionary complexes ("shear-fracture fabric" of Cowan, 1974; "pervasively sheared" fabric of Hsü, 1974). Scaly foliation is developed in pelitic sediments in cores from Legs 66, 67, 78A, and 84 (see Fig. 4 for examples).

The anastomosing parting surfaces that make up scaly foliation are slip surfaces, as shown by slickensides and gouges that characterize the polished surfaces. Scaly intervals that contain lithologic contrasts also exhibit stratal disruption; primary lithologic layering is typically not resolvable as viewed in the cores, except in irregularly shaped, relict domains bounded by slip surfaces. The crude macroscopic foliation defined by slip surfaces is characterized microscopically by a strong preferred orientation of platy minerals (Fig. 5). In some examples, phyllosilicates are aligned at a low angle to the slip surface (Moore, this volume). The alignment of mineral grains has been accomplished by the reorientation of existing minerals and possibly by the disruption of clay aggregates, rather than by precipitation of new mineral phases (Lundberg and Moore, 1982; Moore, this volume; Schoonmaker, this volume).

Scaly fabrics are also developed in basalts and boninites cored in the Mariana forearc (Fig. 4d) and in serpentinites recovered from the Guatemala forearc (Figs. 4e and 4f). Scaly basalt and boninite are pervasively fractured, the fractures lined with altered rock that is dark green and lustrous, appearing like serpentine. Chips of scaly basalt resemble chips of serpentinite until they are broken open to reveal cores of unaltered basalt. A number of intervals of serpentinite from Guatemalan cores have scaly textures, although many cores also show well-preserved relict igneous textures.

A macroscopically similar fabric that has been confused with scaly foliation has been described as "microflakiness," or "microscaliness" in cores from off Guatemala (Aubouin, von Huene, and others, 1982). Pieces of firm mud or soft mudstone with this fabric break open along parallel parting surfaces, or exhibit the fabric when broken at high angles to it, as by the core-splitting wire. Where we have examined this fabric in detail it is more akin to fissility than to scaly foliation. We interpret this microflakiness as an incipient fissility, although it may have been altered by downslope creep as suggested by Baltuck and others (1985).

Interpretation. Scaly fabrics are preferentially associated with biostratigraphically defined faults in the Leg 78A cores, a correlation that can perhaps be used to interpret similar fabrics elsewhere. See Moore and others (this volume) for a detailed investigation of the origin of scaly fabrics in DSDP cores.

Vein Structure

Definition. Vein structure comprises parallel sets of planar to curviplanar, dark, typically clay-rich surfaces or seams (Fig. 6). Individual veins are generally oriented subperpendicular to bedding, but are aligned or nested in parallel sets that make up broad bands or zones, the boundaries of which are subparallel to bedding. Vein structure appears on split core surfaces as nested sets of linear, curved, or sigmoidal traces, which commonly bifurcate both up- and downcore into fairly regular patterns of distributary or anastomosing networks. Individual seams contain sediment that appears finer grained than the surrounding sediment. Because at least some of the vein "filling" is altered in situ sediment, the term "vein" is, in a strict sense, somewhat misleading.

Description. Various names and origins have been given previously to vein structure. We have established that features originally described as (1) dewatering veins on Legs 56 and 57, (2) vein structure on Legs 67 and 84, and (3) sigmoidal examples of spaced foliation on Leg 66 all represent the same structure.

The distribution of vein structure is restricted largely to trench upper slopes. We have found vein structure in cores from all active margins transected by DSDP, and in a range of lithologies, including carbonate deposits as well as the more typical green hemipelagic mud and mudstone (Fig. 6e). Vein structure is most commonly developed in sediment cored in upper-slope environments, and only sparsely or not at all in lowermost-slope sites. It is weakly developed in sediment from one site drilled in a trench (Site 582 in the Nankai Trough) and not present at all in undeformed control sites located in tectonically inactive settings. We have found no reference to features similar to vein structure in passive-margin cores, despite the presence of similar lithologies. Similar structures have been observed locally in onland exposures of sedimentary rocks, most of which are best interpreted as having been deposited in upper-slope or shallow-water environments of active margins. These include forearc terranes of Japan (Ogawa, 1980) and Great Britain (R. J. Knipe, personal communication, 1984) and Miocene mudstones of the Monterey Formation of California (J. Helwig, personal communication, 1984) and similar Miocene mudstones of coastal Ecuador (A. G. Fischer, personal communication, 1984).

Microscopic study indicates that individual seams of vein structure are composed mainly of in situ sediment that has been reoriented and stained, rather than material that has migrated in from the surrounding sediment. Vein filling appears very similar in composition to the wallrock in plane-polarized light, and the two can be distinguished mainly because one is darker than the other. Typically the veins are lighter than the wallrock, unless they show a very dark staining or submicroscopic coating of grains; this may reflect recrystallization of fine-grained clayey matrix to coarser phyllosilicates. Coarse-grained laminations that act as markers in otherwise fine-grained sediment are crosscut by veins that contain coarse grains only at or very near their mutual intersection, indicating that the vein-filling has not traveled far (Lundberg and Leggett, 1986). Phyllosilicates within veins show a preferred orientation parallel to the vein boundaries, whereas phyllosilicates in the wallrock are oriented subparallel to bedding (nearly perpendicular to veins). The dark staining or coating of

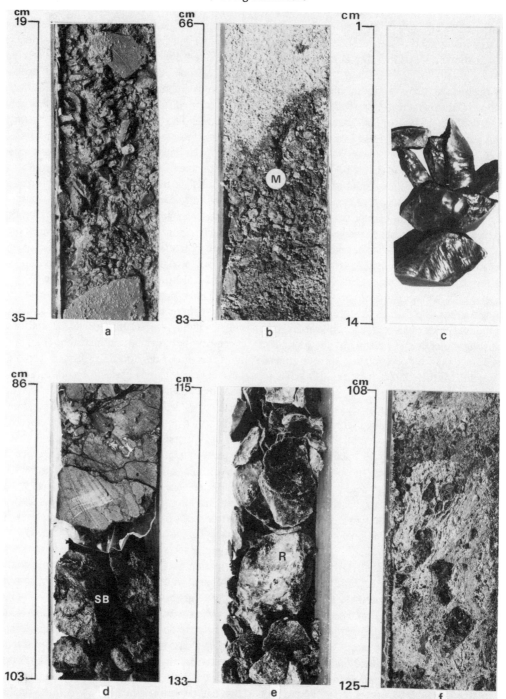

Figure 4. Scaly fabrics. a) Scaly chips of slope mudstone at Interval 568-33-5, 19 to 35 cm (Guatemala).
b) Chips of scaly mudstone (M) and unconsolidated sand interpreted as uplifted and deformed trench
deposits, at Interval 492B-1-5, 66 to 83 cm (southern Mexico). c) Chips of scaly mudstone (slope
deposits) that exhibit well developed pervasive fabric of anastomosing polished and slickensided fracture
surfaces, at Interval 490-60-1, 1 to 14 cm (southern Mexico). d) Scaly basalt (lower half of photo; SB)
and web structure in basalt (upper half of photo) at Interval 459B-70-1, 86 to 103 cm (Marianas).
Polished and slickensided surfaces in scaly basalt are pervasive on a mm scale. Web structure is defined
by cataclastic shear zones of variable orientation and in cores can be confused with fracture patterns
commonly developed in pillow basalts. Curved surficial striations are saw marks. e) Serpentinite-like
phacoidal chips of scaly boninite (high-Mg bronzite andesite) at Interval 458-36-2, 115 to 133 cm
(Marianas). Chips have lustrous, light to dark green, soft alteration rinds (R) that coat cores of relatively
nonfractured volcanic rock. f) Light-colored serpentine-rich matrix encloses angular clasts of hard rock,
mainly serpentinized peridotite, at Interval 567A-16-1, 108 to 125 cm (Guatemala).

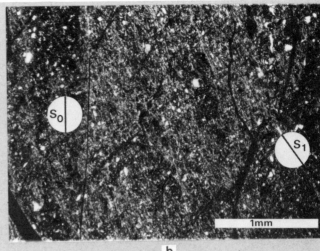

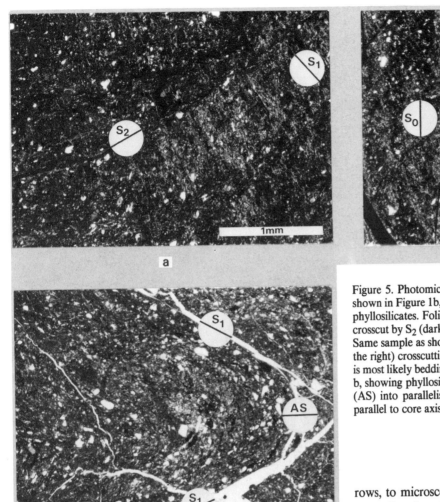

Figure 5. Photomicrographs of scaly fabrics. a) Thin section of sample shown in Figure 1b, showing two secondary foliations defined by aligned phyllosilicates. Foliation S_1 (light fabric, inclined steeply to the right) is crosscut by S_2 (dark fabric, inclined gently to the left). Crossed nicols. b) Same sample as shown in a, showing S_1 (light fabric, inclined steeply to the right) crosscutting compositional layering (subvertical in photo) that is most likely bedding. Crossed nicols. c) Same sample as shown in a and b, showing phyllosilicates parallel to S_1 bent around a fold axial surface (AS) into parallelism with S_2. Plane polarized light; thin sections cut parallel to core axis and split core surfaces.

grains within veins is apparently a result of fluid movement, and not an insoluble residue of pressure solution. We have observed no clear evidence of pressure solution and have found individual veins that have wound sinuous courses around quartz grains rather than dissolving through them (Lundberg and Moore, 1982).

   Interpretation. Explanations for vein structure include hydrofracturing or faulting in the presence of tectonically elevated fluid pressure (Arthur and others, 1980), normal faulting (Lundberg and Moore, 1982), and extensional fracturing with subsequent modification by dewatering (Cowan, 1982b). Following Cowan (1982b), we interpret vein structure as a response to extension, based on the following clues and constraints provided by its distribution, microscopic characteristics, and geometry.

   Vein structure has apparently formed by passive dilation (disaggregative extensional failure) rather than by hydrofracturing or the forceful expulsion of fluids. Evidence for displacement is common, ranging from core-scale offsets of bedding and bur-

rows, to microscopic sigmoidal fabrics in vein-filling phyllosilicates. On the other hand, evidence for fluid flow is limited. Sediment within veins commonly appears to be slightly finer grained than the surrounding sediment, suggesting that perhaps clays from the "wallrock" have been introduced into veins by percolating fluids. Vein structure developed in sediment with abundant carbonate foraminiferal tests appears to contain more fine-grained carbonate matrix than does the wallrock (E. C. Beutner, personal communication, 1984), suggesting either that fluid flow has transported carbonate into the zones, that granulated carbonate is more obvious there, or perhaps that carbonate has been preferentially precipitated in the veins. No other evidence of concentrated fluid flow or injection has been observed; slow expulsion of fluids along pathways generated by deformation is our favored hypothesis for the abundance of fines within veins. We have often observed delicate fossils intact within vein structure seams, however, suggesting low effective stresses (high fluid pressures).

   The geometry of vein structure suggests that it forms early in the deformation history of affected sediment, by bedding-parallel extension. Individual seams are oriented subperpendicular to bedding, and are nested into bands of veins that are generally oriented parallel to bedding, and that often follow particular beds. Down-dip striations on opened seams indicate dip-

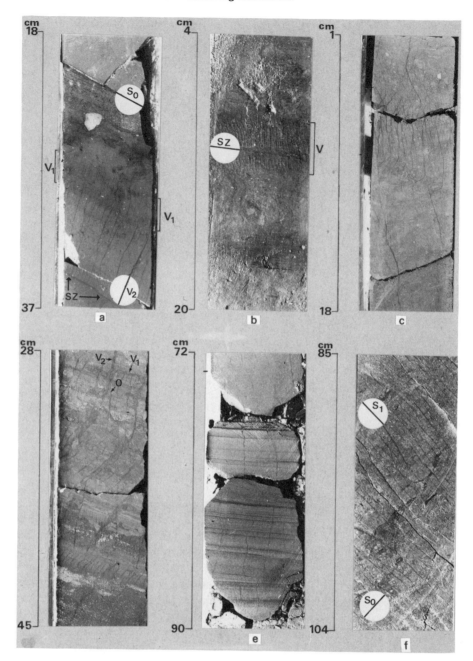

Figure 6. Vein structure and spaced foliation. a) Sigmoidal to nearly planar traces of veins oriented subperpendicular to bedding (S_0) at Interval 584-95-1, 18 to 37 cm (Japan). Early formed veins are short and are concentrated along a specific horizon (V_1). They are sigmoidal, although they may have formed as initially planar features, as tension gashes (see Cowan, 1982b). They have been crosscut by longer, more planar veins (V_2). Note bedding-parallel shear zone (SZ) immediately below set of long veins; shear zone truncates veins both below and above it, and shows micro-offsets itself. b) Small sets of slightly sigmoidal, bifurcating veins (V) above and below a bedding-parallel shear zone (SZ) (Interval 497-26-3, 4 to 20 cm, Guatemala). c) Sets of branching vein structure in mudstone conglomerate at Interval 439-9-5, 1 to 18 cm (Japan). Irregular geometry of traces is a result of the core having been split oblique to veins rather than orthogonal to them. d) Broad, irregular vein structure in siliceous mudstone interbedded with sandy tuff (light-colored beds) at Interval 459B-58-1, 28 to 45 cm (Marianas). Some veins (V_1) end at contacts with coarser layers (more porous and permeable, less cohesive) whereas other veins (V_2) extend into coarser material. Offset (O) is visible macroscopically along some veins. e) Poorly developed vein structure perpendicular to bedding in (mainly) parallel-laminated nannofossil chalk at Interval 459B-48-1, 72 to 90 cm (Marianas). f) Long, continuous, subplanar spaced folia (S_1) cut bedding (S_0) at nearly right angles at Interval 489A-11-4, 85 to 104 cm (southern Mexico).

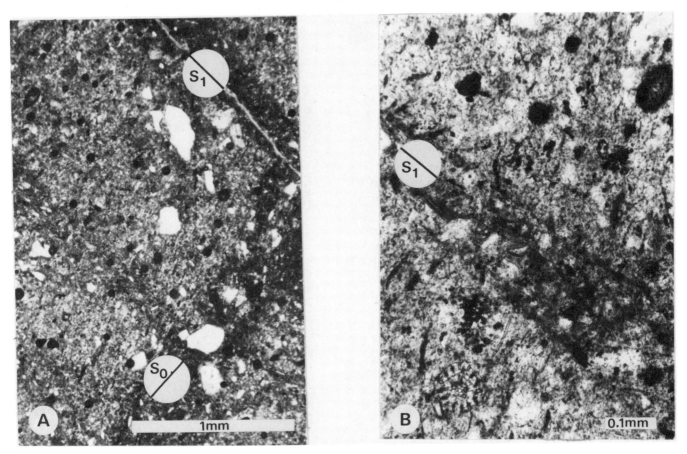

Figure 7. Photomicrographs of spaced foliation sample shown in Figure 6f. a) Bedding (S_0) crosscut by dark zones defining spaced foliation (S_1). Plane polarized light, section cut normal to bedding and foliation. b) Close-up of foliation selvage (S_1) in sample shown in a, showing alignment of phyllosilicates parallel to foliation selvage. Plane polarized light, section cut normal to bedding and foliation.

slip displacement, but macroscopic offsets are typically minute. These offsets indicate normal-fault movement along some seams and reverse-fault movement along others. Common bifurcation into distributary-like branches suggests that vein structure is also accompanied by movement of fluids. Vein structure typically represents the earliest fabric developed in complexly deformed cores, because it is almost invariably crosscut by other faults or fractures affecting a given interval. Vein structure apparently forms at shallow depths prior to tilting, because (1) veins are very nearly perpendicular to bedding, regardless of the dip of bedding; and (2) they dip toward the opposite azimuth (i.e., veins intersect bedding along a subhorizontal line, which approximates the strike of both).

Spaced Foliation

Definition. Spaced foliation is composed of planar dark surfaces or seams oriented subperpendicular to bedding, that occur in sets of closely spaced, parallel surfaces. Spaced foliation resembles vein structure, except that the folia are more planar and form through-going potential parting surfaces (Fig. 6f).

Description. A visually striking spaced foliation cuts bedding at nearly right angles in several cores from off Mexico and Japan (Fig. 6f). Spaced foliation is spatially associated with vein structure and is geometrically similar, although individual folia are more planar and continuous than are the "veins" of vein structure. The parallel, thin, dark selvages are defined microscopically by staining composed of concentrations of fine-grained black to brown material (Fig. 7a). Within these selvages, perfectly aligned fine, elongate phyllosilicates define the spaced foliation (Fig. 7b; Lundberg and Moore, 1982). Radiographs of slabs show reduced penetration by x-rays through the selvages or dark zones that define the foliation, suggesting that these zones are of higher density than the sediment outside the selvages. Some of the dark surfaces were open when the cores were split, but most were not; the core can easily be broken along the intact or "healed" surfaces. Both open and healed surfaces display well-developed down-dip striations, presumably slickenlines.

Interpretation. Examples of spaced foliation grade into sigmoidal nested sets of vein structure with the same orientation, and may be formed by the same mechanism as is vein structure. The dark staining of the folia may be an insoluble residue of pressure solution or a precipitate left by fluids migrating through the selvages; we favor the latter because of the lack of clear evidence for pressure solution.

Kink Bands

Definition. Kink bands are asymmetric, microscopic-scale deformation zones in which bedding has been rotated along sharp hinges; rotation is consistently in the sense of a reverse fault. Kink bands are subtle features when viewed in the cores. The bands comprise faint, dark surfaces, 2 to 5 mm thick, that are oriented at a high angle to bedding. Kink bands are very planar, and they commonly occur in widely spaced, parallel sets and exhibit a regular internal fabric of asymmetrically nested strands (described below). Kink bands superficially resemble vein structure or spaced foliation macroscopically; however, kink bands are extremely planar, are more widely spaced, and show a distinctive internal fabric quite unlike the irregular anastomosing or distributary patterns of vein structure.

Description. We have found kink bands in cores from both the lowermost slope landward of the Nankai Trough and the lower slope landward of the Aleutian Trench (Fig. 8). The three DSDP holes that have been drilled on the lowermost Nankai slope to a sub-bottom depth exceeding 350 meters (Holes 298, 583F, and 583G) have recovered kink bands (Lundberg and Karig, 1986). The dark, planar surfaces that comprise kink bands are difficult to pick out in the dark greenish gray, fine-grained mudstones (Fig. 8a); the small-scale rotation of primary features through the kink bands is typically not resolvable macroscopically (for an exception, see Fig. 8c). More often the kink bands appear simply as very straight traces of dark planar zones on split core surfaces, generally occurring in sets of parallel traces that cut across otherwise featureless mudstone.

Kink bands are typically inclined at about 60 degrees to essentially horizontal bedding, although dips range from 36 to 79 degrees. Several cores exhibit two conjugate sets of kink bands that dip in opposite directions (Fig. 8b). In all cases one set is much more strongly developed than the other, and the conjugate sets typically dip at relatively shallow angles (<45°). Acute angles between the two orientations vary between 59 and 89 degrees; the bisector of the acute angle varies in dip from 1.5° to 12.5°, averaging 6° (n = 5).

In detail, an internal fabric is discernible in some kink bands (Fig. 8b). This fabric is very regular, defined by nested, curviplanar dark surfaces or strands, which probably represent individual movement zones (Lundberg and Karig, 1986).

In thin section, each macroscopically distinct strand of a kink band comprises a zone of reoriented phyllosilicates, kinked in the sense of a reverse fault (Fig. 8d). In a given sample, phyllosilicates within all strands show a single preferred orientation, apparently reflecting a geometric limit to rotation. Boundaries of kink bands are very sharp fold hinges.

Interpretation. Kink bands result from horizontal shortening. Similar features can be seen at a much larger scale in seismic

Figure 8. Kink bands in DSDP cores from the inner slope of the Nankai Trough. a) Multiple subparallel kink bands at Interval 298-12-2, 104 to 121 cm. Some kink bands branch into strands that may join adjacent kink bands. b) Internal structure of kink bands well displayed by kink bands at Interval 583G-15-1, 75 to 79 cm. Earlier-formed kink band in conjugate orientation shows rotation by principal kink bands better than does essentially horizontal bedding in Nankai cores. c) Broad kink band with typically regular internal structure rotates bedding and bedding-parallel parting surface at Interval 298-13-5, 107 to 112 cm. d) Photomicrograph of kink bands at Interval 583F-24-3, 84 to 88 cm. Dark, parallel strands of kink band (S_1) rotate silt lamina in mudstone (S_0). Plane polarized light, section cut normal to bedding and kink bands.

reflection profiles of the Nankai Trough. In the landward portion of the Nankai Trough, just south of the drill sites that recovered kinked sediment, there are high-angle seismic discontinuities geometrically similar to the core-scale kink bands (Nasu and others, 1982). These discontinuities, which may be faults or sharp

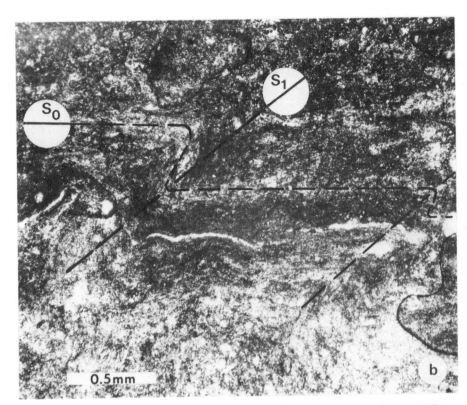

Figure 9. Crenulation folds. a) Crenulations (S_1) in laminated (S_0) diatomaceous mudstone and diatomite at Interval 440B-43-3, 36 to 54 cm (Japan). b) Photomicrograph of crenulations shown in a; plane polarized light, section cut approximately normal to bedding and crenulation fabric.

flexures, have apparent dips of approximately 60° to the north and offset trench sediments with consistently reverse displacement, defining a "protothrust" zone. The kind bands may represent structures that were formed when the kinked sediment was in a tectonic setting analogous to the protothrust zone of the Nankai Trough, marking the initial horizontal shortening of trench deposits in response to plate convergence. Alternatively, the kink bands may have formed where they were found, produced by layer-parallel shortening associated with thrusting.

Crenulation Folds

Definition. Crenulation folds are asymmetrical microfolds with smooth, broad hinges occurring in closely spaced sets with parallel axial surfaces. Crenulation folds crinkle primary lithologic layering in laminated sediment, forming a fabric pervasive on a scale of mms to cms that is similar to some types of crenulation cleavage in ancient rocks.

Description. Crenulation folds have developed in laminated diatomaceous sediment at Site 440, located on the lower slope landward of the Japan Trench. The crenulation fabric strongly rotates bedding into a series of asymmetric folds with parallel axial surfaces (Fig. 9). The geometry of the crenulation folds in Japan cores is similar to that of the kink bands found in cores from the Nankai lower slope, in that both comprise asymmetric microfolds with axial surfaces inclined at a high angle to bedding. The hinges of crenulation folds are broad and smooth, however, as opposed to the very sharp hinges of kink bands. In addition, panels formed by the short limbs of crenulation folds are spaced more densely and evenly than are the kink bands, and are not uniformly dark in color as are the kink bands. Furthermore, bedding in the crenulated sediment in Japan cores has been steeply tilted (Fig. 9a), whereas the kinked Nankai strata are essentially flat-lying. It is unclear whether the crenulation folds formed prior to, synchronously with, or after tilting. Crenulations may be much more common than our data suggest, because without the fine laminations shown by this interval they would be very difficult to distinguish.

In thin section, a strong alignment of diatom frustules parallel to bedding allows the discrimination of mm-scale folds. With increased displacement, these folds yield along axial surfaces to produce microfault zones filled with strongly aligned diatom fragments. In some examples, a second, minor set of crenulations has developed conjugate to the major set, symmetric with respect to bedding. The conjugate crenulations are poorly developed and are not obvious macroscopically.

Interpretation. The crenulations record bedding-parallel shortening. They are intimately associated with disharmonic folding that is likely the result of slumping, however, which is restricted to a short interval in an otherwise uniformly dipping section. We interpret the crenulations to have formed in a compressional region of a slump, probably at the nose of a slump body.

Fissility

Definition. Fissility is defined by fairly continuous parting surfaces oriented parallel to bedding and pervasive on a scale of millimeters.

Description. Macroscopically, fissility is distinguished from scaly fabrics by consistent orientation of parallel parting surfaces, and by the fact that these also lie parallel to bedding. In the absence of bedding traces, incipient fissility potentially can be confused with incipient scaly fabrics. In thin section, however, fissility can be readily identified by a distinct, orderly, and pervasively developed, preferred orientation of platy minerals, commonly accompanied by parallel, discontinuous dark traces of stained surfaces. Fissility is not characterized by the anastomosing nature characteristic of scaly fabrics. Bedding-parallel fissility is commonly exhibited by mudstone from the deeper sections of DSDP sites, generally at depths greater than 150 m (see sediment between kink bands in Figs. 8b, c, and d for examples).

Interpretation. We interpret fissility to be the result of gravitational compaction, enhancing a primary depositional alignment of platy minerals. A primary alignment must be important because there is a strong inverse correlation between the development of fissility and the degree of bioturbation in DSDP cores. Fissility is absent or only weakly developed in strongly bioturbated mudstone, but is common to ubiquitous in non-bioturbated mudstone that has been buried beyond a critical depth. This inverse correlation can be observed in the core from a single site (e.g., Site 493), in which laminated, fissile mudstone (bordering on becoming shale) is interbedded with bioturbated mudstone that shows no fissility.

Stepped Foliation

Definition. Stepped foliation is defined by a set of parallel, discontinuous parting surfaces, each less than 1 cm in length and oriented at a distinct angle to bedding. Macroscopically stepped foliation appears similar to fissility that is not bedding parallel, but in thin section it shows no evidence of mineral alignment.

Description. Stepped foliation has been found locally developed in slope sediments off southern Mexico (Lundberg and Moore, 1982), and in uplifted trench deposits landward of the Nankai Trough ("fracture cleavage" of Moore and Karig, 1976). In thin section the folia show no evidence for offset, and there is no staining or mineral realignment associated with this fabric (see Plate 1, Fig. 2 and Plate 5, Fig. 1 of Lundberg and Moore, 1982).

Interpretation. Stepped foliation cannot be attributed to simple gravitational compaction because it dips more steeply than does the bedding it crosscuts. Stepped foliation may be, in part, a drill-induced feature, and may reflect in situ stresses; this feature remains poorly understood.

Web Structure

Definition. Web structure is a three-dimensional network of diversely oriented cataclastic shear zones. It is developed in basalt and boninite in basement cores from the Mariana forearc. Web structure was originally defined by Cowan (1982a) as an irregular network of dark veins in sandstones, and the term was used by Byrne (1984) for randomly oriented cataclastic shear zones in sandstone. We have not carried out microscopic studies of the web structure developed in these volcanic rocks.

Interpretation. Because web structure is found in volcanic rocks in the DSDP cores, it is clearly a hard-rock phenomenon. Small offsets along individual seams indicate that the seams or veins are displacement zones. Several examples appear to grade progressively into scaly volcanic rock, and web structure may indeed be a precursor of this more intense fabric (Fig. 4d).

Faults

Faults in DSDP cores exhibit a wide variety of appearances, geometries, and senses of displacement. They range from clean, open fractures to broad, intact shear zones filled with black, comminuted sediment (Fig. 10). Open fractures without well-developed slickensides are commonly difficult to distinguish from artificial fractures produced during drilling and handling (see Drilling Deformation, Appendix). Healed fractures are unequivocally in situ features, exhibiting a dark seam of comminuted sediment, which in thin section displays a very strong preferred orientation parallel to the fault surface (Fig. 11). In healed fault zones of considerable width (1 to 10 cm), lenses of relict sediment may show asymmetric tails, possibly recording the sense of relative displacement (tails point in the direction of relative motion).

Biostratigraphically defined reverse faults recovered in cores from Barbados typically have associated intervals of deformed sediment characterized by scaly fabrics and stratal disruption. A conspicuous thrust fault at 276 m subbottom at Site 541 emplaces green, upper Miocene mud over light gray, nannofossil-rich, middle Pliocene mud (Fig. 12). There is only microscopic-scale mixing of the two units at the fault surface, which is itself locally contorted, suggesting that faulting occurred prior to lithification. The fault surface was deformed by drilling, cut by horizontal drilling "laminations"—dark, clay-rich surfaces or planar zones of rotational failure during drilling (see Drilling Deformation, Appendix).

Most faults observed in thin sections have a large component of dip slip and are 10s to 100s of microns in thickness (Fig. 11). In thin section both margins of a given fault zone are typi-

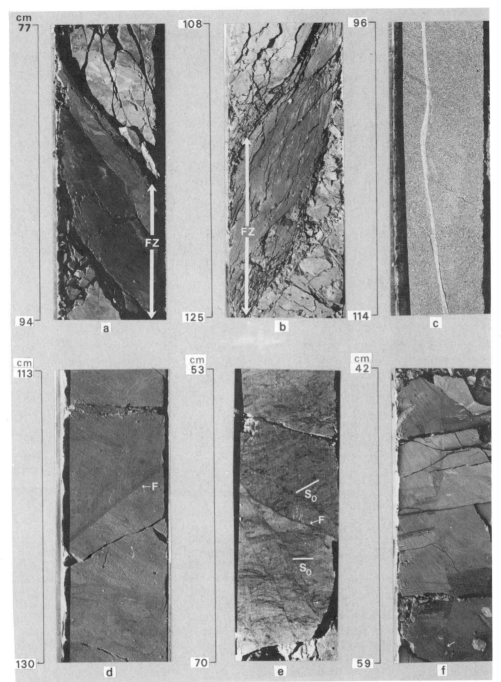

Figure 10. Faults. a) Broad, steeply inclined fault zone (FZ) in mudstone at Interval 584-93-1, 77 to 94 cm) Japan). Dark color stems from fine-grained comminuted material in fault zone. b) Broad fault zone in mudstone at Interval 440B-66-3, 108 to 125 cm (Japan). Light-colored sigmoidal lenses within fault zone are fault-bounded bodies of intact mudstone. Open cracks result from drilling, handling and desiccation of the cores. c) Curviplanar fault with white gouge in sandstone at Interval 439-32-1, 96 to 114 cm (Japan). d) Healed fault (F) in mudstone at Interval 584-34-2, 113 to 130 cm (Japan); curved striations are saw marks. e) Healed faults in mudstone at Interval 584-44-5, 53 to 70 cm (Japan). The main concave-upward fault surface (F) is interpreted as a listric normal fault: bedding dips in the opposite direction as does the fault surface, and bedding dip is steeper above the fault than below it. f) Strike-slip fault (arrow) in mudstone interbedded with volcaniclastic turbidites and tuff layers at Interval 459B-28-1, 42 to 59 cm (Marianas). This and many other faults in the Mariana forearc cores are (1) oriented essentially vertical, normal to subhorizontal bedding (and thus cannot accomplish layer-parallel extension or shortening) and (2) exhibit slickenlines that had a subhorizontal in situ orientation. Curved striations are saw marks.

b

Figure 11. Faults. a) Thick healed fault zone in mudstone at Interval 584-80-2, 125 to 142 cm (Japan). Fault (FZ) is characterized macroscopically by small lenses of relict mudstone aligned parallel to fault and set in dark, fine-grained comminuted fault filling. Above the main fault zone is a 1-cm-thick fault breccia (B), made up of angular clasts of mudstone that have been cemented together; below the main fault zone minor splays (F) disrupt the footwall. The boundaries of the main fault zone are irregular in detail. b) Photomicrograph of fault zone shown in a. Alignment of mineral grains parallel to fault is shown by light-colored fabric (S_1) inclined to the right. Lens (L) of relatively intact mudstone runs through center of photo from upper left to lower right; some fault-parallel alignment surfaces extend through it, whereas most are truncated by its boundary. Crossed nicols; thin section cut normal to fault, parallel to core axis.

cally defined by clays that are strongly oriented parallel to the fault surface (Fig. 11; Knipe, this volume). Within most fault zones, clays, larger detrital grains of high aspect ratio, and diatom frustules are all moderately to weakly oriented at a low oblique angle (15° to 30°) to the fault walls. This orientation agrees in sense with slip as determined by macroscopic offset; most fault zones broad enough to be analyzed in this fashion were normal faults. Overall, these fault zones are remarkably similar to zones produced in simple-shear experiments on unconsolidated clays (Morgenstern and Tchalenko, 1967) and on granular materials

(Mandl, deJong, and Maltha, 1977). Fossils within the fault zones themselves are often intact, reflecting either the heterogeneous distribution of deformation or low confining pressures.

Clastic Dikes

Our core examination revealed only one locality with clastic dikes: Site 584, located on a mid-slope terrace landward of the Japan Trench (Fig. 13). These seams are generally 1 to 3 mm across, with sharp and planar, parallel boundaries, although one example is over 3 cm across and tapers downward to less than 1 cm. The clastic dikes are filled with a lithified mixture of fine sand, silt, glass shards, and clay, which clearly formed a slurry during emplacement. Angular chips of mudstone, apparently derived from the wallrock, are set in the sandy fill of the broad dike mentioned above; the mudstone was clearly lithified during emplacement of the sandy matrix. Most of the clastic dikes form a single set of parallel fractures, which are oriented 66° to bedding and spaced every 15 cm or so, as measured along bedding (Lundberg and Leggett, 1986). There is no obvious offset across these seams. The absence of injection features and the regular, planar geometry suggest initial extensional fracturing, followed by emplacement of a slurry of sandy sediment. A fine sand bed of similar color and texture immediately above the interval that contains the seams is a likely source for the sand, and the fractures were probably filled from above. These sand-filled fractures constitute evidence of brittle failure of mudstone under layer-parallel extension and high fluid pressure.

Breccias

The origin of breccias and intervals of loose rubble can be difficult to distinguish in cores, because drilling deformation can overprint and obliterate features of naturally fragmented rock (Fig. 14). Loose clasts of lithified rock may be, in part, gravels derived from upslope areas, but may show effects of brecciation caused by drilling as well. Natural breccias we have found in DSDP cores range from clearly tectonic breccias to clearly sedimentary breccias. Tectonic breccias may show intervals that were recovered intact despite pervasive fracturing, whereas sedimentary breccias contain rounded clasts of varied lithologies embedded in a lithified, commonly mud-rich matrix. Most commonly, however, intervals of breccia are difficult to interpret. These typically consist of poorly recovered cores, filled with loose clasts, commonly sub-angular to angular, that show effects of some fracturing due to drilling and essentially lack matrix. A further complication is that these loose breccias strongly resemble drill cavings, comprising loose chips and lumps derived from collapse of overlying units into the drill hole (see Drilling Deformation, Appendix). Largely because of the difficulty in interpreting these variously disrupted cores, we can say little about structural features in sites from the lower slopes of the Mariana, Guatemala, and Japan transects (see section on Distribution of Structural Fabrics).

Folds

Small-scale folds have been noted in a number of DSDP cores during shipboard examination. These fall mainly into two categories: (a) individual "folds" with planar limbs and near-horizontal axial surfaces, which are probably artifacts of rotation by drilling (see Drilling Deformation, Appendix) and (b) intervals over which bedding has been disharmonically folded, which are generally identified as slump features (Fig. 15). In several

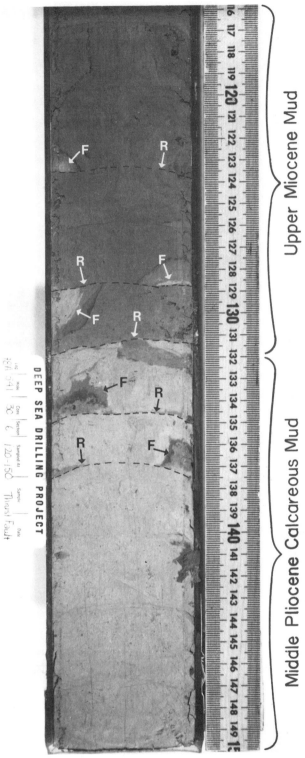

Figure 12. Thrust fault emplacing upper Miocene hemipelagic mud (dark gray) over middle Pliocene nannofossil and foraminifer-rich calcareous mud (light gray) at Interval 541-30-6, 116-150 cm (Barbados). The fault surface has been deformed by drilling (see Cowan and others, 1984 for detailed discussion of this fault). F denotes fault surface; R indicates rotational slip surfaces due to drilling that disrupts fault. Fault was apparently folded prior to disruption by drilling.

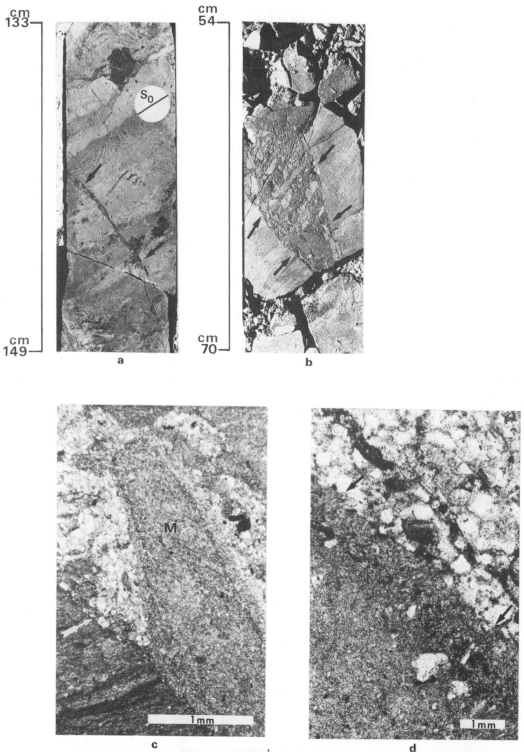

Figure 13. Clastic dikes. a) Sand-filled fracture (arrows) oriented subperpendicular to bedding (S_0) in mudstone at Interval 584-81-3, 133 to 149 cm (Japan). Fracture filling includes mudstone clasts as well as sand. Sand beds of similar composition are interbedded in this core. b) Large sand-filled fracture (arrows) in mudstone at Interval 584-71-2, 54 to 70 cm (Japan). Crack tapers downward; injected sand is mixed with angular clasts of mudstone apparently derived from walls of crack. c) Photomicrograph of sample from interval shown in b. Crack-fill boundary (arrows) separates surrounding dark, laminated sediment (at lower left) from mudstone clasts (M) and sand; plane polarized light. d) Close-up of lower boundary of crack-fill shown in b and c. Boundary is irregular, and surrounding mudstone is stained near crack-fill; plane polarized light.

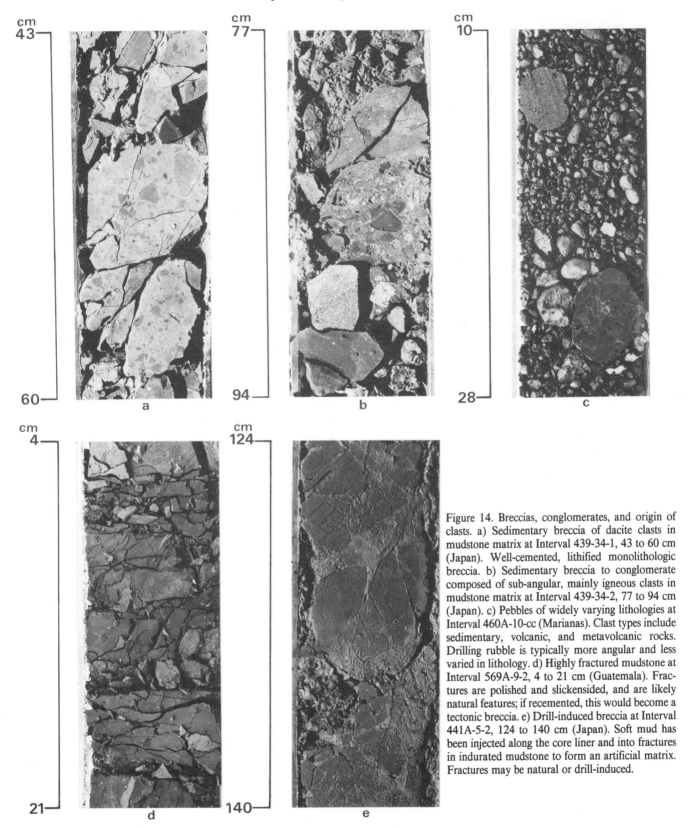

Figure 14. Breccias, conglomerates, and origin of clasts. a) Sedimentary breccia of dacite clasts in mudstone matrix at Interval 439-34-1, 43 to 60 cm (Japan). Well-cemented, lithified monolithologic breccia. b) Sedimentary breccia to conglomerate composed of sub-angular, mainly igneous clasts in mudstone matrix at Interval 439-34-2, 77 to 94 cm (Japan). c) Pebbles of widely varying lithologies at Interval 460A-10-cc (Marianas). Clast types include sedimentary, volcanic, and metavolcanic rocks. Drilling rubble is typically more angular and less varied in lithology. d) Highly fractured mudstone at Interval 569A-9-2, 4 to 21 cm (Guatemala). Fractures are polished and slickensided, and are likely natural features; if recemented, this would become a tectonic breccia. e) Drill-induced breccia at Interval 441A-5-2, 124 to 140 cm (Japan). Soft mud has been injected along the core liner and into fractures in indurated mudstone to form an artificial matrix. Fractures may be natural or drill-induced.

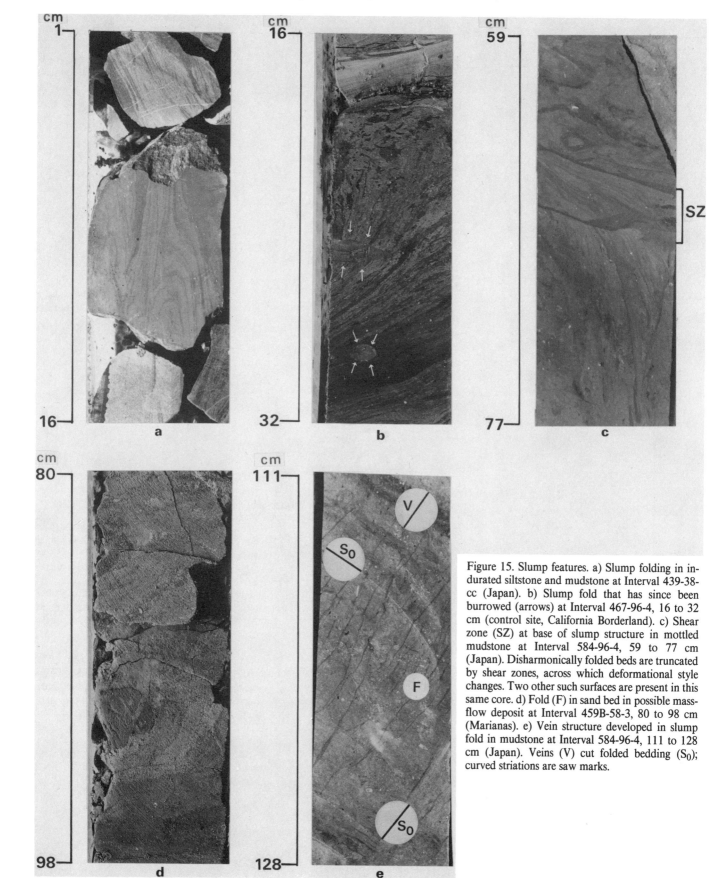

Figure 15. Slump features. a) Slump folding in indurated siltstone and mudstone at Interval 439-38-cc (Japan). b) Slump fold that has since been burrowed (arrows) at Interval 467-96-4, 16 to 32 cm (control site, California Borderland). c) Shear zone (SZ) at base of slump structure in mottled mudstone at Interval 584-96-4, 59 to 77 cm (Japan). Disharmonically folded beds are truncated by shear zones, across which deformational style changes. Two other such surfaces are present in this same core. d) Fold (F) in sand bed in possible mass-flow deposit at Interval 459B-58-3, 80 to 98 cm (Marianas). e) Vein structure developed in slump fold in mudstone at Interval 584-96-4, 111 to 128 cm (Japan). Veins (V) cut folded bedding (S_0); curved striations are saw marks.

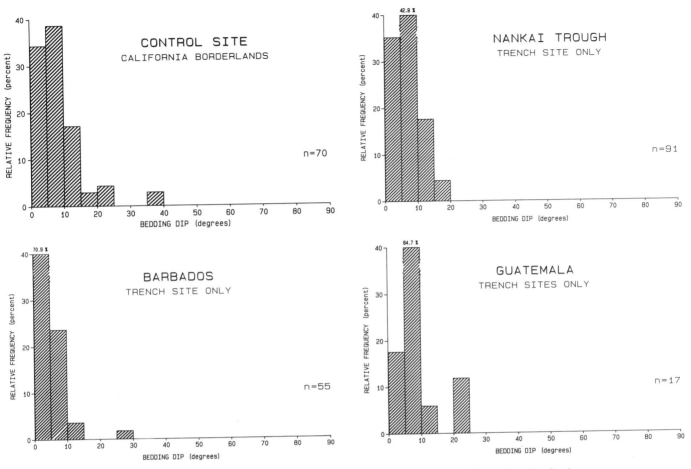

Figure 17. Bedding dip histograms for control sites: undeformed sequence from submarine fan in southern California Borderlands; trench fill from Nankai Trough; sedimentary section from Tiburon Rise seaward of deformation front of Barbados Ridge Complex; and trench fill from Middle America Trench off Guatemala.

cases of the latter type, disharmonic folding is accompanied by curved shear surfaces, apparently basal shears of slumps (Fig. 15c; Lundberg and Leggett, 1986). In some cases, slump features can be confused with stratal disruption (compare Figs. 2, 3, and 15) or with drill-induced features (see Drilling Deformation, Appendix). One unequivocal indicator of natural, near-surface, soft-sediment deformation is the presence of burrowing that post-dates folding (Fig. 15b).

PART 2. ANALYSIS OF STRUCTURAL DATA FROM DSDP CORES

Re-examination of all the DSDP cores provides a basis for the analysis of the distribution of structural features across the widely varied geology of modern convergent margins. The majority of the sediments and rocks recovered by DSDP in forearc regions are slope deposits. These deposits overlie basement terranes, that vary from recently accreted trench and oceanic deposits (Mexico, Barbados, Nankai) and older (pre-Neogene) accreted

deposits (Japan) to imbricated ophiolitic rocks (Guatemala), arc volcanic rocks (Marianas), and continental crust (upper slope, Mexico). We have analyzed structural features developed both in slope deposits and in the underlying terranes. Comparisons of the lateral distribution of these features must consider both whether they are located in the slope sediments or the underlying terrane, and the nature of the underlying terrane. In this part of the paper we use the data presented in the graphic structural logs to interpret the kinematic significance of the distribution of bedding dips, faults, and structural fabrics across the various margins.

Analysis of Bedding Dips

Bedding dips constitute one of the most fundamental fabric elements of forearc DSDP cores and indeed any deformed sequence. During re-examination of the DSDP cores true bedding dips were measured directly from the cores and have been displayed in graphic structural logs (Fig. 16, located in pocket inside back cover) and summarized in histograms (Figs. 17 to 19). Here we examine deformation displayed by bedding from largely un-

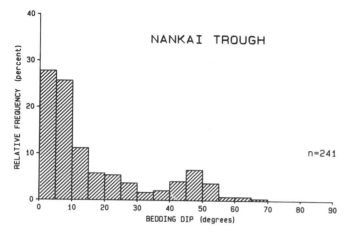

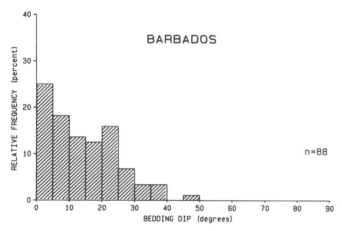

Figure 18. Bedding dip histograms for cores from imbricate-thrust zones near deformation fronts of Nankai Trough (Site 583) and Barbados Ridge Complex (Sites 541 & 542).

deformed sediments lying on the oceanic plate, from accreted sedimentary sequences, and from inner-slope deposits.

Oceanic Reference Sites. Sediments on the oceanic plate from the Nankai Trough, the Middle America Trench off Guatemala, and east of the Barbados ridge provide control on the structural state of material entering subduction zones. Additionally we have documented the bedding dips and other structural features of a site in the California Borderlands where no deformation is presently occurring (Site 467, Leg 63; Fig. 16). Most of the shallow bedding dips in the Nankai Trough (Figs. 16 and 17) are due to a hole deviation of as much as 9° (Lundberg and Karig, 1986). The modal value of bedding dips for the Barbados control site is about 4° (Figs. 16 and 17). Higher dips near the base of the hole probably record faulting of the oceanic crust early in the history of pelagic sediment accumulation. The median bedding dip at Sites 499 and 500 in the Middle America Trench off Guatemala is 8°, with values up to 21° attributable to normal faulting of the oceanic crust just prior to its underthrusting (Figs.

16 and 17). Data are few in the trench off Guatemala; a thicker trench fill would probably record more very-low-angle dips in comparison to those disturbed by normal faulting of the oceanic crust. The bedding dip histogram from the deep (1042 m) hole in the California Borderlands shows a modal value of between 5 and 10°, with a few significantly higher dips (as much as 40°) attributable to slumping (see Figs. 15b, 16, and 17).

Offscraped Sedimentary Sequences. The only penetrations of significantly long intervals of offscraped sedimentary sequences have occurred landward of the Nankai Trough and near the deformation front of the Barbados Ridge Complex (Fig. 18). The bedding dips from the accreted deposits off southern Mexico and the eastern Aleutian Trench are too few in number and too variable to be considered representative and therefore are not included in the following discussion.

Bedding dips from the offscraped sediment of the Nankai and Barbados transects are low, with modal values between 0 and 5° (Fig. 18). These low bedding dips are consistent with the imbricate thrusting inferred for both localities from associated seismic data (see Moore and Lundberg, this volume). Locally higher values are probably due to coring on the flanks of fault-bend folds. For example, in the Nankai data the secondary mode between 45 and 50° reflects penetration of the seaward limb of a hanging-wall anticline at the base of the slope (see section on Faulting).

Slope Deposits. By virtue of having accumulated in place, slope deposits constitute strain recorders for the deformation of the forearc regions. Patterns of bedding dips of inner-trench slope deposits provide a measure of the intensity of structural processes in this environment.

Sites on the lower slopes landward of the Japan Trench and the Middle America Trench off southern Mexico show a broad range of dip inclinations and high mean values of dip (Figs. 16 and 19). The graphic structural logs reveal zones of inconsistent dip, which off southern Mexico are probably associated with faults cutting the slope apron (Lundberg and Moore, 1982). The lower-slope deposits off southern Mexico and northern Japan overlie Neogene accretionary wedges (Moore and Lundberg, this volume). Apparently the continuing deformation or kneading of these tectonically consolidating wedges accounts for the relatively intense deformation of these slope sequences.

In comparison to slope aprons overlying Neogene accretionary wedges, upper-slope deposits off southern Mexico, northern Japan, and the Mariana arc show relatively little deformation. The Mariana forearc represents an end-member of this style of deformation, and bedding dips are comparable in magnitude to those of the control sites (compare Figs. 17 and 19). Most of the dip data for the Mariana histogram are derived from upper-slope sites overlying igneous basement (Hussong and Uyeda, 1982). Similarly, shallow bedding dips are observed in penetrations of the upper slope of the Japan Trench and the upper slope off southern Mexico. The Japan Trench upper slope is underlain by an intruded and presumably relatively rigid Cretaceous and Paleogene accretionary wedge (von Huene and others, 1982),

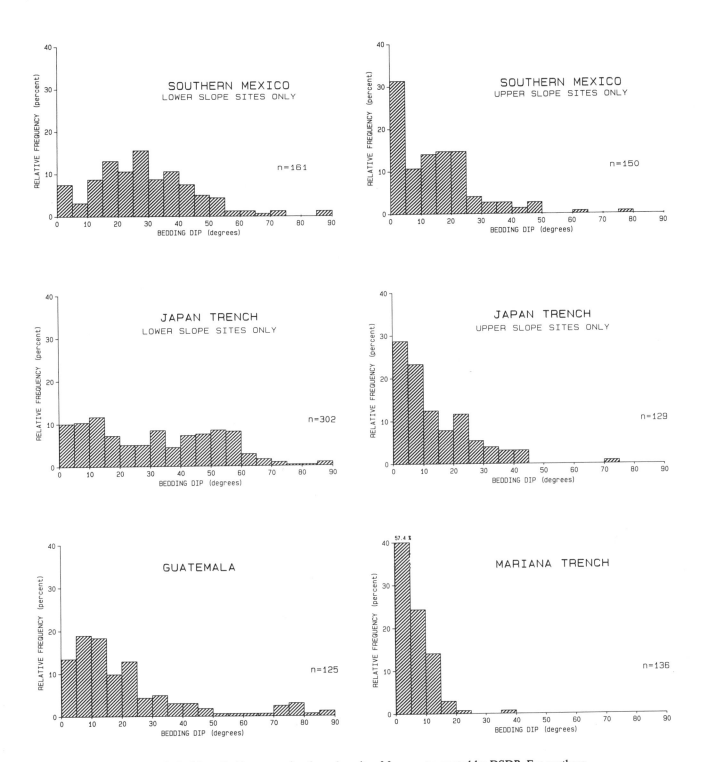

Figure 19. Bedding dip histograms for slope deposits of forearcs transected by DSDP. For southern Mexico and Japan localities lower-slope sites include all those seaward of trench-slope break including sites located in "transition zones." Upper-slope sites encompass those sites landward of trench-slope break and transition zones.

TABLE 1.   TILT-RATE (DIP/AGE) DATA: SLOPE SEDIMENTS FROM DSDP FOREARC SITES

Margin (covergence rate in km/m.y.)	Site	Mean Dip/ Age	S.D.	N	Distance from Trench (km)	Comments
Japan: (104)						
Leg 56-7	434	.17	.24	2	12.5	lower slope*
	435	1.88	.11	2	37	transition zone*
	440	8.16	7.17	121	27.5	transition zone
	441	6.25	3.80	4	15	lower slope*
	438	1.53	2.14	90	116	upper slope
	439	1.26	0.50	39	111	upper slope
Leg 87	584AB	3.61	1.77	173	41	transition zone
Marianas: (71)						
Leg 60	458	1.05	2.21	21	89	upper slope
	459	0.21	0.26	111	46.5	upper slope
	460	6565	10771	3	21	lower slope*
	461	38	----	1	10.5	lower slope*
Guatamala: (74)						
Leg 67	494	3.17	4.65	7	2.96	toe of slope*
	498A	189.9	85.14	2	2.78	toe of slope*
	496	1.18	1.65	15	43.3	seaward of FOR
	497	3.81	3.18	33	36.7	seaward of FOR
Leg 84	566	461.10	253.75	10	22.2	seaward of FOR, extreme values due to young age and moderate dips, few data*
	567	2.54	2.18	7	3.3	toe of slope*
	568	1.95	1.26	19	42.2	seaward of FOR
	569	1.44	0.87	15	36.6	seaward of FOR
	570	4.49	5.01	17	48	seaward of FOR
494-498-567		25.9	66.7	16	~3	combined data, extreme SD*
494-567		2.86	3.51	14	~3	combined data, acceptable SD
Mexico: (67)						
Leg 66	488	43.90	25.47	14	3.5	toe of slope
	491	8.44	5.07	114	13.2	lower slope
	492	3.09	2.03	33	20.5	lower slope
	490	7.17	3.56	96	21.5	transition zone
	489	1.68	0.91	20	33	upper slope
	493	1.08	1.27	130	51	upper slope
Aleutian: (65)						
Leg 18	181	79.40	60.84	12	11	on arcward side of large high at toe of slope, only used dips from slope sediments

Notes: Tilt rate data from trench slopes. For completeness, sites are listed that include too few data to meaningfully average. In cases, dips from nearby sites were combined to produce acceptable numbers of measurements with reasonable standard deviations (S.D.). Figures 21 and 22 include only means from sites or combinations of sites with greater than 10 data points (N) and standard deviations of less than twice the mean. Accordingly, we have not plotted sites (indicated by *) with very few data or highly variable dips. Morphologic subdivision of Guatemala is based on forearc outer high (FOR), seaward of which all sites occur. This feature approaches shelf depth here, making upper and lower slope designations inappropriate. No significant slope sediments were recovered at Nankai or Barbados transects. Convergence rates from Table 1 in Moore and Lundberg, this volume.

whereas upper-slope deposits off southern Mexico overlie a basement of continental igneous and metamorphic rocks (Watkins, McMillen and others, 1982). These less-deformed sedimentary sequences both are farther from the active trench and overlie structurally rigid basement; thus, it is unclear which of these two variables is the principal factor controlling deformation.

Rate of Deformation. Consideration of deformation rate rather than total magnitude of dip provides a more quantitative view of the kneading of slope deposits. To obtain a measure of deformation rate we have divided each dip measurement by the age of the sediment and therefore determined the mean tilting rate at its location (Table 1). Normalizing the dip data in this manner tends to accentuate the differences between the actively deforming, young, lower-slope sequences and the generally older, less deformed upper-slope sediment piles.

Southern Mexico and Guatemala are the only DSDP transects of contrasting basement types for which sufficient dip data exist to compare tilting rate of slope sediments in morphotectonically similar locations seaward of the trench slope break (Fig. 20). The comparison is strengthened by the near coincidence of convergence rates but weakened by the fact that the lower slope off Guatemala is somewhat wider than that off Mexico. A site-by-site comparison at various distances from the trench is not feasible because of lack of sufficient data off Guatemala. The histograms show a significantly lower rate of deformation for the Guatemala region, suggesting that the more rigid igneous basement is an inhibiting factor. A small percentage of the tilt-rate values (mainly from Site 566) are extremely high, however, due to the presence of moderate to steep dips in very young sediments. Clearly, an active deformation zone, perhaps a fault or slump surface, penetrates nearly to the sediment surface here. Overall, we believe that the deformation of the relatively rigid Guatemala slope is not as intense as that occurring in the slope apron of the macroscopically ductile accretionary wedge off southern Mexico. Furthermore, we would argue on less complete data that the concept of rigid versus macroscopically ductile forearcs can be applied to the remainder of the DSDP transects, with the Mariana forearc and the upper slope off Japan being rigid, and the lower slope off Japan and the Nankai, Eastern Aleutian, and Lesser Antilles regions being macroscopically ductile.

The availability of sediment seems to be the principal control on whether or not an accretionary wedge is built and therefore whether a macroscopically ductile wedge is available for deformation. Notable examples of relatively sediment-starved forearcs underlain by igneous basement include the extreme case of the Marianas and, to a lesser degree, Guatemala. In contrast, the Nankai Trough, Eastern Aleutian Trench, Middle America Trench off southern Mexico, and the Lesser Antilles are sediment dominated and have constructed macroscopically ductile accretionary wedges.

Tilt rates across the slope. Given that regions with differing basement types show contrasting intensities of deformation, how might rates of kneading of slope sediments vary across each of these different types of trench slopes? To approach this problem

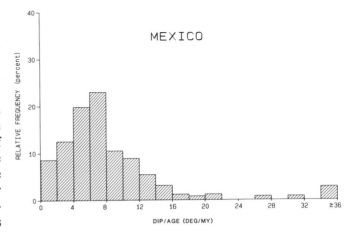

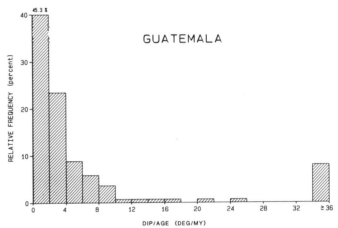

Figure 20. Histogram of tilting rates for slope sediments recovered at inner-slope sites off southern Mexico and Guatemala.

we have determined mean values for the tilt-rate data at individual sites (Table 1) and plotted these values against distance from the trench (Figs. 21 and 22). Because of the range in values, the standard deviations of the tilt-rate means are large; nevertheless, meaningful trends are apparent. For example, over the accretionary wedge off southern Mexico the tilt rate falls off exponentially with distance from the trench (Fig. 21). Rates of deformation over the continental basement are lower than those over the accretionary wedge and appear to vary at a different rate with distance from the trench. In order to compare tilting rates at all DSDP transects we have plotted the means from all forearc slope sediments (Fig. 22). In general the Neogene accretionary wedges and associated transition zones are deforming rapidly, with a pronounced decrease in deformation rate with distance from the trench. Conversely, forearc sites underlain by igneous or metamorphic basement (including the lithified Cretaceous accretionary wedge off Japan) deform more slowly with little variation in rate with distance from the trench. Intuitively, we expect localities with higher convergence rates to deform faster; unfortunately the comparable sets of bedding-dip data are not available from margins with differing convergence rates but similar basement types.

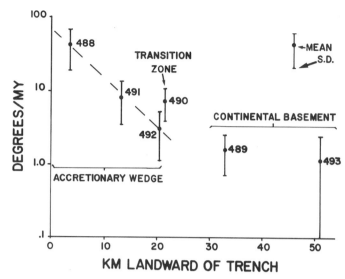

Figure 21. Means and standard deviations of individual dip values of slope sediments divided by age for DSDP sites drilled off southern Mexico. Mean value for each site represents average tilting rate of slope sediments at that point. Note apparent exponential decrease of tilting rate over accretionary wedge.

Tectonic versus gravitational control on surficial slope deformation. How do the tilt-rate data bear on the perennial question of tectonic versus gravitational deformation of trench slopes? The inclination of the slopes off southern Mexico and Guatemalan drilling areas are both 8 to 9°, and sediment lithologies are very similar. If the angle of the slope were the controlling factor, the amount of deformation should be the same. The lower slope off southern Mexico is in fact more deformed than the morphotectonically correlative sites off Guatemala (Fig. 20). Furthermore, the slope off southern Mexico is uniformly inclined through Sites 491 and 492 with a lower dip at Site 488 near the base of the slope. The deformation rate is highest at 488, however, and systematically decreases at 491 and 492 with distance from the trench (Fig. 21). Comparative pore pressure data are not available for both the Mexican and Guatemalan slopes. Higher pore pressure off southern Mexico could account for the more intense deformation even though slope inclination is equivalent to that off Guatemala. In the absence of pore pressure information, however, we tentatively conclude that the kneading of slope deposits here is more likely to be related to tectonic rather than gravitational forces.

Distribution of Faults

With the exception of tilted bedding surfaces, faults are the most common structural features developed in sediment and rock cored by DSDP at active margins. All conceivable geometries of displacement are represented: dip-slip, strike-slip, and oblique-slip faults are all common, and some fault surfaces show evidence of more than one type of displacement. Reverse faults range from

high-angle faults to low-angle thrust faults inferred from biostratigraphic and seismic evidence. Likewise, normal faults include high-angle, low-angle, and listric geometries. Offsets across faults vary from microscopic or barely discernible displacements to offsets greater than the trace of a fault in a core.

Regional Patterns of Faulting. Faults in DSDP cores from active margins are easier to interpret on a regional scale than a core scale. With the notable exceptions of the biostratigraphically documented thrust faults in Barbados cores, individual faults observed in the cores are less informative than are patterns seen throughout sites, especially throughout margins. For this reason we have summarized patterns of faulting on a margin-by-margin basis.

Mexico. The distribution of fractures in cores off southern Mexico can be correlated to the major subdivisions of the margin: accretionary wedge, transition zone, and continental crust (Fig. 23; see Moore and Lundberg, this volume, for description of subdivisions of the margin).

Three sites drilled on the lower slope all show similar patterns of fracturing and record a systematic age progression across strike. The age of the youngest sediment exhibiting fracturing in the three sites increases up the slope, from 0.6 m.y. at Site 488 to 3.3 m.y. at Site 491, to 8.6 m.y. at Site 492. The youngest fractured sediment in these sites has been interpreted as a slope deposit in all cases, with overlying intervals of sand and mud interpreted as offscraped trench deposits (Moore, Watkins, and Shipley, 1982). Fractures are typically moderately to steeply inclined and are dominated by dip-slip faults. In many cases the sense of displacement cannot be determined, although striations allow distinction of the line of most recent motion. Zones of pervasive fracturing (on a scale of millimeters to centimeters) are present in cores from Sites 488 and 492, and an in situ tectonic

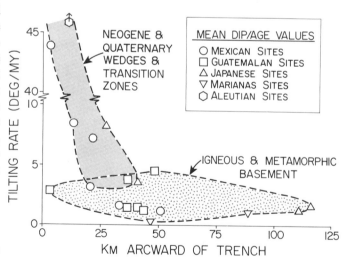

Figure 22. Mean tilting rate of slope sediments for all DSDP sites with a significant slope apron. Note that Neogene and Quaternary wedges and transition zones show rapid variation of tilt rate with distance arcward of trench whereas forearcs underlain by igneous and metamorphic basement show much less variability in tilting rate.

breccia at Site 488 contains partially cemented, angular clasts of hemipelagic mudstone.

Cores from sites drilled on the upper slope also show internally consistent patterns of fracturing. Dip-slip faults predominate at both Sites 489 and 493, but oblique-slip and strike-slip faults are present as well. The youngest fractured sediment at Site 493 is 8.0 Ma, recovered at 275 m, whereas the youngest fractured sediment at Site 489 is 17.3 Ma, recovered at 69 m. This latter occurrence is unusually old and is shallow as a result of Quaternary erosion; an angular unconformity recovered at 45 m from Site 489 represents a missing section of middle Miocene to lower Quaternary sediment that is present elsewhere on the upper slope (Watkins, Moore, and others, 1982).

The enigmatic transition zone was drilled at Site 490, and yielded a pattern of faulting strikingly different from that found at the other sites off Mexico. Here, oblique-slip faults predominate over dip-slip and strike-slip faults (Fig. 23). We interpret this as a result of oblique displacements between the contrasting crustal types that underlie the lower and upper slopes (Lundberg and Moore, 1982). The transition zone may have absorbed much of the oblique component of plate convergence. The youngest fractured sediment at Site 490 is Pliocene (2.7 Ma) mudstone at 315 m, younger than that at all other sites except Site 488, which is located only 3 km from the base of the trench slope. Discrete fractures are absent or indistinguishable in cores from the trench and the outer trench slope of the southern Mexico margin.

Marianas. Both sites drilled in the Marianas forearc that recovered fractures are located in a broad forearc basin: Site 458 was drilled near an uplifted block of basement, and Site 459 near the seaward edge of the forearc basin (Hussong and Uyeda, 1982). We found no discrete fractures in sediment cored at Sites 460 and 461, which were drilled on the lower slope. These two sites recovered only minor amounts of slope mud and loose angular rubble, in part drilling breccia but in part rounded sedimentary clasts of hard rock. We also found no fractures in sediment cored at Site 60, which was drilled (and only spot-cored) in the forearc basin to the south.

Site 458 recovered one core of fractured sedimentary rocks and a number of cores of fractured volcanic rocks. Core 27 (247 m) contains 2.3 m of fractured sandstone and siltstone, approximately 33 Ma. Volcanic basement was encountered directly beneath this sediment and was recovered in Cores 28 to 49 (Hussong, Uyeda and others, 1982). The volcanic rocks comprise boninite and tholeiitic basalt (Wood and others, 1982) and locally display abundant discrete fractures as well as two other fabrics generated by more complex faulting: scaly fabrics and web structure (see Part 1).

Basement cores from Site 459, located at the trenchward edge of the broad forearc basin, do not show scaly fabrics or web structure, despite more than 130 m of penetration into basement. Discrete fractures are abundant, however, both in sedimentary rocks and in the underlying volcanic rocks. We noted a single fracture in 12 Ma vitric mudstone at 122 m, and consistently fractured rock below 245 m, in rocks older than about 16 Ma.

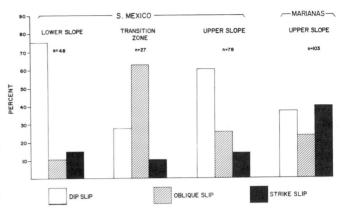

Figure 23. Relative abundances of dip-slip, oblique-slip, and strike-slip faults in southern Mexico and Mariana cores.

Normal faults are not as common in the Mariana cores as originally indicated by shipboard observations. Discrete fractures in cores from Sites 458 and 459 show abundant strike-slip and dip-slip faults, and numerous oblique-slip faults as well (Fig. 23). Given the nearly vertical orientation of many of the strike-slip faults, we surmise that they are actually much more common than indicated by our data compilation (see Appendix). Reports based on initial shipboard studies of the Mariana forearc cores emphasized the abundance and importance of normal faults (Hussong and Uyeda, 1982). Some features that were initially interpreted as normal faults in cores from Site 459 are subvertical strike-slip faults that exhibit subhorizontal striations; others are actually vein structure, displaying typical layer-parallel extension and minor offsets along "veins" that are oriented essentially perpendicular to bedding (see Part 1). The offsets, although locally striking, thus accomplish little or no extension. The seams that form the vein structure do reflect mild extension, but this is likely restricted to upper sediment layers and probably is not indicative of extension at depth (see Knipe, this volume).

In view of geochemical arguments that the Mariana forearc was initially broader (Meijer and others, 1982; Wood and others, 1982), the reportedly abundant normal faults were used as evidence supporting tectonic (subduction) erosion of the forearc (e.g., Hussong and Uyeda, 1982). Although seismic profiles suggest normal faulting in the Mariana forearc (Mrozowski and Hayes, 1980), the abundance of strike-slip faults in the cores suggests removal of part of the forearc by strike-slip faulting. If this were accomplished along a subvertical fault zone, however, some sedimentologic or subduction erosion would still be required in order to thin the remaining forearc crustal wedge. The wedge is tapered at present, and the recovered sections at Sites 458 and 459 preclude substantial thinning by uplift and surficial erosion since middle or late Eocene time.

Japan. Off northern Japan, patterns of faulting in slope sediments vary, depending on whether the sediments overlie the lithified Cretaceous to Paleogene accretionary wedge (upper slope) or the active, modern accretionary wedge (lower slope) (see Moore and Lundberg, this volume). Cores from the lower-most slope (Sites 434 to 441) are characterized by locally intense fracturing and by very poor recovery. Both aspects are probably results of intense pre-drilling brecciation of slope sediment, and the combination has precluded significant recovery of other secondary structures. What little material was recovered is commonly a loose breccia similar in appearance to cavings or drill breccia. It can be demonstrated in several cases that brecciation predated drilling, however, because clasts have been recemented together, something that has not been found in cores from control sites. In the minor coherent intervals recovered, there are comparable numbers of dip-slip, strike-slip, and oblique-slip faults.

Excellent recovery at Site 440, located on a mid-slope terrace, reveals abundant faults and fractures. Relatively few of these display striations; of those that do, strike-slip faults predominate, with nearly as many dip-slip faults and a smaller number of oblique-slip faults. Our interpretation is that Site 440, like Site 490 off Mexico, was drilled in a region that has accommodated an oblique component of convergence.

Site 584 was drilled 60 km north of Site 440 along the strike of the margin, in a position nearly analogous to that of Site 440 at the landward end of a mid-slope terrace (Karig, Kagami and others, 1983). In contrast to those at Site 440, most striated faults in cores from Site 584 are dip-slip faults, and most of these are normal faults. Some appear to be listric, with bedding in the hanging wall dipping into the fault surface at a steeper angle than the bedding in the foot wall (Lundberg and Leggett, 1986). Bedding dips at Site 584 cluster into discrete intervals of consistent dip (Fig. 24). The boundaries between these intervals probably reflect growth faulting, with episodic displacement along listric normal faults causing previously deposited strata to tilt at a progressively steeper angle. Dips measured in cores from between 250 and 830 m sub-bottom make up six discrete intervals of consistent dip, apparently reflecting six episodes of rotation, each of 11 to 14°, all in the same sense. This is consistent with the suggestion that regional-scale, listric normal faulting has tilted much of the section drilled at Site 584 (Karig, Kagami and others, 1983).

At Sites 438 and 439 no discrete fractures are developed in cores from depths shallower than 834 m, reflecting a relatively inactive tectonic setting. Dip-slip faults predominate, although oblique-slip faults are also abundant. Normal faulting on a large scale is seen in reflection profiles in this region (Nasu and others, 1980).

Nankai. Cores recovered from the Nankai Trough itself (Site 582) exhibit faults, unlike those from most other trenches sampled by DSDP. All these faults are normal faults, and all are found in Shikoku Basin deposits that underlie muddy turbidites of the trench fill. Most of these faults are healed and occur between 635 and 661 m subbottom, in sediment about 1.3 Ma; one open normal fault was found at 528 m in mudstone 0.8 Ma. Weakly developed vein structure is also present between 635 and 661 m (Lundberg and Karig, 1986). These extensional features have

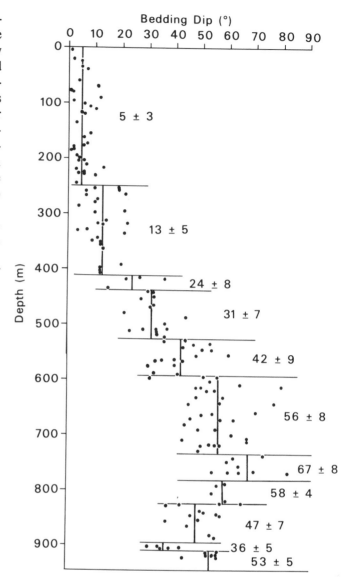

Figure 24. Bedding dips at Hole 584 (midslope terrace, Japan). Means and standard deviations over intervals interpreted as internally consistent. Modified from Lundberg and Leggett (1986).

been related to flexure of the subducting Philippine plate (Bray and others, 1986).

Discrete striated faults in cores that sample trench fill, which has been accreted onto the lower slope, are dominated by dip-slip faults. Processed seismic reflection profiles clearly show an imbricate system of thrust faults underlying the lower slope (Nasu and others, 1982), which progressively scrape off and stack up trench deposits (Karig, 1986). Sites drilled on the lower slope did penetrate through two of the seismically defined splays of the basal thrust. Both faults occur in intervals of poor recovery and there is no indication of the fault surfaces themselves in the cores, but the faults are reflected in downhole changes in bedding dip (Lundberg and Karig, 1986).

Barbados. In the Leg 78A area of the Barbados Ridge, detailed biostratigraphy identified six reverse faults (see graphic log, Fig. 16). These reverse faults have been interpreted as low-angle thrust faults on the basis of seismically defined structural style. Only one of these reverse faults is identifiable in the cores as a single fault surface, although three others are associated with zones of scaly foliation, stratal disruption, and/or intense fracturing, reflecting distributed brittle deformation (Cowan and others, 1984; Moore and others, this volume).

Seven other discrete faults found in our examination of cores from the Barbados drilling are all fairly steep, with dips ranging from 30 to 78°; averaging 54°. This conflicts with the interpretation of the major structural style as stacked low-angle thrust faults (Moore and Biju-Duval, 1984), especially in view of the sampling bias toward recovering shallow-dipping planar features. The low bedding dips observed in the Barbados cores suggest that the steep faults are not associated with significant fault-bend folding.

Guatamala. Discrete faults are only present locally in cores from the slope off Guatemala. The relatively few striated faults are predominantly dip-slip faults, with roughly half as many oblique-slip faults and very few strike-slip faults. Zones of relatively intense fracturing are common, however, as distributed slickensided surfaces on a cm scale at Sites 494 and 567 located at the base of the slope, and at Site 569 on the upper slope.

Fault zones may be represented by intervals of serpentinite in the cores. Beneath sediments of a slope apron, Leg 84 penetrated igneous basement, comprising mafic and ultramafic rocks interpreted as a dismembered ophiolite (Aubouin, von Huene and others, 1982). Intervals of peridotite, gabbro, metagabbro, diabase, basalt, and metabasalt are typically separated in the cores by serpentinite. These zones of serpentinite may mark important fault zones along which basement rocks have been imbricated, either during initial accretion of ocean crustal rocks or during later telescoping of an already emplaced forearc basement. Alternatively, some of these zones of serpentinite might represent the matrix of large-scale surficial debris flows, with clasts of basement rocks several meters across. Serpentinitic mud is present at Site 567, and occurs as a matrix in a probable debris flow deposit; large-scale examples are known in onland olistostromal deposits with mafic and ultramafic clasts and serpentinite matrix (Lockwood, 1971).

Distribution of Structural Fabrics

The distribution of structural fabrics in active-margin cores provides key information on how forearc deposits respond to stresses applied at modern subduction zones. Structural features of forearc regions represent the early stages of development of fabrics found in ancient subduction complexes, and samples from modern active margins have known tectonic settings. We can constrain their age, lithology, physical properties, sedimentation rate, and burial history. Additionally, we know their large-scale structural context, as provided by seismic reflection data. Constraints from the modern environment are especially valuable because many of the secondary fabrics are controlled by composition, texture, degree of induration, and structural regime.

Structures Reflecting Layer-Parallel Compression or Layer-Parallel Shear. A number of the structural features of active-margin cores record layer-parallel compression or shear. The crenulations that crinkle bedding in laminated diatomaceous sediment on the Japan slope, for example, accommodate layer-parallel shortening. The kink bands found in hemipelagic mudstone from the lowermost slope of the Nankai Trough likewise record layer-parallel shortening. We believe that the scaly foliation and stratal disruption represent layer-parallel shear. Where we have independent evidence of structural regime (Barbados and Mexico), these fabrics are found within large-scale shear zones in regions of thrust faulting (horizontal shortening). In the lower slope off Barbados, high resolution biostratigraphy and varied lithology allow reverse faults to be pinpointed in the cores; and the zones of scaly foliation and stratal disruption are consistently located near these reverse faults. Off Mexico, scaly foliation and stratal disruption are restricted mainly to areas with regional evidence for thrust faulting (Moore, Watkins, and Shipley, 1982).

Structures Reflecting Layer-Parallel Extension. We believe vein structure and spaced foliation reflect layer-parallel extension. These features have been referred to as dewatering veins, but microstructural work by Knipe (this volume) indicates that they form as zones of disaggregation during layer-parallel extension, and apparently subsequently collapse under layer-parallel compression. Once formed, they may serve as dewatering conduits, originally suggested by Cowan (1982b). Vein structure has not been reported in passive margin cores, nor have we found examples in control sites. Vein structure occurs in cores from all active margin transects, in carbonate deposits as well as in siliceous and hemipelagic mudstone. Spaced foliation is a macroscopically similar fabric, probably related to vein structure (see section on Vein Structure), and may also reflect initial layer-parallel extension (Knipe, this volume). Spaced foliation in cores off Mexico is spatially associated with normal faulting; here all folia display fine dip-slip striations.

In addition to semi-penetrative fabrics, many cores are also cut by discrete faults, some of which are closely associated with vein structure. These are bedding-parallel, healed shear zones that constitute basal shear zones for bands of vein structure that are restricted to stratigraphic horizons. These shear zones are low-angle detachment surfaces along which upper layers of sediment have apparently moved downslope (Knipe, this volume). Extensional faulting, postdating vein structure, is also recorded by listric normal faults found in cores off Japan (Lundberg and Leggett, 1986).

Distribution of Structural Fabrics. Structures that record layer-parallel compression or shear versus those that record layer-parallel extension occur in contrasting tectonic regimes, commonly across a single active margin. Structures characteristic of layer-parallel compression on shear typically dominate sites on lowermost slopes, whereas those indicative of layer-parallel extension are mainly found at sites on upper slopes (Fig. 25). The

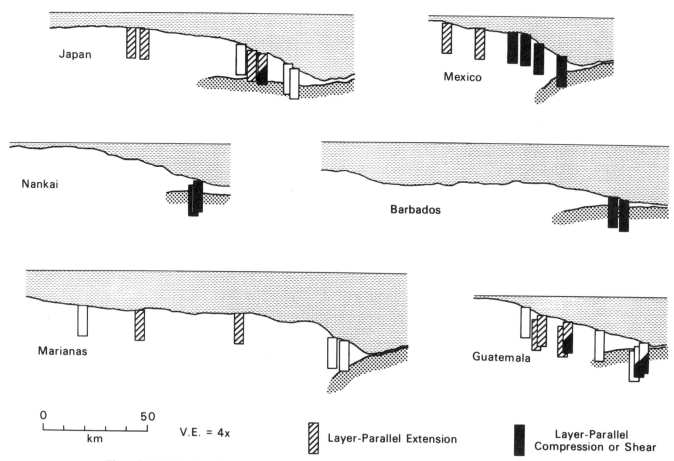

Figure 25. Distribution of compressional and extensional structures in forearc sites. Bathymetric profiles for the six active margins transected by DSDP are shown at the same scale and vertical exaggeration for comparison. The landward portions of the various forearcs regions are not shown; some, especially the Nankai and Barbados forearcs, extend considerable distances arcward of the depicted region. All forearc drilling sites are located on their respective slopes and have been classified by the predominance of compressional or extensional structures. Sites that lack sufficient structural data to be classified (indicated by empty rectangles) are generally sites with poor recovery; the lack of data is a result of the lack of cored sediment.

well-sampled transect off Mexico shows lower-slope sites dominated by structures of layer-parallel compression or shear and upper-slope sites dominated by extensional structures. The other five transects cannot be characterized as completely as a result of poor recovery and lack of drill sites, but the results are consistent with the fabric distribution off Mexico. In the Nankai and Barbados zones there is abundant evidence in fabrics of horizontal shortening or layer-parallel shear in the lowermost slope, which is consistent with seismically defined thrust faulting (Nasu and others, 1982; Westbrook, 1982). The upper and mid-slope regions of these forearcs, however, remain unsampled. In contrast, it is the lower slope that remains poorly known in the Mariana transect, and to a lesser extent the Guatemala and Japan transects. At these margins extensional features occur in cores from upper slope sites; we have little information on structures in lower-slope sediment.

Causes of Fabric Distribution. We believe that the kink

bands found at the base of the Nankai slope formed in the proto-thrust zone located in the landward portion of the Nankai Trough (see Part 1; also Lundberg and Karig, 1986). These kink bands represent layer-parallel shortening associated with initial accretionary processes. We ascribe the majority of stratal disruption, cataclastic fabrics, and scaly foliation in active-margin cores to compression and shearing due directly to subduction. These fabrics are developed in slope sediments deposited on lowermost trench slopes, as well as in off-scraped trench deposits in growing accretionary wedges. Their development in slope apron sediment reflects "kneading" of slope deposits by the subjacent accretionary wedge.

Surficial gravity sliding and associated layer-parallel extension may explain the observed extensional features in the cores (Knipe, this volume). Knipe proposes that most of the extensional features found in active-margin cores form as a result of downslope movement of the upper layers of sediment along low-angle (layer-parallel) detachment surfaces. Because slide scarps are typically not seen on these slopes, the amount of displacement on any one detachment surface would necessarily be relatively small. Displacement apparently does not break through to the surface and may not be restricted to a single fault surface. A related process of distributed creep may be occurring off Costa Rica (Baltuck and others, 1985).

Gravity sliding may produce compressional features in the down-slope portions of slide masses as well (Knipe, this volume). The crenulations found off Japan, at Site 440 on the mid-slope terrace, may represent such a feature. Associated sediments are slump folded (see Part 1) and the remainder of the section recovered at Site 440 shows abundant vein structure.

SUMMARY

Our mesoscopic and optical microscopic review of structural features of DSDP cores from forearcs reveals the following.

1) Scaly mudstones and stratal disruption with associated cataclasis most commonly reflect tectonic deformation (usually thrust faulting) beneath lower slopes of forearcs.

2) Vein structure is present predominantly in cores from upper slope sites. Individual seams are oriented consistently normal to bedding, whereas bands of nested seams are typically restricted to specific beds. In intervals of tilted bedding that also exhibit vein structure, the vein structure has been tilted about the same axis, which is essentially the intersection of bedding and vein structure. Vein fillings are principally altered in situ sediment, rather than material that has injected or migrated into the veins.

3) Kink bands in recently accreted Nankai Trough turbidites have accommodated pervasive layer-parallel shortening that may have occurred in the "proto-thrust" zone in the landward portion of the trench.

4) Crenulation folds of laminated sediment in the lower slope landward of the Japan Trench represent layer-parallel shortening that may have occurred in the toe of a slump.

5) Faults are represented in active-margin cores by a wide variety of features ranging from clean, open fractures to centimeter-thick fault zones composed of milled mudstone and tectonic breccias. Faults are abundant relative to those observed in cores from tectonically quiescent control sites. Faults at active-margin sites typically vary widely in orientation and sense of offset, record a complex strain history, and are dominated by dip-slip displacements. Notable exceptions to this general pattern include the dominantly oblique-slip faults in the transition zone of Mexico, suggestive of a zone of crustal decoupling; strike-slip faults in the Mariana forearc, suggesting forearc truncation by transform faulting; and the consistent pattern of normal faults at Site 584 off Japan, reflecting significant extension within the forearc.

6) Analysis of the magnitude of bedding dips reveals more intense tilting of slope sediments across accreted sediment wedges than over forearcs underlain by igneous and metamorphic basement. The rate of tilting over accreted sediment wedges decreases dramatically arcward away from the trench, reflecting the progressive consolidation and developing rigidity of the sedimentary basement.

7) Structural fabrics reflecting horizontal compression or layer-parallel shear (thrust faults, scaly mudstone, stratal disruption, and kink bands) are preferentially concentrated in lower-slope regions, whereas extensional features (vein structure, normal faults) occur most commonly in upper-slope regions.

ACKNOWLEDGMENTS

We gratefully acknowledge the Submarine Geology and Geophysics Program of the National Science Foundation for financial support of this research (grants OCE8110394 and OCE8315836 to Moore). We thank the staff of the Deep Sea Drilling Project for their assistance during Lundberg's extended visits to the core repositories. We thank Gene Gonzales for his skillful preparation of thin sections of partially lithified sediments. We have benefited from discussions with a number of people, notably Ed Beutner, Darrel Cowan, Rob Knipe, and Steve Lucas of the structural synthesis group; shipboard colleagues Dan Karig and Jeremy Leggett; and Mike Arthur, Tim Byrne, Bobb Carson, and Roland von Huene. Tim Byrne and Othmar Tobisch provided helpful reviews of the manuscript.

APPENDIX: METHODS, ORIENTATION ERRORS, AND DRILLING DEFORMATION

Methods

All measurements of bedding, faults, and fabrics are true dips. Additionally, for fractures and faults we measured the true dip and dip azimuth of the fracture surface and the trend and plunge, or rake and rake reference direction, of each resolvable set of striations. Where possible, we also determined the sequence of striation development and noted offsets. In order to classify striated faults, we call faults with striations that rake 70 degrees or more dip-slip faults, those with striations that rake less than 20 degrees strike-slip faults, and the remainder oblique-slip faults.

We measured dip azimuths and plunges using a convention with reference to the split core surface. Using this approach, and noting the extent of coherent intervals through which drill-induced rotation had not taken place, allowed us to compare the orientation of bedding, fault surfaces, and striations on different fault surfaces. This approach also permits us to integrate our data with paleomagnetic measurements, which provide absolute azimuthal orientations.

Orientation Errors

Errors in orientation data may arise from a number of sources.

Although the angular deviation of the drill holes (and thus of the cores) from true vertical is known, they generally cannot be oriented with respect to azimuthal measurements due to their rotation during drilling. Locally, portions of cores may be azimuthally oriented by reference to their paleomagnetic declination; in addition, cores recovered using the hydraulic piston corer are commonly oriented in situ with respect to azimuth by use of a downhole camera. Errors in the physical measurement of planar surfaces, accomplished by collecting two apparent dips on orthogonal faces (both vertical in situ), are estimated at less than 2 to 3° (based on replication of measurements, comparison of measurements by various operators, and comparison with hole deviation data through seismically defined flat-lying beds). More significant errors may result from the assumption of a vertical hole. Hole deviations of as much as 9° have been recorded, but deviations are commonly only a few degrees (G. Foss, personal communication, 1982). Overall, we believe a reasonable error estimate on any measurement may be about 5°; conclusions are most reliably drawn from patterns of bedding dips or from statistical summaries of dip data.

A pitfall in interpreting the distribution of bedding and faults arises from coring through variably oriented planes. A strong bias occurs in the orientation of discrete planar features encountered in a one-dimensional drill hole. Horizontal surfaces are sampled much more often than equally abundant vertical ones, which must be pervasive on a scale of tens of cm or so in order to be likely to be sampled. Therefore, steeper orientations are probably more common than indicated by core data, whereas horizontal surfaces will have been missed only by a lack of recovery.

Drilling Deformation

Features produced during the drilling and handling of cores vary considerably in geometry and appearance and are not always easily identified. Below we summarize criteria useful in identifying drill-induced artifacts that resemble natural deformational features in DSDP cores (see also Arthur and others, 1980; Lundberg and Moore, 1982; Leggett, 1982; and Dengo, 1982). There is clearly an element of subjectivity in the interpretation of such features; we have adopted a conservative approach, noting such features during our data collection but leaving them out of our compiled graphic logs of structural features. The development of deformational features by drilling is clearly dependent on physical properties. In a number of examples, artificial deformation is associated with or overprints natural deformational features.

Artificial Fractures. Artificial features are identified on the basis of symmetry with respect to the core axis. Artificial open fractures occur as conjugate sets, symmetric about the (originally vertical) core axis, or as long, curving fractures subparallel to the core axis. They usually display hackly or rough surfaces with local, poorly developed striations. Some artificial fractures show rough striations of variable orientation.

Natural fractures are characterized by highly planar surfaces and commonly occur in parallel sets. Healed fractures are clearly in situ features, but the origins of open fractures are equivocal. We have interpreted planar open fractures as natural if they show smooth, shiny or slickensided surfaces, especially if they are parallel to healed fractures or show no obvious symmetrical relationship to the core axis.

Artificial Stratal Disruption. Drilling in stiff mud and soft mudstone produces a variety of features by rotation along an originally horizontal surface (drilling laminations, or drilling biscuits; see Leggett, 1982). These dark, fine-grained "laminations" commonly truncate inclined primary features in the cores, producing an artificial disruption of inclined bedding and other structures (Fig. 12). The orientation of drilling laminations perpendicular to the core axis, and their regular spacing, allows them to be recognized as artifacts of drilling. In addition to readily identified drilling artifacts, there is a spectrum of more complex types of drill-induced chaos. These include swirling of primary laminations into a variety of characteristic geometries, which are commonly observed

Figure 26. Stratal disruption that was probably produced by drilling deformation in varicolored mud and silt at Interval 488-29-4, 130 to 147 cm. Most of Core 488-29 exhibits this style of swirling, much of which curves asymptotically down to one side of the core liner. Fabric varies in orientation throughout the core, but steep to vertical (core-parallel) orientations are common. Mud has flowed plastically; some of this may be pre-drilling, natural deformation, as suggested by location just below a major zone of deformation (see Lundberg and Moore, 1982; and Site 488 Chapter in Watkins, Moore, and others, 1982).

within, although not restricted to, drilling biscuits of short to moderate length (3 to 5 cm) (Fig. 12). Characteristic geometries include small, broad to open folds with horizontal axial surfaces, which affect only laminations along one side of the core, and which invariably warp them concavely outward; and doughnut or annulus-shaped swirls, in which the folds just described wrap clear around the core axis. Artificially swirled laminations commonly show a symmetry with respect to the core axis (Fig. 26), but in long intervals of similarly deformed sediment some portions are strikingly asymmetric, suggesting that symmetric structures are produced on a larger scale than that of the core liner, perhaps by the bit itself.

Small-scale Folds. We have interpreted virtually all core-scale folds as either artificial (drill-induced) folds or as slump features (see section on Folds). Artificial folds are produced by a 180° rotation along a horizontal surface (drilling lamination) in an interval of steeply inclined bedding. Drilling laminations cannot always be identified as such in sediment of a tacky consistency, complicating fold interpretation.

Artificial Scaly Fabrics. Drilling deformation is difficult to rule out in examples of poorly developed scaly fabrics in partially lithified sediments. This is especially troublesome where chips have "caved" or fallen down the drillhole from fractures or otherwise unstable intervals previously penetrated. These cavings often occur in a clayey drilling matrix, resulting in a "blocks-in-matrix" fabric. In the absence of obvious clues or biostratigraphic evidence, cavings are identified by their concentration in (although not restriction to) the upper sections of any given core. Samples from core catchers also tend to be more deformed than the standard sections, probably resulting from their physical extrusion from the core catcher. Scaly serpentinite and serpentinitic mud in Guatemalan cores are typically strongly deformed by drilling, commonly swirled into curving patterns that are symmetric with respect to the long axis of the core; here it is difficult to interpret how much of the scaly fabric is natural deformation.

REFERENCES

Arthur, M. A., Carson, B., and von Huene, R., 1980, Initial tectonic deformation of hemipelagic sediment at the leading edge of the Japan convergent margin, *in* Scientific Party, Initial Reports of the Deep Sea Drilling Project: Washington, D.C., U.S. Government Printing Office, v. 56, 57, pt. 1, p. 569–614.

Aubouin, J., von Huene, R., and others, 1982, Site 494: Middle America Trench lower slope, *in* Aubouin, J., von Huene, R., and others, eds., Initial Reports of the Deep Sea Drilling Project: Washington, D.C., U.S. Government Printing Office, v. 67, p. 27–73.

Baltuck, M., McDougall, K., and Arnott, R. J., 1985, Mass movement along the inner wall of the Middle America Trench, Costa Rica, *in* von Huene, R., Aubouin, J., and others, eds., Initial Reports of the Deep Sea Drilling Project: Washington, D.C., U.S. Government Printing Office, v. 84, p. 551–570.

Bray, C. J., and Karig, D. E., 1986, Physical properties of sediments from the Nankai Trough, Deep Sea Drilling Project Leg 87A, Sites 582 and 583, *in* Kagami, H., Karig, D. E., Coulbourn, W. T., and others, eds., Initial Reports of the Deep Sea Drilling Project: Washington, D.C., U.S. Government Printing Office, v. 87, p. 827–842.

Byrne, T., 1984, Structural geology of melange terranes in the Ghost Rocks Formation, *in* Raymond, L., ed., Melanges: Their origin and significance: Geological Society of America Special Paper 198, p. 21–51.

Cowan, D. S., 1974, Deformation and metamorphism of the Franciscan subduction zone complex northwest of Pacheco Pass, California: Geological Society of America Bulletin, v. 85, p. 1623–1634.

—— , 1982a, Deformation of partly dewatered and consolidated Franciscan sediments near Piedras Blancas Point, California, *in* Leggett, J. K., ed., Trench-Forearc Geology: Geological Society of London Special Publication No. 10, p. 439–458.

—— , 1982b, Origin of "vein structure" in slope sediments on the inner slope of the Middle America Trench off Guatemala, *in* Aubouin, J., von Huene, and others, eds., Initial Reports of the Deep Sea Drilling Project: Washington, D.C., U.S. Government Printing Office, v. 67, p. 645–650.

Cowan, D. S., Moore, J. C., Roeske, S. M., Lundberg, N., and Lucas, S. E., 1984, Structural features at the deformation front of the Barbados Ridge Complex, Deep Sea Drilling Project Leg 78A, *in* Biju-Duval, B. and Moore, J. C., and others, eds., Initial Reports of the Deep Sea Drilling Project: Washington, D.C., U.S. Government Printing Office, v. 78A, p. 535–548.

Dengo, C., 1982, A structural analysis of cores from Leg 67 transect across the Middle America Trench, Guatemala, *in* von Huene, R., Aubuoin, J., and others, eds., Initial Reports of the Deep Sea Drilling Project: Washington, D.C., U.S. Government Printing Office, v. 67, p. 651–666.

Hsü, K. J., 1974, Melanges and their distinction from olistostromes, *in* Dott, R. H., Jr., and Shaver, R. H., eds., Modern and ancient geosynclinal sedimentation: Society of Economic Paleontologists and Mineralogists Special Publication No. 19, p. 321–333.

Hussong, D. M., and Uyeda, S., 1982, Tectonic processes and the history of the Mariana Arc: A synthesis of the results of Deep Sea Drilling Project Leg 60, *in* Hussong, D. M., Uyeda, S., and others, eds., Initial Reports of the Deep Sea Drilling Project: Washington, D.C., U.S. Government Printing Office, v. 60, p. 909–929.

Hussong, D. M., Uyeda, S., and others, 1982, Site 458: Mariana fore-arc, *in* Hussong, D. M., Uyeda, S., and others, eds., Initial Reports of the Deep Sea Drilling Project: Washington, D.C., U.S. Government Printing Office, v. 60, p. 263–307.

Karig, D. E., 1986, The framework of deformation in the Nankai Trough, *in* Kagami, H., Karig, D. E., Coulbourn, W. T., and others, eds., Initial Reports of the Deep Sea Drilling Project: Washington, D.C., U.S. Government Printing Office, v. 87, p. 927–940.

Karig, D. E., Kagami, H., and others, 1983, Varied responses to subduction in Nankai Trough and Japan Trench forearcs: Nature, v. 304, p. 148–151.

Leggett, J. K., 1982, Drilling-induced structures in Leg 66 cores, *in* Watkins, J. S., Moore, J. C., and others, eds., Initial Reports of the Deep Sea Drilling Project: Washington, D.C., U.S. Government Printing Office, v. 66, p. 531–538.

Lockwood, J. P., 1971, Sedimentary and gravity-slide emplacement of serpentine: Geological Society of America Bulletin, v. 82, p. 919–936.

Lundberg, N., and Karig, D. E., 1986, Structural features in cores from the Nankai Trough, Deep Sea Drilling Project Leg 87A, *in* Kagami, H., Karig, D. E., Coulbourn, W. T., and others, eds., Initial Reports of the Deep Sea Drilling Project: Washington, D.C., U.S. Government Printing Office, v. 87, p. 797–808.

Lundberg, N., and Leggett, J. K., 1986, Structural features in cores from the Japan Trench, Deep Sea Drilling Project Leg 87B, *in* Kagami, H., Karig, D. E., Coulbourn, W. T., and others, eds., Initial Reports of the Deep Sea Drilling Project: Washington, D.C., U.S. Government Printing Office, v. 87, p. 809–826.

Lundberg, N., and Moore, J. C., 1982, Structural features of the Middle America Trench slope off southern Mexico, Deep Sea Drilling Project Leg 66, *in* Watkins, J. S., Moore, J. C., and others, eds., Initial Reports of the Deep Sea Drilling Project: Washington, D.C., U.S. Government Printing Office, v. 66, p. 793–805.

Mandl, G., de Jong, L.N.J., and Maltha, A., 1976, Shear zones in granular material: An experimental study of their structure and mechanical genesis: Rock Mechanics, v. 9, p. 95–144.

Meijer, A., Anthony, E., and Reagan, M., 1982, Petrology of volcanic rocks from the fore-arc sites, *in* Hussong, D. M., Uyeda, S., and others, eds., Initial Reports of the Deep Sea Drilling Project: Washington, D.C., U.S. Government Printing Office, v. 60, p. 709–729.

Moore, J. C., and Biju-Duval, B., 1984, Tectonic synthesis, Deep Sea Drilling Project Leg 78A: Structural evolution of offscraped and underthrust sediment, northern Barbados Ridge Complex, *in* Biju-Duval, B., Moore, J. C., and others, eds., Initial Reports of the Deep Sea Drilling Project: Washington, D.C., U.S. Government Printing Office, v. 78A, p. 601–621.

Moore, J. C., and Karig, D. E., 1976, Sedimentology, structural geology and tectonics of the Shikoku subduction zone: Geological Society of America Bulletin, v. 87, p. 1259–1268.

Moore, J. C., Watkins, J. S., and Shipley, T. H., 1982, Summary of accretionary processes, DSDP Leg 66: Offscraping, underplating, and deformation of the slope apron, *in* Watkins, J. S., Moore, J. C., and others, eds., Initial Reports of the Deep Sea Drilling Project: Washington, D.C., U.S. Government Printing Office, v. 66, p. 825–836.

Morgenstern, N. R., and Tchalenko, J. S., 1967, Microscopic structures in kaolin subjected to direct shear: Geotechnique, v. 17, p. 309–328.

Mrozowski, C. and Hayes, D., 1980, A seismic reflection study of faulting in the Mariana forearc, *in* D. E. Hayes, ed., The Tectonic and Geologic Evolution of Southeast Asian Seas and Islands: American Geophysical Union Geophysical Monograph No. 23, p. 223–234.

Nasu, N., Tomoda, Y., Kobayashi, K., Kagami, H., Uyeda, S., and others, 1982, Multi-channel seismic reflection data across Nankai Trough: IPOD-Japan Basic Data Series, No. 4: Tokyo, Ocean Research Institute, University of Tokyo, 34 p.

Nasu, N., von Huene, R., Ishiwada, Y., Langseth, M., Bruns, T., and Honza, E., 1980, Interpretation of multichannel seismic reflection data, Legs 56 and 57, Japan Trench transect, Deep Sea Drilling Project, *in* Scientific Party, Initial Reports of the Deep Sea Drilling Project: Washington, D.C., U.S. Government Printing Office, v. 56, 57, pt. 1, p. 489–503.

Ogawa, Y., 1980, Beard-like veinlet structure as fracture cleavage in the Neogene siltstone in the Miura and Bosa Peninsulas, central Japan: Science Reports, Department of Geology, Kyushu University, v. 13, no. 2, p. 321–327.

Watkins, J. S., McMillen, K. J., Bachman, S. B., Shipley, T. H., Moore, J. C., and Angevine, C., 1982, Tectonic Synthesis, Leg 66: Transect and vicinity, *in* Watkins, J. S., Moore, J. C., and others, eds., Initial Reports of the Deep Sea Drilling Project: Washington, D.C., U.S. Government Printing Office, v. 66, p. 837–849.

Watkins, J. S., Moore, J. C., and others, 1982, Site 489, *in* Watkins, J. S., Moore, J. C., and others, eds., Initial Reports of the Deep Sea Drilling Project: Washington, D.C., U.S. Government Printing Office, v. 66, p. 107–150.

Westbrook, G. K., 1982, The Barbados Ridge Complex: tectonics of a mature forearc system, *in* Leggett, J. K., ed., Trench-Forearc Geology: Geological Society of London Special Publication No. 10, p. 275–290.

Wood, D. A., Marsh, N. G., Tarney, J., Joron, J-L., Fryer, P., and Treuil, M., 1982, Geochemistry of igneous rocks recovered from a transect across the Mariana Trough, arc, fore-arc, and trench, Sites 453 through 461, Deep Sea Drilling Project Leg 60, *in* Hussong, D. M., Uyeda, S., and others, eds., Initial Reports of the Deep Sea Drilling Project: Washington, D.C., U.S. Government Printing Office, v. 60, p. 611–645.

von Huene, R., Langseth, M., Nasu, N. and Okada, H., 1982, A summary of Cenozoic tectonic history along IPOD Japan Transect: Geological Society of America Bulletin, v. 93, p. 829–846.

Manuscript Accepted by the Society March 10, 1986

Geological Society of America
Memoir 166
1986

Faulting mechanisms in slope sediments: Examples from Deep Sea Drilling Project cores

R. J. Knipe
Department of Earth Sciences
The University
Leeds LS2 9JT, United Kingdom

ABSTRACT

The microstructural features of extensional faults developed in slope sediments from the Mariana trench (D.S.D.P. Leg 60) and the Japan Trench (Leg 87) are reported. The study provides information on faulting mechanisms, fluid flow along faults, and processes of fault zone widening. A wide variety of fault geometries and deformation fabrics are preserved along the faults studied, although the deformation mechanisms involved in each case appear to be disaggregation and particulate flow with and without fracturing. In most cases studied the fault zones are composed of anastomosing micromovement zones of finite porosity collapse. It is suggested that the different fault rock fabrics arise primarily from differences in the strain rate history experienced. Individual faults (e.g. 760 m down hole 584, Leg 87) show some evidence of deformation under a range of strain rates and a range of fault zone widening processes. Evidence for disaggregation and particle sinking along a fault from Leg 60 indicates dewatering via slow fluid expulsion.

INTRODUCTION

Recent studies of faults located at active margins have focused on the geometrical evolution of fault arrays (Karig and Sharman, 1975; Seely, 1977; Moore and Biju-Duval, 1984; Silver and others, 1985). Very few studies have attempted to unravel the mechanisms and processes involved in the development of faults. The Deep Sea Drilling Project (D.S.D.P.) provides an important source of material for the analysis of faulting at shallow depths (<1 km), during the critical stages of lithification, when the sediment properties such as porosity, permeability, and strength are changing rapidly (Shepherd and Bryant, 1983; Bray and Karig, 1985).

In this paper I describe the microstructures of selected faults recovered from D.S.D.P. cores and attempt to assess the mechanisms and history of faulting involved in the development of faults located in slope sediments at active margins. The paper complements the analysis of the distribution of faults at active margins reported by Lundberg and Moore (this volume) and describes the detailed microstructural features of four normal faults. A microstructural study of the scaly fabrics associated with contractional faults is presented by Moore and others (this volume). The regional setting of each fault described is reviewed

before its mesoscopic and microstructural features are described and interpreted.

MARIANA TRENCH-SLOPE FAULTS: LEG 60, SITE 495B, DEPTH INTERVAL 425–500M

Regional Setting and Mesoscopic Fault Geometry

The Mariana trench, forearc, and trough regions form part of a complex margin involving active subduction and backarc spreading, which has evolved from the Eocene to the present (Karig, 1971; Hussong and Uyeda, 1982). No significant accretion of Pacific plate sediment or crustal rocks has been found, and the area appears to have experienced a long history of extensional deformation producing steep faults associated with vertical and strike slip movements (see Hussong and Uyeda, 1982; Lundberg and Moore, this volume).

The faults described here were recovered from Site 459B, located approximately 50 km from the trench axis at the seaward edge of the forearc basin near the trench-slope break (see Hussong and Uyeda, 1982). The upper 559 m of this hole recovered

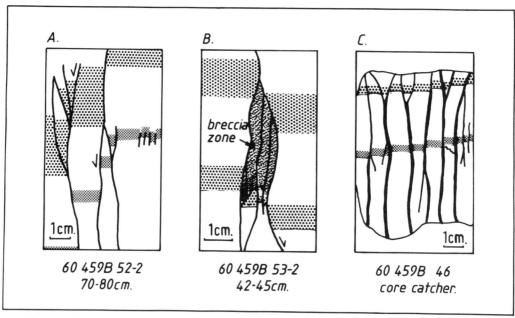

Figure 1. Mesoscopic geometry of faults located in Mariana forearc sediments. The faults include A) narrow, approximately planar zones, B) irregular, anastomosing zones enclosing breccias, and C) regularly spaced fracture arrays. The location of each fault in its core is indicated.

sediments consisting primarily of vitric mud and ooze with ash layers (late-early Pleistocene) overlying a thick pile of late Oligocene to mid-Miocene turbidites and early Eocene to early Oligocene claystones. These sediments overlie pillow basalts and basalt flows. Fractures are common below 245 m in Hole 459B and include strike-slip, dip-slip, and oblique-slip movements (see Lundberg and Moore, this volume). Three faults, located between 425 m and 500 m, have been selected for detailed analysis. These faults occur within a turbidite sequence with nannofossil chalk, vitric muds, laminated silts, and sandstones. The porosity at these depths varies from 50 to 60% (Hussong and others 1982, p. 326) and the cores contain evidence of pre-burrow slumping (core 53.2 12–15 cms) and faulting (core 46 cc) together with the more common post-burrow faulting. The latter faults are described in detail.

The faults within the selected interval occur as narrow discontinuities dipping at angles of between 60 and 90° from the sub-horizontal bedding and exhibit measurable separations of as much as 10 cms. The geometry of the faults varies from sharp, planar single fractures less than 0.2 mm wide to non-planar anastomosing fracture networks where the material located between the boundary fractures is internally brecciated to various degrees (Fig. 1A, B). Fault zones marked by wider, dark features up to 2 mm wide are also present (Fig. 1C). These latter features often occur in arrays with a regular spacing of approximately 1 cm and are very similar to the vein arrays described by Arthur and others (1980), Cowan (1982), Carson and others (1982) and Knipe (this volume).

Fault Microstructure

The microstructural characteristics of the fabrics preserved adjacent to and within the selected faults have been studied using optical and transmission electron microscopes. Ultra-thin sections were prepared by grinding in oil after impregnating specimens with a low viscosity epoxy resin. Areas of these thin sections were then selected for electron microscopy in a JEOL 200CX fitted with analytical and scanning transmission electron microscopy (S.T.E.M.) facilities. The microstructures of each fault studied are described and interpreted separately below.

Spaced Normal Fault Array (459B 46 cc; depth 435 m). The fault array preserved in the core catcher of core 46 is developed in an olive gray mudstone with silt layers of early Miocene age. The sub-vertical fractures are regularly spaced (approximately 1 cm apart), have displacements of 3–8 mm, and occasionally branch or have sub-horizontal connecting fractures (see Fig. 1C). The majority of faults in the array are delineated by 1–2 mm wide dark zones.

The fault zones show a variety of structures in thin section: some appear as approximately parallel-sided domains exhibiting no internal structure but others are made up of irregular anastomosing networks of thin (0.5 mm) movement zones. Within the fault zones characterized by a lack of internal fabric, the total loss of distinctive beds (Fig. 2) suggests either a) the material now occupying the fault zone has been introduced during dilation and displacement or b) the fault zone marks the site of large scale disaggregation where in situ material has been disrupted.

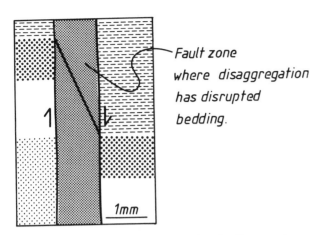

Figure 2. Sketch from thin section illustrating the disaggregation zone where bedding is absent from the fault present in 459B 46cc. The line across the fault zone represents the separation across the fault.

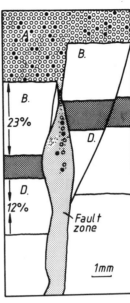

Figure 3. Sketch from an optical montage of a normal fault zone (459B 46cc). Note the evidence for the sinking of grains from bed A, the relative extension of bed B (23%), and the shortening of bed D (12%).

The internal structure of one of the fault zones within the array suggests that a combination of disaggregation and material influx is possible. Sections of this fault zone contain grains with the shape, size, and compositions characteristic of beds adjacent to the fault at higher levels (Fig. 3). The loss of bedding, together with the fault geometry, strongly suggests that a mixing of material along the fault zone has occurred by the sinking of grains through a disaggregated zone. Rapid dewatering and fluid streaming is unlikely along this fault as the flow velocity was insufficient to carry material up along the fault or to prevent large particles from sinking. If we assume a particle size of 100 μm and a density of 5 gm/cm^3, Stokes Law suggests that the flow velocity did not exceed 6 mm/sec.

Variation in the separation along the fault provides some additional information on faulting history and suggests that beds adjacent to the fault have experienced changes in thickness, both extensional and shortening, during the propagation and displacement of the fault. Figure 4 illustrates two ways of producing the displacement magnitude variations, and associated relative strains; one during the propagation of the fault and the other during displacement along the fault.

Normal fault at 494 m (53.2.42–45 cm). This fault developed in late Oligocene marly nannofossil chalk/mudstone with thin silty, vitric layers and graded sandstone units. The fault has a separation of approximately 1 cm and is composed of irregular sub-vertical fractures that dip between 60 and 90° to produce a braided fault zone (see Fig. 1b). The fault zone is up to 1 cm wide; blocks enclosed by the sub-vertical main fractures are brecciated into fragments a few millimeters in diameter. The detailed microstructures revealed by a transmission electron microscopy (T.E.M.) traverse across the fault within a claystone layer are described in detail here and reviewed in Figure 5.

The units traversed contain feldspar, quartz, fossil fragments, and phyllosilicates (illite, chlorite, and mixed layered clays). The

proportion of these components varies with the grain size within the units.

Outside the fault zone the unit is made up of detrital grains and fossils, which range in size from 1 to 100 μm, together with equidimensional clay mineral aggregates, up to 10 μm in diameter, and a fine-grained matrix composed primarily of sub-micron–sized phyllosilicates. The preferred orientation of grains is poor and only the large elongate detrital components are oriented sub-parallel to the mesoscopic bedding. The fine-grained matrix grains are arranged in open frameworks where the individual

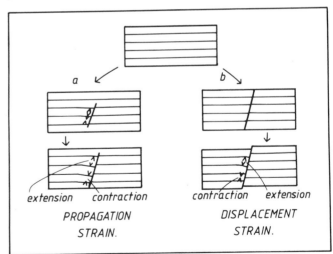

Figure 4. Possible development of strains present along the fault shown in Figure 3. Assuming that the strain is located in the hanging wall, a) shows the development of strain during the propagation of the fault and b) illustrates how strain may be produced after propagation but during displacement.

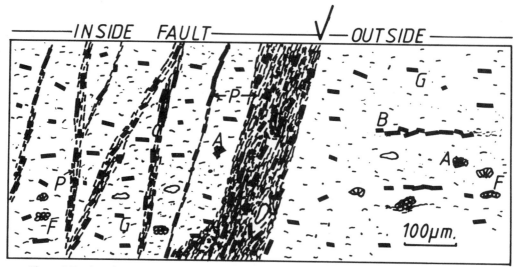

Figure 5. Review sketch of the microstructures present in the normal fault at 494 m from 459B, Leg 60. The fault zone is made up of alignment zones (P). Large detrital grains (G) and fossils (F) are often aligned parallel to the horizontal meso-bedding. Aggregates of new phyllosilicates (A) are also present.

mineral plates are connected (cemented?) at high angles to their neighbours and a large number of grains are oriented with their (001) planes at high angles to the mesoscopic bedding (see Fig. 6). The grain arrangements and preferred orientations within these frameworks are variable but tend to be constant over areas of approximately 3–4 square microns. The porosity of the frameworks also varies with the internal grain arrangement and changes from approximately 50–60 % in areas with poor preferred orientation to <30 % in areas with a more marked preferred orientation. Thin, discontinuous bands sub-parallel to the meso-scopic bedding are also present and contain densely packed phyllosilicates aligned approximately parallel to the bands. The origin of these bands as compaction-induced collapse is discussed in the paper on vein structures by Knipe (this volume). Dense equidimensional aggregates of phyllosilicates up to 10 μm in size and with poor internal preferred orientation are occasionally ob-served and are composed of chlorite and/or illite.

The fault zone is approximately 1 mm wide, and electron microscopy reveals the presence of a domainal structure together with a concentration of pyrite. The domains present may be distinguished by differences in porosity.

The domains with a good preferred orientation have a lower porosity, are oriented sub-parallel to the fault zone and are com-posed of grains aligned sub-parallel to domain boundaries. Most of these domains are less than 10 μm wide but the faulting zone adjacent to the footwall is marked by a domain ~100 μm wide, which contains both large detrital grains and fossil fragments aligned parallel to the fault (see Fig. 7). Occasionally the internal fabric of these domains is deformed into open folds that post-date the fabric evolution and generate small new dilation sites (Fig. 7). The localized bending of the internal fabric may have developed during the final stages of a movement pulse along the zone. High

porosity sites are also present adjacent to the larger grains within the domain. The concentration of fine-grained pyrite (Fig. 8) contributes to the dark color of the fault zone and indicates the movemnt of sulphur-rich fluids along the fault zone.

The domains exhibiting a poor internal preferred orientation of grains are lens-shaped and bounded by the domains with well-aligned grains described above. These domains are characterized by grains arranged in high porosity frameworks similar to those found outside the fault zone. Fossil fragments and rare large detrital grains oriented sub-parallel to the mesoscopic bedding are present, together with aggregates of new phyllosilicates (Fig. 9).

The frequency of the two domains described above changes across the fault zone studied. Domains with the well-developed internal preferred orientation decrease in frequency away from the wide domain that marks the main fault contact (Fig. 5).

Discussion and Interpretation

The microstructural features outlined above for the fault at 494 m indicate that deformation was due to disaggregation and particulate flow involving grain boundary sliding that led to the rotation of grains within the movement zones. The domainal structure reported reveals that displacement was concentrated into localized movement zones, which separated lenses of mate-rial suffering less shear and preserve textures similar to those found outside the fault zone. This preservation suggests that the aggregate was strengthened by some lithification before deforma-tion. The presence of numerous localized movement zones within the fault indicates that new movement zones were generated because existing ones were not able to accommodate the continu-ing deformation. This situation can arise from a hardening of individual zones during the porosity collapse associated with their

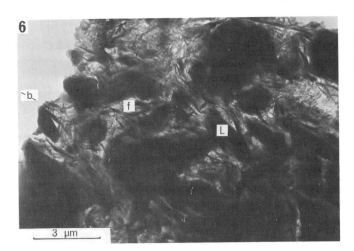

Figure 6. Electron micrograph of the microstructure outside the fault zone shown in Figure 5, illustrating the framework of grains. Note the open framework of fine grains (f). Large grains (L) tend to be parallel to the bedding (b).

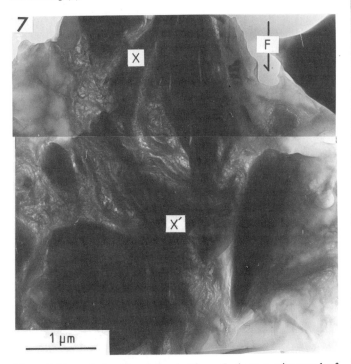

Figure 7. From the location shown in Figure 5, electron micrograph of the fault zone edge illustrating the alignment of detrital particles. Note the bending of the fabric between x and x'. The fault orientation is parallel to [F].

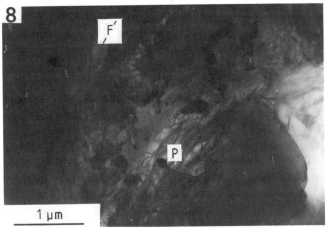

Figure 8. Concentration of pyrite aggregates within the fault zone. The fault orientation is parallel to (F).

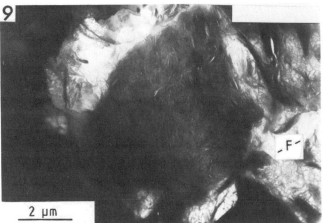

Figure 9. An aggregate of new illite grains present within the fault zone.

evolution (see also Moore and others, this volume) or may arise from an increase in the overall displacement rate on the fault. In the latter situation the existing zones do not harden but are incapable of accommodating the higher strain rate—thus necessitating the generation of new movement zones.

The finite alignment of grains along the movement zones is undoubtedly due to the collapse of the porosity. However, the timing of this porosity collapse relative to that of displacement remains unclear (see also Knipe, chapter 5, this volume). The problem of interpretation arises because of the difficulty in separating an initial extension failure from a localized shear failure in the aggregate. With an initial extension failure the preferred orientation may have developed after a large proportion of the displacement (Fig. 10). The origin of the extension may either be related to high fluid pressures or to a regional extension caused, for example, by slope instability. If the initial failure was by shear failure, then the preferred orientation within the fault zone may have developed during a porosity collapse that accompanied displacement (Fig. 10). Note that the latter evolution does not necessarily involve a high fluid pressure. In both cases the fault zone represents a zone of finite volume loss, although in the case of an initial extensional failure, the fault marks a transient site of volume increase. The distinction between these two modes of failure, although not possible at present in the faults studied, is important as the amount and duration of fluid flow along the fault, together

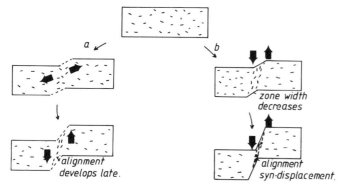

Figure 10. Possible timing of preferred orientation development within movement zones; a) illustrates a preferred orientation developed late during the displacement after extension and b) shows a preferred orientation developed during displacement and collapse of the movement zone.

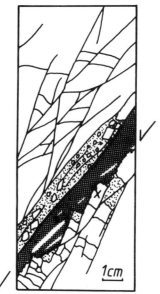

Figure 11. Sketch of the normal fault at 760 m in hole 584 from the Japan trench. Note the fractures and breccias on each side of the main central fault. See text for details. X marks the location of Figure 13.

with the permeability across fault zones, depends critically on the history of porosity within the zone.

The growth of new minerals (illite and pyrite) within the fault zone has important implications for fault sealing. However, the timing of the growth of these phases relative to the timing of displacement is not clear. The concentration of pyrite within the fault zone implies that sulphur-rich fluids have been preferentially channeled along the fault during displacement. On the other hand, the occurrence of new illite aggregates inside and outside the fault zone indicates that these new phases represent part of the general lithification process, which continues after the fault displacement.

JAPAN TRENCH-SLOPE FAULTS, LEG 87.

Regional Setting

The upper slope of the Japan trench forearc area is underlain by a Cretaceous and Palaeogene basement terrane, which may represent an accretionary wedge (von Huene and others, 1982; Karig and others, 1983; and Leggett and others, 1986). This upper slope basement is overlain by a middle to late Cenozoic slope apron. The lowermost slope off Japan has the characteristcs of an active accretionary wedge (von Huene and others, 1982). Drilling of the inner trench slope during Legs 56/57 and 87B revealed a variety of fractures and vein structures (see Leggett and others, 1985; Lundberg and Moore, this volume; Knipe, this volume). The holes in the lower slopes (434–441) were characterized by poor recovery and brecciation of slope sediments, and the mid-slope site (440) exhibited abundant faults of strike-slip, dip-slip, and oblique-slip types. Lundberg and Moore (this volume) have interpreted this latter area as having accommodated oblique convergence. A drill site (584) on the deep sea terrace, some 43 km from the trench, contains abundant veins and dip-slip faults (primarily normal). Lundberg and Leg-

gett (1985) and Leggett and others (1986) argue that the geometries of these arrays are indicative of an extensional listric array, which agrees with the regional interpretation of Karig and others (1983) and the reflection profile data reported in Nasu and others (1980).

One of the most distinctive faults recovered from Site 584 was selected for detailed analysis. The fault occurs at a depth of 760 m and is located in mid-Miocene diatomaceous mudstones. Fractures and veins are common in adjacent sections of the core and the bedding dips at ~60° approximately parallel to the fault.

Mesoscale Geometry of the Fault at 760 m (584. 80.2 70 cm).

The fault at 760 m was chosen for detailed analysis because of the variety of deformational features developed within a single fault zone. Figure 11 summarizes the geometry of the fault seen in the core. The fault dips at ~50° to core axis and is represented by a zone of concentrated deformation 2–3 cms wide. The central part of the fault zone is marked by a dark banded unit ~1–1.5 cm wide. The upper boundary of this central unit, the contact with the hanging wall, is planar while the lower boundary, the footwall contact, is irregular and stepped.

The intensity of deformation features present in the hanging wall differs from the intensity in the footwall. The hanging wall contains two sets of minor fractures. One set is sub-parallel to the main fault and is marked by thin (0.1 mm), dark, planar discontinuities 1–2 cm apart. These fractures are linked by a second set approximately perpendicular to the first set. The most distinctive feature of the hanging wall is a 1-cm-wide breccia zone (Fig. 11). This breccia zone is separated from the rest of the hanging wall by a thin (0.1 mm) fracture. Fragments in the breccia zone are equidimensional, generally less than 4 mm in diameter, and range in shape from angular to semi-rounded.

The contact of the footwall with the central zone is stepped with the long sections of the steps dipping in the same direction as, but steeper than, the main fault zone. Unlike the planar hanging wall base, this contact is lobate on a millimeter scale. The steps in the contact define part of a steeper fracture array, which appears to pre-date some of the movement on the main central fault zone and may represent an array of early Riedel shears. The sediment between these fractures is brecciated by cross-fractures within 2 cm of the main fault. In contrast to the hanging wall breccia, the angular block size ranges in size up to 5 mm thick, and the more intact nature of the zone suggests an earlier stage of brecciation.

Optical and Electron Microstructure

A thin section across the lower part of the fault zone was selected for detailed microstructural analysis (Fig. 12). The fault zone border here can be divided into three regions, each with a different micro-fabric orientation and intensity.

Region 1. The external region is characterized by localized, narrow (0.1 mm wide) planar deformation features. The micro-fabric of the sediment outside these deformation features is composed of fossil fragments, which commonly exceed 10 μm, set in a fine grained (2 μm) matrix of phyllosilicates (illite, chlorite, and mixed layered clays). The orientation of grains in the matrix is variable, with domains where the plates are sub-parallel to the mesoscopic bedding existing alongside domains where a high percentage of the plates are at a high angle to bedding (Fig. 13a,b). The narrow deformation features present in this region occur parallel and perpendicular to the main fault zone. The most extensive of these features are parallel to the main fault, usually extend for up to 10 mm, and are concentrated in the highest few millimeters of this external region. Internally these zones are identical to the main fault zone fabric described below and are marked by a good preferred orientation of grains or plates parallel to the zone border. The zones appear to have originated from localized shear movement parallel to the main fault. The second set of deformation features (fbi) in this external region, which are aligned at right angles to the fault zone, are more discontinuous and irregular than the first set. Both these sets cross-cut one another. The fault-perpendicular set in this external border region has microstructures identical to the vein structures present in the Japan Trench area (see Knipe, chapter 5, this volume). The microstructures contain internal domains where grains are aligned parallel to the borders of the feature and appear to arise from disaggregation associated with localized extension (Knipe, chapter 5, this volume). It should be noted that the preferred orientation in these zones may have been enhanced or developed during subsequent contraction of these features.

Region 2. The fault border zone is approximately 3 mm wide and separated from adjacent regions by fault-parallel movement zones (Fig. 12). The internal structure of this region differs from that of Region 1 in that it contains an oblique fabric (fb) oriented at ~30° to the main fault fabric (fa). This fabric appears to represent the rotated equivalent of the fault-perpendicular set in the external zone. The sense of rotation is consistent with the shear sense predicted for the normal fault. Region 2 also contains fault parallel movement zones, which form anastomosing network and are more common here than in Region 1 (see Fig. 12).

Region 3. The main fault zone, which appears as a dark, banded feature in the core, is designated as Region 3. Optically the region appears to have an almost perfect alignment of grains parallel to the fault trace. Electron microscopy reveals that the internal fabric is composed of a low porosity zone with a good, but not perfect, alignment of phyllosilicates (illite, chlorite, and mixed layered grains) and fossil fragments (Fig. 13c). Large fossil fragments, common outside the main fault zone, are rare within the main fault zone, indicating that test breakage has accompanied fault movement. Rounded aggregates of phyllosilicates are also present, although whether these represent pre- or post-displacement growth features is uncertain.

Discussion

All the fault fabrics described are generated by disaggregation, particulate flow and the fracturing of fossils. The different fault fabrics preserved arise from differences in the distribution and relative importance of these processes and are perhaps indicative of different slip rates on this single fault. The breccias may represent generation during rapid displacement compared to the slower displacement phase, which may have created and rotated the fabrics (fbi) near the footwall boundary zone. It is possible that the different fault fabrics reflect a time sequence, with the rotation of the perpendicular fabric (fbi) developed during the slowing down of the fault slip rate. The edges of the fault zone (Regions 1 and 2) will therefore have been part of the active fault for a shorter period of time than the central portion of the fault and may have experienced a different strain rate history with a lower maximum strain rate and a different fluid pressure history (Knipe, chapter 5, this volume).

Detailed microstructural analysis of the lower part of the fault zone provides an insight into the processes involved in fault zone widening. This widening may arise when either an increased cohesion (hardening) develops along the fault zone, restricting movement, and/or when the accommodation of an increased rate of slip is required. Three different processes appear to have been involved in the widening in the fault studied (Fig. 14).

1) Disaggregation and extension create localized zones at high angles to the fault trace. These vein features may develop where variations in the "ease of slip" occur along the fault edge. In this situation, increased cohesion across the slip plane leads to the production of an extension zone in the footwall. These disaggregation and extension zones at a high angle to the fault trace may also have been initiated by transient high fluid pressures in

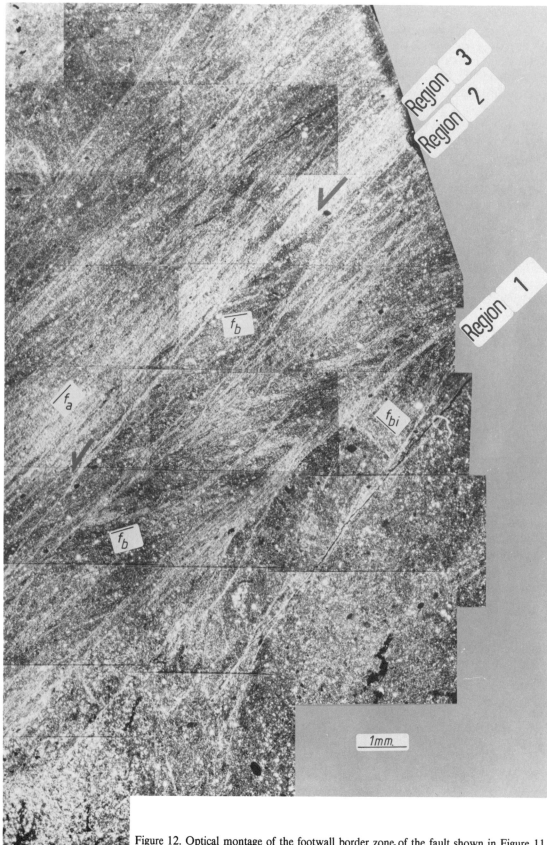

Figure 12. Optical montage of the footwall border zone of the fault shown in Figure 11. The three regions indicated are described in detail in the text.

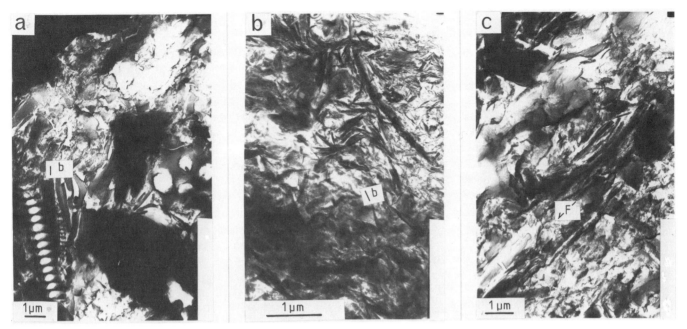

Figure 13. Electron micrographs from outside the fault zone: a) shows fossil fragments, some of which are aligned parallel to the bedding (b); b) illustrates the range of orientations of phyllosilicates in the matrix; and c) electron micrograph of the internal structure of the zone. The movement zone is made up of well-aligned fossil fragments and phyllosilicate grains. The fault orientation is indicated by (F).

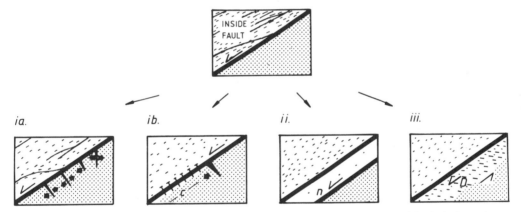

Figure 14. Possible model for the development of the microfabrics at the border of the fault shown in Figure 12. The widening of the fault zone may involve: i) Development of extension zones by a) high fluid pressure induced fracture or b) changes in the cohesion of the active fault plane. The latter situation may be created by "sticking" of sections of the fault plane (c). ii) Development of additional movement planes (n) parallel to the main fault, or iii) Development of a zone of distributed strain (D). See text for details.

the fault zone. Although initiated by extension parallel to the fault, these features may experience shortening during subsequent movement on the fault.

2) The development of new localized movement zones occurs parallel to the main fault. The cross-cutting relationships between extensional features (1) and movement zones indicates that these modes of widening may alternate during the faulting history.

3) The shearing and rotation of the early deformation fea-

tures occurs by widespread disaggregation and straining by particulate flow. This mode of widening is indicated in the fault studied by the rotation of the fabric developed at the fault zone margin.

Why these different modes of fault extension have occurred is unclear at present, although they may be caused by different strain rates and fluid pressure histories. The preferred orientation fabric in the central part of the fault zone may thus be a combination of two processes: a) the development of movement zones parallel to the main fault and b) the development and rotation of extension zones initially at high angles to the main fault zone.

CONCLUSIONS

1) The main mechanisms of deformation in the faults studied include disaggregation and particulate flow.

2) The different geometries and microfabrics preserved reflect variations in the strain histories and, more importantly, variations in the strain rate history of the faults.

3) Evidence for large-scale, rapid dewatering and rapid fluid streaming along the faults studied was not found. Nor is the preferred orientation of grains along the fault zones necessarily created by high fluid pressures.

4) The fault zone microstructures are similar to the vein microstructures described by Knipe (this volume), indicating that the two represent part of a continuous series of deformation responses.

5) The fault from the Japan trench reveals the range of processes that can be involved in fault zone widening. Three widening mechanisms are noted: 1) development of local extension at high angles to the main slip plane, 2) development of local slip planes parallel to the main fault, and 3) distributed particulate flow created a ductile deformation zone at the fault boundary.

ACKNOWLEDGMENTS

The author would like to acknowledge discussions with Drs. Casey Moore, Neil Lundberg, Ed Beutner, Darrel Cowen, and Jerry Leggett, as well as colleagues at Leeds. The work was part of a N.S.F. sponsored research grant, which is gratefully acknowledged. The paper was first presented at a Penrose Conference on Accretion, held in Eureka, California, in May 1984.

REFERENCES CITED

Arthur, M. A., Carson, B., and von Huene, R., 1980, Initial tectonic deformation of hemi-pelagic sediments at the leading edge of the Japan convergent margin, *in* Langseth, M., Okada, H., and others, eds., Initial Reports of the Deep Sea Drilling Project: Washington, D.C., U.S. Government Printing Office, v. 56, 57, p. 569–713.

Bray, C. J., and Karig, D. E., 1985, Porosity of sediments in accretionary prisms and some implications for dewatering processes: Journal of Geophysical Research, v. 90, p. 768–778.

Carson, B., von Huene, R., and Arthur, M., 1982, Small scale deformation structures and physical properties due to convergence in the Japan trench slope sediments: Tectonics, v. 1, p. 277–302.

Cowan, D. S., 1982, Origin of "Vein Structure" in slope sediments on the inner slope of the Middle America Trench off Guatemala, *in* Aubouin, J., von Huene, R., and others, eds., Initial Reports of the Deep Sea Drilling Project: Washington, D.C., U.S. Government Printing Office, v. 67, p. 645–650.

Hussong, D. M., and Uyeda, S., 1982, Tectonic processes and the history of the Mariana Arc: A synthesis of the results of Deep Sea Drilling Project Leg 60, *in* Hussong, D. M., Uyeda, S., and others, eds., Initial Reports of the Deep Sea Drilling Project: Washington, D.C., U.S. Government Printing Office, v. 60, p. 909–929.

Hussong, D. M., Uyeda, S., and others, eds., 1982, Initial Reports of the Deep Sea Drilling Project: Washington, D.C., U.S. Government Printing Office, v. 60, 929 p.

Karig, D. E., 1971, Structural history of the Mariana Island Arc system: Geological Society of America Bulletin, v. 83, p. 323–344.

Karig, D. E., Kagami, H., and others, 1983, Varied responses to subduction in the Nankai Trough and Japan Trench Forearcs: Nature, v. 304, p. 148–151.

Karig, D. E. and Sharman, G. F., 1975. Subduction and accretion in trenches. Geological Society of America Bulletin, v. 86, p. 377–384.

Leggett, J. K., and others, 1986, Extensional Tectonics in the Honshu forearc, Japan: Integrated results of Deep Sea Drilling Project Legs 57, 87, and reprocessed seismic reflection profiles: Geological Society of London Special Publication Extensional Tectonics (in press).

Lundberg, N., and Leggett, J. K., 1985, Structural features in cores from the Japan Trench, Deep Sea Drilling Project Leg 87b, *in* Karig, D. E., Ingle, J. C., Jr., and others, eds., Initial Reports of the Deep Sea Drilling Project: Washington, D.C., U.S. Government Printing Office, v. 87.

Moore, J. C., and Biju-Duval, B., 1984, Tectonic synthesis, Deep Sea Drilling Project Leg 78A: Structural evolution of off scraped and underthrust sediment, northern Barbados Ridge complex, *in* Biju-Duval, B., Moore, J. C., and others, eds., Initial Reports of the Deep Sea Drilling Project: Washington, D.C., U.S. Government Printing Office, v. 78, p. 601–621.

Nasu, N., and others, 1980, Interpretation of multichannel seismic reflection data Legs 56 and 57, Japan Trench transect, Deep Sea Drilling Project, *in* Lee, M., and others, eds., Initial Reports of the Deep Sea Drilling Project: Washington, D.C., U.S. Government Printing Office, v. 56-57, pt. 1, p. 489–504.

Seely, D. R., 1977, The significance of landward vergence and oblique structural trends on trench inner slopes, *in* Talwani, M., and Pitman, W. C., eds., Island Arcs, Deep Sea Trenches, and Back Arc Basins: American Geophysical Union, Maurice Ewing Series 1, p. 187–198.

Shepard, L. E., and Bryant, W. R., 1983, Geotechnical properties of lower trench inner-slope sediments: Tectonophysics, v. 99, p. 279–312.

Silver, E. A., Ellis, M. J., Breen, N. J., and Shipley, T. H., 1985, Comments on the growth of accretionary wedges: Geology, v. 13, p. 6–9.

von Huene, R., and others, 1982, A summary of Cenozoic tectonic history along the IPOD Japan Transect: Geological Society of America Bulletin, v. 93, p. 829–846.

MANUSCRIPT ACCEPTED BY THE SOCIETY MARCH 10, 1986

Geological Society of America
Memoir 166
1986

Scaly fabrics from Deep Sea Drilling Project cores from forearcs

J. Casey Moore
Department of Earth and Marine Sciences
University of California, Santa Cruz
Santa Cruz, California 95064

Sarah Roeske
U.S. Geological Survey
Mail Stop 904
345 Middlefield Road
Menlo Park, California 94025

Neil Lundberg
Department of Geological and Geophysical Sciences
Princeton University
Princeton, New Jersey 08544

Jane Schoonmaker
Hawaii Institute of Geophysics
University of Hawaii
Honolulu, Hawaii 96822

Darrel S. Cowan
Department of Geological Science
University of Washington
Seattle, Washington 98195

Eugenio Gonzales
Department of Earth and Marine Sciences
University of California, Santa Cruz
Santa Cruz, California 95064

Stephen E. Lucas
Department of Earth and Marine Sciences
University of California, Santa Cruz
Santa Cruz, California 95064

ABSTRACT

Scaly fabrics are present in DSDP cores from the Barbados, southern Mexico, Guatemala, and Mariana forearcs. Where independently documented, the scaly fabrics occur adjacent to faults. Scaly foliation surfaces in mudstone are planes of slip comparable to surfaces experimentally produced in shear boxes at low confining pressures. Microscopic and scanning electron microscope (SEM) images of scaly folia in sediments indicate strong preferred orientation of phyllosilicates both parallel to and at low angles to the slip surfaces. The clays within the slip surfaces are not new mineral phases but are produced by the reorientation of existing minerals and perhaps the disruption of clay aggregates. SEM studies and physical property data indicate loss of porosity during the development of scaly fabrics in sediments. At DSDP sites, scaly mudstone formed at temperatures of less than 25 °C, pressures less than 4 MPa, and strain rates of about 10^{-13}; scaly fabrics develop typically in underconsolidated sediment. Scaly fabrics preferentially occur in weak smectitic mudstones as opposed to stronger calcareous or silty mudstones.

In sediments, scaly fabrics apparently develop by the lateral propagation of faults in which individual slip surfaces are formed and abandoned after a limited amount of displacement. Slip may cease on scaly folia because of increasing coefficient of friction, because of decrease in pore pressure, or because of reorientation of the slip surface relative to the stress field. The propagation of scaly fabric occurs because the surrounding undeformed sediment matrix is weaker and/or has more favorably oriented potential failure surfaces. Conversely, in hard rocks fault zones would be less likely to propagate laterally and develop broad scaly fabric zones because they would not exceed the strength of the country rock.

INTRODUCTION

Scaly clays commonly occur in orogenic belts. Perhaps scaly clay units (argille scagliose) are best known from the Apennine Mountains where they include large blocks of exotic compositions and have been classically interpreted as gravity glide deposits (Page, 1963; Abbate and others, 1970; Elter and Trevisan, 1973). In many convergent-margin terranes, scaly clays constitute the matrix to stratally disrupted sequences (melange) considered to be of tectonic origin (e.g. Franciscan Complex, California, Cowan, 1974; Bachman, 1982; southern Alaska, Byrne, 1984; southwestern Japan, Taira and others, 1982; Indonesia, Moore and Karig, 1980; Hamilton, 1979). Scaly fabrics may also occur in olistostromes (Boles and Landis, 1984). Although scaly clays are widespread, they are studied little and are usually only parenthetically mentioned. Notable exceptions are the work of Vollmer and Bosworth (1984) and Lash (1985) in the Taconic orogenic zone of the Appalachians and work in progress by Byrne in the Kodiak accretionary complex of southern Alaska. Here we review the occurrences of scaly foliation in Deep Sea Drilling Project (DSDP) cores from forearc regions (Table 1). We also report on new scanning electron microscope (SEM) studies from the northern Barbados Ridge and selected ancient examples. The presentation runs from the more completely to less completely studied occurrences, rather than the chronological order of the drilling leg.

Definitions

For purposes of this paper we define *scaly foliation* as a fabric of anastomosing, curviplanar fracture surfaces that define phacoids. Fracture surfaces occur on a millimeter scale and are commonly polished and striated, hence they are usually faults. Scaly foliation shows an overall planar orientation. In zones of *incipient scaly foliation,* in the DSDP cores fractures occur locally on approximately a cm scale and in aggregate show no preferred planar orientation in the narrow core. We use *scaly fabric* inclusively to refer to both *scaly foliation* and *incipient scaly foliation.* *Stratal disruption* refers to discontinuous bedding pulled apart in the style of boudinage. In zones of lithologic contrasts, stratal disruption is commonly associated with scaly foliation. In the DSDP cores, scaly foliation occurs predominantly in mudstone, but is developed also in volcanic rocks and serpentinite. Discrete fractures and faults or sets of closely spaced, relatively planar non-anastomosing fractures are not included in our definition of a scaly foliation (e.g. see sets of fractures and faults in Plates 3 to 8 of Arthur and others, 1980).

Gravitational consolidation (termed compaction in geological literature) describes porosity reduction due to vertical overburden. In *normally consolidated sediment* the overburden is supported completely by the sediment fabric, and fluid pressures are hydrostatic. In *underconsolidated sediment* the overburden is supported partly by the sediment fabric and partially by excess fluid pressure. Underconsolidated sediments often develop during rapid sedimentation in which interstitial fluids are unable to escape. The fabric of an underconsolidated sediment will collapse if fluid pressure is reduced. An *overconsolidated sediment* has been subjected to an effective stress higher than that at the depth at which it is sampled; therefore, its fabric is collapsed to a larger degree than that of a normally consolidated sediment. Overconsolidation may result from the uplift and erosion of previously more deeply buried sediment.

In engineering literature, consolidation refers to porosity reduction solely due to the vertical effective stress. In the geological literature (e.g. Carson, 1977) *"tectonic consolidation"* describes a process in which sediment becomes "overconsolidated" due to the effects of both vertical gravitational and tectonic effective stresses.

DISTRIBUTION AND MACROSCOPIC CHARACTERISTICS OF SCALY FOLIATIONS

The macroscopic synthesis (Lundberg and Moore, this volume) indicates that scaly foliation occurs in cores from the northern Barbados Ridge area (Leg 78A), southern Mexico (Leg 66), Guatemala (Leg 67), and the Marianas (Leg 60) (see Table 1). Our work has concentrated on prime examples of scaly fabrics from the northern Barbados Ridge and southern Mexico.

Barbados, Leg 78 A

Scaly foliations in the Leg 78A area (northern Barbados Ridge) are invariably associated with faults defined either by biostratigraphic inversions or a combination of drilling and seismic data (Figs. 1 and 2). Scaly foliation is intensely developed for tens of centimeters above the fault at 276 m at Site 541 (Fault A, Fig. 1). This scaly foliation grades up-core into a fabric characterized by cm-scale polished and striated surfaces (Fig. 3). This zone of incipient scaly foliation extends about 55 m above the fault at 276 m and includes another fault of prominent throw (Fault C, Fig. 1). Incipient scaly foliation occurs at Site 542 in faults of 32 to 70 m throw (Faults B and D, Fig. 1; Fig. 2).

All of the above-mentioned examples of scaly foliation and incipient scaly foliation occur in a smectitic mud that is highly susceptible to deformation. The lithologic control of deformation is well illustrated by the fault at 276 m at Site 541, in which the well-foliated upper Miocene smectitic mudstone overlies a middle Pliocene calcareous mudstone. The calcareous mudstone directly below the fault is unfoliated (see microscopic characteristics, below) and is cut by only a few diversely oriented cm-scale surfaces and several discrete steeply dipping faults. Faults in calcareous mud and mudstone at 72 and 172 m subbottom are not associated with foliations, probably because of the more calcareous lithology and because fault throws are of no more than 20 m.

At the base of Site 541 the cores grade from tilted but otherwise undeformed mudstone to strongly foliated scaly mud. Locally the foliation is so well developed that it resembles fault

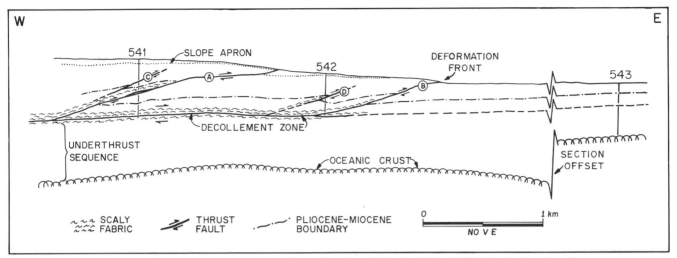

Figure 1. Cross section of deformation front of northern Barbados Ridge highlighting the location of scaly fabrics relative to faults defined biostratigraphically or seismically. Faults A and B are major packet-bounding faults; whereas faults C and D are of markedly smaller displacement and probably are responsible for intrapacket thickening. To account for the required thickening true section probably includes additional faults of small displacement.

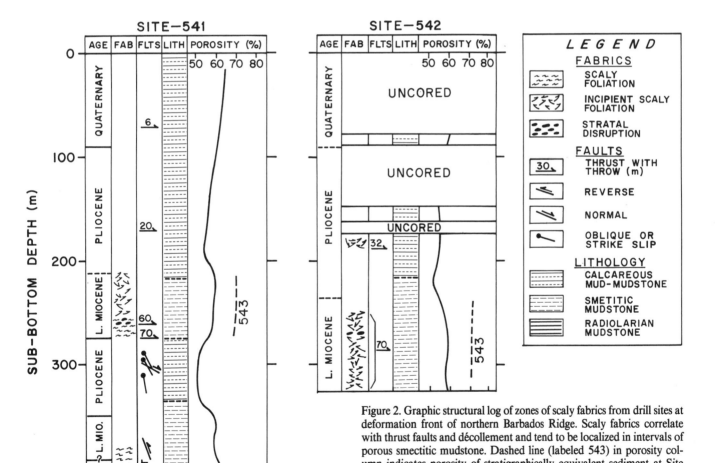

Figure 2. Graphic structural log of zones of scaly fabrics from drill sites at deformation front of northern Barbados Ridge. Scaly fabrics correlate with thrust faults and décollement and tend to be localized in intervals of porous smectitic mudstone. Dashed line (labeled 543) in porosity column indicates porosity of stratigraphically equivalent sediment at Site 543 and illustrates the magnitude of porosity reduction occurring during development of the scaly fabrics. The higher porosity of the scaly zones relative to the adjacent carbonate-rich mud is due to differences in lithology. Structural data from Cowan and others, (1984); lithologic, age and physical property data from Marlow and others (1984).

TABLE 1. SCALY FABRICS AND STRATAL DISRUPTION IN DSDP FOREARC SITES AND SELECTED ANCIENT EXAMPLES

Location and References	Macroscopic Description	Age	Clay Mineralogy S/I/K+C	Grain Size Sd/Slt/Cly	Porosity	Vane Shear Strength (kPa)
Barbados, Leg 78A (1, 2, 3, 4)						
Site 541, ~216-276 m (fault A)	**Scaly Foliation, Stratal Disruption, Cm-scale Polished and Striated Surfaces:** Structures are developed in a smectitic mudstone in a 60-m-thick zone associated with faults at 262 and 276 m with biostratigraphically defined throws of 60 and 70 m respectively. Well developed scaly foliation only apparent a few tens of cm above the fault at 276 m. Stratal disruption locally developed. Cm-scale polished and striated surfaces are ubiquitous throughout the interval.	L. Mio.	55/15/30	9/6/85	55-60	>125
Site 541, ~387-459 m (decollement)	**Scaly foliation, Stratal Disruption:** Scaly foliations commonly occur in 10- 20-cm-thick zones (locally 1 m thick) separating intervals of stiff, but fractured bioturbated mudstone. Locally, deformation is so intense that mudstone has been converted into a soft clayey gouge. The scaly foliation is predominantly horizontal with local variations in orientation probably due to drilling deformation. Some probably stratal disruption. Deformation fabrics developed both in smectitic and radiolarian mudstones. Deformed section lies both above and within decollement zone between offscraped and underthrust sedimentary sequences.	M.-E. Mio.	73/7/20	5/8/87	55-60	>125
Site 542, ~173-181 m (fault D)	**Cm-scale Polished and Striated Surfaces:** A minimum of 10 m of deformed nannofossil-rich mudstone at base of Hole 542 lying above a reverse fault with a displacement of 32 m. The fault occurs in an uncored section between 183 m in Hole 542 and 202 m in Hole 542A.	E. Plio.	35/30/35	5/15/80	55-60	>125
Site 542, ~240-325 m (fault C)	**Cm-scale Polished and Striated Surfaces, Locally Scaly Foliation:** Deformation is developed in a reverse fault zone of about 70 m displacement in smectitic mud. Fault zone is overpressured and probably lies just above decollement between offscraped and underthrust sediments.	L. Mio.	65/10/25	6/10/84	57-62	>125
Southern Mexico, Leg 66 (5, 6, 7, 8)						
Site 488, ~210-240 m	**Stratal disruption and Scaly Fabric:** Zone of stratal disruption shows foliation defined by weakly to strongly oriented elongate lenses of silt to sand. Locally, this foliation is also defined by thin dark zones of fine-grained material which may bound and truncate elongate silt and sand bodies. Scaly fabric is weakly developed. Stratal disruption at Site 488 is apparently accomplished largely by particulate flow (see Lucas and Moore, this volume). Stratal disruption at Site 488 is thought to be associated with a fault cutting slope deposits (see Shepard and others, 1982).	Quat.	3/62/35	10/55/35	~35	>125
Site 491, ~170-200 m	**Local Cm-scale Polished and Striated Surfaces and Local Stratal Disruption:** Scaly zones are locally developed through this 30-m section of deformed core material.	E. Plio.	2/65/33	13/62/20	~40	>125
Site 492, ~260-290 m	**Scaly Foliation and Stratal Disruption:** Intense stratal disruption and scaly foliation developed in sequence of silty muds and sands. Stratal disruption occurs by both cataclasis and particulate flow (see Lucas and Moore, this volume).	L. Mio.	12/75/13	9/62/29	29-42	>125
Site 490, 364 m, 410 m, 445 m	**Scaly Foliation:** Zones of scaly foliation consisting of an astomosing striated and well polished surfaces.	E. Plio.	10/58/32	5/55/40	33-45	>125

TABLE 1. (CONTINUED)

Location and References	Macroscopic Description	Age	Clay Mineralogy S/I/K+C	Grain Size Sd/Slt/Cly	Porosity	Vane Shear Strength (kPa)
Guatemala, Legs 67 and 84 (9, 10, 11, 12)						
Site 494, 241 m, 304 m	Scaly Foliation: Thin intervals of scaly mudstone.	Mio./Eoc.	88/10/2	8/57/35	50-55	>200
Site 494, 285 m	Stratal Disruption: Firm dark gray mudstone with irregularly distributed wisps and layers of lighter gray, more clay-rich, slightly more calcareous mudstone. Thin sections indicate no microfracturing along the lithologic boundaries of the included mudstone pieces. This irregular lithologic pattern is overprinted by healed shear fractures marked by a <1-mm-thick zone of dark cohesive "gouge." Stratal disruption occurred when the rock was soft and the later fracturing when it was a consolidated mudstone. Earlier soft deformation probably is a sedimentary mass flow. Here stratal disruption is conspicuous in not being associated with at least weakly developed scaly foliation.	M. Eoc.	90/10/0	30/25/45	55	>200
Site 567, 176-477 m	Faulting, Brecciation, Locally Scaly Zones, Blocks in a Matrix: All partially affected by drilling but with probably original tectonic and perhaps sedimentary fabrics. Not comparable to scaly fabric developed on cm-scale in Barbados cores, for example. Scaly zones and blocks-in-matrix are in serpentinite, except at 256 m, where a serpentinitic mud occurs. Most brecciation and some faulting is also in serpentinite, below 319 m.	Plio.- L. Cret.	---	---	---	---
Site 569, 150-250 m	Faults: Section locally riddled with faults, some of which are polished. Not exactly an anastomosing scaly foliation, however.	E. Mio.- L. Olig.	73/5/22	7/29/64	60-70	>60
Site 569, 334 m	Scaly Fabric in Mudstone.	U. Eoc.	96/3/1	8/22/70	40	>60
Mariana Forearc, Leg 60 (13)						
Site 458, 335, 420, 447, 457 m	Scaly Fabric in Basalt: Small chips of striated polished andesite and bsalt occurring in restricted zones, probably faults.	Eoc.?			30-37	

References:
1) Biju-Duval, Moore, and others (1984)
2) Cowan and others (1984)
3) Marlow and others (1984)
4) Pudsey (1984)
5) Watkins, Moore, and others (1982)
6) Lundberg and Moore (1982)
7) Shepard and others (1982)
8) Schumann and Nagel (1982)
9) Aubouin, von Huene, and others (1982)
10) Kurnosov and others (1982)
11) von Huene, Auboin, and others (1985)
12) Helm (1985)
13) Hussong, Uyeda, and others (1982)

Figure 3. Example of incipient scaly foliation consisting of slickenlined surfaces on about a cm-scale with diverse orientations; northern Barbados Ridge, Site 541, 229 m subbottom. Piece in lower portion of photo is viewed from the side whereas piece in upper half of photo is view from top.

gouge (Fig. 4). This scaly foliation has a flaky texture and can be disaggregated into innumerable small lenticular polished chips. Overall the foliated material is qualitatively less cohesive than that associated with the thrust faults at 276 and 262 m at Site 541. The foliation at the base of Site 541 occurs in zones commonly 10 to 20 cm thick, but locally up to 1 m thick, separated by about equal thicknesses of stiff, fractured, bioturbated mud-

stone. This well-developed scaly foliation occurs in a radiolarian-bearing mud and marks the décollement zone between offscraped and underthrust sediments. Where it is not deformed by drilling, the foliation is subhorizontal and accompanied by small-scale stratal disruption.

Southern Mexico, Leg 66

Well-developed scaly foliation occurs at Sites 492 and 490, respectively, at the landward margin of the accretionary wedge and in a transition zone between the accretionary wedge and the adjacent continental crust (see Moore and Lundberg, this volume, Fig. 7). The scaly foliation is characterized by polished and striated surfaces and occurs in indurated mudstone of Pliocene and late Miocene age (Fig. 5). At Site 492 the scaly foliation is associated with well-developed stratal disruption and cataclasis (Lucas and Moore, this volume). At Site 490, scaly foliation is locally developed at depths greater than 350 m in a non-disrupted interval cut by a large number of discrete faults.

At Sites 488 and 491, at the toe and in the mid-slope region, respectively, incipient scaly foliation occurs with stratal disruption. The scaly fabric between 210 and 240 m at Site 488 occurs in a fault zone defined by stratal disruption, anomalous physical properties, and hydrocarbon content (Moore, Watkins, and others, 1982; Shepard and others, 1982).

Guatemala, Legs 67 and 84

Off Guatemala scaly fabric occurs in cores from Sites 494 and 567A (located at the base of the slope) and from Sites 569 and 570 (located in the mid to upper slope region) (Moore and Lundberg, this volume, Fig. 9). Only two zones at Site 494 show scaly foliation. The cores from Site 494 also show locally clay-rich, stratally disrupted fabric developed during mass movement that is in turn cut across by healed, gouge-filled fractures (Site 494, 285 m, Aubouin, von Huene and others, 1982). Cores from both Sites 567 and 570 contain serpentinite and serpentinitic mud with scaly fabric. Scaliness was produced by deformation of the crystalline basement underlying the Guatemala slope. At Site 569 in the mid-slope region, scaly fabric occurs in the slope deposits probably in association with faults.

Marianas, Leg 60

In the Mariana forearc scaly fabric occurs at Site 458 from 335 to 458 m subbottom in four zones ranging from 10 to 150 cm thick. The scaly material consists of small chips of polished and striated andesite and basalt that are part of the upper slope basement complex of probably Eocene age. The sequence, including the scaly intervals, contains no sediments but shows many discrete faults. The scaly intervals probably represent faults of somewhat larger displacement than their thinner, discrete counterparts. Scaly fabrics in the hard rocks of the Mariana forearc occur in notably thinner zones than scaly fabrics in sediments at other forearc localities.

Figure 4. Example of scaly foliation from décollement zone at base of Site 541 (458.6 m). Note pinch and swell texture (arrows) that may represent stratal disruption, but in part may also be drilling effects.

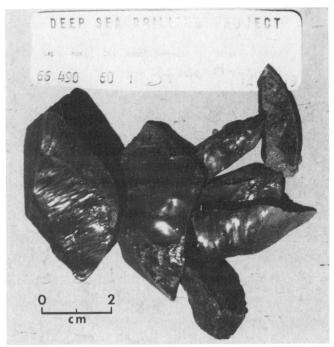

Figure 5. Example of large pieces of scaly mudstone from 541 m, Site 490, southern Mexico.

MICRO- AND ULTRAMICROSCOPIC FABRICS

Sample Preparation

Microscopic and SEM studies have been carried out on scaly fabrics from Legs 66 and 78A and selected subaerially exposed examples. Thin sections were prepared from samples impregnated with low viscosity epoxy and ground in oil with final thinning by hand. The SEM samples were removed from the cores by being fractured while still wet, mounted, air dried, and gold coated.

In the analysis of soil fabrics, shrinkage effects due to air drying and the effect of fracturing may disturb textures (Tovey, 1974). As our observations were made on consolidated mud-stones with water contents of 20 to 40 percent (as opposed to over 100 percent in soils) shrinkage does not significantly disturb the small-scale fabric. Many observations were made on natural fractures, such as slicked and polished surfaces, obviating the problem of fracture disturbance. These slicked and polished surfaces were apparent in hand lens examination of the wet sediment and cannot be due to drying. Finally, many of our observations are of a comparative nature on sets of consistently prepared samples; we believe the differences are real and that the strongly oriented phyllosilicates cannot be related to shrinkage or fracture disturbance processes, which may disorder the extremely porous fabrics of soils.

Samples taken on board ship or in a remotely located repository cannot always be referred back to the orientation of other fabric elements of the core from which they originated. Typically the best samples of scaly mudstone were derived from loose chips in a core disoriented by drilling and splitting. Moreover, the core represents a limited sample volume that is destroyed during continued sampling and analysis. As a consequence, our thin sections and ultramicrographs are not as well oriented as we might wish with respect to some features of the cores. For example, thin sections are not necessarily parallel to shear directions since in many cases this was not apparent during core sampling.

Microfabrics Adjacent To Thrust Faults, Barbados

Several fault surfaces were clearly defined in cores from Site 541 in the Leg 78A area, providing an excellent opportunity to study their relationship to scaly fabrics. Samples from about 220 to 276 m subbottom at Site 541 in an interval of thrust faulting (Fault A, Fig. 1) show scaly partings that are microscopically characterized by anastomosing thin zones of strong preferred mineral orientation (Cowan and others, 1984; Fig. 6). Phyllosilicates are oriented parallel to the boundaries of the thin (~10 micron) scaly folia. Thicker folia (~100 microns) are often composite with mineral orientation parallel to their margins with an internal fabric shallowly inclined (~20 degrees) to the zone. A thin section directly across the fault at 276 m shows local thin zones of well-oriented minerals (Fig. 6A). Elsewhere in this thin

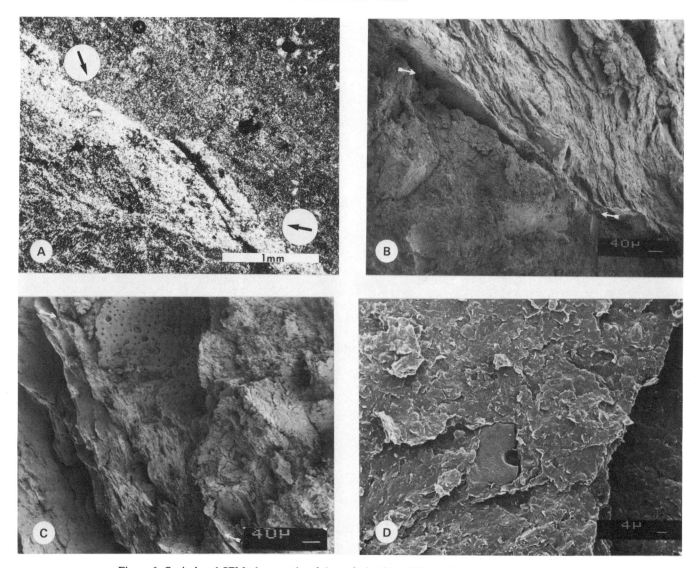

Figure 6. Optical and SEM photographs of thrust fault "A" at 276 m, Site 541, northern Barbados Ridge (Fig. 1). A. Optical view of fault. Fault trends from upper left to lower right (marked by arrows). Sediment on upper right is Pliocene calcareous mudstone and upper Miocene mudstone on lower left. Note strong birefringence (strong preferred orientation) of upper Miocene mudstone, especially adjacent to fault. Photographs A, B, and C are inverted from overall orientation in core (Miocene over Pliocene) because they are from a local fold in the fault surface. B. SEM view of contrasting fabric in foliated upper Miocene mudstone (to right and above discontinuity) and unfoliated middle Pliocene calcareous mudstone. Discontinuity (marked by arrows) post dates faulting and may be due to drilling. C. SEM view of fault contact. Strongly foliated material to left is upper Miocene mudstone. Poorly foliated material rich in foraminifer fragments to right is middle Pliocene calcareous mudstone. Fault is marked by arrows. D. View is perpendicular to foliation surface adjacent to fault. Note small fragment of foraminifer and flattened nature of clay fabric.

section, the Miocene mudstone includes domains of variable orientation, producing a patchy extinction pattern. In contrast, the Pliocene calcareous mudstone in the same thin section shows no clear zones of strong preferred orientation. SEM photos (Fig. 6B, C, and D) also demonstrate the strong orientation of phyllosilicate in the Miocene mudstone near the fault surface, in contrast to the less well-developed fabrics in the Pliocene calcareous

mudstone. In this sample, fabric evolution is apparently influenced by lithology.

At 263 m subbottom at Site 541, a scaly sample from a zone of stratal disruption 8 m above a fault with 60 m throw illustrates both the preferred orientation of the phyllosilicate minerals and the heterogeneity in this fabric (Fig. 7A). Less than 100 microns away from a scaly parting plane, there is little preferred orienta-

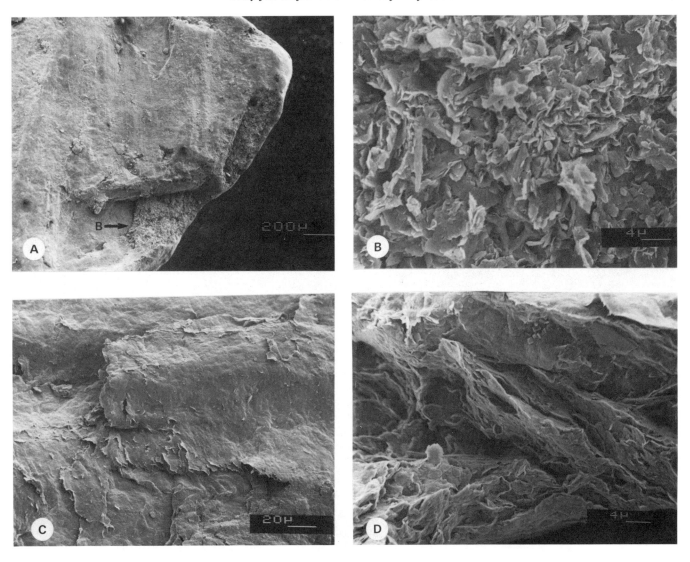

Figure 7. SEM photos of disrupted zone above fault, 245 m, Site 541, northern Barbados Ridge. A. Far view of scaly flake. Note faintly striated vertical surfaces and areas of rougher texture. B. Close-up of rough textured areas in A (arrow) showing porous fabric with preserved discoasters and coccolith plates. C. Detail of slicked surface showing strong preferred orientation of clays with sculptured appearance. Photograph is from different SEM sample but same macroscopic sample as A and B. D. Edge view of C showing strong preferred orientation from upper left to lower right of photograph. Note development of preferred orientation and porosity reduction fabric changes from B to C and D. Overall this sample illustrates well the reduction in porosity associated with the development of the scaly slip surfaces.

tion with good preservation of coccolith plates and the delicate star shapes of discoasters (Fig. 7B). In contrast, a scaly parting surface from the same sample shows strong preferred orientation of the clays parallel to the parting surface (Fig. 7C). An edge view of the parting surface exhibits some degree of orientation extending irregularly 20–25 microns away from the parting surface (Fig. 7D). The heterogeneity of fabric in this sample cannot be attributed to lithology but reflects non-penetrative deformation on a small scale. The collapse of the more open, less oriented fabric (Fig. 7B) to form the strong preferred orientation apparent in

Figures 7C and 7D must involve a substantial reduction of porosity. This ultramicroscopic case for porosity reduction is further supported by lower porosity of the scaly fabric intervals relative to their undeformed equivalents on the oceanic plate (see comparative porosity curves, Fig. 2).

Microfabrics From the Décollement Zone, Barbados

The scaly fabric of the décollement zone at Site 541 in the Leg 78A area is characterized microscopically by anastomosing

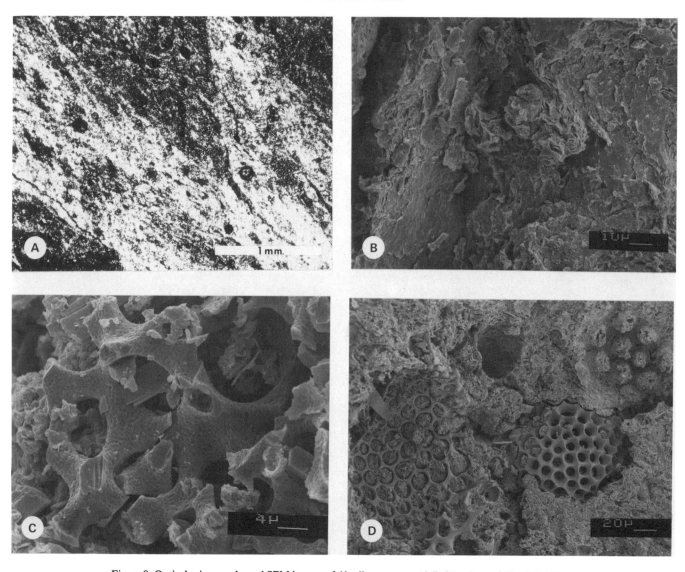

Figure 8. Optical micrographs and SEM images of décollement zone (A,B,C,) at base of Site 541 (458.6 m) and approximately stratigraphically equivalent undeformed sediment (D) from adjacent site on oceanic crust (Site 543). A. Optical photomicrograph of strongly oriented phyllosilicates (bands of high birefringence) with residual pods of low birefringent (less deformed) matrix. B. View down on two surfaces of preferred orientation. C. Close-up of radiolarian collapsed during deformation. Note euhedral authigenic mineral, probably clinoptilolite. D. Tectonically undeformed sediment from oceanic reference site showing porous clay structure and only minor fracturing of partially dissolved radiolarian. During tectonic deformation (transition from D to A-C) bulk porosity is reduced from about 72 percent to 60 percent.

zones of strongly aligned phyllosilicate minerals (Fig. 8A). Thin (6 micron), highly birefringent zones show mineral orientation parallel to their length. Thicker zones (>800 microns) are composite, including subzones with mineral orientation inclined 10 to 20 degrees to the zone boundaries as well as thin zones of strong mineral orientation parallel to the margins of the zones. SEM photos show moderately strong mineral orientation (Fig. 8B) that is, however, less well-developed than that observed in the more smectitic-rich mudstones between 220 and 276 m at Site 541. (Compare Fig. 7C and 7D with 8B).

Initial observations on thin sections from the décollement zone at Site 541 indicate a considerable number of intact radiolarians (Fig. 8A). Careful optical studies, and especially SEM investigations, however, reveal evidence of collapsed and imploded radiolarians (Fig. 8C) and small fossil fragments distributed in the clay matrix. Stratigraphically equivalent samples from the oceanic reference site (Site 543) showed much less intense fracturing of microfossils (Fig. 8D). The intense deformation therefore appears to be responsible for the fragmentation of a portion of the fossils.

Microfabrics, Southern Mexico

Off southern Mexico, a strong preferred orientation characterizes only the microfabrics of scaly foliation in the inner portion of the accretionary wedge (Site 492) and transition zone (Site 490); scaly fabrics from sites nearer the trench (488 & 491) do not show a strong preferred orientation microscopically. At Site 492, in a zone of intense stratal disruption (260–290 m subbottom), phyllosilicates form a nearly pervasive microscopic fabric that is folded and overprinted by a second foliation (Lundberg and Moore, 1982; Plate 8; Fig. 9). The scaly fabrics at Site 492 off southern Mexico are associated with stratally disrupted medium- to coarse-grained sands that deformed by both particulate flow and cataclasis (Lucas and Moore, this volume).

At Sites 488 and 491 near the trench, the incipient scaly foliation shows no microscopic or SEM evidence for preferred orientation along the macroscopically apparent shear zones. Based on transmission electron miscroscope analyses and physical property data, Shepard and others (1982) argue that a bedding fabric has been disrupted and densified to produce the macroscopically scaly zone from 210–240 m subbottom at Site 488.

Clearly, true scaly foliation occurs earlier in the structural evolution of northern Barbados Ridge than off southern Mexico. Vane shear tests indicate that the Barbados scaly sediments are weaker, probably because they are finer-grained and richer in smectite (Table 1). Accordingly, they are more susceptible to failure and development of a scaly fabric.

Microfabrics of Onland Examples

SEM studies have been conducted on scaly samples from the Joes River Mudstone of Barbados (Speed and Larue, 1982), the island of Savu in the forearc region of the Banda arc, Indonesia, and the Eocene Sitkalidak Formation of the Kodiak accretionary complex (Moore and Allwardt, 1980). All samples showed well-developed preferred mineral orientation parallel to the scaly partings. The Joes River sample from Barbados is quite similar to the materials recovered from Leg 78A with slicked parting surfaces being smoothly sculptured (Fig. 10A). The very fine-grained pelagic clays from the island of Savu exhibit very smooth parting surfaces with at least the local continuation of strong preferred mineral orientation well away from parting surfaces (Fig. 10B). In the Kodiak accretionary complex, zeolite facies rocks with less than 10 percent porosity have scaly surfaces with an intense macroscopic polish. Ultramicroscopically, the parting surfaces are locally very smooth or striated with a "hard" appearance (Fig. 10C, D), in contrast to the more sculptured aspect of scaly partings in the DSDP and Joes River samples.

TEXTURAL, MINERALOGICAL, AND DIAGENETIC PROPERTIES

Do the textural and mineralogical aspects of sediments influence their tendency to develop scaly fabric? Do diagenetic

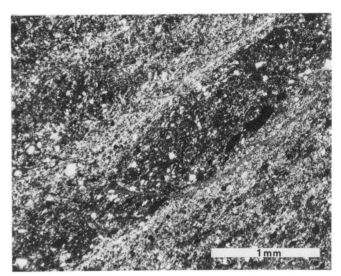

Figure 9. Optical photomicrograph of well-developed scaly foliation at Site 492, off southern Mexico. Bands of high birefringence trending from upper right to lower left are zones of minerals with a preferred orientation along scaly surfaces, with intervening areas of less modified compaction fabric.

changes occur during the formation of scaly fabric? These questions can be addressed in part through mineralogical and textural data available on samples from southern Mexico, Barbados, and Guatemala (Table 1).

The scaly zones associated with thrust faults in the Leg 78A area are preferentially developed in smectitic clay. The scaly foliations associated with the décollement zone in the Leg 78A area are also found in smectitic mudstone that is slightly coarser grained due to the presence of radiolaria. The scaly zones in the Barbados cores occur in sediments with 55 to 60 percent porosity. Vane shear measurements from more coherent mud between scaly intervals indicate undrained shear strength of up to about 125 kPa.

The scaly zones off southern Mexico are principally composed of silty mud with silt percentages averaging 55 to 60 percent and clay-sized grains less than 40 percent (Table 1). The clay mineralogy of the scaly zones is dominated by illite with subsidiary kaolinite and smectite. Porosities range from about 30 to 40 percent. The scaly intervals are too consolidated to obtain meaningful vane shear strengths; however, the strengths probably exceed the 125 to 150 kPa maximum values measured at shallower depths at each site.

Do mineralogical changes occur during the development of scaly foliation? Are the phyllosilicates, oriented along scaly partings, simply reorinted matrix material or have new phases crystallized? In the Barbados area these questions were addressed by detailed X-ray diffraction and chemical analyses of samples collected from intensely scaly zones near faults, on less scaly samples variable distances from faults, and on stratigraphically equivalent sediments sampled at the oceanic reference site (Site 543)

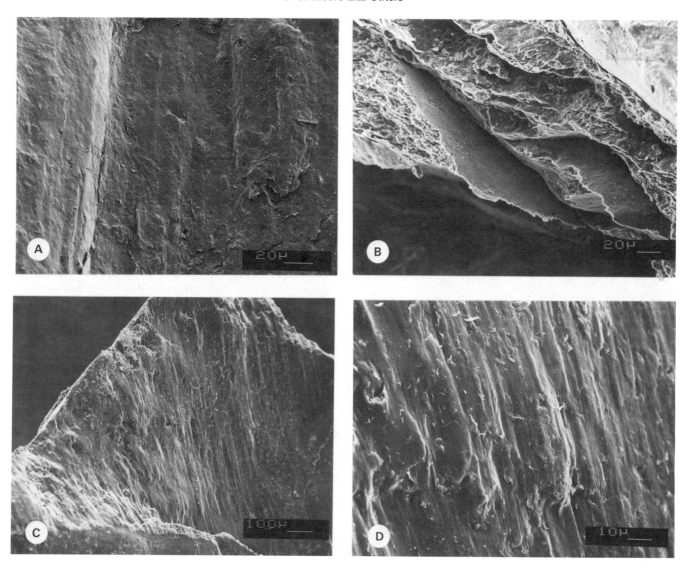

Figure 10. SEM photos of microfabric from onland examples of scaly foliation. A. Scaly foliation surface from the Eocene Joes River Formation, Barbados Island. B. Highly polished surfaces from scaly pelagic melange matrix of Miocene are Savu Island, Indonesia. C. Polished surface from scaly mudstone from Eocene Sitkalidak Formation, Kodiak Islands, Alaska. D. Close-up of C.

(Schoonmaker, this volume). All samples analyzed have similar compositions and are smectite-rich. In some samples of scaly mudstone, the smectite is trioctahedral (a saponite) and has very little or no mixed layering. In other samples from scaly zones and in all samples from the oceanic reference site (Site 543) the smectite appears to be a mixed layer phase and in some cases has both di- and trioctahedral characteristics (Schoonmaker, this volume). Apparently some alteration is occurring in the fault zones in which the scaly fabric preferentially occurs, but scaly foliation itself (which is much more widespread than the alteration) does not directly reflect a mineralogical change. Our SEM observations reveal no evidence of mineralogical changes in the samples we have studied, though new phases have been imaged by transmission electron microscopy in DSDP cores from forearcs else-

where by Knipe (this volume). Our tentative conclusion is that the scaly fabrics form by reorienting matrix material, but that other independent mineralogical alterations may occur in the fault zones in which the scaly fabrics are found (Schoonmaker, this volume). The Barbados samples provide the only rigorous comparison because they are the only scaly samples for which undeformed lithologically and time-equivalent deposits have been recovered.

GEOTECHNICAL OBSERVATIONS ON NATURALLY AND EXPERIMENTALLY PRODUCED SHEAR ZONES IN SOILS AND SEDIMENTS

Surficial earth movements involve fine-grained deposits of

similar or lesser consolidation states than those of the DSDP cores described herein. Not surprisingly, geotechnical results from studies of soils provide interesting parallels to fabrics observed in subduction zones.

The basal slip plane of landslides may be a slickenlined clayey material and can develop a scaly foliation (e.g. Christiansen, 1983). Earth flows (Zaruba and Mencl, 1982) and mud volcanoes (Higgens and Saunders, 1967) locally develop spectacularly slickenlined surfaces. Mud diapirs consist of scaly mudstone and may be the precursor of some types of melanges (Williams and others, 1984). The liquefaction of quick-clays involves pervasive particulate flow and does not produce a scaly fabric (e.g., Kerr and Drew, 1968).

Experimentally produced shear zones in clays (e.g., Tchalenko, 1968) show the development of Riedel shears and thrust shears in addition to the through-going principal displacement shear. The interconnection of these three shear types isolates lenses of shear-bounded but less deformed material that produces a fabric representing an incipient scaly foliation along a shear zone about 2 cm thick.

As indicated by optical examination, experimentally produced shear zones have fabrics very similar to the scaly fabrics observed in the DSDP cores. Typically these studies show high birefringence (strong preferred orientation of minerals) along slip surfaces (Morgenstern and Tchalenko, 1967). The phyllosilicate minerals may be aligned parallel to the slip surfaces in thin zones along their margins (Tchalenko, 1968) but typically are inclined 25 to 30 degrees to the margins of the slip surface (Maltman, 1977; Carson and Berglund, this volume). These inclined zones of minerals with a preferred orientation within the shear zones verge in the direction of shear; accordingly the inclined and margin-parallel mineral orientations respectively mimic the "C-S" fabrics of ductile shear zones in rocks (e.g. Simpson and Schmid, 1983). Experiments have developed structures variously described as kinks, crenulations, and creases that develop with axial surfaces at high angles to the shearing direction (Tchalenko, 1968; Maltman, 1977; Carson and Berglund, this volume).

Experimental shear zones in clays (Tovey, 1974; Fig. 8.26, Mitchell, 1976) and natural slip surfaces in slightly consolidated tills (Quigley and Ogunbadejo, 1974) have phyllosilicate minerals oriented parallel to the slip surfaces as indicated by SEM observations. The individual zones of strong orientation may be very thin (2 microns), discontinuous, and directly adjacent to clays with a random fabric (Tovey, 1974).

Clearly the zones of minerals with a strong preferred orientation in the DSDP cores correspond to the slip surfaces of similar optical characteristics seen in the experimentally produced shear zones. The DSDP samples are more likely to have minerals oriented parallel to the foliation surfaces, probably because these natural shear surfaces have been subject to higher strains than those attainable in shear boxes or triaxial test equipment. The ultramicroscopically deduced preferred orientation of phyllosilicates in experimental shear zones is generally similar to that seen in the DSDP cores. However, none of the experimentally produced shears show the intense sculpturing of clays noted on some of the slickensided surfaces in the Leg 78A area. The latter effect may also be due to high strain.

TEMPERATURE, PRESSURE, STRAIN RATE, CONSOLIDATION STATE, AND POROSITY CHANGES DURING DEVELOPMENT OF SCALY FABRIC

The conditions of development of scaly fabrics are relatively well known for the northern Barbados Ridge locality with progressively lesser information available for examples from southern Mexico and Guatemala. In the northern Barbados Ridge area the temperatures are higher than would be expected from normal burial probably because of the upward advection of warm waters along the fault zones (Table 2). Due to the probable high fluid pressures along the faults, the vertical effective stress may have been substantially lower than that stated in Table 2. The pressures and temperatures quoted for the northern Barbados Ridge probably constitute an upper limit for conditions during the formation of the scaly fabrics off Mexico. The strain rates at the Barbados locality are nearly "geologic" although they might be as much as an order of magnitude higher than quoted due to conservative estimates of fault-zone displacement and time of movement.

In the northern Barbados Ridge area, consolidation tests show that the sediments entering the subduction zone are underconsolidated, as are their offscraped equivalents at Site 541 (Marlow and others, 1984). Similarly, sediments entering the Middle America Trench off southern Mexico are underconsolidated (Shepard and others, 1982). Trench turbidites off Guatemala tend to be underconsolidated; however, the underlying pelagic to hemipelagic sediments are overconsolidated (Fass, 1982). In general one might expect rapidly deposited trench or abyssal-plain deposits to be underconsolidated when they begin to be deformed in a subduction zone.

The SEM photos from the northern Barbados Ridge suggest porosity collapse during the formation of scaly fabric. Here, the porosity is reduced to about 60 percent in the scaly intervals from about 71 percent in the undeformed stratigraphic equivalent (Fig. 2). The resultant volume reduction is about 28 percent; much of this volume decrease is attributable to greater burial (normal vertical consolidation), with the remainder being a true tectonic effect. Off southern Mexico, the incipient scaly foliation at Site 488 occurs in a fault zone cutting slope deposits in which porosity has decreased from a background value of 48 percent to a low of 38 percent with a consequent volume reduction of 16 percent. This volume reduction is entirely of a tectonic nature since the fault zone involves slope sediments deformed in situ. Because the microfabrics show no evidence for preferred orientation (see above), the densification process must be achieved by packing adjacent grains more tightly without shearing them into parallelism as in the Barbados samples. Silt contents average over 55 to 60 percent for the Mexico samples, perhaps preventing develop-

TABLE 2. CONDITIONS OF FORMATION OF SCALY MUDSTONES
NORTHERN BARBADOS RIDGE

	Temperature (degrees C)	Effective Vertical Stress (MPa)	Shear Strain	Strain Rate (/ sec)
Site 541 220-276 m	~20	<2.1	18	6 x 10-13
Site 541 380-460 m	20-25?	<3.5	4	3 x 10-13

Notes: Temperature modified from Davis and Hussong (1984). Vertical effective stress is a maximum value calculated from the buoyant bulk density of the overlying sediment column (Marlow and others, 1984). The probable high fluid pressures active during faulting could reduce the effective stress to near zero values. Shear strain is calculated by dividing the displacement on a fault zone (estimated from the cross section in Figure 1 and/or from the throw) by the thickness of the associated shear zone. Given errors in estimation of fault displacement, the values of shear strain could be in error by a factor of two. The estimates of shear strain are for an entire fault zone; the strain is not homogeneously distributed across the fault zone. The duration of faulting could be in error by a factor of five; therefore, the strain rates could vary by an order of magnitude from the values listed above.

ment of a strong preferred orientation similar to that observed in the uniformly clayey sediments of the Barbados area.

KEY OBSERVATIONS AND CONCLUSIONS

The key observations and conclusions of our study of scaly fabrics in DSDP cores are as follows.

1) Scaly fabric preferentially develops in fault zones. Biostratigraphic and seismic evidence directly associates the scaly fabric of the Barbados area with thrust faults. Circumstantial evidence suggests that the scaly fabric off southern Mexico is associated with faulting. Where faults have been recognized, the scaly fabrics may occur as much as 40 m from these surfaces.

2) Scaly fabric surfaces are slip surfaces. The macroscopic slickenlines suggest slip. Moreover, comparisons of the microscopic and SEM views of DSDP scaly fabric surfaces to known experimentally produced slip surfaces in clay supports slip origin for the former.

3) Microscopic and SEM images of the scaly foliation surfaces indicate strong preferred orientation of phyllosilicates, both parallel to and at low angles to the foliation surfaces. The pattern of mineral orientation in the foliation surfaces locally resembles the C-S fabrics of ductile shear zones. The SEM images and comparative porosity measurements indicate porosity loss attendant with the development of preferred orientation.

4) Formation of new mineral phases need not occur during the development of scaly foliation surfaces. The foliation forms by mineral reorientation and perhaps disruption of clay aggregates.

5) In the DSDP cores, scaly fabrics form at very low temperatures and pressures at near "geologic" strain rates. The

sediment in which scaly foliation develops is probably initially underconsolidated.

ORIGIN OF SCALY FOLIATION IN PARTIALLY CONSOLIDATED MUDS

Model for Development of Scaly Fabric

By reviewing the history of a mud as it develops a scaly foliation, we can integrate our observations into a concrete model for fabric evolution (Fig. 11) that can in part by evaluated by experimental data. Our model pertains only to mud protoliths; the development of scaly fabrics from crystalline materials remains unstudied.

1) Muddy sediment that develops a scaly foliation will either be derived from the incoming oceanic sedimentary section or, in some cases, the overlying slope sediment blanket. Incoming trench sediments and rapidly deposited slope deposits are likely to be underconsolidated. That is, they are unusually porous for their depth of burial and their pore pressures are anomalously high. Such materials have substantial potential for porosity collapse during deformation providing that the pore fluid can escape.

2) Sediment is tectonically stressed and excess fluid pressure develops because of the low permeability of the mud.

3) The sediment mass fails by faulting due to the increase in deviatoric stress and fluid pressure.

4) The relatively open clay fabric collapses along the failure surface, porosity is locally decreased, the coefficient of friction is increased, and fluid is expelled (the shear dewatering process of Karig, this volume).

5) The increase in the coefficient of friction causes the failure

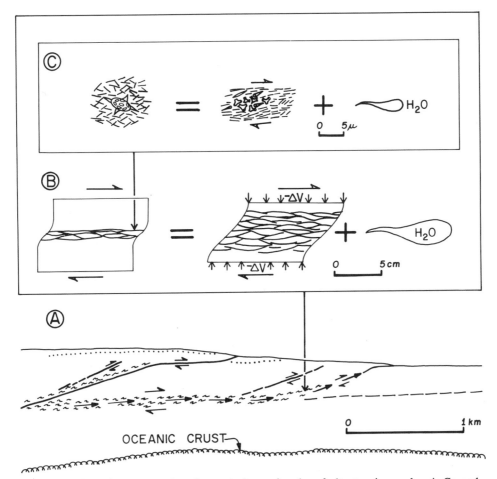

Figure 11. Schematic representation of tectonic dewatering along faults at various scales. A. Generalized cross section of initial deformation of offscraped material showing faults and associated distributed deformation. Single arrows in fault zones show fluid movement; whereas, pairs of single barbed arrows indicate relative movement in fault zones. B. Enlarged view of shear zone showing its widening with progressive strain, volumetric collapse, and fluid expulsion. C. Schematic SEM view of fabric collapse along a single shear surface with development of preferred orientation in phyllosilicates, associated porosity reduction, and crushing of a microfossil.

surface to lock or strain harden. Slip may also stop due to reorientation of the slip plane relative to the stress field.

6) The deviatoric stress increases again and failure occurs not on the existing failure plane but in the adjacent mud matrix that retains a more open (weaker) framework. Repetition of steps 3 to 5 causes the propagation of failure planes and the development of the thick scaly fault zones.

Evaluation of Proposed Model

A critical element of the preceding model for the development of scaly foliation is that failure planes are abandoned after limited slip with the propagation of yet another failure surface. In order for the failure planes to be abandoned, they must become stronger than the surrounding matrix by increasing their frictional resistance to sliding or rotating such that the applied stress will no

longer cause displacement. The shear stress (τ) necessary to cause sliding on a surface equals the cohesion of the material (c) plus the product of the coefficient of friction on the sliding surface (μ) and the effective normal stress along the surface (T_n-T_f, the total stress less the fluid pressure):

$$\tau = c + \mu(T_n-T_f)$$

Some experimental data are available for the evaluation of the effects of cohesion and changes in the coefficient of friction on continued sliding. The role of fluid pressure in the above relationship is considered independently on the basis of observational, experimental, and theoretical data.

Cohesion and Coefficient of Friction. Both triaxial and direct shear experiments on soils typically have stress-strain curves characterized by an initially steep slope in which strain increases slowly relative to stress, followed by an interval of significant strain in which stress increases slowly, not at all, or decreases. The change in slope of the curve is interpreted as the breakdown of the initial cohesion of the soil, after which the yielding of the material is controlled by its coefficient of friction. The slope of the stress-strain curve during this continued yielding indicates whether the material is strengthening (strain hardening), not changing in strength, or weakening.

In soils, the shape of the stress-strain curve seems to be related to whether the sediment being deformed is confined at stresses less than or greater than its previous effective overburden stress in the natural environment. Drained triaxial and direct shear tests on soils at confining stresses equal to or less that their past effective stress (simulating deformation of normally to over-consolidated soils) are characterized by attainment of a peak strength at relatively low strains with subsequent decrease to a lower residual strength (Fig. 12A; Skempton, 1964; Morgenstern and Tchalenko, 1967; Lambe and Whitman, 1969). These experiments are usually characterized by dilation of the sediment.

Triaxial and direct shear experiments on muds at low confining stresses (but exceeding previous effective stress) tend to show continuous strengthening with increasing strain and volume reduction with no pronounced ultimate strength (Crawford, 1959; Bjerrum and Landva, 1966; Fig. 12A). As these experiments are conducted at constant confining stress and pore pressures, the strengthening of the material reflects an increasing coefficient of friction of the deforming soil. The increasing angle of internal friction (or coefficient of friction) is illustrated by the progressive steepening of the Mohr envelopes with increasing strain (Fig. 12D). Experiments on fault gouge (Morrow and others, 1982) and porous siltstones and claystones (Hoshino and others, 1972) at higher confining pressures also show strengthening with continuing deformation (Fig. 12B, C). The collapse of the framework by particulate flow and grain breakage at higher confining pressures is thought to account for the strengthening of these materials (Bjerrum and Landva, 1966; Morrow and others, 1982; Hoshino and others, 1972). The triaxial experiments all involve axial strains to a maximum of 30 percent, so that one might question whether the peak strength of material had been reached. The experiments with fault gouge were extended to shear strains of about 900 percent with continuing strain hardening, however.

All of the experiments mentioned above are drained or dry; that is, any pore fluid could be readily expulsed from the deforming material. Equivalent undrained experiments show peak strengths and failure at low strains as the trapped fluid cannot support shear stress (Lambe and Whitman, 1969). The liquefaction of a sensitive clay dramatically illustrates the reality of a peak and subsequently diminished strength during deformation with no fluid loss (Mitchell, 1976, p. 198).

Trench and hemipelagic sediments entering subduction zones are typically underconsolidated, that is, part of their overburden is being supported by the pore fluid. Consequently the sediments have an unusually porous sediment fabric. SEM photos and porosity data presented herein indicate collapse of the sediment fabric during development of scaly fabrics. This collapse of an open sediment fabric during deformation suggests comparisons to the second group of experiments discussed above, where fabric collapse was accompanied by increasing coefficient of friction. If during deformation in the subduction zone the strength of the sediment in the shear zone increases only slightly, then it will exceed the strength of the adjacent undeformed sediment matrix and allow propagation of a new shear surface through the weaker material. Hence the width of the scaly fabric zone would grow.

Fluid Pressure. In addition to the increase in the coefficient of friction, a drop in pore pressure will also cause strengthening of the failure surface. We have no specific data on variation of fluid pressures during development of scaly fabric, however some speculations are possible based on other observations. Clearly, fluid must be lost to permit fabric to collapse and a scaly surface to develop. Since the overall pattern in accretionary complexes is one of anomalous densification (Bray and Karig, 1985), then fluid must be lost from the entire deforming mass, probably along active faults in the case of the northern Barbados Ridge area (Westbrook and Smith, 1983; Moore and Biju-Duval, 1984). For the fluid to move from the matrix to the faults, a fluid potential (head) drop must exist. Since the intergranular permeability of the less porous scaly mudstone in fault zones would be lower than that of the undeformed sediment matrix, the fluids would probably move along faults largely through fracture porosity. If the fluid pressures are lower in the fault zones relative to the matrix, then the faults would tend to be stronger than the surrounding matrix, would grow at the expense of the matrix, and would produce broad zones of scaly fabric.

Rotation of Slip Surfaces. In homogeneous materials, failure occurs in preferred orientations due to the appropriate combination of normal and shear stresses. In a rotational strain regime in soft materials, the planes of failure are likely to rotate from this failure orientation and therefore no longer have the correct stress combination to continue slip. Moreover, any deformation of a failure plane could lead to geometric locking, quite apart from any stress variation. We believe that this rotation of slip planes may be an important factor in slip-surface propagation during shear-zone deformation.

Lithologic Control. Lithologic control on the development of scaly foliation in the northern Barbados Ridge area is well shown by the preferential development of this fabric in the smectitic mudstone rather than the adjacent calcareous mudstone (Fig. 2). Both lithologies are underconsolidated (Marlow and others, 1984) but the calcareous mud is about 10 percent less porous and significantly higher in vane shear strength (based on comparison of sections of equivalent depth of burial but different lithologies at Site 541 and 543, Marlow and others, 1984). The calcareous mud also has a coarser grain size than the smectitic mud due to the microfossil content of the former. Apparently the more open framework, more uniform grain size, and lower strength of the smectitic mud allows localization of the deformation in this lithology.

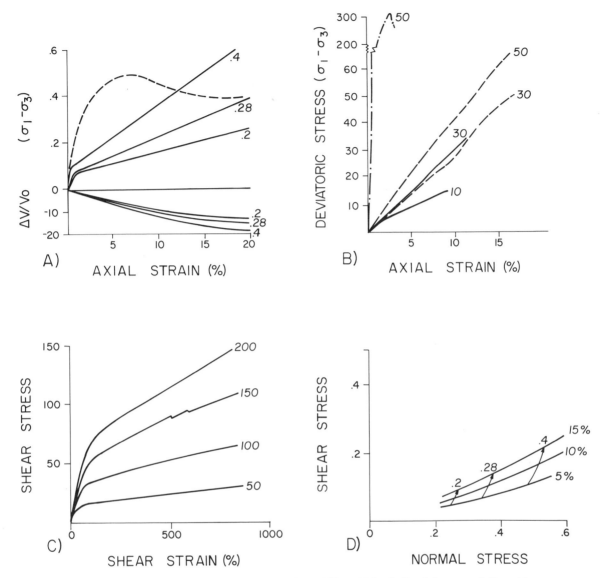

Figure 12. Experimental data. All stress in MPa (1 MPa ~10 bars). Confining stress indicated by numbers at end of stress-strain curves. A. Results from drained triaxial experiments on a sensitive clay (Crawford, 1959). Note substantial volume reduction associated with strengthening of clay structure. For comparison a typical stress-strain curve from a drained triaxial test of an overconsolidated clay is shown by dashed line (Lambe and Whitman, 1969; Skempton, 1964). This latter sample was deformed at an effective confining stress less than its previous effective overburden stress. Note how strength peaks and decreases in contrast to sensitive clay. Additionally, overconsolidated clay shows a volume expansion during deformation. B. Data from dry triaxial experiments on claystone (solid line, 60 percent porosity), siltstone (dashed line, 64 percent porosity), and shale (dot-dashed line, 11 percent porosity). Note that low porosity sample behaves as a brittle rock whereas more porous samples tend to increase in strength without any indication of a yield point (Hoshino and others, 1972). C. Stress-strain curves from drained triaxial experiments on fault gouge deformed in thin shear zone between hard rocks. Note that even at considerable strains the gouge continues to strain-harden (Morrow and others, 1982). D. Mohr envelopes constructed from data in A. Since curves in A do not show ultimate strengths, envelopes are constructed for various degrees of strain, shown in percent at the end of each envelope. Note that envelopes tend to become steeper with increasing strain, therefore indicating an increase in internal friction (or coefficient of friction). Arrows show stress paths defined by points of tangency between the Mohn circles and envelopes for each of the stress-strain curves in A. Each stress path proceeds through failure envelopes with progressively steeper slope or greater internal friction. Hoshino and others (1972) has constructed Mohr envelopes from data in B that also become steeper with increasing strain. Moreover, Morrow and others (1982) has pointed out that the coefficient of friction becomes greater with increasing strain in the experiments shown in C.

Comparisons to Hard Rocks. This distributed deformation inherent in the development of scaly fabrics is one of the unique characteristics of accretionary complexes and is distinct from the pattern of deformation in hard rocks. Compare, for example, the relatively orderly patterns of faulting in fold and thrust belts (Price, 1981) to the exceedingly intricate structure of mature accretionary complexes. In hard rocks, fault planes are weak surfaces that continue to be utilized for subsequent displacements, except in the case of locking due to geometric constraints. At low confining pressures the initial cohesion of hard rocks is high relative to the frictional resistance to sliding along an existing fault plane. Therefore, faults in rocks tend to be the locus of continuing deformation. At the same confining pressures the cohesive strength of sands and muds is much lower and frictional effects within fault planes tend to be more important.

ACKNOWLEDGMENTS

Research reported herein was supported by grants (OCE8110394 and OCE8315836) from the Submarine Geology and Geophysics Program of the National Science Foundation. Dan Karig, Cindy Bray, Mark Brandon and Dave Larue provided thoughtful comments on various drafts of the manuscript. Don Reid contributed the sample of scaly pelagic clay from Savu Island imaged in Fig. 9B. Moore acknowledges the hospitality of the Department of Geological Sciences at Cornell University where the initial manuscript preparation occurred.

REFERENCES CITED

Abbate, E., Bortolotti, V., and Passerini, P., 1970, Olistostromes and olistoliths: Sedimentary Geology, v. 4, p. 521–557.

Arthur, M., Carson, B., and von Huene, R., 1980, Initial tectonic deformation of hemipelagic sediment at the leading edge of the Japan convergent margin, *in* Lee, M., and Stout, L., eds., Initial Reports of the Deep Sea Drilling Project: Washington, D.C., U.S. Government Printing Office, v. 56, 57, pt. 1, p. 569–613.

Aubouin, J., von Huene, R., and others, eds., 1982, Initial Reports of the Deep Sea Drilling Project: Washington, D.C., U.S. Government Printing Office, v. 67, 799 p.

Bachman, S. B., 1982, The Coastal Belt of the Franciscan: Youngest phase of northern California subduction, *in* Leggett, J. K., ed., Trench-forearc geology: Sedimentation and tectonics on modern and ancient active plate margins: Geological Society of London Special Publication No. 10, p. 401–417.

Biju-Duval, B., Moore, J. C., and others, eds., 1984, Initial Reports of the Deep Sea Drilling Project: Washington, D.C., U.S. Government Printing Office, v. 78A, 621 p.

Bjerrum, L., and Landva, A., 1966, Direct simple-shear tests on a Norwegian quick clay: Geotechnique, v. 16, p. 1–20.

Boles, J. R., and Landis, C. A., 1984, Jurassic sedimentary melange and associated facies, Baja, California, Mexico: Geological Society of America Bulletin, v. 95, p. 513–521.

Bray, C. J., and Karig, D. E., 1985, Porosity of sediments in accretionary prisms and some implications for dewatering processes: Journal of Geophysical Research, v. 90, p. 768–778.

Byrne, T., 1984, Early deformation in melange terranes of the Ghost Rocks Formation, Kodiak Islands, Alaska: Geological Society of America Special Paper 199, p. 21–51.

Carson, B., 1977, Tectonically induced deformation of deep-sea sediments off Washington and northern Oregon: Mechanical consolidation: Marine Geology, v. 24, p. 289–307.

Christiansen, E. A., 1983, The Denholm landslide, Saskatchewan, Part I, Geology: Canadian Geotechnical Journal, v. 20, p. 197–207.

Cowan, D. S., 1974, Deformation and metamorphism of Franciscan subduction zones complex northwest of Pacheco Pass, California: Geological Society of America Bulletin, v. 85, p. 1623–1634.

Cowan, D. S., Moore, J. C., Roeske, S. M., Lundberg, N., and Lucas, S. E., 1984, Structural features at the deformation front of the Barbados Ridge complex, Deep Sea Drilling Project Leg 78A, *in* Biju-Duval, B., Moore, J. C., and others, eds., Initial Reports of the Deep Sea Drilling Project: Washington, D.C., U.S. Government Printing Office, v. 78A, p. 535–548.

Crawford, C. B., 1959, The influence of rate of strain on effective stresses in sensitive clay: American Society for Testing and Materials Special Technical Publication 254, p. 36–48.

Davis, D. M., and Hussong, D. M., 1984, Geothermal observations during Deep Sea Drilling Project Leg 78A, *in* Biju-Duval, B., Moore, J. C., and others, eds., Initial Reports of the Deep Sea Drilling Project: Washington, D.C., U.S. Government Printing Office, v. 78A, p. 593–598.

Elter, P., and Trevisan, L., 1973, Olistostromes in the tectonic evolution of the Northern Apennines, *in* De Jong, K. A., and Sholten, R., eds., Gravity and Tectonics: New York, John Wiley and Sons, p. 175–188.

Fass, R. W., 1982, Gravitational compaction patterns determined from sediment cores recovered during the Deep Sea Drilling Project Leg 67 Guatemalan Transect: Continental slope, Middle America Trench, and Cocos Plate, *in* Aubouin, J., von Huene, R., and others, eds., Initial Reports of the Deep Sea Drilling Project: Washington, D.C., U.S. Government Printing Office, v. 67, p. 617–638.

Hamilton, W., 1979, Tectonics of the Indonesian region: U.S. Geological Survey Professional Paper 1078, 355 p.

Helm, R., 1985, Mineralogy and diagenesis of slope sediments offshore Guatemala and Costa Rica, Deep Sea Drilling Project Leg 84, *in* von Huene, R., Aubouin, J., and others, Initial Reports of the Deep Sea Drilling Project: Washington, D.C., U.S. Government Printing Office, v. 84, p. 571–594.

Higgens, G. E., and Saunders, J. B., 1967, Report on 1964 Chatham mud island, Erin Bay, Trinidad, West Indies: American Association of Petroleum Geologists Bulletin, v. 51, p. 55–64.

Hoshino, K., Koide, H., Inami, K., Iwamura, S., Mitsui, S., 1972, Mechanical properties of Japanese Tertiary sedimentary rocks under high confining pressures: Chishitsu Chosajo, Geological Survey of Japan Report 244, 200 p.

Kerr, P. F., and Drew, I. M., 1968, Quick-Clay Slides in the U.S.A.: Engineering Geology, v. 2, p. 215–238.

Kurnosov, V., Murdmaa, I., Kazakova, V., Mikhina, V., and Shevchenko, A., 1982, Mineralogy of sediments from the Middle America Trench (Guatemala Transect), *in* Aubouin, J., von Huene, R., and others, Initial Reports of the Deep Sea Drilling Project: Washington, D.C., U.S. Government Printing Office, v. 67, p. 515–528.

Lambe, T. W., and Whitman, R. V., 1969, Soil Mechanics: New York, John Wiley and Sons, 553 p.

Lash, G., 1985, Accretion-related deformation of an ancient (early Paleozoic) trench-fill deposit, central Appalachian orogen: Geological Society of America Bulletin, v. 96, p. 1167–1178.

Lundberg, N., and Moore, J. C., 1982, Structural features of the Middle America Trench slope off southern Mexico, Deep Sea Drilling Project Leg 66, *in* Watkins, J. S., Moore, J. C., and others, Initial Reports of the Deep Sea Drilling Project: Washington, D.C., U.S. Government Printing Office, v. 66, p. 793–805.

Maltman, A. J., 1977, Some microstructures of experimentally deformed argillaceous sediments: Tectonophysics, v. 39, p. 417–436.

Marlow, M. S., Lee, H., and Wright, A., 1984, Physical properties of sediment from the Lesser Antilles Margin along the Barbados Ridge: Results from

Deep Sea Drilling Project Leg 78A, *in* Biju-Duval, B., Moore, J. C., and others, Initial Reports of the Deep Sea Drilling Project: Washington, D.C., U.S. Government Printing Office, v. 78A, p. 549–558.

Mitchell, J. K., 1976, Fundamentals of soil behavior: New York, John Wiley and Sons, 442 p.

Moore, G. F., and Karig, D. E., 1980, Structural geology of Nias Island, Indonesia: Implications for subduction zone tectonics: American Journal of Science, v. 280, p. 193–223.

Moore, J. C., and Alwardt, A., 1980, Progressive deformation of a trench slope, Kodiak Islands, Alaska: Journal of Geophysical Research, v. 85, p. 4741–4756.

Moore, J. C., and Biju-Duval, B., 1984, Tectonic synthesis Deep Sea Drilling Project Leg 78A: Structural evolution of offscraped and underthrust sediment, northern Barbados Ridge complex, *in* Biju-Duval, B., Moore, J. C., and others, eds., Initial Reports of the Deep Sea Drilling Project: Washington, D.C., U.S. Government Printing Office, v. 78A, p. 601–621.

Moore, J. C., Watkins, J. S., and others, 1982, Site 488, *in* Watkins, J. S., Moore, J. C., and others, eds., Initial Reports of the Deep Sea Drilling Project: Washington, D.C., U.S. Government Printing Office, v. 66, p. 59–105.

Morgenstern, N. R., and Tchalenko, J. S., 1967, Microscopic structures in kaolin subjected to direct shear: Geotechnique, v. 17, p. 309–328.

Morrow, C. A., Shi, L. Q., and Byerlee, J. D., 1982, Strain hardening and strength of clay-rich fault gouges: Journal of Geophysical Research, v. 87, p. 6771–6780.

Page, B. M., 1963, Gravity tectonics near Passo della Cisa, Northern Apennines, Italy; Geological Society of America Bulletin, v. 74, p. 655–671.

Price, R. A., 1981, The Cordilleran foreland thrust and fold belt in the southern Canadian Rocky Mountains, *in* McClay, K. R., and Price, N. J., eds., Thrust and Nappe Tectonics: Geological Society of London Special Publication No. 9, p. 427–448.

Pudsey, C. J., 1984, X-ray Mineralogy of Miocene and older sediments from Leg 78A, Deep Sea Drilling Project, *in* Biju-Duval, B., Moore, J. C., and others, eds., Initial Reports of the Deep Sea Drilling Project: Washington, D.C., U.S. Government Printing Office, v. 78A, p. 325–341.

Quigley, R. M., and Ogunbadejo, T. A., 1974, Soil weathering, soil structure and engineering properties, Sarnia clay crust, *in* Rutherford, G. K., ed., Soil Microscopy: Proceedings of the Fourth International Working-Meeting on Soil Micromorphology: Kingston, Ontario, The Limestone Press, p. 165–178.

Schumann, D., and Nagel, U., 1982, Appendix I. X-ray mineralogical analysis, *in* Watkins, J. S., Moore, J. C., and others, eds., Initial Reports of the Deep Sea Drilling Project: Washington, D.C., U.S. Government Printing Office, v. 66, p. 853–857.

Shephard, L. E., Bryant, W. R., and Chiou, W. A., 1982, Geotechnical properties of Middle America Trench sediments, Deep Sea Drilling Project Leg 66, *inn* Watkins, J. C., Moore, J. C., and others, eds., Initial Reports of the Deep Sea Drilling Project: Washington, D.C., U.S. Government Printing Office, v. 66, p. 475–504.

Simpson, C., and Schmid, S. M., 1983, An evaluation of criteria to deduce the sense of movement in sheared rocks: Geological Society of America Bulletin, v. 94, p. 1281–1288.

Skempton, A. W., 1964, Long-term stability of clay slopes: Geotechnique, v. 14, p. 77–101.

Speed, R. C., and Larue, D. K., 1982, Barbados: Architecture and implications for accretion: Journal of Geophysical Research, v. 87, p. 3633–3643.

Taira, A., Okada, H., Whitaker, J., and Smith, A., 1982, The Shimanto Belt of Japan: Cretaceous-lower Miocene active-margin sedimentation, *in* Leggett, J. K., ed., Trench-forearc geology: Sedimentation and tectonics on modern and ancient active plate margins: Geological Society of London Special Publication No. 10, p. 5–26.

Tchalenko, J. S., 1968, The evolution of kink-bands and the development of compression textures in sheared clays: Tectonophysics, v. 6, p. 159–174.

Tovey, N. K., 1974, Some applications of electron microscopy to soil engineering, *in* Rutherford, G. K., ed., Soil Microscopy: Proceedings of the Fourth International Working-Meeting on Soil Micromorphology: Kingston, Ontario, The Limestone Press, p. 119–142.

Vollmer, F. W., and Bosworth, W., 1984, Formation of melange in a foreland basin overthrust setting: Example from the Taconic Orogen: Geological Society of America Special Paper 198, p. 53–79.

von Huene, R., Aubouin, J., and others, 1985, Initial Reports of the Deep Sea Drilling Project: Washington, D.C., U.S. Government Printing Office, v. 84, 967 p.

Watkins, J. S., Moore, J. C., and others, 1982, Initial Reports of the Deep Sea Drilling Project: Washington, D.C., U.S. Government Printing Office, v. 66, 864 p.

Westbrook, G. K., and Smith, M. J., 1983, Long décollements and mud volcanoes: Evidence from the Barbados Ridge Complex for the role of high pore-fluid pressure in the development of an accretionary complex: Geology, v. 11, p. 279–283.

Williams, P. R., Pigram, C. J., and Dow, D. B., 1984, Melange production and the importance of shale diapirism in accretionary terrains: Nature, v. 309, p. 145–146.

Zaruba, Q., and Mencl, V., 1982, Landslides and their control: New York, Elsevier Scientific Publishing Co., 324 p.

MANUSCRIPT ACCEPTED BY THE SOCIETY MARCH 10, 1986

Geological Society of America
Memoir 166
1986

Microstructural evolution of vein arrays preserved in Deep Sea Drilling Project cores from the Japan Trench, Leg 57

R. J. Knipe
Department of Earth Sciences
The University
Leeds LS2 9JT, United Kingdom

ABSTRACT

The geometry and microstructural features of veins preserved in D.S.D.P. cores from Leg 57 (Japan Trench) are described, based on a combination of optical and transmission electron microscopy. The veins represent a localized failure and show a range of geometrical patterns, which may relate to the strain rate history involved in their evolution. The microstructures associated with the veins are complex and indicative of a range of strain paths. Disaggregation and grain boundary sliding (particulate flow) are the most important processes involved in vein development. It is suggested that (i) although a high pore fluid pressure would aid the initiation of the veins, alternative mechanisms of failure, including collapse during shearing, are also possible, and (ii) the preferred alignment of grains within the veins was probably not formed by "streaming" fluids but by rotation during the porosity reduction and slow fluid expulsion late in the history of vein development. The larger-scale implications of veins are discussed; the range of strain paths associated with veins is suggested to arise from the location of veins in a complex down-slope movement system.

INTRODUCTION

Vein arrays are a common deformation feature of D.S.D.P. cores recovered from the top kilometer of slope sediments at active margins (Arthur and others, 1980a; Cowan, 1982; Carson and others, 1982; Lundberg and Moore, this volume). These features, which represent some of the earliest deformation features produced in the sediments from such tectonic locations, appear as dark, planar to curviplanar structures. They are as much as a few millimeters in width, generally less than ten centimeters in length and show little or no vein-parallel displacement. A detailed study of the distribution of vein structures at the various margins sampled is reported by Lundberg and Moore (this volume). The veins have been interpreted by Arthur and others (1980a) as dewatering features associated with tectonic overpressuring and by Cowan (1982) as representing dewatering channels developed during early burial but unrelated to convergence-induced compressive tectonic stresses. In this paper I have concentrated on the microstructural characteristics of vein structures as revealed by optical and transmission electron microscopy and have attempted to use the information obtained to assess the deformation mechanisms and histories involved in their

evolution. The microstructures of veins from D.S.D.P. Legs 57, 60, and 66 have been studied using the above methods. The results of the analysis of the Leg 57 (Japan Trench) veins presented in detail here are typical of the microstructures preserved at other margins. Some of the optical features of veins present in Leg 67 (Middle America Trench) have been presented by Cowan (1982). Before describing the microstructures observed from Leg 57 specimens, the setting and properties of sediments of Leg 57 containing the veins are reviewed.

Setting and Properties of Veined Sediments

An overview of the tectonic setting and structure of the Japan Trench has been given by von Huene and others (1980) and Leggett and others (1985), and a review of the sedimentary evolution, including deposition and subsidence rates of the fore-arc, has been presented by Arthur and others (1980a). Veins were recorded in all of the drill sites that penetrated through the unlithified sediment apron on the Japan Trench. These sites included the deep sea terrace (a shelf-like structure with a surface dip of

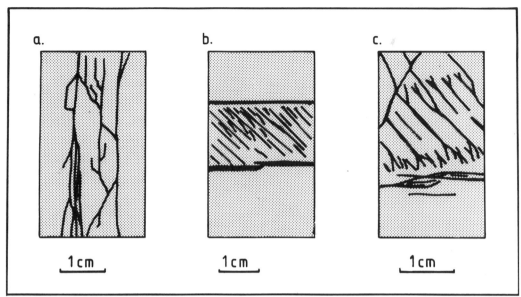

Figure 1. Review of the geometrical characteristics of vein arrays. Bedding in each case is sub-horizontal in the sketches. a) shows an irregular array where a vertical set dominates (From 57, 440B 55.5 85–90 cm sub-bottom depth: 659.4 m.); b) illustrates a regular vein array with a tension gash geometry composed of a large number of closely spaced veins, in this case bounded by features approximately parallel to bedding (from 57, 439 4.3 80-84 cm sub-bottom depth 745.8 m.); c) shows a regular vein array with tension gash geometry and associated sub-horizontal features. Note the bifurcation of veins in this example. (from 57. 439 9.2 110–120 cm sub-bottom depth 890.1 m.).

<1° towards the trench, i.e. sites 438 and 439), the mid-slope terrace (site 440), and the trench lower slope with an average surface dip of 4–7° (sites 441 and 434). The area has a complex tilting history, with the deep sea terrace area having a period of landward tilting during the late Oligocene to Late Miocene as well as oceanward tilting from Late Miocene onwards, which the whole forearc experienced. The cores recovered from this margin show periods of extensional and compressional faulting as well as evidence of down-slope movement (Arthur and others, 1980b; Leggett and others, 1985). There is more evidence of deformation and down-slope movement in the lower slope sites. Veins occur in the "lithified" Miocene and Pliocene diatomaceous mudstones and claystones ("lithified" in this context meaning too hard to be cut with a cheese-slicer). The veins are concentrated at subbottom depths ranging from ~600–800 m on the deep sea terrace (sites 438 and 439) and to below 260 m on the lower slope (sites 441 and 434) (see Arthur and others, 1980b). Where fractures are present in the cores above the veins, they tend to be open fractures.

Bedding dips tend to be more variable in the vicinity of veins reflecting their association with faults. In cores from the deep sea terrace, the maximum dips recorded are 30°, but in the faulted sections of the lower slope, dips may reach 70° (see Lundberg and Moore, this volume).

The porosity of the specimens containing veins varies from 50–70%, although a few sediments in this depth interval do have porosities as low as 30% (Carson and Bruns, 1980). It should be emphasized that these measurements represent the finite or current porosity and not necessarily the porosity at the time of vein formation. Despite the high porosity, these sediments have enough strength to require sawing for sample collection.

The mineralogy of sediments at the depth interval containing the veins has been studied by Aoyagi and Kazama (1980) and found to contain montmorillonite, illite, chlorite, quartz, plagioclase, and pyrite, in addition to diatoms and secondary silica (Moore and Gieskes, 1980).

HAND SPECIMEN GEOMETRY AND ASSOCIATED STRUCTURES

The veins tend to be concentrated in certain lithologies (sediment types) and at certain depths in the cores (see Lundberg and Moore, this volume). The geometrical arrangement of veins from Leg 57 (as well as 60 and 67) varies from irregular networks to regular arrays; their occurrence is often related to the appearance of other deformation features such as faults in the cores. The exact geometry of each of these 'end-member' vein types is outlined below and also in Figure 1.

Irregular arrays occur where the spacing and orientation of veins is highly variable. Vein arrays with these characteristics often give the core a brecciated appearance, where angular blocks (up to 4 cms) of intact sediment are delineated by veins (Fig. 1a; Arthur and others, 1980a, Plate 3). Veins oriented at a high angle to bedding often (but not always) dominate the array. The longest veins tend to be the thickest, forming an anastomosing array in 3D. There is a complete transition from these irregular vein arrays to microfault arrays.

Regular arrays, composed of veins with approximately constant spacing and thickness, are particularly common in the D.S.D.P. cores (Fig. 16; Cowan 1982, Plate 1; Lundberg and Moore, this volume, Fig. 6). As noted by Cowan (1982), these often have tension gash geometries with the XZ plane approximately vertical. In sections cut approximately parallel to the shear plane, the vein arrays either form an overlapping arrangement or an anastomosing network. The truncation and rotation of some veins in the array by others suggests the sequential evolution of veins within the array. Another characteristic of the regular vein arrays is the bifurcation at the ends of individual veins into the "horse tail" structures (Fig. 1c). The significance of these features is discussed later.

Associated Structures

The vein structures described above are often spatially associated with other deformation features in the cores (see Lundberg and Moore, this volume). Faults marked by dark seams with visible offsets of bedding are characteristic of core sections containing veins. The association of the faults and veins is clearly illustrated in Plates 2–6 of Arthur and others (1980a). A more localized association of deformation features with veins is also commonly encountered where shallow dipping dark seams form either the lower or upper boundary of the vein arrays (Fig. 1b).

MICROSTRUCTURES

The microstructures characteristic of the veins have been investigated using optical and electron microscopy. Optical work was conducted on ultra-thin sections produced from specimens impregnated with low viscosity epoxy resin and ground in oil. These sections were then used to select critical areas for the preparation of 3 mm-diameter discs used in transmission electron microscopy (T.E.M.). The T.E.M. results reported were conducted on a Jeol 200CX with scanning transmission electron microscopy (S.T.E.M.) and X-ray detection facilities.

Optical Microstructures

In thin section the veins appear as light-colored, lenticular to planar zones, which in some cases link or truncate each other (Fig. 2). The veins are as much as 1 mm wide and exhibit a range of boundary and internal structures. The boundaries of the veins with the host sediment range from extremely sharp contacts, (<30 μm, commonly defined by a zone of increased preferred orientation) to diffuse, gradational zones (perhaps extending over 0.1 mm). These different boundaries may be present along the different sections of the same veins and often mark a change in the thickness of the vein (Fig. 2). However, it should be emphasized that many veins show no optical evidence of bending of the

bedding fabric at the vein edge. Displacements across the veins seldom exceed a few millimeters. The displacement pattern across veins varies from those with the opposite sense of shear parallel to the boundary, producing graben-like structures, to veins with a constant sense of shearing, producing normal/vertical fault geometries (Fig. 3).

The most important internal feature of the veins is the occurrence of the larger detrital mineral grains and fossil fragments characteristic of the material outside the veins (Fig. 2). The presence of these fragments in what appears to be the same density and frequency as outside is critical to the origin of the veins, as it suggests that the internal vein material represents a modification of the existing sediment and is not totally composed of new, introduced material.

Two types of veins may be recognized, depending on the structures within the veins. The first type includes veins with an internal domainal microstructure where thin (<0.05 mm), discontinuous, and anastomosing domains, approximately parallel to the vein, enclose lenticular domains. The lenticular domains appear to preserve the fabric characteristic of the sediment outside the vein (Fig. 3d). The second type of vein contains no clear internal domainal structure or preservation of the external fabric. The only zones of high preferred orientation are located at the boundaries of the vein (Fig. 3c). The latter type of internal structure, where the characteristics of the fabric outside the vein are not preserved, appear to be more commonly associated with the irregular vein arrays.

The optical microstructures of the shallow dipping features often associated with the regular vein arrays are similar to those of the veins themselves. That is, they contain large detrital grains and fossil fragments. In addition, the internal structures range from examples with domainal features sub-parallel to the boundaries, to other examples with little or no internal fabric. The displacement sense and magnitude is difficult to assess, but the shallow dipping zones appear to represent zones of concentrated slip. The example shown in Figure 2 shows a subsidiary steep movement zone at F with the same sense of shear as inferred for the overlying regular tension gash array. Evidence that the regular vein array represents a tension gash array above the movement zone in Figure 2 is from the truncation and inferred rotation of early veins within the array.

Electron Microscopy

The transmission electron microscope (T.E.M.) was used to study the detailed grain arrangements and microstructures present both inside the veins, and in the sediments adjacent to the veins. Outside the veins, the T.E.M. revealed the complexity of the rock microstructures despite the homogeneous appearance of the hand specimen (see Fig. 4). The fabrics often exhibit a bimodal grain size distribution with the large size fraction, made up of mineral and fossil fragments greater than 3 μm in diameter, "floating" in a fine <1 μm) aggregate. Where the coarse grains or fragments are elongate (>1.5:1), they are aligned sub-parallel ($\leqslant 20°$) to ma-

R. J. Knipe

Figure 2. Optical montage of a regular vein array. (from 57. 439 4.3 95–102 cm sub-bottom depth 890.1 m.). Note the change in individual vein thickness along their length, the truncation of early (rotated) veins (E) by later ones (L), and the associated sub-horizontal zone (M). The small fault (F), together with the overall geometry of the veins, indicates that the array is part of a sinistral tension gash array. Note also the appearance of large detrital fragments within the veins and inside zone M.

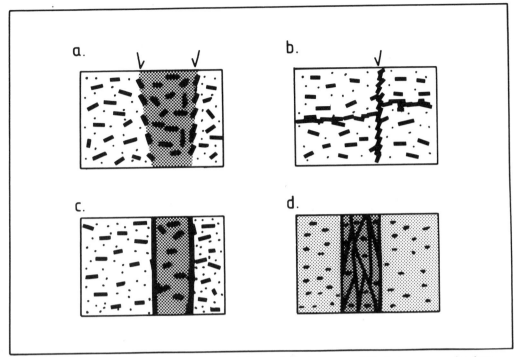

Figure 3. Review of vein characteristics revealed by optical microscopy, a) illustrates an example where bending of the bedding fabric indicates the concentration of shear at the vein margin and the generation of a graben structure; b) shows a narrow vein marking the site of localized displacement; c) illustrates a vein where no evidence of displacement is present and the external fabric is not clearly preserved inside, and d) illustrates a vein with an internal structure of anastomosing domains. The field of view of each sketch is approximately 3 mm, and diagrams are based on examples from 57, 439 cores 8 and 9 sub-bottom depth interval 878–897 m.

croscopic bedding. The larger mineral fragments, primarily quartz, have an irregular, and possibly corroded surface morphology. Also present are local equidimensional clusters of randomly oriented phyllosilicates (usually illites) up to 2 μm in diameter. These clusters appear to represent new grains growing during the burial history.

In general the finer grain size fractions (<1 μm) have a much lower preferred orientation than the coarser fragments, and platy grains aligned perpendicular to the macroscopic bedding are not uncommon (see Fig. 4). The packing and alignment of the fine-grained fraction produces a porous framework of interlocking platy grains. Given the 'delicate' nature of this structure, support, anchors, or "welds" at grain contacts are needed to account for the sediment strength (requiring sawing for sample preparation). The open framework is often modified near large detrital fragments where both the packing and alignment of the fine-grained particles are enhanced. Thin discontinuous zones, composed of well aligned, closely packed phyllosilicate grains oriented parallel to the macroscopic bedding are also present. Such zones are usually less than 2 μm thick and 10 μm long and appear to represent domains where the open framework structure has collapsed during burial. These zones often extend on either

side of large detrital particles and in the optical microscope appear to be single grains.

The heterogeneity of the fabric on the micrometer scale is particularly marked and leads to large variations in the physical properties at this scale. The pore shape and density (i.e. the porosity) varies from area to area and is only homogeneous over a few microns. The contrast in the porosity and permeability is often dramatic between domains with open framework structures and low preferred orientations, and discontinuous domains composed of well-aligned grains sub-parallel to bedding. A study of how the frequency and size of these bedding parallel domains increase with depth of burial has not yet been completed.

Inside the veins the microstructural domains observed optically are recognizable in electron micrographs. The domains composed of well-aligned phyllosilicates, oriented sub-parallel to the vein wall, were found to be more common. As expected, this is particularly true of the thinner (<1 μm), shorter (<5 μm) domains. These alignment domains define a well-developed anastomosing network within the vein, where the width and frequency of the domains vary within individual veins and between different veins. The microstructure within these domains is illustrated in Figure 5, which shows the alignment of large and small

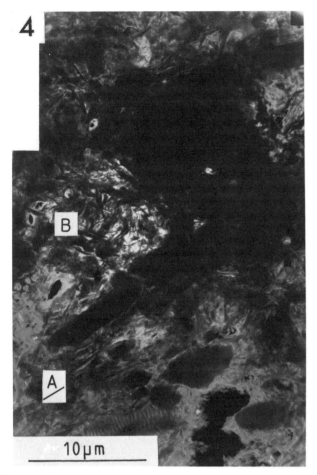

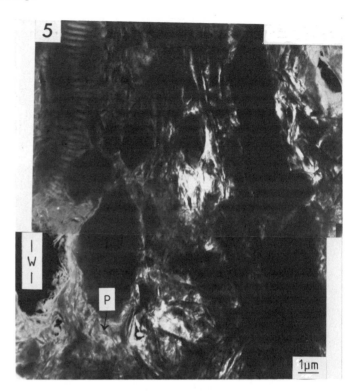

Figure 5. Electron micrograph from inside an alignment zone located at a vein margin. Note the alignment of small and large grains parallel to the vein wall [w] and the pressure shadow areas at the ends of the large grains (e.g.p.). Specimen from 57. 439 9.2 140-144 cm. Sub-bottom depth 890.4 m.

Figure 4. Electron micrograph illustrating part of the microstructure outside a vein. Note the well-aligned grain fabric in sub area A oriented subparallel to the macroscopic bedding and the more open structure in sub-area B. Specimen from 57, 439 8.2 53-57 cm sub-bottom depth 879.3 m.

grains sub-parallel to the domain and vein wall. Small pockets (up to 8 μm in diameter) within the fine grain fraction exhibiting a lower preferred orientation are also present and usually occur in pressure shadow locations at the ends of large fragments (see Fig. 5). The larger fragments within the alignment domains have identical shapes and sizes to the fragments outside the veins and are undoubtedly rotated grains. The grains, which made up the fine fraction of these alignment zones also have size and shape characteristics identical to the fine fraction outside the vein, although their origin as rotated and/or introduced grains is not so easily demonstrated because of the problems of identifying newly grown phyllosilicates. The packing and preferred alignment of the fine grained fraction is more strongly developed in these vein parallel alignment domains.

The anastomosing network described above encloses lenticular domains (microlithons) where the large detrital fragments are oriented sub-parallel to the bedding outside the

vein. The preferred orientation pattern of both large and small grains within these domains is very similar to that present outside the vein, indicating the preservation of the external fabric. The additional microstructure present in these domains, compared with those outside the vein, is the occasional small (<1 μm) discontinuous alignment zone, oriented sub-parallel to the vein wall. these appear to represent incipient displacement zones (Fig. 6). Although the relative distribution of illite clusters inside and outside the veins proved difficult to assess, pyrite appears to be more common within the veins. This concentration of pyrite grains, usually less than 1 μm in diameter, would help account for the dark coloration of the veins in hand specimen.

The gently dipping movement zone associated with veins in the cores contain similar microstructures to the veins. That is, they contain domains of well-aligned phyllosilicates (<4 μm thick) parallel to the zone boundary, which encloses domains of less well-oriented grians. Again the relative frequency and detailed geometry of the two domains varies within individual zones and between different zones. The alignment domains, where present, are more continuous than the equivalent zones occurring outside these structures. The large detrital or fossil fragments within the zone often exhibit pressure shadow features, where the local, fine-grained fabric wraps around the large inclu-

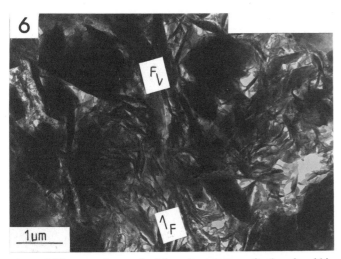

Figure 6. Electron micrograph of the microstructure of a domain within a vein that preserves most of the characteristics of the external fabric. The central zone, F, marks the site of an initial vein and is associated with a good preferred orientation along the displacement zone. Specimen from 57. 439 8.2 53–57 cm sub-bottom depth 890.4m.

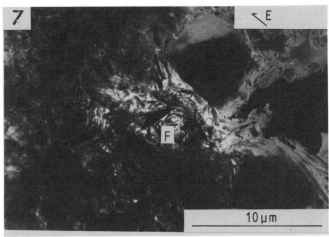

Figure 7. Electron micrograph of a sub-horizontal movement zone. Note the variation in the grain orientation, which appears to define a micro-fold at F. Specimen from 57. 439 9.2 74–79 cm sub-bottom depth 889.75. The edge of the zone is parallel to E.

sions (see Fig. 7). However, these pressure shadows are not always parallel to the zone border; this reflects the variation in the orientation of large elongate fragments. Small sub-regions (10 μm × 10 μm) with different orientations of both large and small grains can often be identified and in some cases appear to define microfolding of the bedding fabric (see Fig. 7).

INTERPRETATION OF MICROSTRUCTURES AND DISCUSSION

Selective aspects of the vein evolution are discussed in this section of the paper with an emphasis on the interpretation of the microstructures preserved and the implications of these features for the conditions and mechanisms of vein development. The following topics of vein evolution are discussed separately below: 1) the deformation mechanisms and microstructural evolution, 2) the strain and strain-rate histories, 3) dewatering processes and water pressure conditions, and 4) large scale implications.

Deformation Mechanicsm and Microstrauctural Evolution

There is little doubt that the veins preserved in the D.S.D.P. cores represent zones where the original sediment has been disaggregated during deformation; they do not represent zones of simple infill. The consistent shape and size of particles inside and outside the veins implies that the preferred orientation domains inside veins represent disaggregation zones where frictional grain boundary sliding (particulate flow) has been the dominant deformation mechanism. (Frictional grain boundary sliding is taken here to describe the deformation process by which uncemented aggregates of rigid grains can flow at low temperatures and confin-

ing pressures. It is equivalent to the independent particulate flow of Borradaile, 1981).

The presence of the veins at depths where the sediment is "lithified" suggests that the sediments had been strengthened before deformation. Two processes are probably involved in this strengthening, which accompanies burial; the first is related to the progressive interlocking of grains and the second is associated with the growth of cement "anchors" or "welds" between grains. Evidence for the growth of new phyllosilicates, together with the possibility of silica growth (Moore and Gieskes, 1980), support this latter strengthening. However, it is emphasized that the microstructure observed is a finite feature composed of different features, which may have developed at different times during the sediment's depth-time history. The illite clusters, for example, occur both inside and outside the veins and may represent the continued growth of material after the deformation.

The disaggregation associated with the vein development is likely to have involved fracturing of the cemented contacts between grains, that is, failure of isolated cement "anchors" distributed over the grain boundaries. No evidence for transgranular failure was observed in these veins. The fracturing along grain boundaries needed to weaken the aggregate and induce pervasive independent particular flow could have been aided by either an increase in the pore fluid pressure and/or by an increase in the stress on the sediment. The potential causes of high fluid pressures and the origin of high shear stresses at shallow depths have been discussed in detail by many authors (e.g. Saxov and Niewenhuis, 1982; Arthur and others, 1980a, p. 583; Westbrook and Smith, 1983) and may be associated with down-slope gravity-driven movement or the propagation of a fault through the sediment. The evidence pertinent to the role of pore fluid pressure in the

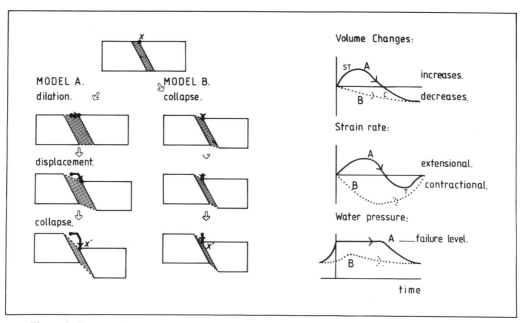

Figure 8. Two 'end-member' models for the evolution of the vein structures. Model A involves a dilation-displacement-collapse history and Model B involves a collapse and displacement history. The changes in the displacement vector from X–X' for each model is shown, together with the possible volume changes, strain rates and water pressure history. The alignment of grains in the zones may have developed either by streaming (ST) during the volume increase stage or if fluid flow was slow during the late collapse. The strain-rate graph illustrates the longitudinal strain-rate history of a line parallel to the displacement vector. The water pressure history for each model emphasizes that the failure level is only reached in Model A.

development of the veins is discussed in more detail in a separate section. Whatever the cause of the fracturing across grain boundaries, the linking of such failures will create a weak zone of disaggregation with different properties where grain boundary sliding (particulate flow) is enhanced, thus allowing strain accommodation by displacement. Given the small displacement associated with the veins, together with their mutual truncation, each vein may represent a small strain feature associated with a short-lived event.

Strain Paths and Strain-Rate Histories

The microstructural features associated with the veins, such as the displacement patterns at vein edges, are indicative of a large range of strain paths. Figure 8 reviews the different histories inferred from the observed microstructures, which include 1) coaxial extension, approximately parallel to the bedding, producing micro-graben structures, and 2) non-coaxial extension leading to the development of veins with micro-fault geometries and tension gash arrays.

The exact strain paths associated with the vein development have yet to be established. Two possible 'end-member' strain behaviours are outlined here and illustrated in Figures 8 and 9. First, the strain history may involve an early dilation and extension of the microfabric. This may arise from the fluid pressure

exceeding σ_3 by an amount greater than the cohesion of the sediment or it may be induced by a tensile regional stress. The magnitude of this extension may be extremely small and, if caused by a high fluid pressure, may be followed by a displacement in the weakened disaggregation zone, the sense of which will be controlled by the larger scale, regional stress system. The late closing of the disaggregation zones in this case gives the vein evolution a three stage evolution (dilation-displacement-collapse). The second possible strain history involves a progressive collapse of the open sediment framework due to an increase in the 'regional' stress on the aggregate. This arises when the stress exceeds the sediment strength and does not require high fluid pressures but involves the collapse (porosity reduction and fluid expulsion) during displacement. Both the strain paths outlined above involve a volume reduction (porosity collapse) within the deformation; the possible influence of such shortening across the vein is discussed in more detail in the section on fluid pressure.

The variation in the geometry of the vein arrays on a hand specimen scale described earlier in the paper can be interpreted in terms of different strain-rate histories. That is, during the deformation event producing the veins the strain rate will have increased, reached a maximum, and then decreased. The different patterns possible in this increase and decrease of strain-rate during the deformation event (i.e. the strain-rate/time path) will have an important effect on the microstructures produced. Microstruc-

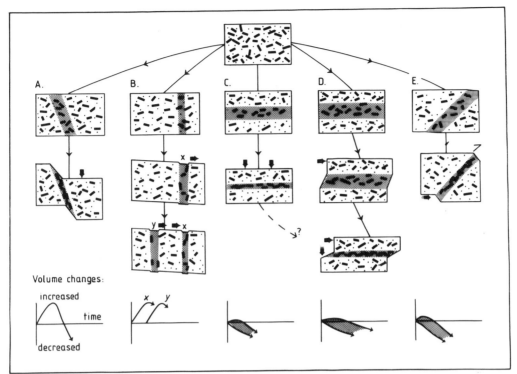

Figure 9. Review of the possible strain histories associated with vein evolution. The graphs at the base of each of the strain histories shown track the possible volume changes in the disaggregation zones with time and illustrate that the veins may experience an initial volume increase followed by a volume decrease in during collapse of the disaggregation zone. A) illustrates the development of a vein with a normal fault geometry, where there is an initial volume decrease in the vein width and a later reduction of the vein porosity during the late stages. B) shows the possible evolution of a vein during an overall coaxial extension developed during the migration of strain wave during down-slope movement. In this case the initial extension zone X develops by displacement of the block on the right of the specimen area shown. This disaggregation may induce movement of the central block, extension in zone Y and a decrease in the width of zone X. In this way the down-slope creep process involves the passage of an extensional strain wave up slope; that is from X to Y followed by a small contractional strain wave that migrates in the same direction. Note that the initial extension may be generated by fluid overpressuring and the late shortening associated with collapse during fluid removal from the zone. C) illustrates the generation and collapse of a disaggregation zone generating a bedding parallel fabric. The overall coaxial shortening (compaction) may have been initiated by a small dilation due to disaggregation because of fluid overpressuring or collapse associated with an increased stress (see volume change graph). D) Evolution of a sub-horizontal movement zone. The development may involve either a small initial volume increase followed by collapse or just a volume loss during displacement. E) Development of a disaggregation zone during an overall shortening deformation. Note the suggested late stage collapse in the disaggregation zone.

tures produced at different strain-rates may be modified by later deformation and the final microstructures left may contain remnants of different deformation responses produced at different strain-rates during the single deformation event. The breccias and irregular and regular vein arrays, together with the internal microstructural variations may therefore reflect evolution during differing strain-rate/time paths. The different deformation responses expected as a result of different strain-rates in poorly or unlithified sediments are discussed in Knipe (chapter 10, this volume). Figure 10 presents a possible distribution of vein types in strain-rate/time space for a sediment with these properties. The

diagram outlines the different hand specimen scale structures, which may develop at different strain rates, and highlights the possible changes in deformation response at different times during one deformation event. At present the fields shown on the diagram are only approximate but are a useful aid in the interpretation of deformation features. For example, consider the initiation of a deformation event in the "lithified" material. The different strain-rate histories will control the deformation responses and the structures that develop. If the strain-rate builds up very rapidly there is little alternative for the material other than to develop a single fault surface on which subsequent displacement

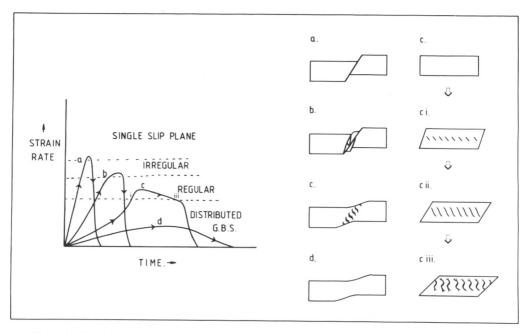

Figure 10. Possible distribution of vein types in strain-rate/time space. Four possible deformation events (a to d) are illustrated, and the features associated with them are shown in the block diagrams (see text for details). C illustrates the changes in vein geometry associated with the strain rate history.

will be concentrated. When the strain-rate is particularly slow the material may accommodate deformation over a wider volume by distributed grain boundary sliding or particulate flow. Between these two extremes we can expect a varying amount of localization of deformation, creating irregular or regular vein arrays. The differences in behaviour may be considered to relate to the materials' ability to absorb or distribute the deformation. Thus, at rapidly accelerating strain-rates, any obstacle to the propagating deformation zone—for example, a large grain or fossil—is simply fractured or by-passed, while at a much lower strain-rate build-up, the deformation may be significantly diverted or spread out around such obstacles.

A number of possible strain-rate/time paths (shown in Figure 10) demonstrate the potential use of these diagrams and illustrate the possible interpretation of two geometrical aspects of the vein arrays seen in the D.S.D.P. cores. In path 'b' a rapid build-up of strain-rate to a high level induces the development of an irregular fracture array. Once initiated, this array is likely to act as a location for the strain accommodation during the decreasing strain-rate at the end of the event. In the example illustrated by path 'c', the evolution of a tension gash array is considered. In this case the strain-rate build-up is lower and reaches a maximum in the regular vein array field. The regular vein array is initiated around point 'ci' (see Fig. 10). As the deformation continues, the veins propagate and the central, older portions are rotated. During a slow decrease of the strain-rate towards the end of this deformation event, the propagation of the single veins making up the array will be more difficult because obstacles that did not

affect the early, faster propagation cannot be by-passed, forcing the vein to split into a horse tail arrangement (Fig. 10). The last stages of deformation associated with the event will be the distributed grain boundary sliding at low strain-rates; this occurs as the deformation is forced to spread out along the weak features (grain boundaries) near the vein tip. This interpretation of evolution vein geometry in terms of changing strain rates is applicable to the tension gash arrays shown in Figure 1c and probably to other tension gash arrays developed in more cemented rock. The model emphasizes the likelihood that different parts of the vein experienced different strain rate histories. Microstructures associated with tips of fractures are likely to be representative of the dying stages of the deformation and fracture propagation and may not yield information on the vein initiation mechanisms. It is possible that the variations observed in individual vein thickness and microstructure also reflect variation in the propagation behaviour of individual veins.

Dewatering Processes and Fluid Pressures

The high water content of the sediments containing veins makes the fluid behavior an important factor in the vein development. Previous works discussing the origin of the veins have all suggested that water plays a key role, although the exact influence of the water has not been determined. Arthur and others (1980a) suggested that the veins represent high fluid pressure dewatering channels, oriented perpendicular to the tectonic compressive stress at the margin, and that the preferred orientation of grains along the margin of the vein arose from either shearing and movement or fluid flow. Cowan (1982) suggested an alternative model for the origin of veins during down-slope creep (subhorizontal extension) and favored a "streaming fluid" hypothesis for the generation of the preferred orientation.*

It is suggested here that a range of processes may be responsible for the preferred orientation within the veins, and that different mechanisms may be reflected by the different types of veins present in the cores. Each of the models suggested below involves the operation of different mechanisms in generating the grain alignment, and each has a different fluid behavior and deformation history. Shown in Figure 8, these models are discussed separately.

Model A. Sediment disaggregation is caused by extension associated with the fluid pressure exceeding the sediment cohesion. Such an increase in fluid pressure can induce a selective orientation of the fracture produced because of its interaction with the more regional stress pattern. That is, as soon as the strength of the sediment is reduced by the initial disaggregation and extension, the propagation of the fracture will be influenced by the regional stress pattern. The strength of the sediment is decreased and the sediment is forced to respond to a stress it was once able to support. There are two possible fluid histories that may follow this situation and generate the preferred orientation of grains with veins. (See also Knipe, Chapter 10, this volume).

Model Ai: Reorientation by Streaming After High Fluid Pressure-induced Failure. Once the increasing fluid pressure has induced disaggregation and dilation of the sediment, reorientation of particles by the fluid flow (streaming) is possible. This process is most likely within the vein systems, which are extensive, or connected to high permeability horizons, where fluid migration is possible. The extensive vein systems tend to be irregular arrays or microfaults. Streaming is an unlikely cause of alignment in the short discontinuous vein arrays where the easy/rapid fluid flow path is not extensive. If streaming was possible at the very start of the deformation event producing these isolated short veins, streaming microstructures—such as bending up of the bedding fabric on both sides of the vein—may be expected to remain in the oldest part of the veins. These microstructures have not been observed.

Model Aii: Reorientation During Porosity Collapse. In this case the alignment fabric arises during the porosity collapse associated with the expulsion of water from the disaggregation zone. This situation is favored when the fluid removal rate from the disaggregation zone is higher than the fluid influx and may be caused by a drop in the fluid pressure. This event may follow a long period where the disaggregation zone is held open by a high fluid pressure (but where the fluid flow did not reorient grains) or may be induced immediately after disaggregation by the removal of fluid from the zone. This latter condition may occur when the

fluid involved with initial disaggregation migrates to create a new disaggregation at the propagatory tip zone, and replacement fluid is not available. In other words, the period of increased porosity and high fluid content and pressure is a short-lived event. In this process the migrating fluid creates zones of dilation and disaggregation and then induces a porosity collapse, grain rearrangement, and shortening across the disaggregation zone as it propagates (see Fig. 8). Thus the deformation is associated with a strain wave passing through the material, inducing an increase and then a decrease in the strain-rate experienced. The shortening need not take place primarily as a result of non-fluid replacement but may also be induced by the passage of a contractional strain wave through the vein. The migration of such strain waves in slump sheets is described by Farrell (1984).

Model B. Sediment disaggregation is a result of the increased shear and/or tensional stresses associated with a larger, more regional stress system and not a result of high fluid pressure. Such stresses may arise from either slope instability or tectonic origin, or both. The alignment of grains is created by structural collapse and fluid expulsion. The disaggregation zones so created may act as channelways for dewatering. However, as no evidence of rapid streaming has been recorded, dewatering along such zones, if it took place, appears to have been via a slow expulsion, which does not align grains.

Figure 8 contains a review of the two models presented above and provides a link with the discussion section on strain paths and strain rate histories. An important aspect of each of the above models (A, and B) is a period of decreasing fluid pressure and content, together with a strain-rate drop during the vein evolution. Similar events may also have contributed to the development of the shallow-dipping movement zones and the bedding-parallel zones of low porosity and high grain alignment present outside the veins. Both these features may also have evolved during the collapse of the sediment aggregate either because of disaggregation by over-pressuring of the fluid or by an increase in the regional stress magnitude. That is, the local collapse and preferred orientation develops behind a migrating fluid concentration. Such a process is likely to be an important contribution to the development of the bedding-parallel fabric during burial and may even be enhanced in the vicinity of veins where the release of fluid pressure and initial dilation is one way of promoting fluid migration and collapse of the adjacent sediment framework.

Large Scale Implications

The veins represent disaggregation and dilation zones produced in lithified sediments with a high porosity and as such can develop near large faults in response to the local stress patterns, as suggested by Arthur and others (1980a), or during slow down-slope creep, as proposed by Cowan (1982). These are not regarded as alternatives but as different responses, both of which are possible during down-slope movement.

The range of vein structures described above, together with the associated features, are likely to develop in different positions

---

*Footnote added after revision. A recent paper by Ritger (1985) has suggested a model of vein development incorporating both the ideas of Arthur and others (1980) and Cowan (1982). The model presented by Ritger is similar to one of the models (Aii) presented here.

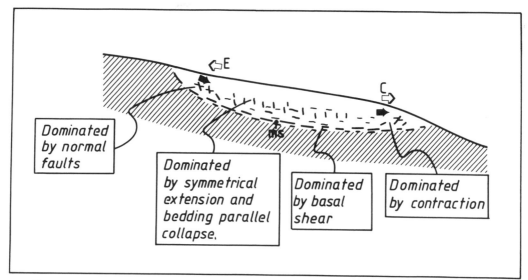

Figure 11. Distribution of deformation features in a down-slope movement system. The vein structures preserved have primarily normal fault, shallow shear, or extensional geometries and are thus likely to have developed in the central and upslope section of the system. Note that the migration of extensional (E) and contractional (C) strain waves need not propagate large distances in this system and that a similar distribution of strain features will develop associated with microshears (e.g. MS). Note also that the individual strain events can be complex, as shown in Figure 8.

in an active down-slope movement system (see Fig. 11). Where strain associated with down-slope movement is distributed over a large depth range, veins with simple sub-horizontal extension histories are likely to concentrate in the center of the system, while vein systems indicative of sub-horizontal shear (e.g. the tension gash arrays) are more likely to develop near the base of the system, and veins (steeply inclined to sub-vertical) with normal fault displacements will dominate the back of the movement zone.

No localized detachment is required for this system of vein distribution, which may be characteristic of the early stages of down-slope movement, and/or where the permeability is high enough to prevent large scale overpressuring.

In situations where the slope angle increases more rapidly or the decrease in permeability and over-pressuring is faster, the resulting down-slope creep may be faster and may promote the development of more faulting, microfaulting, and irregular vein arrays in the system. This second situation of faster down-slope movement may evolve from the initial slow down-slope creep processes as an increased number of potential slip planes (low angle, discontinuous, collapse zones) evolve. That is, no change in the slope development rate or over-pressuring rate is needed, but the changing sediment strength associated with the increased bedding parallel fabric is the cause of failure. Such a failure will, of course, be opposed by the synchronous cementation processes working to increase sediment strength. It should be noted that the distribution of strain paths and strain rates outlined above is likely to be a simplified model of the real situations, where variations in both strain paths and strain-rates are possible during the migra-

tion of strain waves associated with down-slope movement. The result will be a more complex situation where different strain paths (extension and compression), together with different strain-rate patterns, are superimposed on each other.

CONCLUSIONS

1) The vein arrays studied developed by a process of disaggregation accompanied by grain boundary sliding and particulate flow and represent sites of localized failure.

2) The most likely vein evolution models involve either a dilation-displacement-collapse sequence or a displacement-collapse sequence.

3) The range of vein geometries and microstructures preserved may be indicative of different strain-rate histories. Some individual veins exhibit features that can be related to the changing strain-rate during their development.

4) A range of strain paths is indicated from the vein geometries, all of which may be incorporated into a scheme of downslope movement. However, the detailed microstructural analysis reported indicates that the strain events generating the veins are complex and have involved early extension and late shortening.

5) Although high fluid pressures may help promote the disaggregation and initiation of veins, other causes of failure initiation are also possible.

6) No evidence of rapid fluid expulsion along the veins has been found, and although some veins may have acted as a concentrated location for a transient fluid expulsion, fluid flow in the majority of veins appears to have been a slow process.

ACKNOWLEDGMENTS

The author would like to acknowledge discussions with Drs. Casey Moore, Neil Lundberg, Ed Beutner, Darrel Cowan, Alex Maltman, and Jerry Leggett. The work was part of two N.S.F.–sponsored research grants (Nos. OCE8110394 and OCE8315836) that are gratefully acknowledged. The results published here were first presented at a Penrose Conference on Structural Styles and Deformational Fabrics of Accretionary Complexes, held in Eureka, California in May 1984.

REFERENCES CITED

Aoyagi, K., and Kazama, T., 1980, Sediment mineralogy of argillaceous sediments from the Deep Sea Drilling Project holes 436, 438A, and 439, Japan Trench, *in* Lee, M., Stout, L., and others, eds., Initial Reports of the Deep Sea Drilling Project: Washington, D.C., U.S. Government Printing Office, v. 56, 57, p. 1011–1018.

Arthur, M. A., Carson, B., and von Huene, R., 1980a, Initial tectonic deformation of hemipelagic sediment at the leading edge of the Japan convergent margin, *in* Lee, M., Stout, L., and others, eds., Initial Reports of the Deep Sea Drilling Project: Washington, D.C., U.S. Government Printing Office, v. 56, 57, p. 568–615.

Arthur, M. A., von Huene, R., and Adelseck, C. G., Jr., 1980b, Sedimentary evolution of the Japan fore-arc region off northern Honshu, Deep Sea Drilling Project Legs 56 and 57, *in* Lee, M., Stout, L., and others, eds., Initial Reports of the Deep Sea Drilling Project: Washington, D.C., U.S. Government Printing Office, v. 56, 57, p. 521–568.

Borradaile, G. J., 1981, Particulate flow of rock and the formation of cleavage: Tectonophysics, v. 72, p. 305–321.

Carson, B., and Bruns, T. R., 1980, Physical properties of sediments from the Japan Trench Margin and other Trench Slope, Results from Deep Sea Drilling Project Legs 56 and 57, *in* Lee, M., Stout, L., and others, eds., Initial Reports of the Deep Sea Drilling Project: Washington, D.C., U.S. Government Printing Office, v. 56–57, p. 1187–1200.

Carson, B., von Huene, R., and Arthur, M. A., 1982, Small scale deformation structures and physical properties related to convergence in the Japan Trench slope sediments: Tectonics, v. 1, p. 277–302.

Cowan, D. S., 1982, Origin of "vein structure" in slope sediments on the inner slope of the Middle America Trench off Guatemala, *in* Aubouin, J., von Huene, R., and others, eds., Initial Reports of the Deep Sea Drilling Project: Washington, D.C., U.S. Government Printing Office, v. 67, p. 645–650.

Farrell, S. G., 1984, A dislocation model applied to slump structures, Ainsa Basin, South Central Pyrenees: Journal of Structural Geology, v. 6, p. 727–736.

Leggett, J. K., Lundberg, N., Bray, C. J., Cadet, J. P., Karig, D. E., Knipe, R. J., and von Huene, R., 1985, Extensional tectonics in the Honshu fore-arc, Japan: Integrated results of Deep Sea Drilling Project Legs 56, 57, 87, and reprocessed multichannel seismic reflection profiles: Geological Society of London Special Publication Extensional Tectonics (in press).

Moore, G. W., and Gieskes, J. M., 1980, Interaction between sediment and interstitial water near the Japan Trench, Deep Sea Drilling Project Leg 57, *in* Lee, M., Stout, L., and others, eds., Initial Reports of the Deep Sea Drilling Project: Washington, D.C., U.S. Government Printing Office, v. 56, 57, p. 1269–1276.

Ritger, S. D., 1985, Origin of vein structures in the slope deposits of modern accretionary wedges: Geology, v. 13, p. 437–439.

Saxov, S., and Nieuwenhuis, J. K., eds., 1982, Marine slides and other mass movements: New York, Plenum Press, 353 p.

von Huene, R., and others, 1980, Summary, Japan Trench Transect, *in* Lee, M., Stout, L., eds., Initial Reports of the Deep Sea Drilling Project: Washington, D.C., U.S. Government Printing Office, v. 56, 57, p. 473–489.

Westbrook, G. K., and Smith, M. J., 1983, Long decollements and mud volcanoes. Evidence from the Barbados Ridge Complex for the role of high pore fluid pressure in the development of an accretionary wedge: Geology, v. 11, p. 279–283.

MANUSCRIPT ACCEPTED BY THE SOCIETY MARCH 10, 1986

Geological Society of America
Memoir 166
1986

Cataclastic deformation in accretionary wedges: Deep Sea Drilling Project Leg 66, southern Mexico, and on-land examples from Barbados and Kodiak Islands

Stephen E. Lucas
J. Casey Moore
Department of Earth and Marine Sciences
University of California, Santa Cruz
Santa Cruz, California 95064

ABSTRACT

Microstructural studies of DSDP cores from the lower slope off southern Mexico (Sites 488 and 492) reveal intense cataclastic grain breakage (as much as 37% of grains) in structurally disrupted zones penetrating offscraped trench and slope deposits. In contrast, minimal grain breakage occurs in sands overlying the upper slope basement of southern Mexico and in sands from a reference site in the California Borderland. Grain breakage in the latter is consistent with that developed elsewhere due to burial. The enhanced cataclasis at Sites 488 and 492 correlates with their steep average bedding dips. A percentage of broken grains occurs in zones of coarse grain size at these two sites due to increased stress concentration and loading of grain boundaries. Experimental results and a mechanical analysis indicate that these cataclastic fabrics are not due to gravity sliding and are probably tectonic in origin.

Microstructural studies of rocks from the Barbados and Kodiak accretionary complexes show both cataclastic shear zones, defining and permeating sandstone boudins, and distributed grain breakage similar to that observed in DSDP cores. Early-forming concretions cross-cut the cataclastic shear zones, suggesting that they developed in partially lithified sediment.

Our observations suggest that the sands of accretionary complexes initially deform by particulate flow; individual grains are cushioned by elevated pore fluid pressures. With increased effective confining stress, distributive cataclasis occurs, producing a dense, poorly sorted sediment with an increased coefficient of friction. Continuing deformation and further increases in effective confining stress allows failure along discrete shear zones, which ultimately results in boudinage of sandstone along an anastomosing network of cataclastic shear zones.

INTRODUCTION

Accretionary margins constitute structurally complex geotectonic settings, characterized by a variety of penetrative structural fabrics. Previous studies of stratally disrupted rocks, or melange, from uplifted subduction complexes have produced markedly differing interpretations of deformational mechanisms and their regional tectonic significance. Some workers attribute certain types of stratal deformation to gravity-driven down-slope movement (Maxwell, 1959; Page, 1963; Cowan, 1985; Aalto, 1986). Others, however, suggest that stratal disruption is a primary tectonic fabric due to shearing and mixing of sediment, either within a deforming packet of accreted sediment or in a broad fault zone that separates the upper and lower plates (Dewey and Bird, 1970; Dickinson, 1970a; Hsü, 1971). At present, disagreement hinges not on whether gravitational or tectonic deformation is present in an accretionary environment but on distinguishing between them in the field.

Deep Sea Drilling Project (DSDP) transects drilled across modern active margins allow investigation of in situ deformation within developing accretionary wedges. For example, in cores drilled off southern Mexico (DSDP Leg 66), stratal disruption and numerous other structural features form very early—prior to complete lithification and dewatering of sediments (Lundberg and Moore, 1982). Stratal disruption occurs only in uplifted and accreted trench sediments and in the immediately superadjacent layers of mantling slope-apron deposits; the shallowest examples of stratal disruption at each site are present in progressively older rocks upslope, suggesting that deformation occurs beneath the lowermost trench slope in this accretionary environment. Despite circumstantial evidence linking stratal disruption to this accretionary environment, however, it remains unclear whether the deformation is primarily tectonic (i.e., due to strain from offscraping and underthrusting) or gravitational.

A potentially important clue for distinguishing between these modes of deformation is the presence or absence of cataclastic fabrics in the disrupted sediments. Although cataclasis has been interpreted as an integral component of deformation in disrupted zones from some ancient accretionary complexes (Moore and Allwardt, 1980; Byrne, 1984), its presence in Leg 66 drilling cores is the first known documentation at modern convergent margins. Physical conditions of cataclasis are known from the DSDP cores from southern Mexico; therefore direct comparisons can be made with relevant experiments.

CATACLASIS IN DSDP CORES

Drilling and geophysical data collected during the DSDP Leg 66 transect across the Middle America Trench provided conclusive evidence in support of progressive accretion (Fig. 1; Watkins and Moore and others, 1982). Here, three sites (488, 491, and 492) penetrated the slope apron into a young accretionary wedge consisting of offscraped trench turbidites that have been uplifted as much as 3 km above the present-day trench floor.

In the Leg 66 cores, stratally disrupted sediments are characterized by steep and inconsistent bedding dips and by pervasive bedding discontinuities that cannot be explained by primary deposition, bioturbation, or drilling deformation (Lundberg and Moore, 1982; Leggett, 1982). To determine the frequency, distribution, and possible significance of grain breakage in these stratally disrupted deposits, we have studied samples from Sites 488, 491, and 492 (Fig. 2). To evaluate whether grain breakage is unique to stratally disrupted zones, we have compared samples from these zones to samples from the upper-slope sites off Mexico (489 and 493) and from a reference site in the California Borderland (Site 467). These control samples were buried to depths equivalent to, or greater than, those from the lower-slope sites off Southern Mexico and cover a range of grain sizes and cementation conditions. Twenty-four samples composed of sand- or silt-sized grains were point-counted (Fig. 2; Table 1). Unfortunately, stratally disrupted samples from Site 491 proved too fine-grained

to discern grain boundary relationships, and hence to evaluate cataclasis.

Lower Slope Sites: Southern Mexico

Site 488. At Site 488, located near the toe of the trench slope (Fig. 1), the zone of disruption is located within partially lithified Quaternary slope apron deposits between 220 and 240 meters sub-bottom. This zone is characterized by a sharp downhole increase in bulk density, reduced porosity and water content, and by steep, inconsistent bedding dips (Lundberg and Moore, 1982; Watkins and Moore and others, 1982; Shephard and others, 1982). Disrupted sediments display a macroscopic foliation, dipping about 25 degrees, defined by weakly to strongly oriented, elongate bodies composed of sand and/or silt, enclosed in a dark matrix of fine-grained material (Fig. 3). The boundary between sand bodies and matrix varies from distinct to diffuse, and primary bedding is unrecognizable despite marked lithology contrast.

Microscopically, the disrupted sediment is characterized by a variety of deformational textures. Progressive states of deformation range from (1) initial truncation and displacement of very fine-grained (~0.12 mm) to medium-grained (~0.35 mm) sand bodies in a silty mudstone matrix; to (2) an intermediate stage in which wispy stringers, or apophyses, of sand extend into the matrix; to (3) almost complete homogenization of sand, silt, and clay. Sand bodies in the early stages of dismemberment are transected by arrays of cross-cutting and anastomosing microfaults that offset boundaries on the order of a few millimeters. Internally these microfaults are marked by a weak alignment of inequant sand grains that have rotated into parallelism with the plane of movement. There is only a slight indication of grain-size reduction across these fault zones. In more deformed areas, indicated by increased microfault density, individual clusters and stringers of sand become increasingly separated and are bounded by dark zones composed of subparallel concentrations of clay and silt. The internal fabric of sand clusters in these areas grades from grain-supported, arenaceous, randomly oriented, medium-sized sand to matrix-supported, clay-rich zones of finer-grained sand and silt with slightly aligned elongate particles along their boundaries. Sand grains near the edge of sand bodies often appear to be spalling off into the matrix, and when inequant, have long axes roughly parallel to the trace of the sand body. The most advanced stage of stratal disruption occurs in areas of high microfault density and is characterized by a nearly homogeneous mixture of matrix-supported sand and silt (Fig. 4). In these areas, microfaults or shear zones show a pronounced alignment of elongate sand grains as well as a reduced grain size. At this stage of deformation the original outline of individual sand bodies is difficult to resolve.

Microscopic point-counts of four stratally disrupted samples from Site 488 indicate a minor, but significant, amount of cataclastically broken grains. Grain breakage is as high as 12% (sample 1) but averages 9% ±6% (Table 1). Broken grains are most common well within partially dismembered medium-grained sand bodies (Fig. 5), although grain-size reduction is most

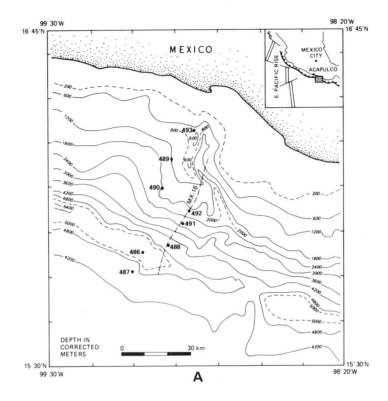

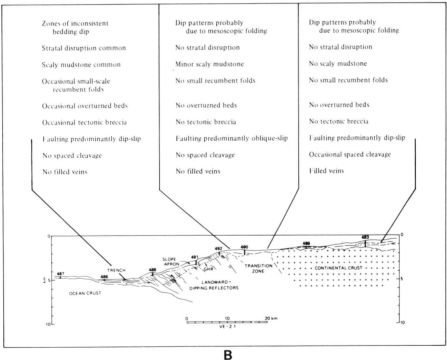

Figure 1. Location map and profile of DSDP Leg 66 spanning the Middle America Trench off southern Mexico. a) DSDP Leg 66 drilling sites. Dashed lines indicate the extent of seismic lines OM-7N and MX-16 (from Watkins and Moore and others, 1982). b) Distribution of structural features in Leg 66 cores. Note that stratal disruption is limited to lower slope sites underlain by landward dipping reflectors (from Lundberg and Moore, 1982).

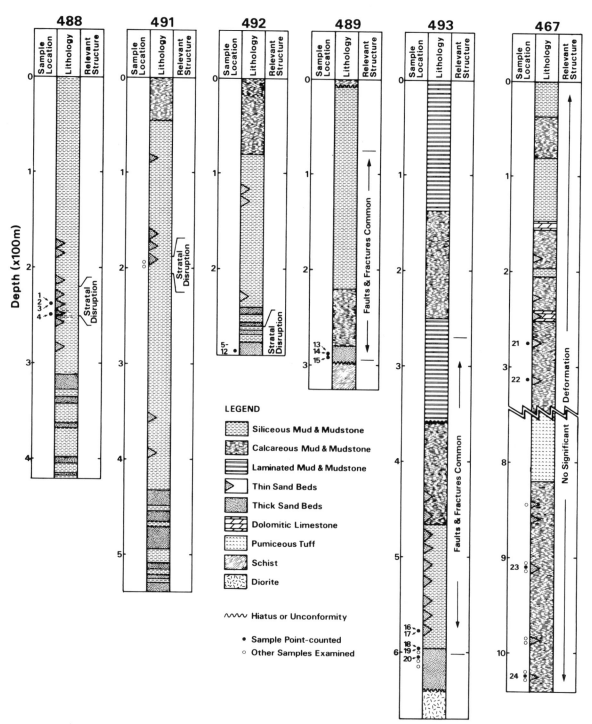

Figure 2. Sample locations lithology, and relevant structural features of DSDP drilling cores studied: Leg 66 lower-slope sites 488, 491, and 492; upper-slope sites 489 and 493 after Watkins, Moore and others, 1982, and control site from the California Borderlands, Leg 63 Site 467 after Yeats and Haq and others, 1981.

pronounced near the borders of sand clusters. The apparent lack of grain breakage near the borders of sand clusters and within microfaults, despite the obvious grain-size reduction, may be due in part to post-cataclastic dispersal of grain fragments. Cataclastic breakdown appears uncommon in very fine-grained sand lenses,

perhaps due to the lack of microscopic resolution. Sand grains of all compositions are cataclastically broken, but commonly grains of feldspar and other minerals with distinct cleavage planes are more thoroughly fragmented and dispersed (compare Fig. 6a, b).

Site 492. A zone of stratal disruption with well developed

TABLE 1. CATACLASTIC GRAIN COUNTS OF DSDP SAMPLES

DSDP Site	Sample	Core/Interval	Depth (m)	Grain Size[a]	Broken Grains (%)	Whole Grains (%)	Total Grains Counted	Mean Broken/ Site	S.D./Site
488	1	26-6/45-48	237.8	fine-med	12	88	218	9	3.6
488	2	26-6/92-66	237.8	fine	11	89	307		
488	3	26-6/133-135	237.8	fine	9	91	284		
488	4	27-1/144-147	249.9	fine	4	96	253		
492-B	5	1-5/84-108	286	coarse	37	63	211	28	7.2
492-B	6	1-5/84-108	286	coarse	31	69	242		
492-B	7	1-5/84-108	286	coarse	27	73	226		
492-B	8	1-5/84-108	286	coarse	24	76	147		
492-B	9	1-5/84-108	286	med-coarse	17	83	118		
492-B	10	1-5/84-108	286	med-coarse	21	79	137		
492-B	11	1-5/84-108	286	med-coarse	26	74	119		
492-B	12	1-5/84-108	286	very coarse	27	63	374		
489-A	13[b]	30-5/86-90	288.8	fine	< 1	>99	302	< 1	1.2
489-A	14[b]	30-5/97-103	288.9	fine	< 1	>99	318		
489-A	15[b]	31-1/0-6	291	fine	2	98	306		
493	16	50-2/35-37	577.8	med-coarse	1	99	173	5	3.1
493	17	51-1/67-70	578.1	med-coarse	3	97	132		
493	18	52-1/11-14	595.1	med-coarse	6	94	147		
493	19	52-2/37-40	596.8	med-coarse	9	91	311		
493	20	53-1/139-143	605.8	med-coarse	6	94	306		
467	21	30-3/5-8	275	fine	2	98	327	1	1.5
467	22	34-2/75-77	313.7	fine	3	97	300		
467	23[c]	97-2/0-1	910	fine	< 1	>99	306		
467	24[c]	109-2/88-91	1024.8	fine	< 1	>99	237		

[a]Grain size range from visual estimates (Wentworth, 1922).
[b]Cemented sample.
[c]Partially cemented sample.

cataclastic textures is located at the base of hole 492B at a depth of about 286 meters sub-bottom. This disturbed interval of mid to late Miocene sediment consists of poorly consolidated, medium- to very coarse-grained sand intermixed with and partially consolidated by a shale and scaly mudstone pseudomatrix (Dickinson, 1970b). The coarse sands are of trench affinity (Watkins and Moore and others, 1982). Macroscopically, disrupted intervals are characterized by small, wispy sand lenses that are dispersed sub-parallel to a semipenetrative planar fabric. This fabric is defined by anastomosing healed fracture surfaces in a matrix of scaly clay. In contrast to samples from Site 488, the boundaries between matrix and sand are always distinct. Although sand is dispersed throughout the matrix, there is little intimate intermixing of the two lithologies. Bedding and other primary sedimentary structures typically are not discernible, although in some cases rootless, isoclinal micro-folds composed of coarse sand are present with axial planes sub-parallel to the pervasive fabric (Fig. 7).

On a microscopic scale, sand bodies are injected between fracture surfaces separating mudstone chips. Segregation of the sand and mudstone suggests substantial consolidation of the mudstone prior to stratal mixing. Unlike samples from Site 488, pulverized sand grains at Site 492 are abundant throughout sand lenses and are present even in thin stringers that extend into the mudstone matrix. Broken grains commonly fail along tensile fractures that propagate between points of impingement with adjacent sand grains.

The majority of grains within sand lenses are angular and range in size from about 4 to 0.025 mm. However, some extensively altered samples display a crude bimodal grain size distribution, with most grains clustering around 1.0 mm and 0.2 mm in dimension (see Fig. 8a). Comparisons of these sands with those from the presumed source, that is, from the Middle America Trench (MAT), (Watkins, Moore, and others, 1982; courtesy of R. H. Enkeboll), reveal that they are compositionally similar, but differ slightly in both grain roundness and size distribution. The MAT sand grains are commonly more well rounded and contain substantially fewer grains in the range of 0.2 mm or less. Although this difference in grain shape and size distribution of these two samples is vivid, only a small proportion of the fine-grained fraction in stratally disrupted sands from Site 492 can be positively identified as cataclastically derived using standard microscopic techniques.

Cathode-luminescence microscopy (CLM) allows correlation of cataclastic fragments and allows us to distinguish whether a cluster of fine-grained material originated via cataclastic or sedimentary processes. For example, CLM indicates that a large percentage of the fine-grained sand fraction at Site 492 is cataclastically derived and mixed to only a minimal extent (compare Fig. 8a, b). Accordingly, our use of optical microscopy to point-count fractured sand grains results in a conservative estimate of grain breakage. Even so, 37% of the sand grains counted in Samples 5 and 12 from Site 492 had been cataclastically degraded. The mean fraction of broken grains for the eight samples point-counted at this site is 28% ±7.2% (Table 1).

Figure 3. Interval of stratally disrupted silt, sand (S), and mud (M). Interval 488-26-6, 126-145 cm (237.8 m below sea floor (BSF). Ruled scale (to the right) is in millimeter increments.

Upper Slope Sites

Site 489. Drilling at Site 489 penetrated about 300 meters of lower Miocene muddy siltstone, siltstone and fine-grained sandstone, which is capped by a thin veneer of Quaternary muddy silt and underlain by metamorphic basement (Watkins and Moore and others, 1982). All samples examined were collected from a zone of well lithified fine-grained sandstone about 290 m below sea floor (BSF). Macroscopically these sands appear stratally coherent, exhibiting both bedding and grading. Grading and grain imbrication, as well as a micro-sparite carbonate cement, are discernible microscopically. An open framework-grain fabric and a paucity of tangential and long contacts between grains indicates early cementation, although signs of dissolution along some grain boundaries suggest that the present fabric may be due in part to diagenetic alteration or dissolution along grain boundaries.

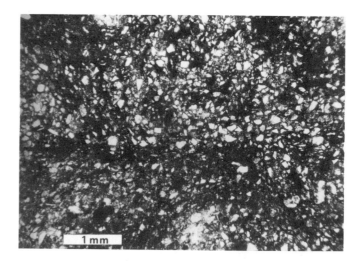

Figure 4. Photomicrograph of an extremely deformed mixture of sand, silt, and clay near the junction of several anastomosing shear zones. Sample no. 3, interval 488-26-6, 133-135 cm (237.8 m BSF). Scale bar equals 1 mm.

Figure 5. Cataclastic grain breakage (B) in stratally disrupted sands from DSDP Site 488. Sample no. 1, interval 488-26-6, 45-48 cm (237.8 m BSF). Bar scale equals 0.25 mm.

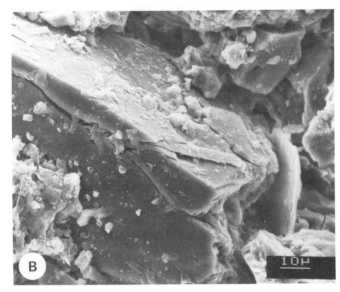

Figure 6. SEM photomicrographs of broken grains from stratally disrupted silt and sand bodies from Site 488; interval 488-26-6, 135-136 cm (237.8 m BSF). a) Fractured mineral (feldspar?) with distinct cleavage planes displaying an abundance of extremely fine-grained fragments. b) Cataclasis of a sand grain (quartz?) lacking distinct cleavage planes typically results in fewer fine-grained fragments (than those with cleavage); moreover the fracture surfaces tend to be irregular and appear resistant to disaggregation.

In three samples point-counted from Site 489, only nine broken grains were observed out of a total of 926 sand grains examined (<1% ±1.2%). All broken grains observed were isolated from other broken grains and were fractured in a similar fashion to most of the broken grains from Sites 488 and 492, that is, extensional fractures propagating from the point of impingement by surrounding sand grains. Fractures are now filled with sparry calcite cement. Broken sand grains were never observed under SEM, presumably in testament to their scarcity.

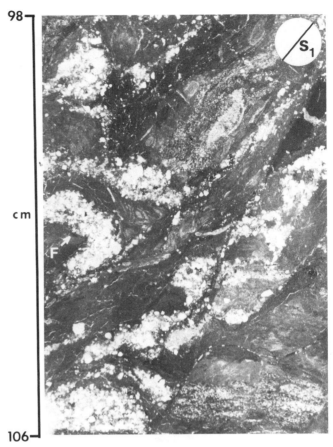

Figure 7. Polished, impregnated slab of stratally disrupted sand and scaly mudstone. A foliation (S_1) is defined by elongate bodies of coarse sand and silt. Note the rootless, isoclinal fold (F) to the left. Interval 492B-1-5, 98-106 (286 m BSF).

Site 493. Site 493 was drilled 25 to 30 km landward of the boundary between continental crust and the accretionary prism. Drilling penetrated 652 m of Quaternary through early Miocene sediment before reaching dioritic basement (Watkins, Moore, and others 1982). Five partially lithified, massive, medium to coarse-grained sandstones buried between 577 and 605 m BSF were sampled and examined for cataclastic grain breakage.

Microscopically, these sandstones exhibit a crude grain imbrication of fairly well-rounded, elongate grains of quartz, feldspar, and small grains of shale. These sandstones appear to have been lithified by a weak muddy-silt pseudomatrix composed of deformed shale fragments, with only limited chemical cementation. As a result a substantial number of long- and sutured-grain contacts are present, indicating substantial overburden and compaction (Taylor, 1950). The percentage of broken grains varies substantially from one sample to another, ranging from 1 to 9%. Three of the sandstones, samples 18, 19, and 20, display a considerable amount of cataclastic alteration, with between 6 and 9% of the sand grains broken. Grain fracturing here differs from that at Site 492 in two ways. First, fracture orientation is approximately

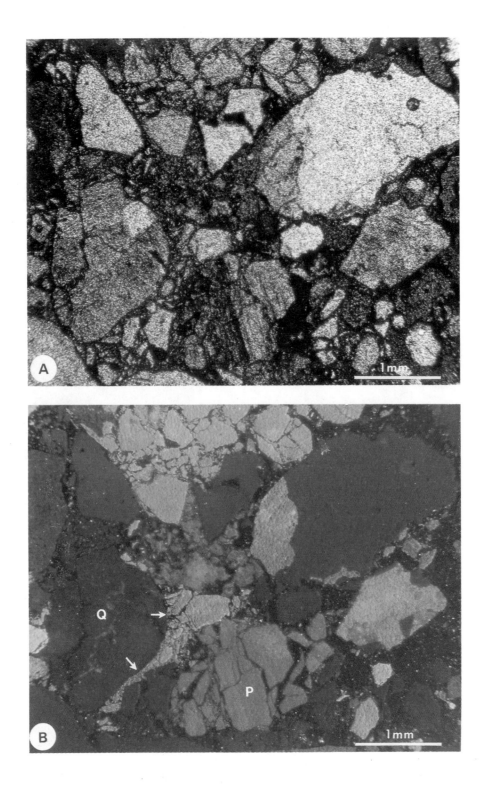

Figure 8. An example of cataclastic texture in stratally disrupted sands from Site 492. A) Photomicrograph of sample no. 7 displaying the abundant relatively large fractured sand grains in a silt sized matrix typical of these stratally disrupted sediments (plane-polarized light); B) Photomicrograph of the same section (above) using cathode-luminescence microscopy. The clusters of fine-grained material that luminesce uniformly were presumably single grains that have suffered extreme cataclasis. Note potassic feldspar (arrows) pulverized and squeezed between quartz (Q) and plagioclase feldspar (P).

bedding normal, as opposed to more or less random orientations at Site 492. Secondly, grain fracture results in large distinguishable sub-grains that do not appear to be dispersed, even when viewed using CLM. The abundance of broken grains in these three samples may be due in part to local tectonism as implied by an increase of small-scale faults at this depth (Fig. 2; Lundberg and Moore, 1982, Fig. 3).

Reference Site: California Borderland

Site 467. Site 467 of DSDP Leg 63, located near San Miguel Gap in the California Borderland east of the Channel Islands was selected as a control site to isolate the effects of an active margin setting. Drilling here penetrated 1041 m of relatively undisturbed sediment and rock that is primarily composed of silty clay and clayey chalk with local intervals of clayey dolomitic limestone and scattered thin sandstone layers (Yeats and Haq and others, 1981). Lithified, fine-grained, bedded sandstone layers were sampled from 275 to 1024 m BSF and examined for cataclastic grain breakage (Fig. 2).

Microscopically, the sandstones are structurally coherent and composed of well-sorted fine sand grains with laminations defined by varying concentrations of clay or neomorphic micritic cement. The four samples point-counted together contain less than one percent broken grains (Table 1). Uncemented samples from shallower depths (275–313 m BSF) contain up to a few percent broken grains, whereas partially cemented samples collected at depths of up to 1 km show almost no grain breakage. Apparently cementation inhibits grain breakage. There is no evidence that later diagenetic alteration or dissolution of sand grains is responsible for the absence of cataclastic fabrics in these deeply buried sandstones.

Discussion of Cataclasis in DSDP Cores

Cataclasis Due to Vertical Loading?. The concentration and style of cataclastic fabrics in zones of stratal disruption (lower slope Southern Mexico) and the paucity of cataclasis elsewhere, indicates that overburden is not responsible for this deformation. A study by Taylor (1950) of porosity reduction due to simple burial and compaction indicates that crushed feldspars first appear at depths of about 1360 m in sandstone from the Shannon Formation (Cretaceous) from Wyoming, depths almost four times greater than cataclastic samples from Sites 488 and 492. The limited amount of grain breakage at Sites 467, 489, and most of Site 493 is comparable to Taylor's findings and may represent background deformation induced by sediment loading.

Cataclasis and Magnitude of Bedding Dips. The concentration of cataclasis at Sites 488 and 492 correlates with the high average bedding dips at these sites relative to the upper slope sites (489 and 493) and the reference site in the California Borderland (Fig. 9). Site 488 shows steeper bedding dips than Site 492, yet the intensity of cataclasis is greater for the latter site (Fig. 9; Table 1): this apparent inconsistency is explained by the me-

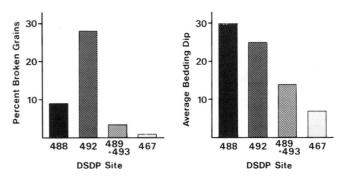

Figure 9. Bar graphs illustrating the mean fraction of grain breakage (of total sand and silt grains) and mean bedding dip for each drilling site. Note the positive correlation between the mean bedding dip (cumulative deformation at each site) and the amount of broken grains present. See text for an explanation of the discrepancy in Quaternary sediments at Site 488.

chanics of grain breakage in particulate materials. In coarser-grained sand, fewer grain contacts per unit area cause higher stress concentrations than in finer-grained sand; accordingly, coarse-grained sands at Site 492 display better developed cataclastic fabrics than do the fine-grained sands of Site 488, even though the latter site has steeper average bedding dips.

Cataclasis During Gravity Gliding: A Mechanical Evaluation. The constraints of the modern setting allow calculation of the gravitational stresses in the deformation zones at Sites 488 and 492 and their comparison to stresses necessary to produce cataclasis experimentally. The great lateral extent and uniform inclination of submarine slopes allows their stability analysis by the method of infinite slopes (Moore, 1961; Lambe and Whitman, 1969, p. 352). This analysis requires only knowledge of the surface slope, the depth of the failure surface, and the fluid pressure. We can specify all but the latter, evaluate slope stability under hydrostatic conditions, and then consider the consequences of increased fluid pressure. For this analysis, hypothetical slump sheets are shown cutting the zones of cataclasis at Sites 488 and 492 (Fig. 10).

The inclination (i) of the hypothetical slump surface through Sites 488 and 492 is taken to be parallel to the surface slope of 10 degrees (Fig. 10). The mean depths (z) of the zones of cataclasis at Sites 488 and 492 are 230 and 285 m, with the average buoyant bulk densities (ρ_B) of the overburden 0.7 and 0.8 gm/cm^3, respectively (Shepard and others, 1982). The vertical effective stress is the product of the buoyant bulk density, depth, and the acceleration of gravity (g). The effective normal (G_N) and the shear (τ) stresses on the failure surface represent the components of the vertical stress with adjustment for the increasing area of the inclined plane (Fig. 10b; Fig. 11b; Lambe and Whitman, 1969, p. 352).

$$\sigma_N = \rho_B g z \cos^2 i$$
$$\tau = \rho_B g z \cos i \sin i. \qquad (1)$$

The states of stress on the inclined failure planes through Sites

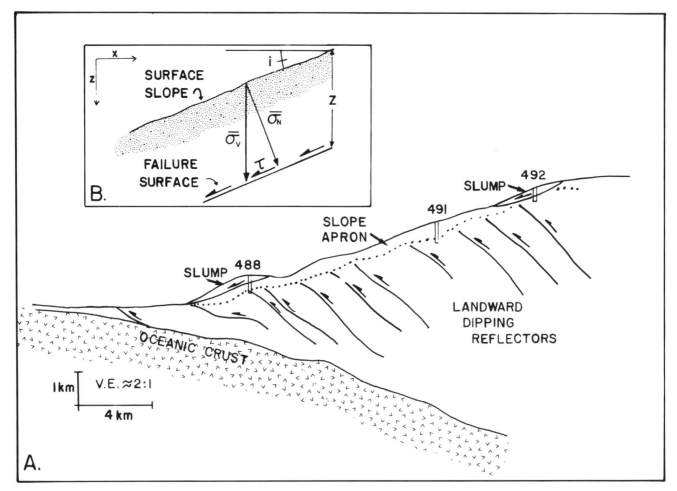

Figure 10. A) Cross section through the lower slope of the Leg 66 area showing hypothetical slumps cutting Sites 488 and 492 at the levels of cataclasis observed in the cores. B) Orientation of vertical effective stress $\rho_B g z$, normal stress (G_N), and shear stress (τ) relative to the failure surface. The vertical effective stress equals the integrated buoyant bulk density of sediment overlying the failure surface.

488 and 492 (points A and B, Figure 11b) lie below the failure envelope, indicating that the sediment beneath these sites will not fail gravitationally along slope-parallel shear surfaces under hydrostatic pore pressure conditions.

The state of stress on planes of all orientations beneath the Sites 488 and 492 is represented by the circumference of the Mohr circles that pass through points A and B in Figure 11b. Although our analysis does not directly specify the magnitude and orientation of the principal stresses, their ratio can be approximated (~0.5) from Poisson's ratio, assuming an isotropic elastic material (see Sowers and Sowers, 1970, p. 324 and 337). Accordingly, the Mohr circle can be graphically constructed since we know (1) that ratio of σ_1 to σ_3 is 0.5, (2) that the maximum principal stress must be slightly greater than the normal stress on the slope-parallel plane, and (3) that the Mohr circle must pass through the states of stress (A and B in Fig. 11b) on the inclined planes. The constructed Mohr circle does not intersect the failure envelope, therefore indicating that the slope is stable for failure planes of any orientation.

Increasing the pore pressure can induce slope failure beneath Sites 488 and 492, an area that otherwise is stable at hydrostatic pore pressures. Since the total stress of the overburden (σ) at Sites 488 and 492 is constant, any increase in the pore pressure (ρ) results in a decrease or counter balancing of the effective stress (σ_E) or

$$\sigma = \sigma_E + \rho. \qquad (2)$$

Because of the hydrostatic nature of the pore pressure, the effective stress decreases equally in all directions. The Mohr circles for the hydrostatic case do not change in diameter but are translated towards the failure envelope; gravitationally induced slumping may occur (Fig. 11b; Hubbert and Rubey, 1960).

The slope of the Mohr failure envelope (ϕ) for sand normally exceeds 30 degrees; the value of ϕ used in Figure 11 (32.5°) is from a medium- to fine-grained sand used in experiments to test for the threshold of cataclasis (Bishop 1966). Experiments reported by Bishop (1966) and De Beer (1965), as well as a review by Vesic and Clough (1968), indicate that grain break-

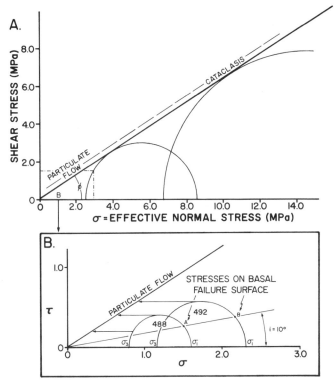

Figure 11. A) Mohr diagram with the Mohr failure envelope showing the experimentally determined range of particulate flow and cataclasis. B) Enlargement of A showing gravitationally-induced stress conditions at Sites 488 and 492 for planes of any orientation (Mohr circles) and stress conditions on the basal failure plane. Horizontal arrows depict movement of Mohr circle toward the failure envelope during increasing fluid pressure. Note that both planes of any orientation, and especially the basal failure plane of the slump, intersect the Mohr envelope well into the field of particulate flow, indicating that cataclasis is unlikely during gravity gliding.

Figure 12. Fragments of stratally disrupted sandstone boudins from the Scotland Formation, Barbados. Cataclastic shear zones are dark colored zones that penetrate the rock. Coin is approximately 2.5 cm diameter.

age does not begin until shear stresses reach about 4 MPa (40 bars), with significant cataclasis not occurring until 10 MPa (100 bars) (Fig. 11). Sands deform by particulate flow at shear stresses below 4 MPa. The Mohr circles in Figure 11b intersect the failure envelope at low shear stresses in the realm of particulate flow. Therefore, even in slumps due to abnormally high fluid pressure, deformation would proceed by particulate flow. Since strain rate has little effect on the strength of brittle rocks at low temperatures and low confining pressures (Paterson, 1978, p. 29–30), the transition from experimental to geologic strain rates would not reduce the stress threshold sufficiently to allow cataclasis.

The preceding analysis indicates that cataclasis is not possible on shallowly inclined slump planes passing through the deformation at Sites 488 and 492. The cataclastic fabrics developed at these sites were produced by tectonic deformation.

CATACLASIS IN SUBAERIALLY EXPOSED ACCRETIONARY COMPLEXES

Cataclastic shear zones are a common feature in stratally disrupted sandstone lithologies from uplifted accretionary complexes (Hsü, 1974; Moore and Allwardt, 1980; Speed, 1983; Byrne, 1984). These shear zones form a network of anastomosing curviplanar surfaces in sandstones undergoing progressive boudinage, presumably in response to layer-parallel shear (Byrne, 1984). Samples with cataclastic shear zones from the Scotland Formation (Barbados) and the Sitkalidak Formation (Kodiak Islands) were chosen for examination because of their lack of or only slight (zeolite facies) metamorphism, respectively.

In the Morgan Lewis area of Barbados, the Scotland Formation (the terrigenous suite of Speed and Larue, 1982) consists of stratally disrupted and boudinaged trench and/or deep sea fan sandstones and shales. Locally these sandstone boudins are crosscut by zones of cataclastic grain size reduction that are generally less than 1.0 cm in thickness (Fig. 12). The Sitkalidak Formation is the youngest (Eocene), seaward-most, subaerially exposed accreted packet in the Kodiak Islands, Alaska, (Moore and

Figure 13. Cataclastic shear zones (dark zones) cross-cutting sandstone from the Sitkalidak Formation (Ugak Island, Alaska). The ruler is 15 cm in length.

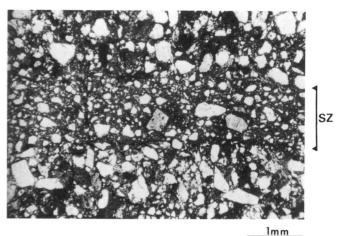

Figure 14. Photomicrograph of a cataclastic shear zone in boudinaged quartzose sandstone from the Scotland Formation (Barbados). The shear zone (SZ), oriented horizontally, is marked by a dark zone and an abrupt reduction in average grain size (arrow). Photographed using plane-polarized light; scale bar equals 1 mm.

Allwardt, 1980). Stratal disruption in the Sitkalidak Formation is characterized by sandstone boudinage with individual boudins both bound and cross-cut by cataclastic shear zones (Fig. 13). Displacement along individual shear zones rarely exceeds a few centimeters. In thin section the microfabrics of sandstone boudins zones from the Scotland and Sitkalidak Formations are remarkably similar; therefore, except where noted, the following fabric description applies to both units.

Microscopically, cataclastic shear zones are easily identified by their slight opaque coloration and reduced average grain size relative to the surrounding rock (Fig. 14). Boundaries of shear zones are usually distinct, but with locally gradational margins. Where gradational boundaries are present, the wallrock sandstone appears to be disaggregating, releasing individual grains into the shear zone in a fashion similar to that observed at Site 488 (off southern Mexico). In addition, thin lozenges of sand (as much as 2 mm wide) trapped between shear zones that splay and reconnect, also appear to be breaking down and releasing relatively large grains. Grains in the process of fracturing are most commonly observed adjacent to, or in lozenges trapped within shear zones, as opposed to central portions of the shear zone itself (Fig. 15). Grain breakage in regions adjacent to a shear zone may be responsible for their distinct bimodal grain-size distribution. In these areas sand grains are forcibly impinged upon from two to three sides (within the plane of a thin section), resulting in tensile fractures propagating from grain to grain, similar to those observed in sands from Site 492. Parent grains can in some cases be reconstructed by fitting together angular boundaries of adjacent grain fragments, like working a jig-saw puzzle. Commonly, numerous fragments within broken grain clusters maintain close optical continuity despite disaggregation. Although it is not entirely clear whether wholesale grain breakage here is related to the same stress field that produced the shear zones, some samples display a crude alignment of sand grains outside and in between

shear zones, suggesting that some grain flow may have occurred prior to, or during, shear zone genesis. In some samples the aligned fabric of sand grains merges almost imperceptibly into the shear zone, suggesting some contemporaneity. Remobilization of sand grains by later deformational events, however, cannot be ruled out.

Cathode-luminescence microscopy shows brightly luminescent sand grains of the Sitkalidak Formation in various stages of disaggregation within shear zones. Small sand lozenges, described in the above, are plucked from the wallrock and subsequently deformed in the shear zone (Fig. 15). Individual sand grains trapped within these lozenges commonly display asymmetric tails indicating the sense of displacement, (Fig. 15b, c). Strikingly, CLM shows an abundance of extremely fine-grained fragments quartz and feldspar within the shear zones. The dark color of the shear zones is due largely to light diffraction within this fine-grained medium and is not the consequence of a clay-rich matrix nor solution residue. Sparse plagioclase feldspars in Barbados sandstones are differentially dispersed across shear zone boundaries. Well outside the shear zones, blue luminescing plagioclase grains are either unbroken or only slightly fractured. Closer to the shear zone, plagioclase feldspars become progressively more deformed until at the shear boundary itself they are dispersed into discrete blue luminescing lenses parallel to shear plane. Within the shear zone, feldspars are completely pulverized and disseminated somewhat randomly throughout the gouge.

Ultramicroscopically (SEM), shear zones from the Scotland Formation contain abundant fine-grained particles that are remarkably uniform in size (~10 microns across) and are locally lined by scaly clay minerals (Fig. 16). This scaly fabric is not found in clay minerals outside cataclastic shear zones within these samples.

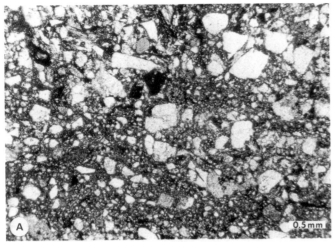

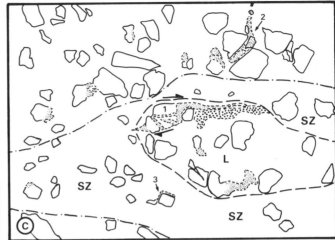

Figure 15. Photomicrographs of a cataclastic shear zone in a stratally disrupted sandstone from the Sitkalidak Formation, Alaska. A) Shear zone, characterized by fine grain size and splaying around a small lozenge of deformed sandstone; plane-polarized light (Scale bar equals 0.5 mm). B) Shear zone from (a) under cathode luminescence microscopy (CLM). Note the fractured grains both within and adjacent to the shear zone, and the shear tails after the cataclastically deformed feldspar grain in the center of the photograph (see Fig. 15c). C) Line drawing interpretation of the previous photomicrographs showing the shear zone (SZ) incorporating and deforming a small sand lozenge (L). Note the fractured grain (1) with shear tails indicating the sense of displacement. The small dots represent comminuted grain fragments (2 and 3) visible only under CLM; large grains are for reference.

Discussion Of Cataclasis in Subaerially Exposed Accretionary Complexes

The localized grain fracturing and grain alignment outside cataclastic shear zones suggest that the initiation and propagation of shear zones occurred roughly contemporaneously with intergranular flow (and minor rotation?) in a sand that was probably weakly lithified at best. We have found no evidence that sandstone inclusions from either of these units were well lithified prior to shear zone genesis. There are no pressure shadows associated with rotated grains, no shear zone breccias, or other fabrics suggestive of mesoscopically brittle behavior. Moreover, Vrolijk and Byrne (1984) note that cataclastic shear zones (web-structure), from the Kodiak accretionary complex are overgrown by early-formed concretions.

The development of discrete shear zones in the Sitkalidak and Scotland Formations implies a change in the structural integrity of the sandstone during deformation and probably reflects a greater degree of consolidation than that present in the DSDP cores. Consolidation of these sands appears to have been achieved by particulate flow and localized cataclasis resulting in a densely packed, hardened material of substantially reduced porosity. At this stage, further deformation could result in mesoscopic failure along through-going cataclastic shear planes similar to those observed in lithified sandstones (discussed below). The development of discrete shear zones may reflect deformation within the accretionary complex at depths greater than those sampled at Sites 488 and 492. Experiments with unconsolidated sands (Mandl and others, 1977; Friedman and others, 1980) indicate that shear zones become progressively more ordered when subjected to increasingly higher confining pressures.

Shear zones within the Sitkalidak and Scotland sandstones are similar to small faults in Entrada and Navajo Sandstones from the San Rafael Desert in southeastern Utah (Aydin and Johnson, 1978). In the latter rocks, individual shear zones (deformation bands) progress to arrays of shear zones (deformation zones), to discrete faults of relatively large displacement (Aydin and Johnson, 1978). These authors argue that strain-hardening, due to grain size reduction, is responsible for the formation and abandonment of a succession of shear zones. As in the sandstones from the Scotland and Sitkalidak Formations, Aydin and Johnson (1978) note that displacement along individual shear surfaces is small, a few millimeters to centimeters at most. Along zones of densely packed shear zones, however, discrete faults form with displacements of as much as 10 m.

Figure 16. SEM photomicrograph of scaly clay and fine silt fragments lining a cataclastic shear zone, Scotland Formation, Barbados (SEM).

In an experimental study, Mandl and others (1977) observed a similar hardening mechanism in unconsolidated material sheared under confining pressure. However, instead of the shear zone being abandoned, it grew symmetrically outward from the initial plane of shear. After a total displacement of approximately 1 m, movement once again returned to the center of the shear zone, developing a smooth slickensided surface. Perhaps a similar mechanism operated to develop the smooth slicked surfaces in the Sitkalidak Formation. Mandl and others (1977) attributed the development of a central through-going fracture surface to "strain-softening." They suggest that limited movement and cataclasis continues within the so-called "hardened shear zone," producing a material with a smaller, more uniform grain size distribution, reducing grain overlap and interlocking. With time

(and continued displacement), the coefficient of friction is reduced and slip returns to the center of the shear plane.

The observations of Aydin and Johnson (1978) and experiments of Mandl and others (1977) offer a novel explanation for the generation of multiple shear zones of both large and small displacement. Neither, however, reported the development of cross-cutting shear planes. The latter probably result from the (high magnitude) of non-coaxial, non-plane strain that occurs in subduction zones.

CONCLUSIONS

The earliest deformation of sand off southern Mexico probably proceeds by non-destructive particulate flow, facilitated by excess pore fluid pressure (Fig. 17b). With increasing effective confining stress, cataclasis begins (Site 488; Fig. 17c), later becoming the dominant deformational process (Site 492). Cataclastic fabrics off southern Mexico developed at maximum burial depths of 300 m and must be due to tectonic rather than gravity deformation. Cataclasis and associated grain size reduction locally increases the coefficient of friction (strain hardening), causing the locus of deformation to migrate away from zones of grain breakage to the adjacent, less deformed matrix. A bulk increase in coefficient of friction within deforming sands, coupled with increasing effective confining stress, apparently concentrates further deformation along discrete cataclastic shear zones (Fig. 17d; Barbados and Kodiak accretionary complexes). The widespread distribution of cataclastic grain breakage in individual accretionary complexes suggests propagation of this deformation mechanism through large volumes of rocks, perhaps by strain hardening and high-magnitude, non-coaxial, non-plane strain.

ACKNOWLEDGMENTS

We thank Ken Aalto, Neil Lundberg, and Othmar Tobisch for careful reviews of versions of this manuscript. Nancy Breen

Increasing Strain & Effective Confining Stress

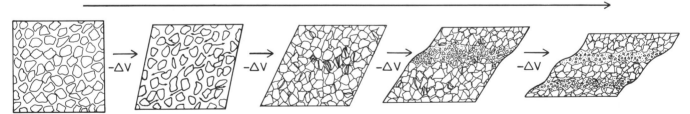

A) Undeformed
   Sediment

B) Non-destructive
   Particulate Flow

C) Incipient Cataclasis

D) Shear Zone For-
   mation

E) Strain Hardening-
   Formation Of New
   Shear Zone

Figure 17. Model for cataclastic deformation and shear zone development in tectonically deformed sandstones. (A) Undeformed water-rich sediments. (B) Internal deformation with particulate flow. (C) Incipient cataclasis. Increasing confining stress inhibits grain boundary sliding and causes localized cataclasis where stress concentrations exceed grain strength (e.g. Sites 488 and 492). (D) Propagation of discrete shear zones. (E) Strain hardening of initial shear zone and development of a new shear zone in weaker adjacent material.

and Steven Ward provided thoughtful comments on the mechanical evaluation of cataclasis. We appreciate Neil Lundberg's assistance with sampling as well as suggestions during laboratory work. Peter Vrolijk provided data on relations between young concretions and web structure in the Sitkalidak Formation. Re-

search on the DSDP cores was supported by the National Science Foundation through grants OCE-8110349 and OCE-8315836. Field studies of cataclastic shear zones in the Kodiak accretionary complex were supported by National Science Foundation Grant EAR-8305883.

REFERENCES CITED

Aalto, K. R., 1986, Structural geology of the Franciscan Complex of the Crescent City area, northern California: Geological Society of America Bulletin (in press).

Aydin, A., and Johnson, A. M., 1978, Development of faults as zones of deformation bands and as slip surfaces in sandstones: Pure Applied Geophysics, v. 116, p. 931–942.

Bishop, A. W., 1966, The strength of soils as engineering materials: Geotechnique, v. 16, p. 91–130.

Byrne, T., 1984, Structural geology of melange terranes in the Ghost Rocks Formation, Kodiak Islands, Alaska, *in* Raymond, L. A., ed., Melanges, Their Nature Origin, and Significance: Geological Society of America Special Paper 198, p. 21–52.

Cowan, D. S., 1985, Structural styles in Mesozoic and Cenozoic melanges in the western Cordillera of North America: Geological Society of America Bulletin, v. 96, p. 451–462.

De Beer, E. E., 1965, The scale effect in transposition of the results of deep sounding tests on the ultimate bearing capacity of piles and caisson foundations: Geotechnique, v. 13, p. 39–75.

Dewey, J. F., and Bird, J., 1970, Mountain belts and new global tectonics: Journal of Geophysical Research, v. 75, p. 2625–2647.

Dickinson, W. R., 1970(a), Second Penrose Conference: The global tectonics: Geotimes, v. 15, no. 4, p. 18–22.

——, 1970(b), Interpreting detrital modes of greywacke and arkose: Journal of Sedimentary Petrology, v. 40, p. 695–707.

Friedman, M., Hugman III, R.H.H., and Handin, J., 1980, Experimental folding of rocks under confining pressure, part VII—Forced folding of unconsolidated sand and of lubricated layers of limestone and sandstone: Geological Society of America Bulletin, v. 91, p. 307–312.

Hsü, K. J., 1971, Franciscan melanges as a model for eugeosynclinal sedimentation and underthrusting tectonics: Journal of Geophysical Research, v. 76, p. 1162–1170.

——, 1974, Melanges and their distinction from olistostromes, *in* Dott, R. J., Jr., and Shaver, R. H., eds., Modern and ancient geosynclinal sedimentation: Society of Economic Paleontologists and Mineralogists Special Publications No. 19, p. 321–333.

Hubbert, M. K., and Rubey, W. W., 1960, Role of fluid pressure in mechanics of overthrust faulting: A reply: Geological Society of America Bulletin, v. 71, p. 617–628.

Lambe, T. W., and Whitman, R. V., 1969, Soil Mechanics: New York, John Wiley and Sons, Inc., 553 p.

Leggett, J. K., 1982, Drilling induced structures in Leg 66 cores, *in* Lee, M., and others, eds., Initial Reports of the Deep Sea Drilling Project: Washington, D.C., U.S. Government Printing Office, v. 66, p. 531–538.

Lundberg, N., and Moore, J. C., 1982, Structural Features of the Middle America

Trench slope of southern Mexico, Deep Sea Drilling Project Leg 66, *in* Lee, M., and others, eds., Initial Reports of the Deep Sea Drilling Project: Washington, D.C., U.S. Government Printing Office, v. 66, p. 793–814.

Mandl, G., de Jong, L.N.J., and Maltha, A., 1977, Shear zones in granular material: Rock Mechanics, v. 9, p. 95–144.

Maxwell, J. C., 1959, Turbidite, tectonics, and gravity transport, northern Apennines, Italy: American Association of Petroleum Geologists Bulletin, v. 43, p. 2701–2719.

Moore, D. G., 1961, Submarine slumps: Journal of Sedimentary Petrology, v. 31, p. 343–357.

Moore, J. C., and Allwardt, A., 1980, Progressive deformation of a Tertiary trench slope, Kodiak Islands, Alaska: Journal of Geophysical Research, v. 85, no. B9, p. 4741–4756.

Page, B. M., 1963, Gravity tectonics near Passo della Cisa, northern Apennines Mountains, Italy: Geological Society of America Bulletin, v. 74, p. 655–672.

Paterson, M. S., 1978, Experimental rock deformation—the brittle field: Springer-Verlag, New York, 254 p.

Shephard, L. E., Bryant, W. F., and Chiou, W. A., 1982, Geotectnical properties of Middle America Trench sediments, Deep Sea Drilling Project Leg 66, *in* Lee, M., and others, eds., Initial Reports of the Deep Sea Drilling Project: Washington, D.C., U.S. Government Printing Office, v. 66, p. 475–505.

Sowers, G. B., and Sowers, G. F., 1970, Introductory soil mechanics and foundations: London, Macmillan, 556 p.

Speed, R. C., 1983, Structure of the accretionary complex of Barbados, I: Chalky Mount: Geological Society of America Bulletin, v. 94, no. 1, p. 92–116.

Speed, R. C., and Larue, D. K., 1982, Barbados: Architecture and implications for accretion: Journal of Geophysical Research, v. 87, no. B5, p. 3633–3643.

Taylor, J. M., 1950, Pore-space reduction in sandstones: Bulletin of the American Association of Petroleum Geologists, v. 34, no. 4, p. 701–716.

Vesic, A. S., and Clough, W., 1968, Behavior of granular material under high stresses: Journal of the Soil Mechanics and Foundations Division, Proceeding American Society of Civil Engineers, v. 94, p. 661–687.

Vrolijk, P. J., and Byrne, T., 1984, Fluid evolution during early melange deformation [abs.]: EOS American Geophysical Union Transactions, v. 65, no. 45, p. 1147.

Watkins, J. S., McMillen, K. J., and others, 1982, Tectonic synthesis, Deep Sea Drilling Project Leg 66, *in* Lee, M., and others, eds., Initial Reports of the Deep Sea Drilling Project: Washington, D.C., U.S. Government Printing Office, v. 66, p. 837–849.

Yeats, R. S., and Haq, B. U., and others, eds., 1981, Initial Reports of the Deep Sea Drilling Project: v. 63, Washington, D.C., U.S. Government Printing Office, p. 967.

MANUSCRIPT ACCEPTED BY THE SOCIETY MARCH 10, 1986

Printed in U.S.A.

Geological Society of America
Memoir 166
1986

Clay mineralogy and diagenesis of sediments from deformation zones in the Barbados accretionary wedge (Deep Sea Drilling Project Leg 78A)

Jane Schoonmaker
Hawaii Institute of Geophysics
University of Hawaii
Honolulu, Hawaii 96822

ABSTRACT

Drilling during DSDP Leg 78A in the Barbados accretionary complex provided an opportunity to study the clay mineralogy and chemistry of sediments in relation to development of structural fabrics in the sediments and location of the samples relative to major structural features in the wedge. The clay mineral suite, comprised of smectite, illite, kaolinite, and chlorite, was generally similar in all samples analyzed from both accretionary wedge sites (541 and 542) and from the Atlantic reference site (543). Differences in the mineralogy of the smectite component were noted, however, for several samples from the accretionary wedge Site 541. In most of the sediments analyzed, the smectite is a trioctahedral, mixed-layer phase. Sediments near a reverse fault and from the basal décollement zone from Site 541, however, contain a trioctahedral smectite with no mixed-layering, probably an Fe-rich saponite. The sediments containing saponite all have well-developed structural fabrics including scaly foliation, fracturing, and stratal disruption. This association, however, is not ubiquitous, and thus it is concluded that the occurrence of saponite is not directly related to development of structural fabrics. It is likely, rather, that the reverse fault and the basal décollement zone, by acting as conduits for upward migration of fluids released at depth in the wedge, provided unique chemical environments in which formation of saponite was favored. Evaluation of the chemical data indicates that the saponite probably formed by alteration of pre-existing mixed-layer smectite.

INTRODUCTION

The clay mineral content of deep-sea sediments is an indicator of depositional and diagenetic processes affecting the sediment column. Depth variations in clay mineralogy may reflect changes in detrital contributions, resulting, for example, from a change in source area or climatic variations. In shallowly buried sediments, diagenetic processes commonly involve dominantly physical changes associated with burial and compaction. Depth-dependent chemical and mineralogical changes can also occur. Diagenetic reactions include alteration or dissolution of existing phases and precipitation of secondary minerals. These reactions may occur at shallow burial depths and do not necessarily require elevated temperatures or pressures. Shallowly buried sediments may also be affected by hydrothermal processes occurring at and below the seafloor.

The influence of tectonics on diagenesis has not been investigated to the same extent as that of other factors such as temperature, burial depth, and sediment age. Many structural fabrics develop in response to stress. It is possible that diagenetic reactions accompany development of fabrics such as scaly or spaced foliation.

Variations in the chemistry and mineralogy of the fine fraction of clay-sized sediments, in association with other evidence, can be attributed to diagenetic processes. In turn, the degree and extent of diagenetic alteration of sediments may help delineate other processes affecting the sediment column such as water circulation patterns, tectonic activity including faulting, and fabric development. For example, Schoonmaker and others (1986) and Larue and others (1985) investigated diagenesis of clay minerals in sediments from the Barbados Ridge Complex. Outcrop and well sediment samples from Barbados Island were interpreted to represent the products of an earlier period of accretion. The diagenetic studies were used to infer original depth of burial of the sediments and to delineate probable thrust-fault zones at depth in the wedge.

Sediments sampled during DSDP Leg 78A in the Barbados accretionary wedge provide an opportunity to evaluate clay mineral diagenesis in a setting undergoing accretion. Drilling at Site 543, located east of the toe of the accretionary wedge (Fig. 1), penetrated 411 m of pelagic and hemipelagic sediments overlying Cretaceous basalt (Biju-Duval, Moore and others, 1984). At Sites 541 and 542, lower Miocene and younger sediments scraped off the Atlantic seafloor and incorporated in the accretionary wedge were sampled (Fig. 1). The 459-m-thick sequence at Site 541 contains reverse faults with coincident, biostratigraphically documented stratigraphic inversions (Biju-Duval, Moore and others, 1984). These sediments and the 325.5-m sequence drilled at Site 542 show development of structural features and textures including fracturing, scaly foliation, and stratal disruption (Cowan and others, 1984; Moore and others, this volume). At both sites 541 and 542, drilling terminated in highly deformed sediment interpreted to be part of the basal décollement zone separating off-scraped from underthrust sediment sequences (Biju-Duval, Moore and others, 1984; see Fig. 1). Hole 541 appears to have actually penetrated the décollement, whereas at Site 542, drilling terminated very near, but not in, the décollement (Biju-Duval, Moore and others, 1984).

In this study, samples have been analyzed from zones of deformation or noted fabric development from Holes 541 and 542A in the accretionary wedge. Structural features of these sediments include stratal disruption (zone A, Fig. 1), scaly foliation associated with reverse faults (zones B and C, Fig. 1), and intense fracturing, foliation, and stratal disruption (zones D and E, Fig. 1). The properties of these sediments have been compared to those of stratigraphically equivalent sediment samples from the tectonically undisturbed Atlantic reference site 543.

METHODS

Mineralogy was determined by x-ray diffraction, using a Philips Norelco x-ray diffractometer and Ni-filtered, CuK_α radiation. To remove organic matter, the samples were first treated with 5% sodium hypochlorite (Clorox) buffered to pH 9.5 with HCl (Anderson, 1963). Amorphous Fe-oxyhydroxides were removed using the Na-citrate-Na-dithionite method of Mehra and Jackson (1960). Size fractionation was done by centrifugation after dispersal by ultrasonication and, if necessary, addition of Calgon.

Oriented mounts were prepared by pipetting the clay suspension onto a glass slide. X-ray diffractograms were run after air-drying and after glycolation to expand smectites. Random mounts were prepared by packing dried clay powder into an aluminum holder from the back. Oriented samples were scanned from $2-32°2\theta$ at a rate of $1°2\theta$/minute and from $58-63°$ at $1/4°2\theta$/minute. Random mounts were scanned from $2-45°2\theta$ at $1°2\theta$/minute.

An estimate of the extent of mixed-layering in the smectites was obtained using procedures developed for mixed-layer illite/smectite (Hoffman, 1976; Reynolds and Hower, 1970). Because the composition of the phase interlayered with the smectite in the Leg 78A samples is not known, these percentages are only approximations; relative variations in percent mixed-layering, however, should be valid. Semiquantitative estimates of the relative percentages of the various clay minerals were made using the method of Mann and Müller (1979).

Samples for chemical analysis were treated to remove amorphous Fe-oxyhydroxides as described above, dispersed, and the $<2-\mu m$ fraction isolated by centrifugation. The samples were then freeze-dried and ground to a fine powder. Chemical analyses were done by atomic-absorption spectrophotometry.

RESULTS

Mineralogy and Stratigraphic Relationships

In general, the mineral contents of all sediments analyzed from Holes 541, 542A, and 543 are similar. As shown in Tables 1 and 2, the clay mineral suite is dominated by smectite, with lesser amounts of kaolinite, chlorite, and illite. Quartz and feldspar are ubiquitous, but present in minor quantities. In the Atlantic reference hole (Site 543) percent smectite increases downhole from the range 40–60% in shallowly buried sediments to 70–90% at depth at the expense of all other clay minerals (Table 1). Samples from Holes 541 and 542A are rich in smectite and have clay mineral distributions similar to those found in samples from the lower half of the sediment column from Hole 543 (Tables 1 and 2). No significant trends in clay mineral distributions with depth are apparent from Site 541 sediments (Table 2).

A combination of mineralogic data, physical properties data (Marlow and others, 1984), and radiolarian dating (Renz, 1984) has been used to identify samples from Hole 543 (133.8 to 193.9 m sub-bottom depth, Table 1) that are approximately stratigraphically equivalent to sediments incorporated in the accretionary wedge at Sites 541 and 542. Comparison of clay mineral distributions, particularly percentage smectite, between the three sites (Tables 1 and 2) shows that sediments from 133.8 m sub-bottom depth and deeper in Hole 543 are very similar mineralogically to sediments from Holes 541 and 542A. A significant change in physical properties of sediments at approximately 200 m sub-bottom depth in Hole 543 marks a horizon thought to correspond to the level of the décollement developed at Sites 541 and 542 (Marlow and others, 1984). If this interpretation is true, sediments shallower than about 200 m at Hole 543 are strati-

TABLE 1. MINERALOGICAL CHARACTERISTICS, LEG 78A, SITE 543

SAMPLE[*]	SUB-BOTTOM DEPTH (m)	AGE	(060)[†]	SMECTITE STRUCTURAL TYPE	V/P[§]	% SM[**]	% IL[††]	% K/C[§§]
543-6-3/35-43,<1	59.9	Plio.	1.49,1.53	Both tri. & di.	47	42	31	27
, b			1.540	Trioct.	40	43	23	34
543-9-4/117-124,<1	90.7	Lt. Mio.-	ndp		45	48	29	23
, b		E. Plio.	1.540	Trioct.	40	50	21	29
543-10-4/110-117,<1	100.2	Lt. Mio.-	ndp		44	55	23	22
, b		E. Plio.	1.54	Trioct.	41	52	18	30
543-11-3/93-100,<1	108.0	?	1.530	Trioct.	38	65	16	19
, b			ndp		32	57	19	24
543-12-4/104-111,<1	119.1	?	1.536	Trioct.	24	65	11	24
, b			1.540	Trioct.	29	73	9	18
543-13-4/120-127,<1	128.8	?	1.540	Trioct.	40	61	7	32
, b			1.530	Trioct.	30	42	19	39
543-14-2/60-67,<1	133.7	?	1.540	Trioct.	27	66	8	26
, b			1.49,1.54	Both tri. & di.	26	60	11	29
543-14-2/78-80,<1	133.8	?	1.535	Trioct.	13	91	0	9
, b			ndp		21	56	12	32
543-15-cc/7-8,<1	150.0	?	1.530	Trioct.	9	92	0	8
, b			ndp		32	57	17	25
543-16-3/40-47,<1	155.0	?	1.531	Trioct.	14	85	5	9
, b			1.544	Trioct.	23	79	9	12
543-18-2/53-57,<1	172.6	E. Mio.	1.524	Tri. w/di. char.	18	87	3	10
, b			1.535	Trioct.	24	86	4	10
543-19-5/12-17,<1	186.2	E. Mio.	nd		25	86	4	10
, b			1.542	Trioct.	25	78	10	12
543-20-3/130-137,<1	193.9	E. Mio.	1.535	Trioct.	20	80	6	14
, b			1.544	Trioct.	30	76	8	16
543-24-3/35-42,<1	230.9	Olig.	1.520,1.540	Tri. w/di. char. & tri.	29	88	0	12
, b			1.540	Trioct.	35	51	13	36
543-29-4/79-86,<1	280.3	Eoc.	1.540	Trioct.	20	90	0	10
, b			1.535	Trioct.	30	40	7	53

*) Samples are identified by hole-core-section/cm interval. Size fractions indicated by <1 (less than 1 μm) and b (bulk).
†) Position of the (060) reflection in Å. Ndp indicates no discernable peak; nd indicates (060) not determined.
§) V/P refers to the valley-to-peak ratio of the (001) smectite peak; see Fig. 2. The number given here is actually an extimate of percent non-smectite interlayers derived from an empirical relationship between V/P and % interlayers for mixed-layer illite/smectite from Hoffman (1976).
**) Percent smectite or mixed-layer clay; all clay percentages are normalized to 100.
††) Percent illite.
§§) Percent Kaolinite and/or chlorite.

graphically equivalent to sediments that have been offscraped and incorporated in the wedge, whereas sediments below this depth are equivalent to those that were underthrust with the underlying crust (see Fig. 1). The Hole 541 and 542A samples analyzed are all Miocene in age (Renz, 1984; see Table 2). The ages of samples from Hole 543 range from Eocene to Pliocene, although a number of samples are barren and undated (Renz, 1984; see Table 2). Samples between 133.8 and 193.9 m sub-bottom depth in Hole 543 are of early Miocene or unknown age. These age relations are consistent with the hypothesis of stratigraphic equiv-alency of these sediments with those analyzed from Holes 541 and 542A.

Nature and Occurrence of Smectite

Although all samples have basically similar mineralogies, differences exist in the characteristics of the smectite between samples. As determined by x-ray diffraction analysis, a number of criteria (Fig. 2) have been employed to describe differences in the nature of the smectites. These criteria include positions of the

TABLE 2. MINERALOGICAL CHARACTERISTICS, LEG 78A, SITES 541 & 542A

ZONE[†]	SAMPLE[*]	SUB-BOTTOM DEPTH (m)	AGE	(060)[*]	SMECTITE STRUCTURAL TYPE	V/P[*]	% SM[*]	% IL[*]	% K/C[*]
A	541-28-4/123-130,<1	253.8	Lt. Mio.	1.543	Trioct.	20	90	0	10
	, b			nd		24	70	7	23
A	541-28-5/3,<1	254.3	Lt. Mio.	1.530	Trioct.	22	88	0	12
	, b			nd		19	70	9	21
--->B	541-29-3/143-150,<1	262.0	Lt. Mio.	1.544	Trioct.	0	87	0	13
	, b			nd		23	73	11	16
C	541-30-6/115-122,<1	275.7	Lt. Mio.	1.524	Tri. w/ di. char.	30	95	0	5
	, b			nd		45	73	15	12
C	541-30-6/124,<1	275.7	Lt. Mio.	ndp		12	76	7	17
	, b			nd		35	78	11	11
C	541-30-6/130,<1	275.8	Lt. Mio.	1.530	Trioct.	19	75	11	14
	, b			nd		38	77	11	12
--->D	541-47-2/64-68,<1	430.7	E.-Mid. Mio.	1.530	Trioct.	0	93	0	7
	, b			nd		5	87	3	10
--->D	541-49-2/55-62,<1	449.6	E.-Mid. Mio.	1.540	Trioct.	0	91	0	9
	, b			1.524		0	83	0	17
--->D	541-50-3/86-92,<1	460.9	E.-Mid. Mio.	1.541	Trioct.	0	78	0	22
	, b			nd		0	79	4	17
E	542A-9-1/85-92,<1	307.4	Lt. Mio.	1.539	Trioct.	8	90	0	10
	, b			nd		30	73	9	18
E	542A-10-5/77-84,<1	322.8	Lt. Mio.	ndp		36	72	9	19
	, b			nd		48	67	6	28

*) See Table 1.
†) Zones refer to location and types of structural features; see Fig. 1. Arrows denote samples in which saponite was detected.

basal reflections (002, 003) on diffractograms from oriented samples. These peak positions may vary somewhat depending on structure and chemistry of the smectite. Significant shifts in the positions of the basal reflections indicate the presence of mixed-layering in the smectite. Another criterion that may reflect the presence of mixed-layering is the breadth and/or skewedness of the (002) and (003) basal reflections (e.g. Reynolds and Hower, 1970). The valley-to-peak ratio of the (001) reflection (V/P, see Fig. 2) may be used to obtain a semi-quantitative estimate of the amount of mixed-layering in the smectite. Theoretically, the valley-to-peak ratio of pure smectite should equal zero. That is, the valley at about $3°2\theta$ in Figure 2 should extend down to the level of the background. Although this ratio (V/P) also reflects other characteristics of the smectite, it has been shown empirically to indicate the extent of mixed-layering in illite/smectite (Hoffman, 1976; Reynolds and Hower, 1970). A final criterion used to characterize the smectites is the position of the (060) reflection (not shown in Fig. 2), which differentiates between the two basic structural types of smectite, di- and trioctahedral. The (060) peak position ranges between approximately $62°2\theta$ (1.49 Å, dioctahedral) and $60°2\theta$ (1.54 Å, trioctahedral) (Bailey, 1980).

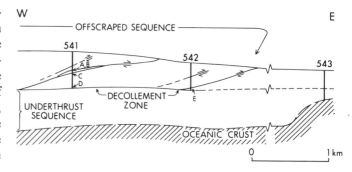

Figure 1. Schematic E-W diagram showing locations of Sites 541 and 542 in the offscraped sediments of the Barbados wedge and of the Atlantic reference Site 543. Site 543 lies to the north of Sites 541 and 542, but has been brought into the line of section for diagrammatic purposes. The dashed line indicates an approximate extension of the stratigraphic horizon along which the décollement forms. Sediments were analyzed from five zones within the accretionary prism: A) a section of stratally disrupted sediment; B) and C) two reverse faults characterized by scaly foliation; D) the basal décollement zone at Hole 541 in which sediments are highly deformed; and E) highly deformed sediment associated with a thrust fault directly above the décollement in Hole 542A. Modified from Moore and others, this volume.

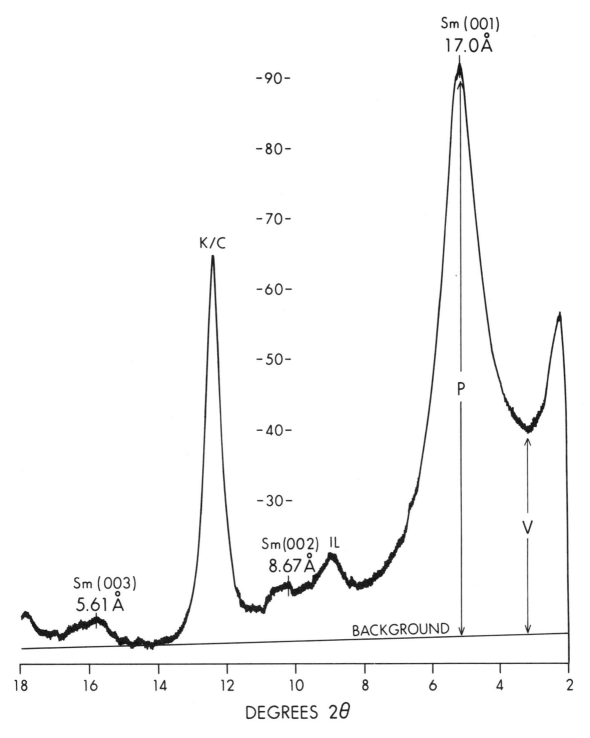

Figure 2. X-ray diffractogram of the <1-μm fraction of a typical sediment from Leg 78A (543-14-2/60-67). Three basal reflections of smectite are indicated (Sm (001), (002), and (003) with d-spacings in angstrom units), as well as an illite peak (Il) and a combined kaolinite and chlorite peak (K/C). The background level determined at higher values of 2θ has been extended linearly to the low 2θ end of the diffractogram. V indicates the height above background of the valley at about 3° 2θ; P is the height of the Sm (001) peak above background. The ratio V/P is used in estimating the extent of mixed-layering in the smectite.

These criteria have been employed to identify variability in the nature of the smectites in Holes 541, 542A, and 543. As shown in Tables 1 and 2, the position of the (060) reflection indicates a trioctahedral structure for all smectites, although a few samples also contain some dioctahedral smectite. In most of the sediments, the smectite appears to be a mixed-layer clay mineral as deduced from the valley-to-peak ratio (Tables 1 and 2) and the positions and shapes of (002) and (003) reflections. For example, Figure 3 shows a series of x-ray diffractograms from Hole 543. The sample depicted in Figure 3A contains significant quantities of illite, kaolinite, and chlorite, as well as smectite. The (001) reflection of the smectite (at 5.2°2θ; 17 Å) has a high valley-to-peak ratio. The (002) and (003) reflections were not detected. These observations suggest that the smectite is a mixed-layer phase with a significant amount of interlayering. Figure 3B illustrates a sediment containing smectite with a moderate degree of mixed-layering as indicated by the smaller valley-to-peak ratio and the broad, skewed (002) and (003) reflections. The low valley-to-peak ratio and the distinct nature and d-spacings of the smectite peaks of the sample shown in Figure 3C indicate smectite with only a small amount of mixed-layering.

The smectites in all samples from Holes 542A and 543, and most of them from Hole 541, are mixed-layer phases. Several sediments from Hole 541, however, contain trioctahedral smectite with no detectable interlayering (as an example, see Fig. 4). During preparation of these sediments for x-ray diffraction analysis, it was noted that the finest fraction, containing the trioctahedral smectite, was dark green and translucent, with a gel-like consistency. When exposed to ethylene glycol vapor, the clay samples expanded slowly over a period of two weeks until constant values for the (001) peak position were obtained. This difficulty in expansion probably results from a high tetrahedral layer charge owing to Al for Si substitution (R. Giese, personal communication). The two most common trioctahedral smectites are saponite and hectorite (Brindley, 1980). Saponite is a Mg- and Fe-rich smectite with variable tetrahedral substitution of Al for Si. Conversely, hectorite derives its layer charge from *octahedral* substitution of Li for Mg. It is likely, therefore, that the trioctahedral smectite detected in several samples from Hole 541 is an end-member saponite in composition. The mixed-layer smectite found in all other samples probably consists of saponite interlayered with another clay mineral. This interlayered mineral could not be positively identified, but peak positions indicate it could possibly be talc (R. C. Reynolds, personal communication). In the following discussion, trioctahedral smectite with little or no interlayering is referred to as saponite to differentiate it from the mixed-layer smectite. Samples containing saponite can be identified in Table 2 by V/P ratios equal to zero and are indicated by arrows.

Saponite was detected in clay mineral samples from two zones of Site 541: the basal décollement (zone D of Fig. 1 and Table 2) and on a reverse fault (zone B, Fig. 1, Table 2). Incipient scaly foliation was noted in the sample from the reverse fault (zone B, Fig. 1), and sediments from the basal décollement (zone

D) are intensely foliated (Moore and others, this volume). The association between development of scaly foliation and the occurrence of saponite, however, is not ubiquitous. Scaly clays from near the basal décollement region of Hole 542A (zone E, Fig. 1 and Table 2) contain mixed-layer smectite. Furthermore, a series of scaly foliated samples near a major reverse fault at Site 541 (zone C of Fig. 1 and Table 2), and a zone of stratal disruption in Hole 541 (zone A) are characterized by mixed-layer smectite. The relationship between fabric development and saponite occurrence, therefore, does not seem to be a direct one. Although these features may be present in the same samples, they appear to develop independently of one another.

The saponite found near the fault of zone B and in the basal décollement region at Site 541 (zone D) was not recognized in any of the stratigraphically equivalent samples of the Atlantic reference site (543). It has not been noted in other investigations of Site 543 mineralogy (Pudsey, 1984; A. Meyer, unpublished data). The occurrence of saponite in Hole 541 sediments may be linked to incorporation of the sediments in the accretionary wedge. This possibility is discussed below.

Chemistry

Chemical analyses of selected samples are reported in Table 3. These data are for the <2-μm size fraction (small sample volume prevented analysis of a finer grain-size fraction), which contains the minerals smectite, kaolinite, chlorite, illite, and, in some samples, quartz and amorphous silica. Although the chemical data reflect this multi-mineral assemblage, some conclusions can be drawn about the smectite composition. Magnesium contents of the sediments are low, especially for saponite-bearing sediments (Kohyama and others, 1973; Seyfried and others, 1978), suggesting that the smectite is an Fe-rich saponite. Amorphous iron phases were removed prior to chemical analysis, so all reported Fe_2O_3 is structural iron, probably from the saponite and chlorite. Lithium contents are typical of detrital clay mineral mixtures (Tardy and others, 1972), confirming the earlier assumption that the trioctahedral smectite in these samples is not hectorite. Perhaps the most notable feature of the chemical data is the lack of consistent significant differences between samples. Sediments from the accretionary wedge Sites 541 and 542 are chemically similar to those from the Atlantic reference Site 543. No consistent differences between samples with saponite and those with mixed-layer smectite are evident.

Discussion

Saponite is an important low-temperature alteration product of oceanic basalt (Andrews, 1977; Scarfe and Smith, 1977; Seyfried and others, 1978). Seyfried and Bischoff (1979) produced Fe-saponite as a product of the experimental reaction of seawater with basaltic glass and diabase at 150°C. Saponite is also commonly found in tuffaceous and volcanic-rich rocks (Sudo, 1954; Iijima and Utada, 1971; Kohyama and others, 1973; Sudo and

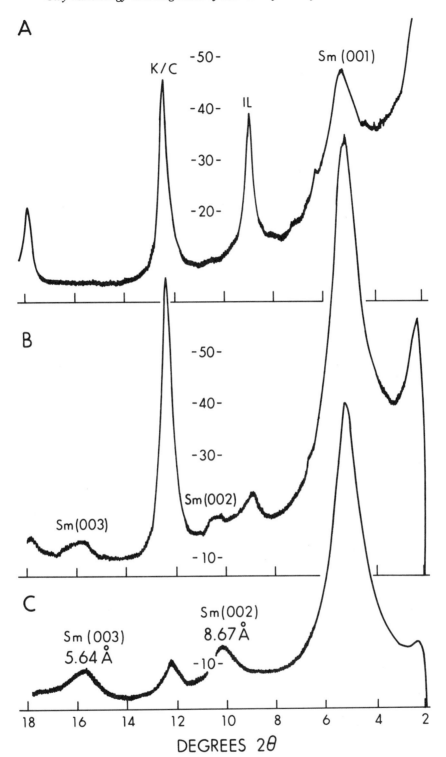

Figure 3. A series of x-ray diffractograms of the <1-μm size fraction of sediments from Site 543 illustrating mixed-layer clay minerals with different percentages of non-smectite interlayers as estimated from the valley-to-peak ratios of the Sm (001) peaks. A) Sample 543-9-4/117-124; % non-smectite interlayers = 45. B) Sample 543-14-2/60-67; % non-smectite interlayers = 27. C) Sample 543-14-2/78-80; % non-smectite interlayers = 13. Peaks are labeled as in Figure 2.

J. Schoonmaker

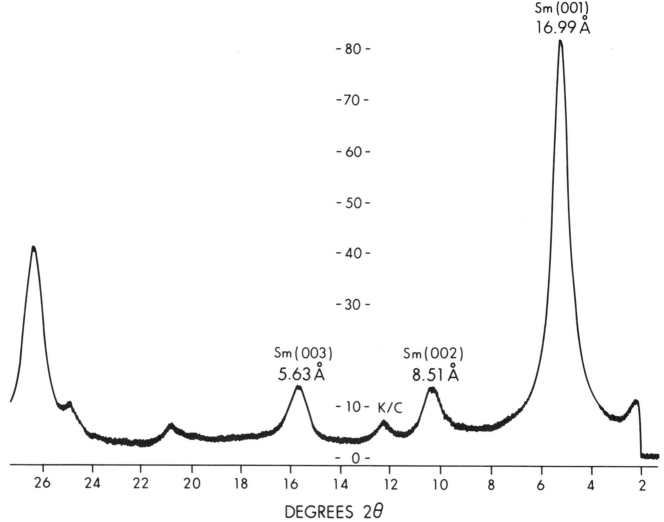

Figure 4. An x-ray diffractogram of the <1-μm size fraction of a sediment from the décollement zone at Site 541 (541-49-2/55-62). This sample consists of smectite with essentially no mixed-layering (V/P = 0; probably saponite) with a small amount of kaolinite. Peaks labeled as in Figure 2.

Shimoda, 1978; and Chang and others, 1986). Iron-rich saponite has been documented as the precursor to mixed-layer chlorite/ smectite in burial sequences of volcanic-rich sandstones (Chang and others, 1986). The hydrothermal (>400°C) alteration of saponite to mixed-layer talc/saponite, chlorite/saponite, and saponite/phlogopite was investigated by Whitney (1983).

Saponite, however, has not been reported as a common component of deep-sea sediments. This is probably a result of the fact that many investigators do not identify the composition or variety of smectite in the sediments studied. The x-ray diffraction pattern of saponite is similar to that of other smectites, and distinction must be based on the (060) reflection, which can be difficult to detect in some samples, and on the chemistry of the phase.

In the sediments from DSDP Leg 78A, saponite was found only in samples from the basal décollement zone and from one

reverse fault in Hole 541. Although the total number of samples analyzed is small, the presence of saponite in 4 out of 11 samples from Sites 541 and 542, and its total absence in the 15 samples from Site 543, suggest that the detection of saponite in the accretionary wedge is not a sampling artifact. As discussed above, it does not appear that the occurrence of saponite is directly related to development of structural textures (scaliness for example) in the sediments. It is likely, rather, that the basal décollement and reverse fault provide unique chemical environments in which the formation of saponite is favored. It is unlikely that the décollement and reverse fault formed preferentially in zones of saponite, because examination of stratigraphically equivalent samples from Hole 543 did not reveal saponite. As sediments are scraped off the incoming oceanic plate and incorporated in the accretionary wedge or, alternatively, underthrust with the oceanic crust, they are compacted and undergo dewatering. The décollement and

TABLE 3. CHEMICAL DATA, LEG 78A, <2 um SIZE FRACTIONS OF SELECTED SAMPLES

SAMPLE*	SUB-BOTTOM DEPTH (m)	SiO_2 (%)	Al_2O_3 (%)	Fe_2O_3 (%)	MgO (%)	CaO (%)	Na_2O (%)	K_2O (%)	TiO_2 (%)	P_2O_5 (%)	MnO (%)	LOI[†] (%)
541-28-4/123-130	253.8	47.8	18.1	8.01	1.86	0.67	1.78	2.04	0.5	0.108	0.129	11.13
--->541-29-3/143-150	262.0	47.2	17.4	8.12	1.82	1.06	2.17	2.24	0.57	0.108	0.258	9.71
541-30-6/115-122	275.7	45.2	18.1	8.92	1.82	0.76	2.00	2.43	0.47	0.304	0.258	10.51
--->541-49-2/55-62	449.6	45.9	18.1	8.81	2.02	0.5	2.60	1.05	0.57	0.115	0.387	16.0
--->541-50-3/86-92	460.9	51.7	18.1	8.58	1.69	0.28	3.06	1.3	0.57	0.059	0.129	11.26
542A-9-1/85-92	307.4	48.4	17.4	8.01	2.02	1.26	3.22	1.83	0.5	0.189	0.258	11.52
543-6-3/35-43	59.9	58.9	20.4	5.72	1.66	0.17	2.95	3.27	0.63	0.117	0.041	9.47
543-11-3/93-100	108.0	55.0	18.9	9.04	1.79	0.25	1.57	2.58	0.57	0.041	0.258	11.39
543-16-3/40-47	155.0	59.9	13.6	8.69	1.92	0.39	2.06	1.19	0.5	0.043	0.258	11.87
543-18-2/53-57	172.6	50.4	17.4	8.47	1.86	0.39	2.89	1.04	0.43	0.045	0.129	12.74

SAMPLE	SUB-BOTTOM DEPTH (m)	Ba (ppm)	Ag (ppm)	Be (ppm)	Cd (ppm)	Co (ppm)	Cr (ppm)	Cu (ppm)	Li (ppm)	Mo (ppm)	Ni (ppm)	Pb (ppm)	Sr (ppm)	V (ppm)	Zn (ppm)
541-28-4/123-130	253.8	120.0	0.9	3.0	0.8	23.0	88.0	50.0	81.0	1.0	57.0	36.0	70.0	310.0	161.0
--->541-29-3/143-150	262.0	180.0	1.2	3.0	0.8	23.0	108.0	48.0	71.0	4.0	45.0	36.0	90.0	220.0	162.0
541-30-6/115-122	275.7	80.0	1.2	3.0	0.5	24.0	84.0	54.0	74.0	1.0	45.0	36.0	75.0	250.0	180.0
--->541-49-2/55-62	449.6	80.0	0.9	2.5	0.8	30.0	70.0	150.0	88.0	3.0	87.0	36.0	60.0	210.0	180.0
--->541-50-3/86-92	460.9	80.0	0.3	3.0	0.8	24.0	88.0	113.0	85.0	1.0	75.0	34.0	60.0	240.0	203.0
542A-9-1/85-92	307.4	120.0	0.3	2.5	0.5	21.0	86.0	41.0	80.0	1.0	45.0	21.0	78.0	350.0	150.0
543-6-3/35-43	59.9	180.0	0.3	4.0	0.8	22.0	96.0	39.0	89.0	1.0	54.0	36.0	71.0	290.0	170.0
543-11-3/93-100	108.0	200.0	0.3	2.5	0.8	30.0	126.0	81.0	63.0	1.0	54.0	30.0	48.0	240.0	206.0
543-16-3/40-47	155.0	80.0	0.3	2.5	0.5	30.0	78.0	78.0	65.0	1.0	52.0	34.0	48.0	230.0	200.0
543-18-2/53-57	172.6	100.0	0.3	2.5	0.5	29.0	86.0	203.0	65.0	1.0	53.0	19.0	35.0	230.0	159.0

*Arrows denote samples in which saponite was detected.
[†]LOI = Loss on ignition at 110°C

fault zones provide conduits for escape of the released fluids; therefore these environments would likely differ chemically from the surrounding sediments.

There is independent evidence for preferential circulation of fluids in these zones. Fluid pressures approximately equal to the lithostatic load at the base of Hole 542A were measured during an inadvertent packer experiment at that site (Moore and Biju-Duval, 1984). A hydrologic model of the wedge in which fluid pressure balances lithostatic load along the entire décollement predicts a systematic pressure gradient and resultant upslope movement of fluids along the décollement with fluid escape along active thrust splays (Moore and Biju-Duval, 1984; see their Fig. 19). In addition, thermal gradients at the toe of the accretionary wedge appear to be abnormally high (Davis and Hussong, 1984). During drilling at Site 541, a temperature of 20.4°C was measured at a sub-bottom depth of 170 m, yielding a thermal gradient of 10.4°C/100 m (Davis and Hussong, 1984). Upslope migration of warm waters along the décollement and through fault zones could explain the steepness of the observed thermal gradient. Interstitial water chemistry provides further evidence for preferential fluid movement along the décollement and fault zones. Although the vertical concentration profiles of several porewater constituents could be interpreted as indicating upward advection of fluids through the relatively impermeable sediment pile, the profiles are best explained by alteration of volcanic matter within the sediment section (Gieskes and others, 1984). Lack of evidence for upward advection of fluids through the sediment column

implies migration of the waters preferentially along specific horizons or through specific zones of higher permeability.

Migration of dewatering fluids along the décollement and other conduits in the wedge has also been evoked as an explanation of several larger scale features of the Barbados complex. Westbrook and Smith (1983) described mud volcanoes seaward of the deformation front of the Barbados accretionary wedge. They suggested that these features formed in response to migration of overpressured pore fluids along the décollement zone toward the toe of the wedge, and then along horizons in the undeformed strata seaward of the complex. At some distance in front of the wedge the vertical stress exceeds the least horizontal stress and diapirs form (Westbrook and Smith, 1983). Cloos (1984) proposed that some landward-dipping seismic reflectors observed in accretionary wedges, including the Barbados complex, are porous fracture zones filled with dewatering fluids.

The above observations support the conclusion that the presence of saponite in the décollement and fault zones of Hole 541 is related to fluid migration through those zones. The saponite probably forms by alteration of pre-existing trioctahedral mixed-layer clay minerals rather than by direct precipitation from pore fluids. This mechanism of formation is supported by the similarity in chemical compositions of all samples (Table 3). It is unlikely that if large-scale dissolution of pre-existing clay minerals, followed by precipitation of a new phase (saponite), had occurred that uniform chemical compositions would have been maintained.

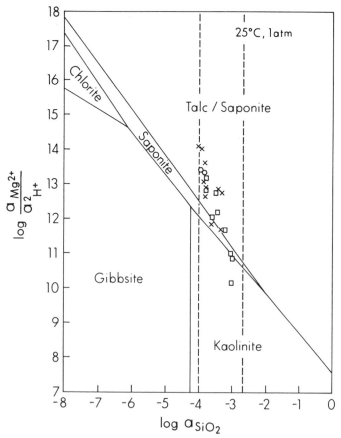

Figure 5. Activity-activity diagram for the system MgO-Na$_2$O-Al$_2$O$_3$-SiO$_2$-H$_2$O at 25°C, 1 atm P. In situ temperatures were close enough to 25°C that the temperature range would not significantly influence the diagram. In addition, pressure effects on equilibrium constants are minimal below temperatures of 300°C, so the diagram drawn for 25°C, 1 atm P adequately describes the system. In constructing the diagram the ratio a_{Na^+}/a_{H^+} was assumed to be $10^{6.90}$ (average value from pore water concentrations, Gieskes and others, 1984). Pore water concentration data from three sites are plotted (X—Site 541; O—Site 542; □—Site 543). Vertical dashed lines at log a_{SiO_2} = –4.0 and –2.7 represent saturation with quartz and amorphous silica, respectively.

Activity-activity diagrams, calculated for minerals of interest and used in conjunction with pore water data, can be useful in determining the feasibility of proposed mineral-solution reactions. Such a diagram was constructed for the Leg 78A sediments (Fig. 5) using the idealized mineral compositions and thermodynamic data of Table 4. The mixed-layer smectitic clay mineral is represented as saponite/talc. The activity-activity diagram shows a narrow field of saponite stability separating the fields of chlorite, gibbsite, and kaolinite from that of mixed-layer saponite/talc. Interstitial water concentration data from Gieskes and others (1984) are plotted on the diagram. These data are generally not from the same cores or sections as the solid-phase data reported here. (Specifically, there are no pore water data from sections in which saponite was found.) The location of the pore water data on the diagram, however, is still useful in evaluating whether

reactions involving saponite/talc and saponite are possible in these sediments. Most of the pore water concentration data from Gieskes and others (1984) fall in the saponite/talc field relatively close to the saponite-saponite/talc boundary, although several data points from Site 543 fall in the kaolinite field. All data plot between the lines for quartz and amorphous silica saturation. The nearly linear distribution of data does not represent a depth trend for any of the sites. It is also not thought to correspond to a particular reaction pathway. Rather, the trend described by the data probably reflects local lithologic variability. For example, the data points falling closest to the line for amorphous silica saturation (log a_{SiO_2} =–2.7) correspond to pore waters from radiolarian-rich sediments (Biju-Duval, Moore and others, 1984). Pore water compositions also reflect alteration of volcanic material in the sediment (Gieskes and others, 1984). The location of most of the pore water concentration data in the saponite/talc field indicates the waters may be saturated with respect to that phase and that the proposed conversion of saponite/talc to saponite is a feasible reaction in the Leg 78A sediments.

The conversion of the pre-existing mixed-layer smectite to saponite is probably primarily a chemically, rather than temperature, controlled phenomenon. If the thermal gradient determined by Davis and Hussong (1984) for the shallow portion of Hole 541 (10.4°C/100 m) is extended to the depth of the décollement zone, the temperature would be in the range 40–50°C. Because of the likely influence of advection on the temperature measurements, this temperature range is probably a maximum. The little work that has been done on the stability of saponite in this temperature range (Chang and others, 1986), and work on other smectites (for example, Perry and Hower, 1970; Hower and others, 1976; Boles and Franks, 1979; Freed, 1980), indicates that diagenesis involves conversion of expandable-clay minerals (smectites) to non-expandable ones via various mixed-layer intermediaries. Investigations of trioctahedral smectite diagenesis at higher temperatures confirm these trends (Iijima and Utada, 1971 and Whitney, 1983). If the reactions in the décollement and fault zones were primarily temperature controlled, it would be expected that mixed-layer phases would be favored over an end-member smectite (saponite).

It is concluded, therefore, that saponite has formed in several specific zones at Site 541 by alteration of pre-existing mixed-layer smectite. This alteration is in response to a changed chemical environment resulting from upslope migration of dewatering fluids through these zones. Questions that have not been resolved involve the limited occurrences of the saponite. Why is it found throughout the décollement zone at Site 541 but not in the sediments very near the décollement at Site 542? Why is it not found in other fault zones within the offscraped sediments? Kinetics possibly play a role. Fault zones have limited periods of activity. Moore and others (this volume) describe how displacement in muddy sediment occurs in limited amounts along any given surface before propagating to another slip surface, creating a broad fault zone. It might also be expected that fluid migration along a specific horizon would be limited in time and that fluid move-

TABLE 4.   THERMODYNAMIC DATA USED IN CALCULATING THE ACTIVITY-DIAGRAM (FIG. 5)

Species or Mineral	Formula	G°f kcal/mole, 25°C, 1 atm P	Source
Mg^{2+}(aq)		-108.70	Helgeson and others (1981)
Na^+(aq)		-62.62	Helgeson and others (1981)
SiO_2(aq)		-199.19	Helgeson and others (1981)
H_2O(l)		-56.68	Helgeson and others (1978)
Gibbsite	$Al(OH)_3$	-276.17	Helgeson and others (1978)
Kaolinite	$Al_2Si_2O_5(OH)_4$	-905.61	Calculated according to Tardy and Garrels (1974)
Chlorite	$Mg_5Al_2Si_3O_{10}(OH)_8$	-1958.60	Calculated according to Tardy and Garrels (1974)
Saponite*	$Na_{0.33}Mg_3Si_{3.67}Al_{0.33}O_{10}(OH)_2$	-1344.6	Calculated according to Tardy and Garrels (1974)
Saponite/Talc**	$Na_{0.264}Mg_3Si_{3.736}Al_{0.264}O_{10}(OH)_2$	-1339.7	Calculated according to Tardy and Garrels (1974)

*An Na-rich, rather than Fe-rich, saponite is used because Fe concentrations in the pore waters were not determined.

**Saponite/talc is 20% talc, 80% composite.

ment would persist longer in some fault zones than in others. The décollement zone is presumably still active at both Sites 541 and 542. The absence of saponite at Site 542 could reflect the location of the samples directly above rather than within the décollement zone. Alternatively, the patterns and persistence of fluid movement through the deformed sediment at the bases of Sites 541 and 542 may differ, resulting in dissimilar extents of alternation of smectites at these two sites.

ACKNOWLEDGMENTS

This research was supported by NSF Grants OCE 83-15836 and OCE 81-10394 to J. C. Moore, U. C. Santa Cruz and by Office of Naval Research N00014-82-C-0380. Samples were provided by the Deep Sea Drilling Project. The author thanks R. C. Schneider for laboratory assistance and P. Sexton and D. Haneda for typing the manuscript. Reviews by M. Baltuck, J. Hein, F. T. Mackenzie and J. C. Moore helped to improve the manuscript. The encouragement of J. C. Moore throughout this project is greatly appreciated.

REFERENCES CITED

Anderson, J. U., 1963, An improved pretreatment for the mineralogical analysis of samples containing organic matter: Clays and Clay Minerals, v. 10, p. 380–388.

Andrews, A. J., 1977, Low temperature fluid alteration of oceanic layer 2 basalts, Deep Sea Drilling Project Leg 37: Canadian Journal of Earth Sciences, v. 14, p. 911–926.

Bailey, S. W., 1980, Structures of layer silicates, *in* Brindley, G. W., and Brown, G., eds., Crystal Structures of Clay Minerals and their X-ray Identification: Mineralogical Society of London Monograph No. 5, p. 1–123.

Biju-Duval, B., Moore, J. C., and others, 1984. Initial Reports of the Deep Sea Drilling Project, Leg 78A: Washington, D.C., U.S. Government Printing Office, v. 78A, 848 p.

Boles, J. R., and Franks, S. G., 1979, Clay diagenesis in Wilcox sandstones of Southwest Texas: Implications of smectite diagenesis on sandstone cementation: Journal of Sedimentary Petrology, v. 49, p. 55–70.

Brindley, G. W., 1980, Order-disorder in clay mineral structures, *in* Brindley, G. W., and Brown, G., eds., Crystal Structures of Clay Minerals and their X-ray Identification: Mineralogical Society of London Monograph No. 5, p. 125–195.

Chang, H. K., Mackenzie, F. T., and Schoonmaker, J. E., 1986, Comparisons between the diagenesis of dioctahedral and trioctahedral smectites, Brazilian offshore basins: Clays and Clay Minerals (in press).

Cloos, M., 1984, Landward-dipping reflectors in accretionary wedges: Active dewatering conduits?: Geology, v. 12, p. 519–522.

Cowan, D. S., Moore, J. C., Roeske, S. M., Lundberg, N., and Lucas, S. E., 1984, Structural features at the deformation front of the Barbados Ridge complex, Deep Sea Drilling Project Leg 78A, *in* Biju-Duval, B., Moore, J. C., and others, eds., Initial Reports of the Deep Sea Drilling Project: Washington, D.C., U.S. Government Printing Office, v. 78A, p. 535–548.

Davis, D. M., and Hussong, D. M., 1984, Geothermal observations during Deep Sea Drilling Project Leg 78A, *in* Biju-Duval, B., Moore, J. C., and others, eds., Initial Reports of the Deep Sea Drilling Project: Washington, D.C., U.S. Government Printing Office, v. 78A, p. 593–598.

Freed, R. L., 1980, Shale mineralogy of the No. 1 Pleasant Bayou geothermal test well—A progress report *in* M. H. Dorfman and W. L. Fisher, eds., Proceedings of the Fourth U.S. Gulf Coast Geopressured-geothermal Energy Conference, v. 1: Austin, University of Texas, p. 153–162.

Gieskes, J. M., Elderfield, H., Lawrence, J. R., and LaKind, J., 1984, Interstitial water studies on Deep Sea Drilling Project Leg 78A, *in* Biju-Duval, B., Moore, J. C., and others, Initial Reports of the Deep Sea Drilling Project:

Washington, D.C., U.S. Government Printing Office, v. 78A, p. 377–384.

Helgeson, H. C., Delany, J. M., Nesbitt, N. W., and Bird, D. K., 1978, Summary and critique of the thermodynamic properties of rock-forming minerals: American Journal of Science, v. 278-A, 230 p.

Helgeson, H. C., Kirkham, D. H., and Flowers, G. C., 1981, Theoretical prediction of the thermodynamic behavior of aqueous electrolytes at high pressures and temperatures: IV. Calculation of activity coefficients, osmotic coefficients, and apparent standard and relative partial molal properties to 600° and 5 kb: American Journal of Science, v. 281, p. 1249–1516.

Hoffman, J., 1976, Regional metamorphism and K-Ar dating of clay minerals in Cretaceous sediments of the Disturbed Belt of Montana [Ph.D. thesis]: Case Western Reserve University, 266 p.

Hower, J., Eslinger, E., Hower, M. E., and Perry, E. A., 1976, Mechanism of burial metamorphism of argillaceous sediments: I. Mineralogical and chemical evidences: Geological Society of America Bulletin, v. 87, p. 725–737.

Iijima, A., and Utada, M., 1971, Present-day diagenesis of the Neogene geosynclinal deposits in the Niigata oilfield, Japan: Advances in Chemistry Series 101, p. 342–349.

Kohyama, N., Shimoda, S., and Sudo, T., 1973, Iron-rich saponite (ferrous and ferric forms): Clays and Clay Minerals, v. 21, p. 229–237.

Larue, D. K., Schoonmaker, J., Torrini, R., Lucas-Clark, J., Clark, M., and Schneider, R., 1985, Barbados: Maturation, source rock potential and burial history within a Cenozoic accretionary complex: Marine and Petroleum Geology, v. 2, p. 96–110.

Mann, U., and Müller, G., 1979, X-ray mineralogy of Deep Sea Drilling Project Legs 51 through 53, Western North Atlantic, *in* Donnelly, T., Francheteau, J., and others, eds., Initial Reports of the Deep Sea Drilling Project: Washington, D.C., U.S. Government Printing Office, v. 51, 52, 53, pt. 2, p. 721–729.

Marlow, M. S., Lee, H. J., and Wright, A., 1984, Physical properties of sediment from the Lesser Antilles margin along the Barbados Ridge: Results from Deep Sea Drilling Project 78A, *in* Biju-Duval, B., Moore, J. C., and others, eds., Initial Reports of the Deep Sea Drilling Project: Washington, D.C., U.S. Government Printing Office, v. 78A, p. 549–558.

Mehra, O. P., and Jackson, M. L., 1960, Iron oxide removal from soils and clays by a dithionite-citrate system buffered with sodium bicarbonate: Clays and Clay Minerals, v. 1, p. 317–327.

Moore, J. C., and Biju-Duval, B., 1984, Tectonic synthesis, Deep Sea Drilling Project Leg 78A: Structural evolution of offscraped and underthrust sediment, Northern Barbados Ridge complex, *in* Biju-Duval, B., Moore, J. C., and others, Initial Reports of the Deep Sea Drilling Project: Washington, D.C., U.S. Government Printing Office, v. 78A, p. 601–621.

Perry, E. A., and Hower, J., 1970, Burial diagenesis in Gulf Coast pelitic sediments: clays and Clay Minerals, v. 18, p. 165–177.

Pudsey, C. J., 1984, X-ray mineralogy of Miocene and older sediments from Deep Sea Drilling Project Leg 78A, *in* Biju-Duval, B., Moore, J. C., and others, Initial Reports of the Deep Sea Drilling Project: Washington, D.C., U.S. Government Printing Office, v. 78A, p. 325–342.

Renz, G. W., 1984, Cenozoic radiolarians from the Barbados Ridge, Lesser Antilles subduction complex, Deep Sea Drilling Project Leg 78A, *in* Biju-Duval, B., Moore, J. C., and others, Initial Reports of the Deep Sea Drilling Project: Washington, D.C., U.S. Government Printing Office, v. 78A, p. 447–461.

Reynolds, R. C., Jr., and Hower, J., 1970, The nature of interlayering in mixed-layer illite-montmorillonites: Clay and Clay Minerals, v. 18, p. 25–36.

Scarfe, C. M., and Smith, D.G.W., 1977, Secondary minerals in some basaltic rocks from Deep Sea Drilling Project Leg 37: Canadian Journal of Earth Sciences, v. 14, p. 903–910.

Schoonmaker, J., Mackenzie, F. T., and Speed, R. C., 1986, Tectonic implications of illite/smectite diagenesis, Barbados accretionary prism: Clays and Clay Minerals (in press).

Seyfried, W. E., Jr., and Bischoff, J. L., 1979, Low temperature basalt alteration by seawater: An experimental study at 70°C and 150°C: Geochimica et Cosmochimica Acta, v. 41, p. 1937–1947.

Seyfried, W. E., Jr., Shanks III, W. C., and Dibble, W. E., Jr., 1978, Clay mineral formation in Deep Sea Drilling Project Leg 34 basalt: Earth and Planetary Science Letters, v. 41, p. 265–276.

Sudo, T., 1954, Iron-rich saponite found from Tertiary iron sand beds in Japan: Journal of the Geological Society of Japan, v. 59, p. 18–27.

Sudo, T., and Shimoda, S., 1978, Clays and clay minerals of Japan: Amsterdam, Developments in Sedimentology 26, Elsevier, 326 p.

Tardy, Y., and Garrels, R. M., 1974, A method of formation of layer silicates: Geochimica et Cosmochimica Acta, v. 38, p. 1101–1116.

Tardy, Y., Krempp, G., and Trauth, N., 1972, Le lithium dans les mineraux argileux des sediments et des sols: Geochimica et Cosmochimica Acta, v. 36, p. 397–412.

Westbrook, G. K., and Smith, M. J., 1983, Long décollements and mud volcanoes: Evidence from the Barbados Ridge Complex for the role of high pore-fluid pressure in the development of an accretionary complex: Geology, v. 11, p. 279–283.

Whitney, G., 1983, Hydrothermal reactivity of saponite: Clays and Clay Minerals, v. 31, p. 1–8.

Manuscript Accepted by the Society March 10, 1986
HIG Contribution 1747

Geological Society of America
Memoir 166
1986

Physical properties and mechanical state of accreted sediments in the Nankai Trough, Southwest Japan Arc

Daniel E. Karig
Department of Geological Sciences
Cornell University
Ithaca, New York 14853

ABSTRACT

The general shape and mechanical behavior of an accretionary wedge can be modeled with a pressure dependent Coulomb rheology, but measurements of physical properties and structural geometries in the Nankai (southwest Japan) wedge demonstrate that a simple, constant property model is inadequate. Porosity in the Nankai prism decreases downward slightly faster than in the correlative trench section, reflecting an increase in effective mean stress as well as a change from uniaxial to biaxial strain. The coefficient of cohesion (C_0) is observed in DSDP cores to increase with decreasing porosity. The dip angles of a conjugate shear fracture set observed in these cores, as well as the frontal thrust, show that σ_1 dips about 5° toward the trench at depths of 400 m to 1000 m, and the coefficient of internal friction (μ_m) is about 0.36, and the fracture strength at 1000 m can be approximated by $\tau = 1\text{MPa} + 0.36\,\sigma_n'$. Pore fluid pressures at this position are estimated to be moderately greater than hydrostatic ($\lambda = 0.75$), leading to a coefficient of sliding friction along the basal décollement of about 0.2

In contrast to the linear surface slope of the non-cohesive, constant property wedge model, the toes of accretionary wedges are generally convex upward. A minor fraction of this convexity can be explained by the effect on the force balance of an arcward decrease in average porosity. Moreover, instantaneous horizontal shortening in the Nankai wedge is more strongly concentrated toward the wedge toe than that in a non-cohesive constant-property model. These observations require an arcward and downward increase in average Coulomb parameters of wedge sediments, largely because of the reduction in average porosity and its effect on μ_m.

Discontinuities in surface slope, which mark zones of persistent thrusting, represent material at a different state of failure than that within the thrust sheets. Concepts developed in soil mechanics suggest that these zones progress through peak strength into a lower strength residual state with a further reduction in porosity and major fabric reorganization.

Although the porosity within these broad shear zones appears less than that outside, some parts of the zones remain zones of weakness. The central parts of these zones may actually become strengthened with continued strain and water loss. This effect would be enhanced if fracture permeability leads to preferential water flow along the fault zones because this would require a pore pressure decrease into the fault zone and thus higher effective normal stresses in that zone.

INTRODUCTION

The mechanics of deformation in thrust belts had intrigued structural geologists and geophysicists for almost a century. The topic has received recent impetus from the expanded knowledge of the geometry and kinematics of these belts, especially of those constituting the accretionary wedges along trench-arc systems. Accretionary wedges are particularly suited to mechanical studies

D. E. Karig

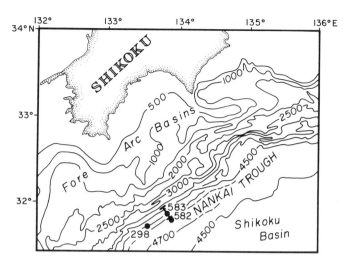

Figure 1. Regional Setting of DSDP Sites in the Nankai Trough. The heavy line shows the location of the seismic profile illustrated in Figure 2.

because, with lower rates of erosion, their shape closely reflects the distribution of deformation and because the rates of deformation are often much higher than those of foreland thrust belts.

Chapple (1978) showed that the basic solution to the paradox of large horizontal transport of weak material in a thrust system is a wedge within which internal deformation is broadly distributed. However, this kinematic condition can be satisfied using a number of constitutive relations, including a Coulomb (pressure dependent) response (Davis and others, 1983), perfect plasticity (Chapple, 1978; Stockmal, 1983), and Newtonian viscosity (Emerman and Turcotte, 1983). To some extent the rheology chosen reflected the objectives and perspective of the investigator, but it is clear that the present knowledge of physical and mechanical properties of the material involved provides grossly inadequate constraints for the discrimination of rheologies. It is important to narrow these constraints by developing a better understanding of the mechanical properties of deforming sediments involved in these zones of thrusting.

Recent geophysical studies and deep sea drilling in the Southwest Japan Arc (Nankai Trough) have produced a wealth of data concerning the physical properties and mechanical state of sediments in the toe of an accretionary wedge (Kagami, Karig, and others, 1986). For this wedge there is also a very well delineated structural framework, from which the distribution of deformation can be closely determined (Karig, 1986a). These combined data provide an unusually complete mechanical picture of the toe of an accretionary wedge. A data set from the Sunda Arc near Nias (Karig and others, 1980; Kieckhefer and others, 1980) provides additional although less complete information that suggests the mechanical picture of the Nankai wedge is not unique, but perhaps typical of accretionary wedges dominated by clastic sediment.

In this paper, data from Deep Sea Drilling Project Leg 87A that bear on the mechanical state of accreted sediments are re-

viewed and their relationships to the state of stress are discussed. The constraints provided by these results can also be used to assess the various rheological models. I have commented here only on the Coulomb model (Davis and others, 1983; Dahlen and others, 1984) because it is couched in terms of parameters measured in our trench studies. In fact, an initial motivation for this study was the recognition that, contrary to the conditions predicted by the simple Coulomb model (Davis and others, 1983; Dahlen and others, 1984), the toes of most accretionary wedges are convex upward. Moreover, the mechanical properties implied by the structural fabric observed in the Nankai wedge are very different from those favored in general by Davis and others (1983).

DATA AND ANALYSIS

General

The Nankai Trough marks the locus of convergence between the Philippine Sea and Eurasian plates along southwestern Japan (Fig. 1). The rate of convergence in the vicinity of the drill sites is uncertain; seismologic data suggest rates between 2.5 (Ranken and others, 1984) and 4 cm/yr. (e.g., Seno, 1977), whereas the geologic data from DSDP legs 31 and 87 suggest 2 cm/yr or less (Karig and Angevine, 1986). For this study a value of 2 cm/yr, assumed to be an average over several 10^5 yr, is used, but the important claims is that the convergence rate is low. This slow convergence is felt to be responsible for the large and well organized structures that were remarkably well-imaged by a seismic reflection profile (Fig. 2) that was used as a reference section for drilling operations (Kagami, Karig, and others, 1986).

Sediments of the trench wedge and uppermost Shikoku basin section are being accreted and deformed in two ways. At least half the total shortening in the toe of the wedge is accomplished by thrusting along well-defined, discrete faults. These initiate 2 to 3 km apart but, as deformation progresses, displacement apparently becomes concentrated on fewer of these faults, forming amalgamated, arcward thickening structural blocks 5 to 7 km wide (Fig. 2). The rest of the deformation occurs as a diffuse, seismically irresolvable sub-horizontal shortening, leading to an arcward thickening of the accreted sections. Thrusting and resulting simple shear is the dominant process near the wedge toe and probably along the basal décollement, whereas a grossly irrotational flattening appears to dominate throughout the rest of the wedge (Karig, 1986b).

This well-defined structural framework in the prism toe permits the calculation of the distribution of cumulative and instantaneous deformation (Karig, 1986a). The instantaneous deformation, of particular importance to this study, is shown to be very strongly concentrated towards the toe of the wedge; about 75% of the instantaneous horizontal shortening is occurring less than 15 km from the deformation front. This distribution of deformation will later be compared with the distribution of deformation predicted by the Coulomb models.

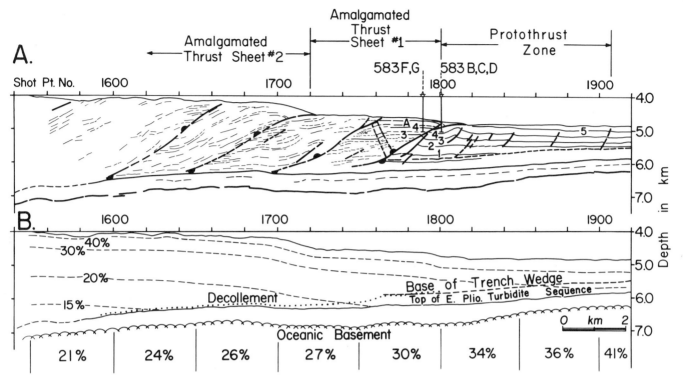

Figure 2. A. Interpretive depth section across the toe of the Nankai accretionary wedge, from seismic profile 55-3-1 (Nasu and others, 1982). The displaced half circles represent estimates of offset along major thrust faults. B. Smoothed contours of bulk porosity, from seismic and drill data (Bray and Karig (1985), and average porosity for wedge columns calculated from the contours. The décollement (dotted line) follows the base of the trench wedge beneath the protothrust zone but drops to the top of the Pliocene turbidites beneath the first thrust sheets.

Porosity

The reduction of porosity during the deformation of accreted sediments is probably the most pronounced change observed in the sediment physical properties, and one that will be argued to exert strong controls on the mechanical state of the sediment. Ironically, this porosity reduction is not obvious in the porosity-depth gradient obtained by drilling across the toe of the Nankai wedge. In the Nankai system, that gradient becomes only slightly steeper from the trench floor to Site 298, about 15 km behind the deformation front and, on the basis of empirical seismic velocity/porosity relationships, continues to gradually increase arcward (Bray and Karig, 1985a). However, the tectonic thickening of the accreted section places originally shallower high-porosity trench sediment in deeper, low-porosity sections of this curve, and leads to a much lower average porosity of columns of accreted sediment than of the incoming section (Fig. 2). For example, the sediment entering the Nankai wedge has an average porosity near 40%, whereas a column of accreted sediment 15 km behind the deformation front has an average porosity of only 20% (Bray and Karig, 1985a).

Although only generalized porosity values can be estimated at present, there is some evidence of local minima of porosity that correspond with zones of strong dislocation (Bray and Karig,

1985a). Later it will be argued that this spatial relationship is a result of post-failure strain and that there are feed-back mechanisms resulting in the progressive strengthening of the deformed and dewatered sediments.

Shear Strength

Another parameter that can be determined from DSDP cores is "shear strength." Shear strength values are measured with various techniques (e.g., Boyce, 1976; Kagami, Karig, and others, 1986), but basically provide the maximum resistive stress at zero effective normal stress. In effect, the data provide values of the constant of cohesion in the Coulomb strength criteria.

These values of cohesion must be considered minimal for several reasons. First, the available tests can only be performed on relatively soft (weak) sediments, which are particularly prone to serious disturbance during drilling and handling as well as from expansion of the contained gas. All these factors destroy fabric and reduce cohesion. Sand-rich sediments are generally highly disturbed but clearly have very little in-situ cohesion, because they are uncemented. Second, the tests require that the sample fail in a specific manner, as along a cylindrical surface; too often, and particularly in the stiffer sediments, samples fail at lower stress levels by extension across the core. A third reason for which the values measured might be considered minimal stems from the difference between true cohesion (C_0), which is measured at $\sigma_n' = 0$, and apparent cohesion (C_a), which is the intercept of the linear Coulomb relation, extrapolated to $\sigma_n' = 0$. Because the $\tau - \sigma_n$ relationship is reality curvilinear, with a slope that decreases as σ_n increases, a linear Coulomb approximation at moderate σ_n' will have an intercept, C_a, at $\sigma_n = 0$ that is greater than C_0. This difference can approach 100 MPa for effective confining stresses of several 100 MPa (e.g., Hoshino and others, 1972).

Values of cohesion measured on small, unfractured samples, on the other hand, are undoubtedly greater than effective bulk cohesion in an accretionary wedge where rocks are generally highly fractured. Bulk effective cohesion probably reflects a number of factors, such as block interlocking, which would combine to produce a pressure-independent component of strength in a Coulomb approximation.

Despite the careful attention paid to these problems during DSDP Leg 87, the measurements were still able to produce a depth-cohesion gradient to depths of only about 200 m. The most obvious result of our shipboard data is a strong increase in the cohesion of clay-rich sediments with depth. Because all tests were done with zero confining stress, this increase in cohesion must reflect primarily the decrease in porosity that accompanies increasing in-situ depth. If the measured values of cohesion are assumed to fall on or beneath the curve defining a cohesion versus depth gradient, an approximately linear relationship between cohesion and depth can be constructed over the depth range of 0 to 200 m (Bray and Karig, 1986). Cohesion continues to increase with depth as illustrated by qualitative measures of stiffness (Bray and Karig, 1986) but numerical values will not be available until tests on preserved and stored samples are run in an apparatus that we are now constructing.

The data from Site 582, in the trench wedge, can be fit by $C_0 = 40 + .53z$ where z is depth in meters and C_0 is cohesion in KPa. Cohesion in the toe of the frontal thrust (Site 583C, D) is $C_0 = 70 + 0.85z$ and further back in this thrust sheet (Site 583E, F) $C_0 = 25 + 0.85z$. The greater cohesion near the surface in the hole through the thrust toe probably results from the demonstrable erosion of surficial sediment there (Kagami, Karig and others, 1986). The more significant observation is that the rate of increase of cohesion in the sediments within the wedge is significantly greater than that in the sediments of the trench fill. This difference in the slopes of the cohesion versus depth gradients is primarily a function of the slightly greater porosity versus depth gradient at Site 583. The very similar curves of cohesion versus porosity for the uneroded sections at both sites (Fig. 3) demonstrates the primary correlation between these two properties and also shows the increasingly rapid increase in cohesion with decreasing porosity (Bray and Karig, 1986).

In summary, we note a marked, roughly linear increase in cohesion with depth as well as a continuing increase in cohesion well beyond the depth range tested on shipboard, although not necessarily with the same linear relationship. Nevertheless, a linear extrapolation would suggest values of cohesion on the order

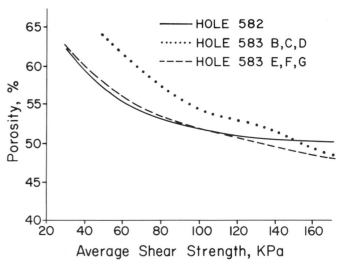

Figure 3. Relationship of porosity and cohesion as determined from shear strength measurements on DSDP samples in the Nankai toe. The higher cohesion at Hole 532B, C, D probably reflects the removal of surficial sediments by erosion (Bray and Karig, 1986).

of 1 MPa at depths of 1 km at the wedge toe. There is also a predictable arcward increase in the gradient of cohesion, reflecting the arcward increase in porosity-depth gradients.

MECHANICAL PROPERTIES FROM STRUCTURAL ANALYSIS IN THE PRISM TOE

At relatively low effective confining stress, most sediments fail in brittle fracture, and the shear strength on these failure surfaces is approximated by the Coulomb criteria. Two important aspects of this approximation are: 1) that the failure strength (τ_m) is a linear function of the effective normal stress on the failure surface (the effective normal stress, σ_n', being the total normal stress minus pore pressure), or $\tau_m = C_0 + \mu_m \sigma_n'$, where μ_m, or alternatively $\tan \phi$, is a property of the material termed the coefficient of internal friction, and 2) that the angle ψ between the failure surface and direction of maximum (compressive) principal stress (σ_1) is a function of μm_m: $\psi = \pi/4 - \arctan \mu m_m/2 = \pi/4 - \phi/2$. In the situation where a conjugate set of failure surfaces develop, the acute angle between fractures is 2ψ and the determination of μm_m follows directly.

Several structural features observed in the DSDP drill cores and on the seismic reflection profile provide evidence for the orientation of stress and for the value of μm_m in the toe of the Nankai wedge. These include a conjugate set of kink or deformation bands, a conjugate set of shear fractures, and well defined dips of the imbricate thrusts that rise from the basal décollement. In addition, the dips of the basal décollement and the prism surface, which are very well defined on a reference seismic reflection profile (Fig. 2; Nasu and others, 1982) help to constrain the magnitude of stress components.

Figure 4. Typical shear surface across a split DSDP core from 350-m sub-bottom in Hole 583F. Surfaces form a conjugate set with reverse offset and dip-slip slickenlines or grooves. The treads on the stepped surface are postulated to be Riedel fractures. Scale is in cm.

Deformation Bands

At depths greater than about 350 m in DSDP holes 298, 583F, and 583G, narrow, steeply dipping zones of minor dislocation with a reverse sense of slip are common features of clay-rich cores (Lundberg and Karig, 1986). These zones are comprised of anastomosing surfaces of dark, finer-grained phyllosilicates, and might be termed kink or deformation bands.

These bands occur in conjugate sets, although one set strongly predominates in any single core sample. Both sets dip about 60°, although the poor statistics permit a variation of several degrees. Because of the reverse slip on both sets, the direction of the maximum principal stress (σ_1) is assumed to bisect the obtuse (120°) angle and to be nearly horizontal.

These small-scale deformation bands in the cores have been correlated with a 60° north-dipping set of seismic discontinuities imaged in the proto-thrust zone (Fig. 2; Karig, 1986a), suggesting that these bands formed in the proto-thrust zone (Lundberg and Karig, 1986). Moreover, the single north-dipping set of seismic discontinuities would suggest first, that the predominant set of deformation bands also dips north, and second, that σ_1 had a very slight dip to the south. This latter inference is suggested by experiments of Gay and Weiss (1974), and would be expected, since σ_1 in this cohesive material should dip southward at least as steeply as the 1.2° surface slope (Dahlen and others, 1984).

A sub-horizontal σ_1 in the protothrust zone would imply

that the shear strength along the décollement just beneath the base of the trench fill is very low in comparison to that within the trench fill clastics. This stress orientation also supports the deformation model of uniform horizontal flow in this region.

Conjugate Shear Fractures

In addition to the deformation bands, a conjugate set of well developed shear surfaces is displayed in cores from DSDP holes 583F and 583G below about 350 m (Lundberg and Karig, 1986) as well as in hole 298, 10 km farther upslope. These surfaces are characterized by down-dip steps, and dip-slip slickenlines and grooves (Fig. 4). The dominant dip of these fractures is near 40° but fractures clearly conjugate to the 40°-dipping set, as well as a moderate percentage of non-conjugate fractures, dip 20 to 34° with an average near 30°. Paleomagnetic data indicate that the intersection of the two fracture sets is horizontal and sub-parallel to the trench axis (Niitsuma, 1986). Reverse offsets (Lundberg and Karig, 1986) and a sub-horizontal acute (70°) interfracture angle indicate that the bisectrix of that angle parallels σ_1 and dips about 5°. The paleomagnetic data, as well as the requirement that σ_1 plunges in the direction of the surface slope, indicate that σ_1 plunges toward the south.

These fractures appear to be surfaces of brittle failure, and the interfracture angle (2ψ) of 70° thus indicates a value of μ_m of 0.36, or $\phi = 20°$ for this clay-rich siltstone. The steps on the fracture surface dip about 10° less steeply than the fracture. Step surfaces penetrate into and die out in the country rock, suggesting that they are Riedel fractures that preceded development of the throughgoing displacement surface (e.g., Morgenstern and Tchalenko, 1967). Because Riedel fractures form at an angle near $\phi/2$ from the major displacement surface (Tchalenko, 1968), another estimate of μ_m, very similar to that above, is obtained.

Frontal Thrust Zone

The frontal thrust zone, which generated the structural terrace on which DSDP Site 583 was drilled, is a major shear surface that probably reflects the bulk strength of the displaced trench fill at failure conditions. Experimental studies of shear zones (e.g., Tchalenko, 1968) suggest that this throughgoing shear developed slightly later than the conjugate shear fractures but with similar stress conditions. Rotation of the stress vector toward the shear surface occurs following failure and reduction of shear strength on the major shear surface (Morgenstern and Tchalenko, 1967). Because Riedel fractures form at an angle near $\phi/2$ from the major displacement surface (Tchalenko, 1968), another estimate of μ_m, very similar to that above, is obtained.

Frontal Thrust Zone

The frontal thrust zone, which generated the structural terrace on which DSDP Site 583 was drilled, is a major shear surface that probably reflects the bulk strength of the displaced

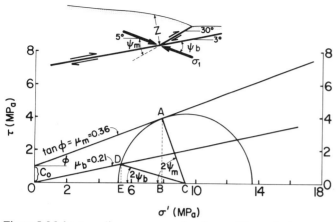

Figure 5. Mohr stress diagram representing the condition at the intersection of the frontal thrust and the basal décollement (see upper diagram). The line tangent to the Mohr circle represents failure at fracture or peak strength on the frontal thrust; $\tau_m = C_0 + \mu_m\sigma_n'$. The lower line represents failure by sliding at residual strength on the décollement; $\tau_b = \mu_m\sigma_n'$. The determination of the stress state is discussed in the text.

trench fill at failure conditions. Experimental studies of shear zones (e.g., Tchalenko, 1968) suggest that this throughgoing shear developed slightly later than the conjugate shear fractures but with similar stress conditions. Rotation of the stress vector toward the shear surface occurs following failure and reduction of shear strength on the major shear surface (Morgenstern and Tchalenko, 1967).

The frontal thrust has a remarkably planar, 30°N dipping surface, which is best seen after a balanced structural section is restored (Karig, 1986a). The lack of folding associated with the thrust, except over the upper ramp corner, indicates that it can be treated as a fracture, again related to the shear strength of the sediment column at the time of fault initiation.

The fault dip is very similar to the shallower, north-dipping fracture set, which would suggest a similar value for μ_m of 0.36 for the bulk sediment section. Even if the inclination of σ_1 decreased between the development of the fractures and the thrust, it must still dip at least as steeply southward as the surface slope (originally 1° – 2°), so that $\psi > 32°$ and $\mu_m < 0.49$.

The series of imbricate or older frontal thrusts rising from the décollement arcward of this basal shear also appear to have originated as shear fractures (Karig, 1986a). Restoration of displacement, although hampered by diffuse deformation, suggests initial dips of 25 to 30° and thus values of μ_m, similar to that of the present frontal thrust.

Basal Décollement

The basal décollement, which forms the base of the accretionary wedge, and from which the imbricate thrusts rise, is also well constrained by the reference seismic profile (Fig. 2). Differential displacement between the wedge and its substrate begins beneath the protothrust zone, apparently close to the contact

between the trench fill and the hemipelagic section of the Shikoku basin (Karig, 1986a). Beneath the first thrust sheet the décollement drops to a position near the top of an early Pliocene turbidite sequence, at which level it remains for at least 25 km. The dip of the décollement over this distance is that of the downgoing plate, which gradually increases arcward, but beneath the toe of the accretionary wedge it averages about 3°.

This constancy of stratigraphic position of the décollement beneath the wedge toe and the low (5°) dip of σ at Site 583 imply a lower shear strength within the décollement than in the surrounding material. The localization of minimum strength just above the Pliocene turbidites (Fig. 2) is probably due in part to a lower fracture strength in the hemipelagic sediments than in the sand-rich turbidites. A second factor, however, is that, after a few cm of displacement, the shear zone would be at a state of residual strength, which is generally less than the fracture strength in sediments that fail brittlely.

STRESS CONDITIONS AT THE INTERSECTION OF THE FRONTAL THRUST AND DÉCOLLEMENT

The intersection of the frontal imbricate thrust with the basal décollement is a unique location where, at initiation of thrusting, sediment is simultaneously at a condition of fracture strength on the imbricate thrust and at residual strength along the décollement. Assuming a brittle Coulomb response, we can use the orientation of the stress in the overlying wedge, together with the mechanical properties deduced from the structures to estimate both the frictional coefficient on the décollement (μ_b) and the effective stress state. The mechanical state of sediment at this position is graphically analyzed with a Mohr stress diagram (Fig. 5). On this diagram both the fracture strength and residual strength are assumed to be linear functions of the effective normal stress, although both curves are, in reality, somewhat non-linear.

Mechanical conditions at the intersection of the frontal thrust and the décollement must be estimated from the structural geometry, as expressed on the reflection profile and as extrapolated from the drilling results at shallower levels. Moreover, the structural geometries must be corrected back to those that existed at the initiation of thrusting.

The frontal thrust developed with a constant 30° dip to a depth as close to the décollement as can be resolved on the seismic section. This geometry strengthens the assumption that the orientation of σ_1 and the value of μ_m do not change markedly between the depth penetrated during drilling ($\approx$500 m) and the décollement. Thus the angles ψ_m and ψ_b, between σ_1 and the frontal thrust and the décollement respectively, are assumed as constant with depth in this analysis. With these conditions, the residual strength along the décollement (τ_b) is:

$$\tau_b = \sigma_n' \mu_b = \frac{\sigma_x' - \sigma_z'}{2} \tan 2\psi_b \tag{1}$$

where the x axis is constructed parallel to the décollement.

A derivation similar to that of Davis and others (1983) can

now be developed to determine μ_b and the state of stress in terms of measured or estimated parameters. Because both fracture and residual strength conditions are occurring at a single stress state, we can relate the mechanical parameters at these conditions through the value of differential stress, $\sigma_1 - \sigma_3$. On the Mohr diagram (Fig. 5), point A represents the fracture strength and D represents residual strength. Trigonometric relationships between triangles ABC and EDC can be used to show:

$$\frac{\sigma_1' - \sigma_3'}{2} = \frac{\sigma_x' + \sigma_z'}{2} \sin \phi_m + C_0 \cos \phi_m \qquad (2)$$

$$\frac{\sigma_1' - \sigma_3'}{2} = \frac{\sigma_x' + \sigma_z'}{2} \sec 2\psi_b. \qquad (3)$$

Combining equations 2 and 3 to eliminate $\sigma_1' - \sigma_3'$, and simplifying,

$$\frac{\sigma_x' - \sigma_z'}{2} = \frac{\sigma_z'}{\sec 2\psi_b \csc \phi_m - 1} + \frac{C_0}{\sec 2\psi_b \sec \phi_m - \tan \phi_m}. \qquad (4)$$

If we substitute equation 4 into equation 1 to eliminate $\sigma_x' - \sigma_z'$, and because $\sigma_n' = \sigma_z'$ in our co-ordinate frame

$$\mu_b = \frac{\tan 2\psi_b}{\sec 2\psi_b \csc \phi_m - 1} + \frac{C_0 \tan 2\psi_b}{\sigma_z' (\sec 2\psi_b \sec \phi_m - \tan \phi_m)}. \qquad (5)$$

We further assume that σ_z' is equivalent to the vertical stress because of the low (3°) dip of the décollement. The value of σ_z' can then be estimated in terms of overburden; $\bar{\rho}_b$, the mean bulk density; g, the gravitational acceleration; and λ, the excess pore pressure factor of Hubbert and Rubey (1959) as modified by Davis and others (1983) for submarine wedges: $\sigma_z' = \bar{\rho}_b g z(1-\lambda)$. Because both forms of failure are assumed to have occurred in the single small region of the fault intersection, λ is assumed to be the same for both failure surfaces. If there are very sharp pore-pressure gradients adjacent to the décollement, this assumption would have to be modified, but, with the available data, any more complicated relationship is as yet unwarranted.

The value of $\bar{\rho}_b$ at the fault intersection, before displacement occurred on the frontal thrust, is estimated as 2.0 g/cm³ (Bray and Karig, 1985a). This value, taken from a point 3 km south of the present intersection, should also represent the density at original depth (1 km) of the fault intersection (z). Substitution of these values and of the values obtained earlier ($\psi_b = 8°$, $\psi_m = 35°$, $\phi_m = 20°$ and $C_0 = 1$MPa) lead to a simple relationship between μ_b and λ (Fig. 6):

$$\mu_b = -.14 + \frac{0.0197}{(1 - \lambda)}. \qquad (6)$$

In this situation, where μ_b bears a known relationship with τ_b (equation 1), the calculated value of μ_b is dependent on the pore fluid pressure because of the effect of pore fluid pressure on the normal stress. Pore pressures have not been measured in the Nankai wedge, but they must at least be hydrostatic, in which case $\lambda = 0.5$ and $\mu_b = 0.18$. Because overpressured conditions

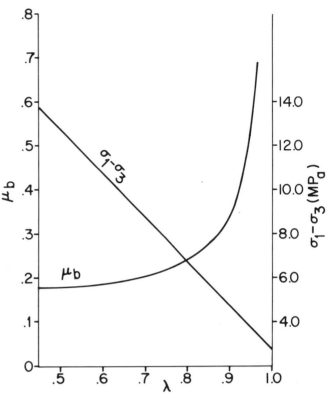

Figure 6. Possible variations of sliding friction (μ_b) and differential stress ($\sigma_1 - \sigma_3$) as functions of λ for the mechanical state at the intersection of the frontal thrust and the basal décollement. If $u_b < = 0.36$, then $\lambda < 0.9$, but local considerations suggest that $u_b \approx 0.2$ and $\lambda = 0.75$.

appear to prevail in accretionary prisms (e.g., Moore and von Huene, 1980), a higher value of λ is likely. The maximum value of λ should be near 0.85, where $\mu_b = \mu_m$, but geotechnical experiments indicate that μ_b is generally significantly lower than μ_b for normally to overconsolidated sediments that fail brittlely (e.g., Mitchell, 1976).

A value of λ between 0.7 and 0.8 is felt most reasonable not only because of the limiting values but also because the rapid dewatering of hemipelagic strata beneath the trench wedge, as deduced from measured porosities and reduction in thickness (Bray and Karig, 1985b, in preparation), lead to an estimate of $\lambda \approx 0.6$ in that setting. Pore fluid overpressure is expected to increase arcward into the prism toe as the tectonically induced load increases. If $\lambda \approx 0.75$, μ_b would be about 0.2 (Fig. 6), which is consistent with laboratory derived values for clays of moderate porosity (e.g., Kenny, 1967).

With these estimated mechanical conditions at the fault intersection, the differential stress level ($\sigma_1' - \sigma_3'$) capable of being supported can also be determined. Either a combination of equations 3 and 5, or examination of triangle ODE on the Mohr diagram leads to:

$$\sigma_1' - \sigma_3' = \frac{2(1 - \lambda) \, \rho_b g z \mu_b}{\sin 2\psi_b}. \qquad (8)$$

The combination of equation 6 with equation 7 to eliminate μ_b, followed by numerical evaluation with parameters estimated in the Nankai Trough produces a simple linear relationship: $\sigma_1' - \sigma_3' = 19.91 \, (1 - \lambda) + 2.80$ (in MPa). Values of λ between 0.7 and 0.8 lead to a supportable differential stress ($\sigma_1' - \sigma_3'$) near 8 MPa (Fig. 6). Higher differential stresses would require lower pore pressures and consequently even lower values of μ_b.

CROSS-SECTIONAL SHAPE OF THE ACCRETIONARY WEDGE

The cross-sectional shape of an accretionary wedge is an important boundary condition because it constrains distribution of deformation of the accreted sediments. In isolation it is, however, a non-unique constraint, in that the shape has been matched by Coulomb, plastic and viscous rheologies with suitable adjustment of parameters.

The simple Coulomb wedge models of Davis and others (1983) and Dahlen and others (1984), with constant physical and mechanical properties, do not match observed profiles of accreting wedges. A model wedge consisting of uniform non-cohesive sediment has a constant slope, whereas a model with constant property, cohesive sediments has a concave upward toe. In reality, the frontal regions (several tens of km) of almost all accreting wedges are convex upward, many of them strongly so.

This apparent contradiction has since been recognized in the lesser Antilles arc by Davis (1984), who suggests that the more porous sediments near the toe behave with perfect plasticity, with a strength dominated by a pressure-independent cohesion. Alternative explanations for the observed convexity can be made by examining variations in porosity and in distribution of deformation across the wedge. Both of these variations imply an arcward increase in strength.

Effect of Porosity Change

One effect of arcward-decreasing average porosity in accreted sediments is an arcward increase in the average density of the accretionary wedge. This density distribution modifies the force balance of columns within a Coulomb wedge and reduces the surface slope as density increases. The effect of density increase was tested by calculating the change in wedge-slope using equation 18 of Davis and others (1983) for columns with constant and varying (observed) bulk density. In this calculation, a constant strength constraint is assumed to separate the effects of simple porosity change from that of increasing strength, which might be caused by a number of processes in addition to decrease of porosity. This calculation shows that even with an exceptionally large increase in density, from 2.0 gr/cm^3 to 2.7 gr/cm^3, the slope would decrease less than 0.5°. The result of this estimate indicates that, although the arcward reduction in porosity is a factor in explaining the wedge profile, it is not sufficient, and that another contributing process must be sought.

Distribution of Deformation

The profile of an accretionary wedge can also be examined in terms of the distribution of deformation. Thus, the more concentrated the horizontal shortening near the wedge toe, the more pronounced would be its surface convexity. In the Nankai wedge, the distribution of deformation has been estimated using a structural analysis of the seismic profile as well as several methods based on the conservation of mass flow (Karig, 1986b). This observed distribution of deformation can be compared with that which can be calculated for a homogeneous non-cohesive Coulomb wedge with a fixed apical angle ($\alpha + \beta$). This approach can also be applied to a cohesive Coulomb wedge, in which the deformation is not as concentrated toward the toe as in a non-cohesive wedge.

A non-cohesive constant-strength wedge has a fixed surface slope if the basal surface is planar (Davis and others, 1983). The slow and gradual increase in the dip of the basal décollement beneath the first 20 to 30 km of the Nankai wedge justifies the simplifying assumption of a constant basal slope beneath the toe and allows a comparison of the surface slope of the Nankai wedge with that of the constant-strength Coulomb model having a similar value of β.

This comparison of the instantaneous distribution of deformation across the wedge toe requires the determination of a function (γ) termed the shortening ratio (Karig, 1986a). The shortening ratio is defined as $\gamma = \ell - \ell_0/\ell$, where ℓ_0 is the original dimension and ℓ the observed (present) dimension. Shortening ratio is analogous to strain, but is referred to the present, observed state of deformation and is positive for a decrease in dimension. The instantaneous rate of horizontal shortening is then $d\gamma/dt$.

The vertical shortening ratio is $\gamma_z = 1 - (z_0/z)$, where z is the thickness at a distance x from the wedge toe and z_0 is the thickness at the toe. The horizontal gradient of γ_z is

$$\frac{\partial \gamma_z}{\partial x} = \frac{z_0 \, dz}{z^2 \, dx} \tag{9}$$

but dz/dx in the simple Coulomb wedge model is $\tan \alpha + \tan \beta$, which is closely approximated by $\tan (\alpha + \beta)$ for small angles. Thus

$$\frac{\partial \gamma_z}{\partial x} = \frac{z_0}{z} \tan (\alpha + \beta). \tag{10}$$

If we consider the model wedge to have constant porosity, volume is conserved, and the horizontal shortening ratio,

$$\gamma_x = \frac{\gamma_z}{1 - \gamma_z}. \tag{11}$$

Substitution of ϕ_z for the non-cohesive Coulomb wedge leads to:

$$\gamma_x = \frac{x}{z_0} \tan (\alpha + \beta). \tag{12}$$

To determine the instantaneous distribution of horizontal

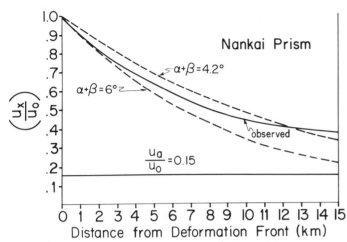

Figure 7. Comparison of the observed distribution of instantaneous deformation across the toe of the Nankai wedge with those calculated for noncohesive, constant strength wedges of different tapers. Instantaneous shortening is proportional to the slope of those curves, $\partial u/\partial x$, where u is the horizontal particle velocity at x, the distance from the deformation front. These curves are normalized to u_0, the subduction velocity. Even in the constant strength wedge, shortening is concentrated toward the wedge toe, but not as much as observed. This difference requires arcward increasing strength across the wedge toe.

shortening, we assume a very simple flow model of uniform horizontal flattening, in which $\partial \gamma_x/\partial_z = 0$. This assumption is violated by the discrete thrust faults and by the trenchward dip of σ_1, but comparison of model and observed distribution of data (Karig, 1968a) show adequate agreement in the toe of the Nankai wedge. A simple form of the continuity equation: $\partial \gamma_x/\partial_t = \partial u/\partial_x$, where u is the horizontal particle velocity, can be recast as:

$$\frac{\partial \gamma_x}{\partial x} = \frac{\partial \ln u}{\partial x} \qquad (13)$$

and integrated from $\mu = \mu_0$ at x = 0 and $\mu = \mu_x$ at x. A plot of velocity (u) versus distance from the deformation front (x) then describes the distribution of instantaneous deformation as the slope of the curve (Fig. 7). In this calculation the normalized ratio, u_x/u_0, is used, where u_x is the horizontal velocity at distance x and u_0 is the subduction velocity acting at x = 0. This normalization avoids the problem of uncertainties in subduction rate and gives fractional values of instantaneous deformation across the wedge.

The exponential nature of this curve shows that even in a constant-strength wedge with a constant taper, the instantaneous horizontal shortening is concentrated toward the wedge toe. However, the curves of velocity versus distance for the constant-strength wedge are less convex upward than the curve derived from observed deformation, indicating that observed instantaneous deformation is more strongly concentrated toward the wedge toe than is predicted by the constant-strength, non-cohesive Coulomb model.

Thus the convexity of accretionary wedge profiles can be

explained principally by the greater concentration of horizontal shortening toward the toe than in a constant property wedge. Because of the relationship between stress and strain, this is equivalent to concluding that there must be greater arcward increase in strength in a real wedge than that which results from the increased mean stress induced by increasing wedge thickness. This increased strength could result from variations across the wedge in either mechanical properties or in effective mean stresses. The nature of those variations and their relative importance is a serious problem because there are very few relevant data. Nevertheless, some constraints can be gleaned from the results of experimental studies of rocks and soil, coupled with observations of structural patterns in the Nankai accretionary wedge.

DISCUSSION

The mechanical properties of the sediments observed in the toe of an accretionary wedge must be interpreted in light of two quite disparate bodies of experimental data collected from geophysical rock mechanics and from geotechnical engineering. Most studies in rock mechanics deal with materials with low porosity at moderate to high differential stress levels ($10^2 - 10^4$ MPa) whereas geotechnical experiments are usually restricted to high porosity "soils" subjected to stresses of 0.1 to 1 MPa. The range of effective differential stress in the sediments studied in the wedge toe is intermediate, from 1 and 10 MPa, a range from which very few data have been collected. This data gap is even more pronounced because the perspectives and objectives in the two disciplines are not easily extrapolated to this intermediate field. In rock mechanics, for example, the porosity remains low and nearly constant during deformation, even if pore fluid is unconfined. On the other hand, the effect of pore fluid during deformation is critical in the range of porosities explored by geotechnical engineers.

Both maximum and residual strengths of rocks and soils are adequately modeled by a pressure-dependent Coulomb criterion, but how the Coulomb parameters of μ and C might vary as functions of porosity, lithology, or other factors is very poorly known. To complicate the situation, the porosity of a sediment is a function of an applied effective stress condition, but for deviatoric stresses in general, even this relationship is not calibrated.

Some idea of the variations of μ and C in porous sediments can be extracted from the two areas of experimentation. When coupled with a yield criteria from soil mechanics, these variations suggest the relative importance of μ and C as functions of porosity and of the underlying relationship between porosity and applied stress. To the extent that these relationships are understood, the observed distribution of porosity and geometry in the toe of the Nankai and several other wedge toes can then serve as powerful constraints.

Coefficients of Friction

Experiments in rock mechanics have led to the conclusion that, for a wide variety of rock types, coefficients of friction vary remarkably little. In particular, for almost all rocks at a residual strength state, where cohesion is very small, μ_b is about 0.85 for mean stresses up to 200 MPa (Byerlee, 1978). Lower values of μ_b for some clay-rich rocks are recognized (e.g., Wang and others, 1980), but these are implied to be anomalous. Coefficients of friction at maximum or fracture strength, μ_m, cannot be as simply summarized but, for effective mean stresses up to 200 MPa, are significantly higher than μ_b (e.g., Byerlee, 1967, 1075).

In contrast, the more porous sediments, for which peak strengths are most often obtained in geotechnical experiments, show values of μ_m that can be less than 0.2 for clay-rich sediment to a maximum near 0.7 for fine sand (e.g., Mitchell, 1976). Tests of the residual state again commonly show a reduced strength that is reflected by a reduction in the coefficient of friction (Kenney, 1967).

One of the few extensive test programs of sediments having a wide range of porosities, by Hoshino and others (1972), produced varied but often high values of μ_m and μ_b, which led Davis and others (1983) and Dahlen and others (1984) to extrapolate the rock mechanics data to sediments in general. The samples of Hoshino and others (1972) were tested dry, however, which generally leads to frictional coefficients of μ_m in clay-bearing rocks that are much larger than those in a saturated condition (Goodman, 1980; Hoshino, 1981).

The values of μ_m and μ_b deduced from the structural fabric of the moderately porous (30–40%) sediments in the toe of the Nankai wedge are clearly much lower than those obtained in rock-mechanics tests and by Hoshino and others (1972). They are much more similar to the values cited as examples by Mitchell (1976), Lambe and Whitman (1969), and Kenney (1967) in the geotechnical literature.

The greater values of frictional coefficients derived from strong, low porosity rocks than from soft, porous sediments might reflect differences in the conditions of stress, in characteristics associated with lithology, or to the state of porosity itself. The greater mean stresses used in rock mechanics cannot be responsible because, for both soft sediment (e.g., Mitchell, 1976) and hard rock (e.g., Byerlee, 1967; Goodman, 1980), the coefficients of friction decrease with increasing mean stress, as reflected in the curvature of Mohr-Coulomb strength envelopes. Differences in mineralogy and grain size (Kenney, 1967; Koerner, 1970; Skempton, 1964) clearly affect frictional coefficients, but these characteristics do not systematically change with the changing physical state of the sediment. The frictional coefficients in a given porous sediment are interpreted as varying primarily with the state of porosity, although this only removes the problem to an understanding of the relationship between the porosity in a sediment and the applied stress responsible for that porosity.

Coefficient of Cohesion

The coefficient of cohesion for porous sediments has received very little attention, and worse, has been measured in several different ways. In addition to true cohesion (C_0), mea-

sured at $\sigma_n' = 0$, and apparent cohesion (C_a), which is the extrapolation of the linear Coulomb relationship to $\sigma_n' = 0$, another measure of cohesion is the difference between fracture strength and frictional strength at a given mean stress (Byerlee, 1967). The Coulomb model for wedges implicitly uses C_a, which is greater than C_0 by the convexity of the observed shear strength versus normal stress relationship. This convexity results in an increase in C_a with increasing mean and normal stress.

Cohesion is also known, if only qualitatively, to vary with lithology and porosity. In highly porous sediments, where cementation is not a major factor, cohesion is much greater for clay-rich than sand-rich material, but it is still very low (Fig. 3). The increase in cohesion with decreasing porosity in argillaceous sediments can be estimated by the data presented previously (Fig. 3) and by analysis of the Mohr-Coulomb fracture strength envelopes generated by Hoshino and others (1972). In the Nankai Trough sediments, C_0 was measured in saturated, high porosity sediments, providing minimum values for C_a, whereas the measurements of Hoshino and others (1972) were made on dry sediments, which should result in much greater cohesion than for saturated clay-rich sediments. These data suggest that C_a increases, perhaps exponentially, from about 0.1 MPa near 55% porosity to something less than 20 MPa at 20% porosity.

In the convex upward sections of the Nankai wedge, most of the sediments have porosities between 50% and 15%, and about half of this material is estimated to be sand-rich (Kagami, Karig, and others, 1986). Moreover, these sediments, particularly the deeper and more highly deformed, can be assumed to be highly fractured. Bulk cohesion should reflect some combination of the intrinsic cohesion of the different lithologies and the resistive effects of the fracture geometry on frictional sliding. Thus, for lightly cemented clastic wedge toes, cohesion appears to be a porosity dependent parameter that probably varies between 0.1 MPa and less than 10 MPa (Fig. 8).

Porosity and Strength

Porosity clearly has a very important effect on sediment strength through its relationship with both C and μ. Sediment porosity, in turn, is dependent on effective mean stress (σ_m'), deviatoric stress ($\sigma_1 - \sigma_3$), and the state of strain, as well as on lithology. For the uniaxial strain conditions of typical basinal strata, the decrease of porosity with increasing effective mean stress is quite well calibrated (see references in Bray and Karig, 1985a). Not as well-known to geologists is that biaxial or triaxial strain will cause a greater porosity decrease than will uniaxial strain at the same effective mean stress (Fig. 9). This porosity reduction in soils begins as soon as the strain becomes biaxial and continues, with complications near peak strength, to a maximum at the residual strength.

Much of this response is embodied in the critical state concept of soil mechanics (Schofield and Wroth, 1968), which theorizes that at a given mean stress a sediment will continue to deform after reaching a unique state of yield strength or support-

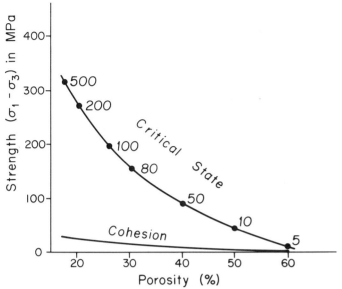

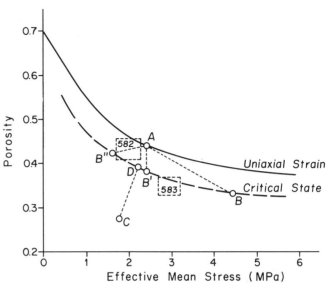

Figure 8. Shear strength versus porosity at critical stage for argillaceous sediments tested dry by Hoshino and others (1972). This very approximate projection of the critical-state line was estimated by assuming that the confining pressure at which the strain became transitional from brittle to ductile defined the critical state. Mean stresses determined at this state are shown along the critical-state line. Although the strength of these dry samples is much greater than for saturated sediments, these data show the very marked, probably exponential increase in shear strength with decrease in porosity at stress-porosity equilibrium. The cohesive component of strength was determined by extrapolating the Mohr strength envelopes of Hoshino and others (1972) to zero normal stress. At stress-porosity equilibrium (critical state), cohesion is a small fraction of total strength for all porosities.

Figure 9. Conceptual diagram of the relationship between porosity and effective mean stress for uniaxial strain and biaxial strain at critical state for a porous sediment (after Kezdi, 1974). The uniaxial curve is generated from the results of an unpublished consolidation test on artificial sediment similar to the silty claystones in the Nankai trough at 400 m in DSDP Hole 582, which are correlative with the sheared sediments at 400 m in Hole 583. The calculated in situ porosity-mean stress condition for the uniaxially consolidated sediment in hole 582 is shown by the upper dashed box. The critical state or yield curve is entirely hypothetical, but is consistent in shape with those generated by soil mechanics experiments (e.g., Schofield and Wroth, 1968) and in magnitude with calculated porosity strength relations for sediment at 400 m in hole 583 (lower dashed box). The three paths from A to B represent possible conditions whereby dewatering could occur as the sediment moved from a position in the trench fill into the toe of the accretionary wedge where it would be at a state of failure. Here the decrease in effective mean stress from B to B' to B" would represent increasing values of over pressure.

able differential stress without change of porosity. This concept has proved very useful in defining the mechanical state of deforming soils, but its applicability to lower porosity, stronger sediments, where the fabric is modified during strain and the modes of deformation may differ, has not been adequately demonstrated (Wood and Wroth, 1979).

These relationships of porosity and strength imply that when a sediment is at a state of shear failure in equilibrium with its porosity, both C and μ are, in effect, pressure dependent. In particular, μ and C at the yield state are not dependent upon pore pressure, except as it is a component of the effective mean stress. Thus, if sediments in the wedge toe were at failure and if their porosities were in equilibrium with the applied stress, no matter how overpressured they might be, their strength and the values of μ and C could be estimated from observed porosities, once yield relationships had been experimentally established. However, if the effective mean stress becomes lower than this equilibrium value, by erosion of overburden or by a subsequent increase in pore-pressure, μ and C do not significantly decrease. Under these conditions the two terms of the Coulomb strength equation become decoupled, and only the frictional term remains dependent on σ_m'.

A very crude estimate of a yield relationship can be deter-

mined from the argillaceous sediment data of Hoshino and others (1972), with the recognition that these dry tests produced exaggerated strength values (Fig. 8). The equilibrium mean stress at failure for each porosity was estimated as that occurring when the deformation fabric and stress-strain curve changed from brittle to ductile. At this transition, the porosity change during deformation is small and the sediment is approaching its critical state. The cohesive component of strength determined from this data set is a small fraction of the total sediment strength at all porosities and one that decreases with decreasing porosity.

Arcward Increase in Prism Strength

The arcward increase in strength across the toe of an accretionary wedge that was deduced from the distribution of deformation might immediately be attributed to the observed arcward decrease in porosity. Before this simple correlation is assumed, however, other factors that might affect the wedge strength, including bulk anisotropy and variations in pore pressure should be considered.

Sediment strength in a wedge must be assumed to be heterogeneous and anisotropic. Heterogeneity stems from the concentration of deformation in zones and from the dependency of strength on strain, before and after initial fracture. Anisotropy results from the layering of sediment with different composition and strength. This effect also is a function of the angle between the layering and principal stresses (McLamore, 1966). In an accretionary wedge the arcward increase in mean stratal dip (Karig, 1986b), will require that a higher proportion of total strain occur within the stronger sands far from the toe than at the toe, where strain may be concentrated in weak clay-rich horizons. The effects of heterogeneity and, in particular, anisotropy are quite probably significant factors in the arcward increase of strength, but the smaller variations in values of μ resulting from changes in these factors than from porosity reduction suggest that they are of secondary importance.

A pressure-dependent strength is also affected by variations in pore pressure through its effect on effective normal stress. The resulting response depends critically on whether or not sediment porosity is in equilibrium with effective stress. If porosity is in equilibrium with applied stress, then cohesion must account for only a small fraction of sediment strength. On the other hand, if pore pressure in a sediment is raised so that effective stress becomes less than the equilibrium stress, then the frictional component of strength would be reduced without significantly reducing the cohesive component. If λ approached 1, a sediment with a given porosity would behave as if it has a pressure-independent strength.

Davis (1984) has suggested that such a cohesion-dominated strength might explain the convex toe of the Lesser Antilles wedge, and he has modeled the sediment as a pressure-independent, perfectly plastic material. The very high λ value (>0.9) inferred from drilling into the décollement (Moore and Biju-Duval, 1984) is cited as support for this condition, but a deformation-induced reduction of porosity in the overlying wedge (Moore and Biju-Duval, 1984) would suggest that these sediments are actively dewatering and thus near porosity-stress equilibrium. If so, the pressure-dependent frictional component of strength must be the dominant factor of strength, at least within the wedge.

The sediments in the toe of the Nankai wedge are more rapidly dewatering than those of the Lesser Antilles (Bray and Karig, 1985a) and should also be in porosity-stress equilibrium. At a depth near 400 m in DSDP Site 583, where porosity of clay-rich strata is about 40% and the structural fabric permits an estimate of mechanical state, the cohesion (~0.4 MPa) is only about 25% of the total shear strength. The sand-rich strata, with a much higher coefficient of internal friction (>0.6) and almost no cohesion, should have a greater shear strength, almost all of which is in the pressure-dependent term.

An arcward reduction in λ has also been proposed to account for the increase in strength required by wedge convexity

(Suppe, 1983; Zhao and others, 1984), but several considerations argue against the application of this idea to the toes of accretionary wedges. There is no simple relationship between porosity and pore pressure, and no reason for decreasing pore pressure across the frontal region of wedges. To the contrary, the dehydration of clay and opaline silica and low-grade metamorphic reactions will generate new pore water that would tend to maintain high pore pressure (e.g., Burst, 1976). Furthermore, the decreased permeability that accompanies decreased porosity would also tend to maintain high pore pressure, even at very low porosity. If λ values do decrease arcward across the wedge, the resultant increased mean stress would lead to enhanced porosity reduction of a sediment element, with attendant increases in C_a and μ_m.

The preceding discussion leads to the conclusion that the required arcward increase in strength across the toe of an accretionary wedge is due primarily to the increase in coefficient of friction that results from a reduction of porosity. Local exceptions, where the sediment is not in porosity-stress equilibrium, are to be expected. This conclusion probably does not extend to sub-aerial thrust belts where massive erosion has reduced the mean stress on previously dewatered sediments.

Some idea of the required magnitude of increase in strength across the toe of an accretionary wedge can be obtained by determining the ratio of (μ_m/μ_b) for a uniform, non-cohesive wedge at different distances from the deformation front using observed values of ρ_b, α, and β. From Davis and others (1983) and Dahlen and others (1984):

$$\alpha + \beta = \frac{(1 - \lambda)\,\mu_b + (1 - \dfrac{\rho_w}{\rho_b})\,\beta}{(1 - \dfrac{\rho_w}{\rho_b}) + (1 - \lambda)\,K}. \tag{14}$$

In this equation ρ_w is the density of water and K is a function dependent on the relative value of μ_m and μ_b. Approximate solutions for K, using either equation 28 of Davis and others (1983) or equation 18a of Dahlen and others (1984) are adequate for the accuracy required here.

With this approach, we are assuming constant values of $\bar{\rho}_b$ and μ_m throughout each column of wedge material at each distance for which the equation is evaluated. Lateral variations in $\bar{\rho}_b$ were shown to have small effects on the slope as does the horizontal variation in μ_m, but the increase in μ_m with depth will be shown to be a more serious problem. As before, λ is assumed to be constant throughout the wedge and on the décollement. Curves relating μ_m to μ_b can then be constructed at different points across the wedge (Fig. 10). This construction, done at points 3 km and 15 km behind the deformation front in the Nankai wedge (assuming a constant λ of 0.75), demonstrates that μ_m/μ_b increases significantly arcward, which requires a large arcward increase in μ_m for laterally uniform or arcward increasing values of μ_b on the décollement.

A similar conclusion is reached for the Sunda wedge using points 10 km and 30 km from the frontal thrust, at least for values of μ_b >0.3. However, the very steep (13°) average surface slope within 5 km of the frontal thrust leads to values of μ_m lower than

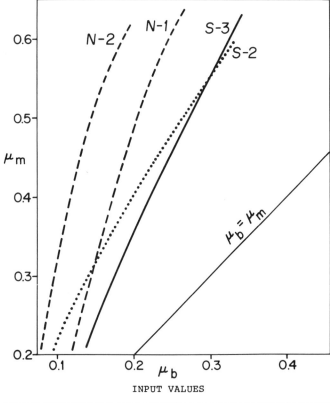

	χ (km)	α (°)	β (°)	ρb	λ
Nankai-1	3	1.5	3	2.0	.75
2	15	1.0	3	2.3	.75
Sunda-1(A)	.5	13	4°	2.1	.75
2(A)	10	5°	4°	2.3	.75
3(A)	30	2°	5°	2.5	.75

Figure 10. Calculated relationship of internal friction (μ_m) to sliding friction (μ_b) at various distances across the Nankai and Sunda wedges, using a constant strength model, but with different parameters at each point. The input parameters are shown in the table above. For most of both wedges, the slopes can be satisfied by a μ_m that increases arcward but is constant with depth ($[\partial\mu_m/\partial x]=0$). At the toe of the Sunda wedge, however, the steep slope would imply that $\mu_m < \mu_b$, which is physically implausible. Such steep slopes can best be explained by a wedge model in which μ_m increases with depth.

μ_b, which is unrealistic if the décollement is to persist. Such steep slopes can be qualitatively explained with a wedge model in which μ_m increases significantly with depth, which is also inferred from the relationships among porosity, depth, and μ_m that were developed earlier.

Variations in Sediment Strength During Strains

Even a wedge model with simply varying properties will not explain observations such as the large discontinuities in surface slope. These might be understood by considering the assumption that a Coulomb wedge is everywhere at a state of internal failure

(Davis and others, 1983). Whereas the amount of strain accumulated in wedge sediments is great enough to justify this approximation, the assumption that the state of failure is everywhere identical must be questioned. The magnitude of differential stress at failure is not only a function of such factors as lithology and porosity, but is also, in most sediments, a function of the state of strain. Consideration of this stress-strain relationship shows it to be a very important factor in the rheologic behavior of accretionary wedges.

The relationships among porosity, strain, and sediment strength are particularly complex and have not received much study. Two aspects of these relationships that are important to deformation in the toes of accretionary wedges are the mode of strain near failure as a function of effective mean stress, and the magnitude of supportable differential stresses at large post-failure strains.

The greater efficiency of sediment dewatering during biaxial strain than during uniaxial strain has already been noted. If a sediment, consolidated by uniaxial strain at some effective mean stress, is then deformed at a biaxial strain condition, porosity reduction can occur over a wide range of associated mean stress values (Fig. 9). If the increased deviatoric stress leading to failure is associated with hydrostatic pore pressures, σ_m' can increase markedly, with a commensurately large porosity drop (path A-B of Fig. 9). However, even relatively high pore pressures (large λ values), which cause a decrease in σ_m', can accompany a reduction in porosity, as shown by path A-B″.

The decrease in volume along the initial parts of these deformation and dewatering paths is accompanied by a ductile distortion without discrete failure surfaces or other observable structural features. The part of the dewatering path approaching peak strength and critical state is more complex and may include both ductile and brittle deformation.

Quite a different response will result if the mean stress exerted on the sediment during biaxial strain is well below that in equilibrium with the porosity at the critical state. This deformation, indicated by path C-D (Fig. 9), will be dilational and involve brittle shear because the sediment in the shear zone attempts to attain the higher equilibrium porosity. Mohr failure envelopes generated by triaxial tests on sedimentary rocks (e.g., Hoshino and others, 1972; Dunn and others, 1973; Byerlee, 1975) are, for most of the confining pressure range used, in this condition of overconsolidation, but wide departures from an equilibrium condition probably occur rarely in the toes of accretionary wedges.

Sediments in the toes of accretionary wedges are subjected to tectonic stresses that produce a nearly biaxial or plane strain. In the Nankai, Sunda, and several other wedges, sediments are generally compacting as they move into and through the wedge toe, which strongly indicates that porosity is in equilibrium with stress. Large strains and apparently pervasive fracturing further imply that most sediments are at failure or yield. Except for very highly strained sediments in shear zones, sediments in wedge toes should therefore be close to their critical states. If critical-state lines were experimentally calibrated, measurements of the in-situ porosity would allow a direct estimation of the effective mean stress, which would constrain the possible range of pore pressure.

The effect of biaxial strain on the dewatering of sediments in the Nankai wedge can be illustrated by comparing the porosity-mean stress states of a sediment element in the trench wedge at DSDP Hole 582 with the correlative element in the accretionary wedge of Hole 583. An element at a depth of 400 m in Hole 582 has an in situ porosity of 40–42% and is estimated to be subject to a hydrostatic pore pressure (Bray and Karig, 1985b and in preparation), which, with an average bulk density of the overlying sediment of 1.75 g/cm^3, leads to a λ value of 0.57. For this uniaxial consolidation, $\sigma_1' = \sigma_z' = 2.9$ MPa and, if K_0—the ratio of horizontal to vertical stress—is about 0.55 (Kezdi, 1974), then $\sigma_2' = \sigma_3' = 1.6$ MPa, and $\sigma_m' = 2.0$ MPa. For the correlative element in Hole 583, also at a depth near 400 m, the in situ porosity is approximately 35%, $\bar{\rho}_b = 2.0$ g/cm^3, and λ has been estimated to be 0.75. At this biaxial strain state, where σ_1' is sub-horizontal, $\sigma_2' = (K_0/[1 + K_0]) (\sigma_1' + \sigma_3')$. If K_0 is 0.5 for these less porous sediments, $\sigma_2' = 2.3$ MPa. The tectonic increment of stress more than offsets the effect of increased pore pressure, leading to an increased σ_m' of 3.1 MPa.

The porosity-mean stress state for the sediment element in Hole 582 falls remarkably close to a uniaxial consolidation curve generated for an artificial sediment of similar composition (Fig. 9). In contrast, that for the sediment in Hole 583 falls well below this curve, as it should be if the biaxial state of strain enhanced the porosity reduction. The critical state curve drawn through this data point is conceptual, but is consistent with those presented by Schofield and Wroth (1968) and Wood and Wroth (1979). This suggests that, at the same effective mean stress, the critical state has porosity about 5% lower than that of the uniaxial consolidation curve. An important inference to be drawn from this illustration is that, if there are extremely high pore pressures in some wedge toes (e.g., $\lambda > 0.9$), the porosity-depth gradients in those regions should be quite low, perhaps even lower than in the correlative undeformed sediments, because of the marked decrease in σ_m'.

Sediments biaxially strained at σ_m' in equilibrium with porosity are compactive before failure, but may display a low peak in shear strength and fail on discrete brittle shears (e.g., Mitchell, 1976). This is particularly true for clay-rich and other cohesive sediments. Data from soil mechanics also indicate that the transition from a brittle to a ductile strain fabric occurs at a higher mean stress for a given sediment than does the transition from dilative to compaction overall volume change. Thus sediments at states slightly below the uniaxial consolidation curve (mildly overconsolidated) will be initially compactive when subjected to biaxial strain at similar mean stresses, but may show discrete brittle shear surfaces and local dilation near a peak failure condition. The observations suggest that the strain fabric of sediments near the equilibrium state is very sensitive to slight variations in σ_m', which in an accretionary wedge could result from minor fluctuations in pore pressure.

Continued deformation after peak strength is reached results in a drop to residual strength or critical state accompanied by a further reduction of porosity (e.g., Skempton, 1964). The additional porosity loss probably occurs primarily in the shear zones where clay platelets become more highly aligned and sand grains may be comminuted. The lower porosity within shear zones of sediments deformed in porosity-stress equilibrium would contrast with the enhanced shear zone porosity in sediments deformed at mean stress lower than equilibrium, as has been well described for overconsolidated soils (Skempton, 1964; Mitchell, 1974).

Although still quite debatable, there is evidence for marked local decrease of porosity in shear zones in accretionary wedges. This condition was deduced from the impedance contrast of the seismic signature of the frontal thrust in the Nankai wedge (Bray and Karig, 1986) and was noted in cores through highly deformed zones in accreted sediments of the Middle American arc (Shepard and others, 1982). This phenomenon was also observed in the basal deformed sections of recent marine slumps (Bohlke and Bennett, 1980). In all these cases the zone of dewatering and shear is not a single surface but is at least several meters thick. Persistence of shear along the décollement, as well as along major imbricate thrusts, requires that strength be lower in these zones than in the surrounding sediment. The existence of convex upward slope sectors between the major active imbricate thrusts further suggests that these act as weak basal zones to Coulomb wedge segments.

We are thus faced with a situation where sediment becomes weaker despite a decrease in porosity. However, the significant thickness of these shear zones and early deactivation of some thrusts within the Nankai toe suggest that the sheared strata may also become strengthened with continued strain, and deformations thus migrate elsewhere or diffuse (Fig. 11). A few high-pressure strain tests on clay-filled shear surfaces (Morrow and others, 1982; Wang and Mao, 1979) also suggest a progressive increase of strength with large strain, perhaps accompanied by continuing porosity decrease.

Not only is this a quantitative question of competing processes affecting porosity and the coefficient of internal friction but also of variations in pore pressure. For lack of better data, λ has been assumed constant through the wedge, but there is reason to suspect that pore pressures may be anomalous in major shear zones. It has been suggested that pore pressures may be very high in major shear zones. Localization of calcareous crusts and thermal springs along the surface trace of such shears (Carson and others, 1984) has suggested that they are also zones of preferential egress of water from the wedge (Moore and Biju-Duval, 1984). Enhanced flow along the shears is quite plausible, even if porosity there is reduced, because permeability could be greatly increased by fracturing. However, if there is fluid flow into and along these shears, a decrease in pore pressure into the zone of fluid flow is required (Fig. 11c). This in turn would lead to local increases in the effective mean stress in the shear zone. Even without an increased coefficient of friction this would increase the strength of that zone.

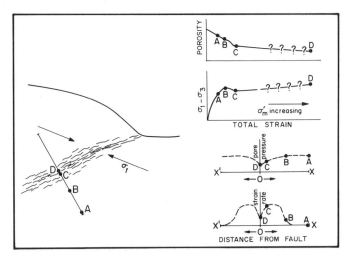

Figure 11. Conceptual diagram illustrating how shear dewatering might lead to strengthening within shear zones and to migration of zones of high strain rate. With continued post-failure strain, the porosity of a deformed sediment is postulated to decrease (panel 1). Because the supportable differential stress increases rapidly with decreasing porosity (at low porosities), the continued strain could lead to a condition where the sediment strength after large strain is greater than its peak strength (compare D with B in panel 2). If in addition, enhanced fracture permeability leads to preferential dewatering along the fault zone, a negative pore pressure gradient must exist approaching the shear zone (panel 3). Finally, if the strain rate is greatest at the position where the shear strength is a minimum, then both the effect of porosity change and differential pore pressure will lead to a strain rate maximum near point C (panel 4) and outward migration of deformation.

The recognized effects of porosity, strain, and pore pressure on strength may thus be combined to produce zones of minimum strength and maximum strain rate flanking the zone that earlier was the focus of maximum deformation (Fig. 11d). How far deformation diffusion might proceed and what conditions must exist before it could occur remain to be discovered.

CONCLUSIONS

The mechanical properties observed in sediments within the toe of the Nankai wedge support a pressure-dependent failure criterion. A simple Coulomb model suffices at present to explain the gross behavior of accretionary wedges, but this is in large part because the mechanical state of these bodies is poorly constrained. Data from the Nankai Trough show that the strength of the porous sediments in the wedge toe is much less than those of

hard rocks in general and from the values favored by Davis and others (1983) in particular. The strength of sediments in the wedge toe, which is primarily a function of porosity, increases both arcward and downward as porosity decreases, so that the Coulomb parameters for dense rock are quite probably applicable to the highly dewatered arcward sections of accretionary wedges.

Discontinuities in wedge profiles, in distribution of deformation, and probably in porosity are interpreted as zones of significantly lower failure strength within the sediment. These zones are identifiable as the persistent thrust fault that bound major amalgamated thrust packets. In such zones the mechanical behavior of sediment appears to be quite peculiar and leads to weakening followed by strengthening as conditions of strain, porosity, and pore pressure evolve. Although much of this behavior is predictable from the concept of critical state soil mechanics, there appear to be additional processes involved.

Improvements in the Coulomb model might include the use of effective bulk properties that vary with depth and position across the arc, as well as the division of the wedge into sub-zones on the basis of the discontinuities of slope and deformation. This more detailed approach to the mechanical analysis of accretionary wedges is not merely a refinement of the Coulomb model but is necessary before local structural observations can be used to generate mechanical coefficients that can be assumed to be valid as bulk properties. Spatial heterogeneities in physical and mechanical properties require that the local values be correctly integrated into the larger system.

As important, a much better understanding of the intrinsic mechanical behavior of porous sediments that dewater during deformation must be acquired. There is a particular need to explore the behavior of these sediments at high strains, as they exist in shear zones. These objectives will require in-situ observations of structures and physical properties of accretionary wedges as well as laboratory experiments in which strain can be correlated with applied stress.

ACKNOWLEDGMENTS

The ideas presented here were developed during lengthy discussions with a number of my graduate students and colleagues, perhaps the most influential of whom were Cindy Bray, Neil Lundberg, and Casey Moore. Dan Davis and Glen Stockmal provided thoughtful reviews, and Tony Dahlen saved me from at least one obvious error. This work was supported in part by NSF grant OCE-8018759.

REFERENCES

Bohlke, B. M., and Bennett, R. H., 1980, Mississippi Prodelta Crusts: A clay fabric and geotechnical analysis: Marine Geotechnology, v. 4, p. 55–82.

Boyce, R. E., 1976, Deep Sea Drilling Project procedures for shear strength measurement of clayey sediment using modified Wykeham Farrance laboratory vane apparatus: in Barker, P. F., Dalziel, I.W.D., and others, eds., Initial Reports of the Deep Sea Drilling Project: Washington, D.C., U.S. Government Printing Office, v. 36, p. 1059–1068.

Bray, C. J., and Karig, D. E., 1985a, Porosity of sediments in accretionary prisms and some implications for dewatering processes: Journal of Geophysical Research, v. 90, p. 768–778.

——, 1985b, Dewatering and extensional deformation of the Shikoku Basin hemipelagic sequence in the Nankai Trough: EOS Transactions of the American Geophysical Union, v. 66, p. 374.

——, 1986, Physical properties of sediments from the Nankai Trough, Deep Sea Drilling Project Leg 87A, Sites 582 and 583, in Kagami, H., Karig, D. E., and others, eds., Initial Reports of the Deep Sea Drilling Project: Washington, D.C., U.S. Government Printing Office, v. 87, p. 827–842.

Burst, J. F., 1976, Argillaceous sediment dewatering: Annual Review of Earth and Planetary Science, v. 4, p. 293–318.

——, 1967, Frictional characteristics of granite under high confining pressure: Journal of Geophysical Research, v. 72, p. 3639–3648.

Byerlee, J. D., 1975, The fracture strength of Weber sandstone, International Journal of Rock Mechanics and Mining Sciences, v. 12, p. 1–4.

——, J. D., 1978, Friction of rocks: Pure Applied Geophysics, v. 116, p. 615–626.

Carson, B., Ritger, S. D., and Suess, E., 1984, Precipitation of carbonate crust associated with subduction induced porewater expulsion: Washington-Oregon continental slope: Transactions of the American Geophysical Union, v. 65, p. 1089.

Chapple, W. M., 1978, Mechanics of thin-skinned fold and thrust belts: Geological Society of America Bulletin, v. 89, p. 1189–1198.

Dahlen, F. A., Suppe, J., and Davis, D., 1984, Mechanics of fold-and-thrust belts and accretionary wedges (continued): Cohesive Coulomb theory: Journal of Geophysical Research, v. 89, p. 10087–10102.

Davis, D. M., 1984, The compressive mechanics of accretionary wedges applied to the Leg 78A study area near Barbados, in Biju-Duval, B., Moore, J. C., and others, eds., Initial Reports of the Deep Sea Drilling Project: Washington, D.C., U.S. Government Printing Office, v. 78A, p. 659–582.

Davis, D., Suppe, J., and Dahlen, F. A., 1983, Mechanics of fold-and-thrust belts and accretionary wedges: Journal of Geophysical Research, v. 88, p. 1153–1172.

Dunn, D. E., LaFountain, L. J., and Jackson, R. E., 1973, Porosity dependence and mechanism of brittle fracture in sandstone: Journal of Geophysical Research, v. 78, p. 2403–2417.

Emerman, S. H., and Turcotte, D. L., 1983, A fluid model for the shape of accretionary wedges: Earth and Planetary Science Letters, v. 63, p. 379–384.

Gay, N. C., and Weiss, L. E., 1974, The relationship between principal stress directions and the geometry of kinks in foliated rocks: Tectonophysics, v. 21, p. 297–300.

Goodman, R. E., 1980, Introduction to rock mechanics: John Wiley and Sons, Inc., 478 p.

Hoshino, K., 1974, Effect of porosity on the strength of the clastic sedimentary rocks, in Advances in Rock Mechanisms: Proceeding in the 3rd Congress of the International Society of Rock Mechanics, v. 2, pt. A, p. 511–516.

——, 1981, Consolidation and strength of the soft sedimentary rocks: Proceedings of an International Symposium on Weak Rock, Tokyo, 1981, Rotterdam, A. A. Balkema, v. 1, p. 155–160.

Hoshino, K., Koide, H., Inami, K., Iwamura, S., and Mitsui, S., 1972, Mechanical properties of Japanese Tertiary sedimentary rocks under high confining pressures: Geological Survey of Japan Report 244, 200 p.

Hubbert, M. K., and Rubey, W. W., 1959, Role of fluid pressure in mechanics of overthrust faulting, I, Mechanics of fluid-filled solids and its application to overthrust faulting: Geological Society of America Bulletin, v. 70, p. 115–166.

Kagami, H., Karig, D. E., and others, 1986, Initial Reports of the Deep Sea Drilling Project: Washington, D.C., U.S. Government Printing Office, v. 87, 985 p.

Karig, D. E., 1974, Evolution of arc systems in the western Pacific: Annual Review of Earth Planetary Science, v. 2, p. 51–75.

——, 1986a, The framework of deformation in the Nankai Trough, in Kagami, H., Karig, D. E., and others, eds., Initial Reports of the Deep Sea Drilling Project: Washington, D.C., U.S. Government Printing Office, v. 87, p. 927–940.

——, 1986b, Kinematics and mechanics of deformation across some accreting

forearcs: Proceedings of the Oji Symposium on the Formation of Ocean Margins, Tokyo, Nov. 21-23, 1983 (in press).

Karig, D. E., Moore, G. F., Curray, J. R., and Lawrence, M. B., 1980, Morphology and shallow structure of the lower trench slope off Nias Island, Indonesia, in Hayes, D. E., ed., The Tectonic and Geologic Evolution of Southeast Asian Seas and Islands: American Geophysical Union Geophysical Monograph 23, p. 179–208.

Karig, D. E., and Angevine, C. L., 1986, Geologic constraints on subduction rates in the Nankai Trough, in Karig, D. E., Kagami, H., and others, eds., Initial Reports of the Deep Sea Drilling Project: Washington, D.C., U.S. Government Printing Office, v. 87, p. 789–796.

Kenney, T. C., 1967, The influence of mineral composition on the residual strength of natural soils: Proceedings Geotechnical Conference, Oslo, Norway, v. 1, pp. 123–129.

Kezdi, A., 1974, Handbook of soil mechanics, v. 1, Soil Physics: New York, Elsevier, 294 p.

Kieckhefer, R. M. Shor, Jr., G. G., Curray, J. R., 1980, Seismic refraction studies of the Sunda Trench and forearc basin: Journal of Geophysical Research, v. 85, p. 863–889.

Koerner, R. M., 1970, Effect of particle characteristic on soil strength: Journal of Soil Mechanics and Foundations Division: Proceedings, American Society of Civil Engineers, SM 4, p. 1121–1233.

Lambe, T. W., and Whitman, R. V., 1969, Soil Mechanics: New York, John Wiley and Sons, 553 p.

Lundberg, N., and Karig, D. E., 1986, Structural features from the Nankai Trough lower slope, Deep Sea Drilling Project Sites 582 and 583, in Kagami, H., Karig, D. E., and others, eds., Initial Reports of the Deep Sea Drilling Project: Washington, D.C., U.S. Government Printing Office, v. 87, p. 797–808.

McLamore, R. T., 1966, Strength-deformation characteristics of anisotropic sedimentary rocks [Ph.D. thesis, University of Texas]: Ann Arbor, Michigan, University Microfilms, 259 p.

Mitchell, J. K., 1976, Fundamentals of Soil Behavior: New York, John Wiley and Sons, Inc., 422 p.

Moore, G. F., and Curray, J. R., 1980, Structure of the Sunda Trench lower slope off Sumatra from multichannel seismic reflection data: Marine Geophysical Research, v. 4, p. 318–340.

Moore, J. C., and von Huene, R., 1980, Abnormal pore pressure and hole instability in forearc regions: A preliminary report: Menlo Park, California, Ocean Margin Drilling Project, 29 p.

Moore, J. C., and Biju-Duval, B., 1984, Tectonic synthesis, Deep Sea Drilling Project Leg 78A, Structural evolution of offscraped and underthrust sediment, northern Barbados Ridge, in Biju-Duval, B., Moore, J. C., and others, eds., Initial Reports of the Deep Sea Drilling Project: Washington, D.C., U.S. Government Printing Office, v. 78A, p. 601–621.

Morgenstern, N. R., and Tchalenko, J. S., 1967, Microscopic structures in Kaolin subjected to direct shear: Geotechnique, v. 17, p. 309–328.

Morrow, C. A., Shi, L. Q., Byerlee, J. D., 1982, Strain hardening and strength of clay-rich fault gouges: Journal of Geophysical Research, v. 87, p. 6771–6780.

Nasu, N., Tomoda, Y., and others, 1982, Multichannel seismic reflection data across Nankai Trough: Tokyo, IPOD—Japan Basic Data Series, No. 4, 34 p.

Niitsuma, N., 1986, Paleomagnetism of the Nankai Trough and the Japan Trench sediments, in Kagami, H., Karig, D. E., and others, eds., Initial Reports of the Deep Sea Drilling Project: Washington, D.C., U.S. Government Printing Office, v. 87A, p. 757–786.

Ranken, B., Cardwell, R. K., and Karig, D. E., 1984, Kinematics of the Philippine Sea Plate: Tectonics, v. 3, p. 555–575.

Schofield, A. N., and Wroth, C. P., 1968, Critical State Soil Mechanics: London, McGraw-Hill, 310 p.

Seno, T., 1977, The instantaneous rotation vector of the Philippine sea plate relative to the Eurasian plate: Tectonophysics, v. 42, p. 209–226.

Shepard, L. E., Bryant, W. R., and Chiou, W. A., 1982, Geotechnical properties of Middle America Trench Sediments, Deep Sea Drilling Project Leg 66, in Watkins, J. S., Moore, J. C., and others, eds., Initial Reports of Deep Sea Drilling Project: Washington, D.C., U.S. Government Printing Office, v. 66, p. 475–504.

Skempton, A. W., 1964, Long-term stability of clay slopes: Geotechnique, v. 14, p. 77–102.

Stockmal, G. S., 1983, The modelling of large-scale accretionary wedge deformation: Journal of Geophysical Research, v. 88, p. 8271–8288.

Suppe, J., 1983, Major changes in fluid pressure and rock strength during deformation in fold and thrust belts: Geological Society of America Abstracts with Programs, v. 15, p. 702.

Tchalenko, J. S., 1968, The evolution of kink bands and the development of compression textures in sheared clays: Tectonophysics, v. 6, p. 159–174.

Wang, C.-Y., Mao, N.-H., 1979, Shearing of saturated clays in rock joints at high confirming pressure: Geophysical Research Letters, v. 6, p. 825–828.

Wang, C.-Y., Mao, H.-H., and Wu, F. T., 1980, Mechanical properties of clays at high pressure: Journal of Geophysical Research, v. 85, p. 1462–1468.

Wood, D. M. and Wroth, C. P., 1979, Rocks and soils under different pressure regimes: University of Cambridge, Department of Engineering Technical Report 70-1979, 14 p.

Zhao, W.-L., Davis, D., and Dahlen, F. A., 1984, Variations in fluid pressure and the shape of convex accretionary wedges: EOS Transactions of the American Geophysical Union, v. 65, p. 285.

MANUSCRIPT ACCEPTED BY THE SOCIETY MARCH 10, 1986

Printed in U.S.A.

Geological Society of America
Memoir 166
1986

Sediment deformation and dewatering under horizontal compression: Experimental results

Bobb Carson
Peter L. Berglund*
Department of Geological Sciences
Lehigh University
Bethlehem, Pennsylvania 18015

ABSTRACT

Experimental deformation of submerged, saturated sediment indicates that under horizontal compression marine deposits fracture, forming conjugate shear sets and, in several cases, imbricate thrust sheets that dip toward the locus of deformation. At the same time, the sediment consolidates by dewatering through the sediment-water interface. Water loss is directly related to duration of compression and proximity to the origin of the stress field. Consolidation results in increased sediment shear strength.

Microfabric studies indicate that deformation induces formation of fractures, faults, and crenulations, ranging in width from 15 μm to 1 mm. The fractures appear to be important dewatering conduits, which may influence the gross permeability of the sediment mass. Fluid escape or differential slip along faults results in reorientation of platy particles defining narrow zones of preferred orientation in soft sediment. If water loss is impeded during deformation, hydrofracturing may occur.

INTRODUCTION

Sediments involved in accretion at convergent continental margins undergo deformation. At margins characterized by slow convergence ($\leqslant 4$ cm/yr) and thick trench fill, deformation commonly takes the form of large-scale folding and thrust faulting (Chase and Bunce, 1969; Silver, 1972; Carson and others, 1974; Seely and others, 1974; Karig and Sharman, 1975; Moore and Karig, 1976). Deformation may also result in small-scale veining, fracturing, and faulting (Moore, 1973, Moore and others, this volume; Moore and Geigle, 1974; Berglund, 1980; Carson and others, 1982; Cowan, 1983) and anomalous overconsolidation (Trabant and others, 1975; Carson, 1977; Carson and Bruns, 1980; Shepard and Bryant, 1983; Bray and Karig, 1985, 1986).

Although seismic reflection studies and samples from modern accretionary zones, as well as studies of ancient subduction complexes (Moore, 1973; Blake and Jones, 1974; Bachman, 1978; Connelly, 1978), have broadly outlined the structural and compositional configuration of convergent margin sediments, they have provided little information on the mechanics of the deformation process. As a result, experimental models have been used to define the gross response of sediments to horizontal compression (Hubbert, 1951; Seely, 1977; Davis and others, 1983). When appropriately scaled, such models can approximate the kinematics and patterns of sediment displacement within the accretionary wedge (Cowan and Silling, 1978). Although the models cited have defined the dynamics of the accretionary zone, they have not considered the phenomenon of sediment dewatering, which occurs during deformation. Because dewatering changes the bulk density of the deposits involved in subduction-accretion, and because overpressuring associated with dewatering probably controls effective stress on fault planes, scale models do not duplicate field conditions and are difficult to interpret. Nevertheless, models are useful in delineating response patterns of sediment to deformation. This paper describes an experiment undertaken to define the pattern of sediment consolidation under horizontal compression and the mechanisms by which dewatering is effected.

TECTONIC DEWATERING: EVIDENCE FROM ZONES OF ACCRETION

Evidence that dewatering of accretion zone sediments is

---

*Present address: Union Texas Petroleum, 1401 E. Iliff Ave., Aurora, Colorado 80014.

influenced by tectonic loading comes from several localities (Shepard and Bryant, 1983). Early consolidation studies (Trabant and others, 1975) of sediment from the Shikoku subduction zone (convergence rate ~2 cm/yr; Karig, 1986) indicated that accreted sediments are highly overconsolidated, relative to their depth of burial. More recent results (Bray and Karig, 1984; Karig, this volume), based largely on seismic refraction data, indicate that sediment at the toe of the Nankai wedge has an average porosity of ~40%, while 15 km landward the average porosity of the sediment has been reduced to 20%. Geometry of fault zones derived from seismic reflection data suggests a concomitant increase in coefficients of cohesion and internal friction with this decrease in porosity.

Japan trench slope sediments exhibit an array of veins, fractures, and microfaults that are thought to be water-release structures uniquely associated with tectonic convergence (Carson and others, 1982; convergence rate 8-10 cm/yr, Minster and Jordan 1978), even though the sediments have not been actively accreted and are not highly overconsolidated. Similar structures, which commonly occur as steeply dipping, sinuous, anastomosing fractures, are observed on the inner slope of the Middle America trench off Guatemala (Cowan, 1983; convergence rate ~7 cm/yr, Minster and Jordan, 1978). Fabric modification related to accretion has been documented in the same trench off Mexico (Lundberg and Moore, 1982 and this volume; convergence rate 10 cm/yr, Molnar and Sykes, 1969).

The areal pattern of tectonically-induced dewatering has been described from surficial lower continental slope samples off Washington and Oregon (Carson, 1977; Barnard, 1978; convergence rate ~2.5 cm/yr). Carson (1977) has shown that at least 18% of the sediment's original interstitial volume has been lost by tectonically-induced consolidation (reduction of average void ratio from 1.04 to 0.85, minimum estimate). Most rapid water loss occurs at the toe of the accretionary wedge, which is defined by the base of the lower continental slope. Dewatering continues across the accretionary wedge, but at a reduced rate. Age determinations based on radiocarbon biostratigraphy indicate that much of the deformation and dewatering have been effected over the past 2.0×10^6 years (Carson, 1977). A gross calculation comparing the void ratios of undeformed (Cascadia Basin) and deformed (lower slope) sediments $\leqslant 2.0 \times 10^6$ years old (as outlined in Carson, 1977, p. 303–304) yields a minimum discharge rate of 170 $cm^3/m^2/yr$, which can be attributed to tectonic loading. The actual rate may be as much as an order of magnitude greater, because the void ratios are maximum estimates.

EXPERIMENTAL DESIGN

The sediment used in the deformation/dewatering experiments was mud derived from physically disaggregating mudstone collected on the lower continental slope off Washington (sample 79-14; Carson, 1977). This sediment consists of clayey silt (59% silt, 41% clay) containing less than 1% fine sand. It has the following parameters: $M_\phi = 7.5\phi$ (fine silt); $\sigma_1 = 2.01\phi$ (very poorly

sorted); $Sk_1 = 0.14\phi$ (positively skewed) (Folk and Ward, 1957). The clay minerals in the $<2\mu m$ fraction include montmorillonoids (25%), illite (45%), and kaolinite/chlorite (undifferentiated, 30%). The silt fraction contains quartz, feldspars (plagioclase and microcline), chlorite, muscovite, and hypersthene. The Atterberg limits are: liquid limit = 47%, and plastic limit = 30%.

To simulate deformation in a convergent setting, sediment was emplaced in a 125 cm long × 20.2 cm wide × 20 cm high Plexiglas trough and horizontally compressed by a rack-and-pinion gear–driven vertical plate (Fig. 1). The sediment was introduced as a thick, water-saturated slurry, and covered by artificial seawater for the duration of each experiment. The submerged deposits were allowed to consolidate by gravitational self-loading for at least two weeks prior to deformation. In consolidation tests, the time required for complete consolidation (T_{100}) under lithostatic load was determined to be 240 hours (i.e. beyond 240 hours no change in column height occurred). The sediment was subsequently deformed at convergence rates of 1×10^{-6} or 10×10^{-6} cm/sec (31.5 or 315 cm/year). The resulting strain rates for the entire sediment mass were either $1 \times 10^{-8}S^{-1}$ or $1 \times 10^{-7}S^{-1}$ depending upon the convergence rate, although locally rates were undoubtedly higher, as strain was not accommodated uniformly throughout the 90 cm long sediment mass. These rates are greater than those for entire accretionary wedges (10^{-13}–$10^{-14}S^{-1}$), but may be less than localized strain rates within the wedge associated with faulting. The height of the sediment column prior to deformation, but after vertical consolidation, was approximately 10 cm.

Prior to and during compression, the bulk density of the sediment in the squeezebox was monitored by gamma ray attenuation (Myers and others, 1974). A frame around the squeezebox held a 50 mCu gamma ray source (C_S^{137}) in front of the box, and a scintillation counter (Harshaw Chemical, Model 6S6/2) behind (Fig. 1). Lead shields defined a 1 cm^2 beam, which passed horizontally through the sediment. Gamma rays were counted on a multichannel analyzer (Northern Scientific NS-700 Series) and the system was periodically calibrated by scanning solutions of known densities (1.0229 - 1.3339 Mg/m^3), which encompassed those found in the sediment. The gamma ray unit could be positioned vertically in 1.9-cm increments, and was adjusted horizontally at 5 cm intervals to define a matrix of locations (Figs. 2–5) at which densities were repeatedly determined during an experimental run.

Bulk densities were determined by linear regression:

$$\gamma_{sat} = b_0 + b_1 (Ln\ counts/min)$$

where b_0 and b_1 are regression coefficients based on determinations of the standard solutions. Bulk densities were empirically converted to water content (percent dry weight) by the equation (Richards and others, 1974):

$$W = 2.9669 \times 10^3 - 4.4817 \times 10^3 \gamma_{sat} + 2.3179 \cdot 10^3 \gamma_{sat})^2 - 4.0551 \times 10^2 (\gamma_{sat})^3$$

Figure 1. Configuration of the squeezebox: (A) Trough containing submerged sediment; (B) rack-and-pinion gears that drive the movable plate (C) in the trough inducing deformation; (D) gamma ray source (C_s^{137}) and detector (E), which bracket the trough and can be adjusted both horizontally and vertically.

Application of counting statistics and error propagation in conversion to water content indicates that real differences of 3.5% water content can be discerned at a 95% confidence level.

Water contents were monitored every 24 hours at the 10×10^{-6} cm/sec convergence rate or 168 hours for the 1×10^{-6} cm/sec convergence rate. At these times, photographs were taken and line drawings made to record the fracture pattern apparent through the front face of the box. We infer that these patterns extend through the interior of the sediment mass, as similar patterns appear on the opposite side of the box, and surface expression of fault planes extending to the sediment-water interface are approximately linear and transverse to the direction of compression. Interstitial pore pressures were monitored at either two or five locations within the sediment mass during three (Runs 6, 7, and 8) of the six experimental runs. Tubes were emplaced either in the moveable plate (at two depths), or ~5 cm from the bottom at approximately 15 cm horizontal intervals from the plate prior to deformation. The tubes were connected to a pressure transducer (Dynisco, Model TCAPT25-1C) through a multiport ball valve. Although the initial pore pressure results are reasonable, development of gas bubbles in the tubes after 48 to 72 hours invalidates the subsequent data.

Upon completion of each deformation experiment, vane shear strength determinations were made at 5 cm intervals along the length of the sediment mass, 1.5 cm below the sediment-water interface. The tests were performed with a Wykham-Farrance vane shear apparatus (2.54 cm vane) rotated at 20°/min. After one experiment (Run 5), 3.5 cm diameter cores were collected by inserting thin-walled (1 mm) plastic tubing into the sediment. The cores were subsequently impregnated with Carbowax 6000 and thin-sectioned for post-deformational fabric studies.

Because sediment was introduced to the box as a slurry, water contents prior to compression, but after vertical (gravitational) consolidation, varied from 83 to 106 percent (dry weight) depending upon (vertical) position in the box and initial water content of the slurry. Obviously, these water contents are greater than those encountered in in situ marine sediments and the associated bulk densities ($1.53-1.46$ Mg/m^3) are lower than densities of much of a sediment column undergoing deformation in a subduction zone. Off Washington/Oregon, for example, bulk density $\approx 1.8-2.0$ Mg/m^3 (Dehlinger and others, 1968; Shipboard Scientific Party, 1973). Furthermore, the strength of the sediment in the model (shear strength 0.8-1.6 kPa) is 1 to 2 orders of magnitude less than shear strengths recorded for convergent margin

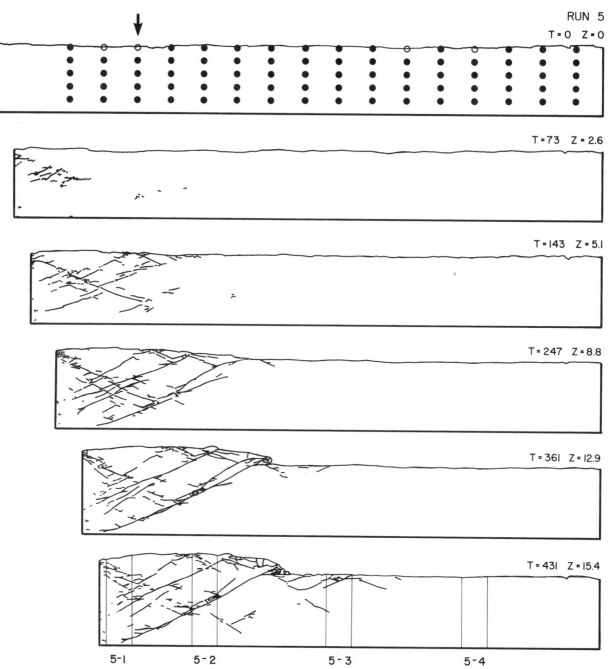

Figure 2. Structural development, Run 5, convergence rate = 10 μcm/sec. T = time in hours; Z = total displacement of driven plate in cm. Dots (at T = 0) indicate positions at which gamma ray determinations were made throughout the experiment. Arrow (at T = 0) marks position of water contents shown in Figure 6. Lines are fractures/faults observed through the front of the squeezebox. Positions of cores 5-1 through 5-4 (collected after completion of deformation) are indicated at T = 431.

sediments (Carson, 1977; Bouma and Moore, 1975; Carson and Bruns, 1980). No attempt has been made to dynamically scale the rheological properties of the experimental sediment because the purpose of this study was not to duplicate accretion zone structural evolution, but to delineate patterns by which the sediment dewaters. As a result, no claim is made for structural similarity between the fault configuration observed in the model, and large-

scale (km) fault patterns developed at convergent margins. The reader will note, however, that the scale (<10 cm length; width ≤2 mm) and subplanar to anastomosing configuration of fractures observed in the model are similar to vein structures observed at several margins (Carson and others, 1982; Lundberg and Moore, 1982; Cowan, 1983).

In all, seven experimental runs were made during this study.

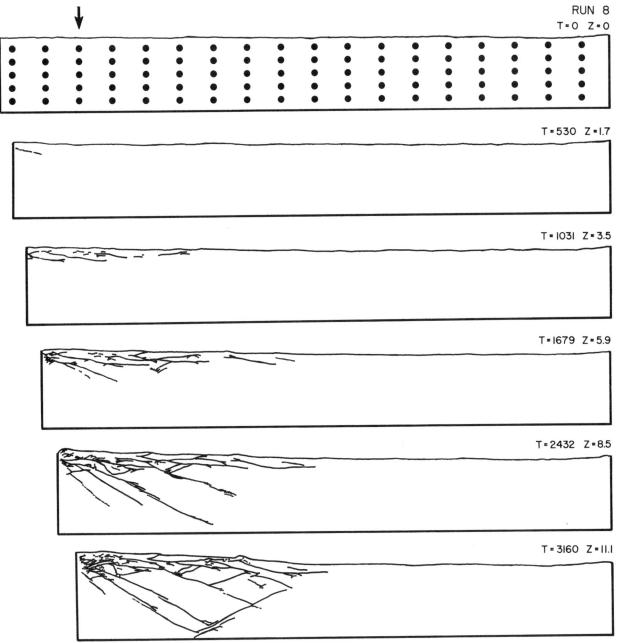

Figure 3. Structural development, Run 8, convergence rate = 1 μcm/sec. T = time in hours; Z = total displacement of driven plate in cm. Dots (at T = 0) indicate positions at which gamma ray determinations were made throughout the experiment. Arrow (at T = 0) marks position of water contents diagrammed in Figure 6. Lines are fractures/faults observed through the front of the squeezebox.

Runs 2 through 7 had a convergence rate of 10×10^{-6} cm/sec; Run 8 was compressed at 1×10^{-6} cm/sec. Runs 2 and 3 were replicates, while 4 through 8 were unique combinations of initial water content, sediment thickness (after vertical consolidation), and/or convergence rate.

EXPERIMENTAL RESULTS

Structural Configuration and Evolution

In all of the experimental runs, cracks appeared in the sedi-

ment mass during deformation, even though the water content exceeded the liquid limit. These features are referred to as fractures in this paper, under the most general definition of that term (American Geological Institute, 1972). That is to say, the term fracture is used to denote any break, whether or not it accommodates displacement. It does not necessarily imply loss of cohesion, and microfabric studies conducted subsequent to deformations (see below) indicate that many of the "fractures" are, in fact, shear zones. Initial opening of the fractures may be a pressure-

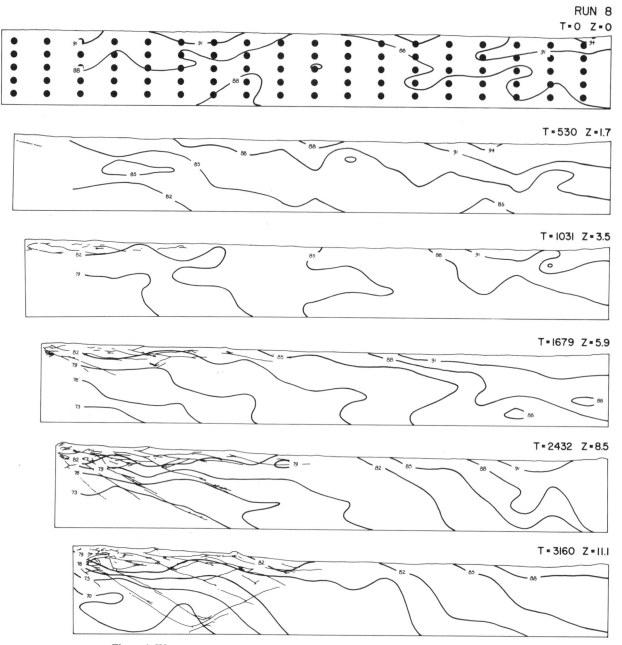

Figure 4. Water content evolution, Run 8. Contour interval, 3 percent (dry weight).

dilation response as described by Ritger (1985).

Although the individual runs differed in water content or convergence rate, the general geometry of fractures developed and their sequence of development were constant from run to run. Line drawings of fracturing induced during Runs 5 (convergence rate = 10×10^{-6} cm/sec) and 8 (convergence rate = 1×10^{-6} cm/sec) are presented in Figures 2 and 3 to represent the generally observed structural evolution.

In all runs at strains less than 0.01 (plate displacement ~0.8 cm), discontinuous fracturing of the sediment mass was observed within 20 cm of the driven plate. Fracturing occurred even though the water content was above the liquid limit. The short, initial joints commonly showed no discernible planar configuration, although many dipped toward the plate (T = 73, Fig. 2). At strains of ~0.03 (T = 73, Fig. 2; T = 530, Fig. 3), however, the joint pattern began to define a plane dipping away from the plate at 17 to 32°. Commonly this plane evolved into a continuous fracture (T = 143, Fig. 2) or set of fractures (T = 1679, Fig. 3).

At strains of 0.05 (high convergence rate; T = 143, Fig. 2) to ~0.09 (low convergence rate; T = 3160, Fig. 3) well-defined fractures dipping (20–28°) toward the plate appeared, forming conjugate shear sets with the pre-existing fractures. Angles of

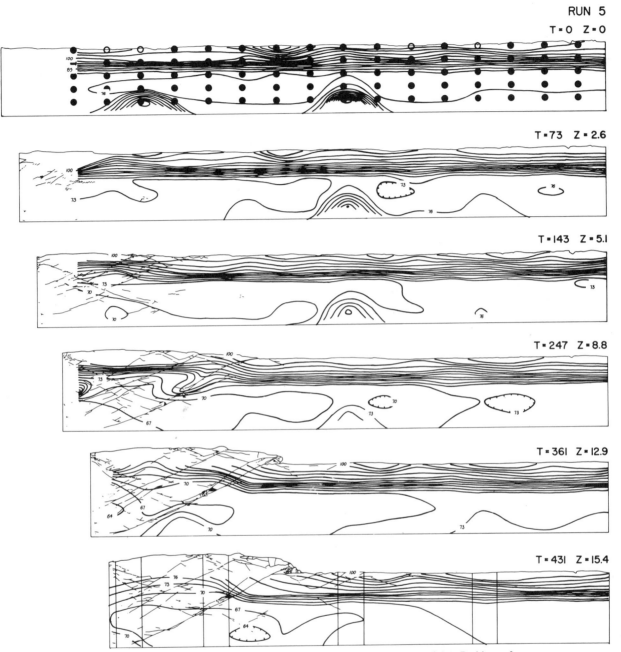

Figure 5. Water content evolution, Run 5. Contour interval, 3 percent (dry weight). Positions of cores
5-1 through 5-4 (as in Fig. 2) are indicated at T = 431.

intersection ranged from 38–57°. At the high convergence rate
these secondary fracture planes eventually extended to the surface, and became the dominant fracture set (T ⩾247, Fig. 2; T
⩾362, Fig. 10).

After the principle fractures were established, active thrusting took place along them, elevating the sediment surface (T =
361, 431; Fig. 2), and accommodating much of the subsequent
shortening. Small normal faults were commonly developed at the
nose and near the surface of the thrust sheets.

Continued convergence resulted in formation of successive

thrust faults in front of the previously established faults (T =
143-247, Fig. 2). As a result, a series of imbricate thrust sheets
were defined, with the oldest sheet situated nearest the plate. This
developmental pattern was observed in all high convergence rate
runs (3-7).

At the low (1×10^{-6} cm/sec) convergence rate (Run 8, Fig.
3), more strain (up to 0.10) was accommodated by fractures
dipping away from the plate than was accommodated by similar
fractures in the other (high convergence rate) runs. These fractures, which were observed in the early stages of all runs, roughly

parallel the principal stress axes and water content contours (see below), and probably reflect direct shearing induced by the plate movement. Fractures dipping in the opposite direction (toward the plate) are much more common at high convergence rates (compare Figs. 2 and 10, with Fig. 3). Their orientation nearly parallel to the expected pressure gradient and at high angle to water content contours, and their dominance in runs where water expulsion rates clearly exceed intergranular permeability (see below, Table 3), suggest that they form to accommodate dewatering. If this is the case, their lesser abundance in Run 8 (Fig. 3) implies that in this run, intergranular permeability was more nearly sufficient to accommodate the rate of pore water discharge.

Sediment Dewatering

Under convergent horizontal stress, unconfined sediments dewater, as indicated by the progressive change in measured water contents (Figs. 4, 5). The dewatering pattern was generally similar for all runs, although variations in initial pore water distributions complicate the results.

Examination of Figure 4 indicates that in all instances after compression has begun (T >O), the lowest water contents are found near the base of the driven plate. From this position, water contents increase upward and outward, defining lines of equal water content that extend horizontally away from the plate, and then dip, with increasing gradient, toward the base of the box (Fig. 4, T = 1679, 2432, 3160). The pattern defined by the water content lines roughly parallels the expected trajectories of the principal stress axes for this experimental configuration (Hafner, 1951). As compression proceeds, the lines of equal water content radiate away from the base of the plate (compare the sequential positions of the 79 percent water content contour; Fig. 4, T = 1031, 1679, 2432, and 3160), reflecting the movement of interstitial water upward through the sediment mass. Water is lost through the sediment/water interface.

When the original distribution of pore water is not homogeneous, but consists of a surface layer of higher water content (Run 5, Fig. 5; formed by initial emplacement of two slurries, the upper one having a higher water content), the dewatering pattern is not as obvious. As before, low water contents appear first at the base of the driven plate, subsequently moving upward and outward from that position (note positions of 70 percent contour line, Fig. 5, T ≥143). The high water content surface layer persists over the duration of the experiment, however, as interstitial water from the lower portion of the sediment is fed to it from below. This is not to say that the surface sediment does not dewater; in the zone of active deformation, surficial water contents decline from ~106% (Fig. 5, T = 0) to less than 100% (T = 431). The base of the upper layer, which is defined by the 79% contour at T = 0, lies between 70 and 73% at 431 hours.

The extent to which the sediments dewatered varied with position in the box and the initial water content. Generally, sediment nearest the plate and with the highest initial water content

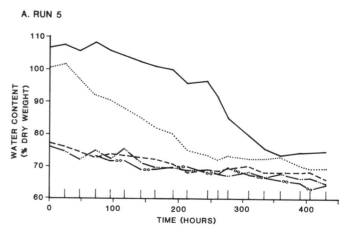

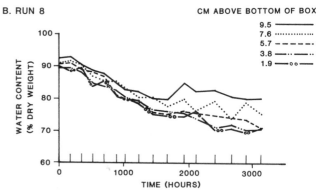

Figure 6. Variation in water content (percent dry weight) with time: (A) Run 5; (B) Run 8. Horizontal positions indicated (by arrow) in Figures 2 and 3.

(Fig. 6a, b) showed the most pronounced reduction (12 to 30% dry weight) in water content, which is a direct measure of the reduction in interstitial void volume. At the opposite end of the box, water contents and void volumes declined not more than 6% during an experiment. This decline, nevertheless, indicates that even those sediments that showed no structural evidence of deformation dewatered due to compressive stress.

The sediment dewaters at different rates depending upon the rate of convergence, initial water content, and position with the squeezebox. Observed rates of water loss near the plate (Fig. 6a, b) range from 0.5–3.1% water content/cm of convergence (0.003–0.11% water content/hour). Step-wise non-linear regression analysis indicates that water content at all locations within the zone of observed deformation is a quadratic function of time (i.e. water content = A-B (time) + (time)^2, where the regression coefficients are unique to each position; A ranges from 60 to 110, B from –0.16 to –0.03, and C from –0.001 to 0.0002). The sediment dewaters most rapidly during the initial stages of deformation (Fig. 6b, T ≤1470 hours, total strain 0.06: rate of water loss ≈2.5 percent water content/cm of convergence), and at lesser rates after initial consolidation (Fig. 6b, T ≥1470 hours, total strain 0.06–0.12: rate of water loss ≈0.8 percent water content/cm of convergence). This pattern implies rapid initial pore

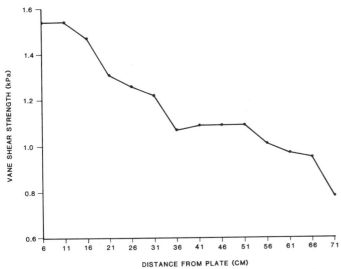

Figure 7. Vane shear strength as a function of distance from the driven plate, Run 5. Determinations made after completion of experiment (T = 431, Fig. 2).

volume reduction and fabric modification under convergent stress, followed by decreasing rates of consolidation as the sediment adjusts to the applied pressure field. There is some evidence that the initial response to compression is dilation, manifested by slightly higher water contents (Fig. 6a, levels 7.6 and 9.5; Fig. 6b), and small, discontinuous extensional joints at total strains of 0.005–0.008.

Pressure determinations at depths of 5 cm during the first 72 hours of Runs 6, 7, and 8 indicate that internal pore pressures never exceeded hydrostatic pressure by more than 0.15 kPa (equivalent to a head of 1.53 cm of water at 4°C). Indeed, in most instances, internal pressures did not exceed hydrostatic pressure by more than 0.07 kPa, the lower limit of resolution of the transducer. Discernible pore pressure highs bore no apparent relationship to incidence or extent of visible fracturing.

The consolidation, evidenced by lowered water contents and induced by convergence, resulted in an increase in sediment shear strength. The post-deformation results from Run 5 (Fig. 7) are representative: shear strength ranged from 1.54 kPa, nearest the plate, to 0.77 kPa at the far end of the box. The pattern, which emerged with each run, was a general decrease in shear strength with increasing distance from the driven plate and with increasing sediment water content.

Sediment Microstructure

In the following discussion x, y, and z refer to the geometric axes of the squeezebox, not the strain axes, which are unconstrained. X is vertical, positive downward; y is horizontal, positive toward the right side of the box, looking in the direction of compression; z is horizontal, the direction of compression.

The microstructure of the squeezebox sediment was examined at four locations (Figs. 2, 5) after completion of the deformation. In thin section, the microstructure is characterized chiefly by severe inhomogeneity; areas in which the fabric is homogeneous are rarely greater than 20 mm^2 in areal extent.

Two types of structures are dominant: shear fractures (Fig. 8a, b) and a domainal structure consisting of narrow, lenticular, alternating domains in which clays are inclined in opposite directions to the axis of the domain (Fig. 8c, d). These latter structures are known as crenulations (Maltman, 1977) when the alternate bands are symmetrical and kink bands when one set of domains dominates and the inclination angles differ markedly (Maltman, 1977; Morgenstern and Tchalenko, 1967; Tchalenko, 1968).

The crenulations consist of lenticular domains, rarely longer than 5 mm, which, when viewed with crossed nicols appear as light and dark zones (Fig. 8c, d), due to opposing orientations within alternate domains. The crenulations are most commonly oriented parallel to the trace of the xy plane. As such, they indicate the maximum principal compressive strain direction. Less often, they are inclined at small angles ($\leqslant 15°$) to the x and y axes, and occasionally can be found nearly parallel to the z axis. The internal angle formed by the junction of clay flakes in the crenulations varies from 60 to 100°. The width of the individual domains is equally variable, ranging from 20 μm (Fig. 8a) to as much as 300 μm (Fig. 8d).

Macro- and micro-shear zones are ubiquitous in the squeezebox sediment and are largely responsible for the inhomogeneity of the fabric. They are commonly inclined 20 to 35° to the z axis, but in some cases this angle is as high as 45° or as low as 0°. They occur in four recognizable size classes characterized by length, width of shear zone, and spacing between adjacent faults:

(1) Macro-shear zones, outlined in Figures 2 and 3, are up to 1 mm wide, range from less than one to greater than 10 cm in length, and are spaced on the order of 1 cm apart. Broad zones of particle reorientation are observed microscopically along some of these zones (Fig. 9a). Shear zones of this class tend to make smaller angles with the z axis than do those of the other three classes, usually 20 to 25°.

(2) The second class of shear fractures range in width from 200 to 300 μm, are on the order of 1 cm in length, and are commonly spaced 300 to 500 μm apart. These zones are frequently parallel, sometimes en echelon (Figs. 8b, 9b).

(3) Shear zones of the third class are typically 50 to 60 μm in width, approximately 2 mm in length, and are spaced approximately 500 μm apart (Fig. 8a).

(4) The smallest shear zones observed are 15 to 20 μm in width, some 200 to 500 μm in length, and are spaced 20 to 70 μm apart (Fig. 8a). Sets of these zones are generally limited to areas of less than 1 mm^2; they are observed even in core 5-4, taken 56 cm from the driven plate (Fig. 2).

Within the outer portions of the largest shear zones, clay flakes are oriented parallel to the direction of shearing. In the central regions, however, they lie at a small angle (10 to 20°) to the plane of shearing. This relationship is also observed in the

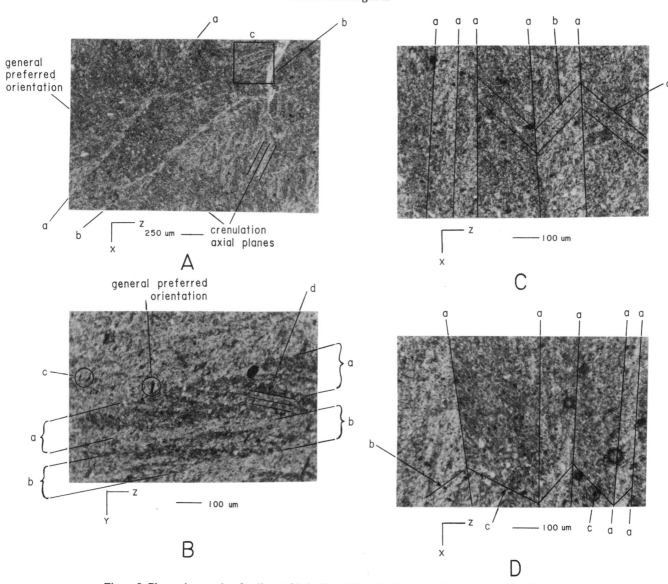

Figure 8. Photomicrographs of sediment fabric, Run 5. Sample (core) positions indicated in Figure 2. (A) Sample 5-1, xz plane; crossed nicols, gypsum plate. Two shear fractures (a, b) inclined 40° and 50° to z. Platelets in surrounding and interlying areas are generally oriented perpendicular to shear fractures. Note, however, crenulations in lower right quarter of plate. These crenulations trend about 15° from the x axis; clay flakes in one set (light areas) are parallel to shear fractures, those in alternate set (dark areas) perpendicular. White area in top of plate is Carbowax; note set of small shear fractures to left (c). (B) Sample 5-2, yz plane; crossed nicols, gypsum plate. Preferred orientation, possibly that due to horizontal compression, 15° clockwise from the y axis, shown also by elongate silts (c). Shear zones (a, b) subparallel (approximately 20°) with z axis, and flakes within are oriented 30° clockwise from z (d). (C) Sample 5-1, xz plane, crossed nicols, gypsum plate. View of crenulations axial planes (a). Flakes in light areas (b) are oriented 50° counterclockwise from z; those in darker areas (c) lie 50° clockwise from z. (D) Sample 5-2, xz plane, crossed nicols, gypsum plate. Crenulations, with dihedral angle of 100°. Flakes in light areas (b) oriented 50° counterclockwise from z; those in dark areas (c) lie 50° clockwise from z.

second class of shear structures; within the shear zones, clay flakes are well-oriented with a rake of 15 to 30° to the shear plane, while they are parallel to shearing along the borders of the zone (Fig. 9b, c). In the smallest two classes of shear fractures, however, due to the extremely narrow width of the shear zones, all of the clays lie parallel to the shear surface (Figs. 8a, 9d).

DISCUSSION

The strain history of the squeezebox is complex. The boundaries of the box affected the compressive stress field, and large amounts of translation and faulting (Table 1), accompanied by some degree of rotational strain, have resulted in a noncoaxial

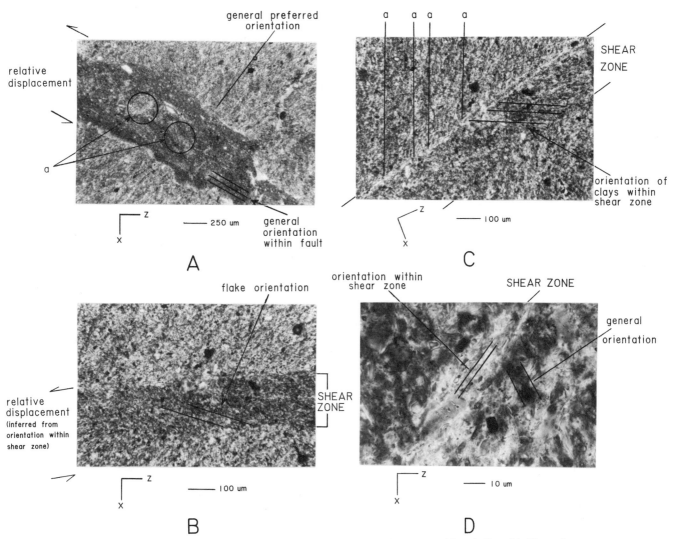

Figure 9. Photomicrographs of sediment fabric, Run 5. Sample (core) positions indicated in Figure 2. (A) Sample 5-2, xz plane, crossed nicols, gypsum plate. Fault zone of macro-fault. Orientation of clay flakes in surrounding area trends 45° counterclockwise from z; some flakes (a) in center of "fault zone" maintain this orientation; majority of clays within zone, however, lie parallel to direction of displacement. (B) Sample 5-1, xz plane; crossed nicols, gypsum plate. Shear zone across bottom of photograph, inclined 5° counterclockwise to z axis. Clay flakes within shear zone are well aligned 30° clockwise from z, indicating probable sinistral displacement. Above shear zone, flakes are dominantly oriented 45° counterclockwise from z. (C) Sample 5-1, xz plane; crossed nicols, gypsum plate. Same field as Figure 9b, rotated 30° counterclockwise. Note narrow plane of clays (light area along top edge of shear zone) oriented parallel to shear displacement (running diagonally lower left to upper right). Domainal structure axial planes (a) are also more apparent in upper left portion of photograph. (D) Sample 5-1, xz plane; crossed nicols, gypsum plate. High magnification view of shear plane (light area) of the type shown in Figure 8a. Note well developed parallelism to shear plane. Oil immersion objective.

path of deformation. Preferred particle orientations, which developed at one time and one position in the box, were modified as that part of the sediment mass was moved into a different area of the stress field. Furthermore, the strain history can be dealt with only qualitatively; the design of the experiment precludes strain determinations that are more accurate than estimates derived from water loss considerations. Despite these complexities, the

experiments reveal something of the process of saturated, soft-sediment deformation under compression.

If the direction of particulate preferred orientation is considered to be equivalent to that of the maximum finite shortening, it is evident from thin sections (Figs. 8, 9) that the maximum strain has assumed widely differing orientations throughout the squeezebox. This pattern is due mainly to shearing at the

TABLE 1. ESTIMATED MINIMUM AND MAXIMUM VALUES FOR
PRINCIPAL COMPRESSIVE STRAIN (e_1), RUN 5
VALUES IN PERCENT

Location	A Minimum volume loss*	B Maximum estimate of e_1**
5-1	-13.2	-32
5-2	-13.2	-36
5-4	-6.6	-6.6

* = minimum estimate of e_1 if increase in sediment
height is neglected.

** sediment height increased by extension.

boundaries of the box and the pervasive shear fracturing within the sediment.

One response to the stress field is the physical rotation of individual grains into paired domains that form crenulations. The rotation of grains, which were presumably subhorizontal after gravitational consolidation, formed crenulations whose axial planes are generally perpendicular to the z-axis. Several authors (Morgenstern and Tchalenko, 1967; Tchalenko, 1968; Maltman, 1977) have described a similar response to horizontal compression directed parallel to an initial preferred orientation formed by vertical consolidation.

Another, more local, source of shortening is faulting. Each thrust fault may be considered a simple shear system resulting in a maximum finite shortening between the upper and lower surface of the shear zone. This shortening results in the alignment of clays at a small angle to the shear plane, as seen in Figure 9a-c.

From water loss measured at various positions in the squeezebox, volume reductions can be calculated. These, in turn, yield strain estimates, which while revealing nothing of strain history, do furnish information on the distribution of total strain within the squeezebox. Using Run 5 as an example, a specific gravity of 2.7 Mg/m^3 for the solid grains, and 1.0229 Mg/m^3 for the fluid (artificial sea water), the volume reductions listed in Table 1 are calculated. Most of the water loss and volume reduction occurred near the plate in the most deformed region. If increase in the vertical dimension is neglected (Table 1a), the volume loss can be taken as the principal compressive strain (e_1) at each location. In reality, however, the vertical dimension experienced considerable change: +28% at position 5-1 (Fig. 2), +35% at position 5-2, and no change at position 5-4. If this change in height is considered to be extensional strain, the compressive strain (e_1) must become considerably larger (Table 1b) to accomplish the volume reductions calculated above. Thus, depending on whether the change in height is ignored or considered to be extensional strain, the estimates for e_1 assume minimum or maximum values.

It is evident, however, that much of the increase in the vertical dimension is the result of uplift by thrusting. If it is assumed that volume loss is accomplished strictly through horizontal compression, and the vertical increase is due entirely to

faulting, the cumulative displacement along thrust faults can be calculated for each location within the box (Table 2a). Comparison of the observed displacement (3.2 cm) along the major thrust fault developed during Run 5 (Table 2b) with the calculated values indicates that this assumption may be essentially correct, since locations 5-1 and 5-2 are cut by several fault planes whose displacements are additive.

Differences in deformation fabric at various locations within the box are largely a function of two variables; distance from the origin of the stress field (the plate) and time. The sediment nearest the plate is deformed first; as preferred orientation begins to develop, in part as numerous micro-shear zones, water is lost. As deformation proceeds, this sediment becomes more coherent, begins to behave as a semi-rigid block, and is thrust over sediment further from the plate. Deformation thus propagates away from the plate with time; the stresses in the more distant sediment, however, are smaller, having been attenuated by grain-to-grain friction. At this greater distance from the plate, the orientation of the stress field also differs from that nearer the plate. With less obvious parallelism of phyllosilicate flakes in the sediment groundmass and fewer micro-shear zones, water loss at positions more distant from the driven plate may occur preferentially along macro-shear zones.

To test the hypothesis that fracturing is an important dewatering mechanism, the observed pore water discharge from sediment deformed during compression was compared with the expected discharge from unfractured, sediment (Table 3). Using an "intergranular" coefficient of permeability, $k = 2.0 \times 10^{-7}$ cm/sec (determined by consolidation test on Run 6 sediment), and the maximum head recorded by the pressure transducers (1.5 cm (0.15kPa), mounted on driven plate), the expected pore water discharge (Q), in the absence of fracturing, is $\leq 5 \times 10^{-5}$ cm^3/sec (Table 3a). This value is about 2 orders of magnitude smaller than the observed discharge, 1.2×10^{-3} cm^3/sec (Table 3b). These results imply that fractures may be important dewatering conduits and control the gross permeability of the sediment mass.

If, in fact, the fractures are integral to the dewatering process, blockage of these zones ought to perturbate the deformation/dewatering pattern. To determine if this occurs, Run 7 (Fig. 10) was conducted to replicate Run 5, with the exception that at T = 145.5 hours, a sediment/water slurry (initial water content = 243%) was introduced that uniformly covered the deforming sediment mass. Although the water content of this "cap" material eventually declined to 180–210% (depending upon position), it remained sufficiently fluid that fractures did not penetrate it (no evidence of displacement at sediment/water interface). The sediment beneath, although it continued to dewater, developed an intensity of fracturing at the nose of the overthrust sheet not observed in any other run (compare T = 431, Run 5, Fig. 2 with T = 408, Run 7, Fig. 10). Expulsion of interstitial water may have been impeded, resulting in dilation of the sediment mass just below the fluid layer. The geometry of the dilated fractures and movement along them indicates that they developed under shear stress, but their density and position suggest that dilation occurred

TABLE 2A. CALCULATED THRUST FAULT DISPLACEMENTS, RUN 5 (ALL VALUES IN CM)

Position (distance from plate [Fig. 2] T = 431)	Increase in sediment height over duration of experiment	Calculated displacement (to account for height increase) along thrust plane dipping		Horizontal shortening accommodated by calculated thrusting	
		20°	30°	20°	30°
5-1 (2.7 cm)	2.8	8.7	5.6	7.7	4.9
5-2 (15.4 cm)	3.5	10.2	7.0	9.6	6.1

TABLE 2B. OBSERVED THRUST FAULT DISPLACEMENT, RUN 5 (ALL VALUES IN CM)

Position	Increase in sediment height attributable to thrusting	Attitude of major thrust fault (in degrees)	Observed displacement at surface	Horizontal shortening accommodated by observed thrusting
23.8-28.1	2.5	25.5	3.2	2.9

TABLE 3. COMPARISON OF CALCULATED AND OBSERVED PORE WATER DISCHARGE, RUN 6

A. Calculated discharge, utilizing measured, intergranular permeability coefficient (k):

$Q = kiA$ (Darcy's Law), where

Q = rate of fluid discharge (cm^3/sec)

k = coefficient of permeability = 2.0×10^{-7} cm/sec

i = hydraulic gradient

$$= \frac{\text{head (cm)}}{\text{Ave. length of travel path (1/2 ave. sediment ht; cm)}}$$

$Q = (2.0 \times 10^{-7})(1.5/5.3)(887)$

$= (1.5/5.3)$

$= 5.02 \times 10^{-5}$ cm^3/sec

A = area of sediment-water interface across which discharge takes place (cm^2)

$= 887$ cm^2

B. Observed discharge

Volume (cm^3) of saturated sediment ultimately modified by fracturing (i.e., within 36 cm of final plate position)		Volume of water lost (cm^3)	Rate of discharge (Q, cm^3/sec)
(1) Initial volume (T = 0 hours)	(2) Final volume (T = 431 hours)	(1-2)	
10277	8431	1846	1.2×10^{-3}

to accommodate water displaced by deformation. No obvious increase in pore pressure was recorded by the transducers (mounted on the driven plate), but the distribution of the fracturing suggests that if excess pore pressures occurred, they may have been restricted to the nose of the overthrust block. This fracture pattern may also imply that the major shear fractures dipping toward the plate are the primary dewatering routes.

IMPLICATIONS OF EXPERIMENTAL RESULTS

Although the fabric observed in artificially deformed sediment (Morgenstern and Tchalenko, 1967; Tchalenko, 1968; Maltman, 1977; Berglund, 1980) is not directly comparable to the veins and fractures in naturally occurring subduction zone sediments (Carson and others, 1982; Cowan, 1983; Lundberg

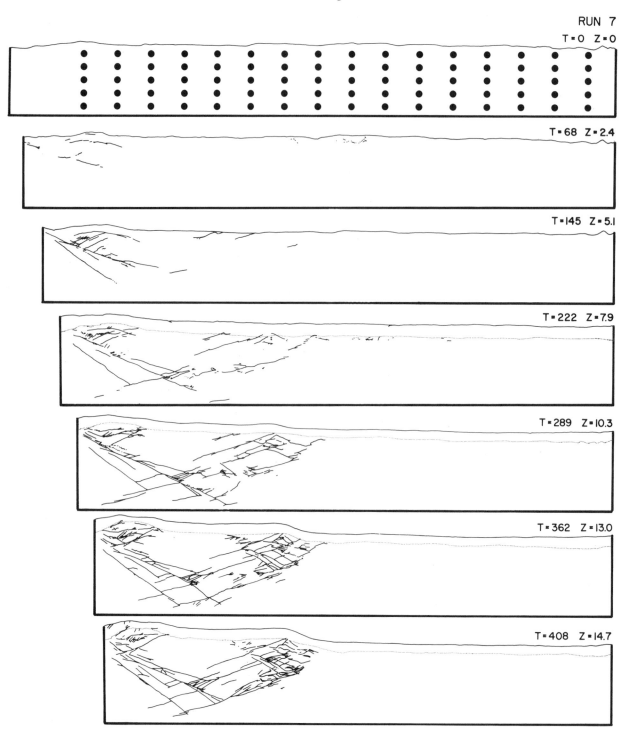

Figure 10. Structural development, Run 7, convergence rate = 10 μcm/sec. T = time in hours; Z = total displacement of driven plate in cm. Slurry was added *after* T = 145. Contact between slurry and preexisting sediment-water interface is indicated by dotted line at T $\geqslant$ 222.

and Moore, this volume), fracturing of sediment is a common response to dewatering under applied tectonic stress. The fractures may result from shearing induced by an inhomogeneous strain field, or from development of abnormal pore pressure generated by convergence (Ritger, 1985). Whatever their origin, the fracture zones apparently become both loci of water escape and zones of differential movement. The degree of fracturing, which may locally range from isolated faults to complex brecciation of the sediment mass, probably reflects the secondary porosity required to accommodate water loss under local overpressure.

It is unclear which mechanism is effective, but either the motion of the escaping fluids (which account for the loss of volume) or the fault motion, result in reorientation of platy particles, defining narrow zones of preferred orientation. These zones may presage (and perhaps control) the development of rudimentary fissility or spaced cleavage, which is common to accretionary zone deposits (Moore and Geigle, 1974; Moore and Karig, 1976; Carson, 1977; Moore, 1980; Carson and others, 1982; Lundberg and Moore, 1982, this volume; Cowan, 1983).

If water loss along fracture zones is retarded, abnormal pore pressures may develop under continued convergence, and hydrofracturing can be expected to result. The situation is most likely to occur at convergent margins, such as the present Japan Margin (Carson and others, 1982), where a thick blanket of low-permeability terrigenous sediment is deposited over the accretion zone. If the model is a reliable predictor, hydrofracturing may be concentrated above the primary, landward-dipping fault zones, near the noses of the overthrust blocks, rather than at great depths within the accretionary complex.

REFERENCES CITED

American Geological Institute, 1972, Glossary of Geology: Washington, D.C.

Bachman, S. B., 1978, Cretaceous and early Tertiary subduction complex, Mendocino coast, northern California: American Association of Petroleum Geologists Bulletin, v. 62, p. 2349.

Barnard, W. D., 1978, The Washington continental slope: Quaternary tectonics and sedimentation: Marine Geology, v. 27, p. 79–114.

Berglund, P. E., 1980, Phyllosilicate fabric in naturally deformed mudstone from the Washington continental slope, and comparison with experimentally induced fabric [M.S. thesis]: Bethlehem, Pennsylvania, Lehigh University, 127 p.

Blake, M. C., Jr., and Jones, D. L., 1974, Origin of Franciscan melanges in northern California, *in* Dott, R. H., Jr., and Shaver, R. H., eds., Modern and Ancient Geosynclinal Sedimentation: Society of Economic Paleontologists and Mineralogists Special Publication 19, p. 345–357.

Bouma, A. H., and Moore, J. C., 1975, Physical properties of deep-sea sediments from the Philippine Sea and Sea of Japan, *in* Initial Reports of the Deep Sea Drilling Project: Washington, D.C., U.S. Government Printing Office, v. 31, p. 535–568.

Bray, C. J., and Karig, D. E., 1985, Porosity of sediments in accretionary prisms and some implications for dewatering processes: Journal of Geophysical Research, v. 90, p. 768–778.

—— , 1986, Physical properties of sediments from the Nankai Trough, Deep Sea Drilling Project Leg 87A, Sites 582 and 583, *in* Kagami, H., Karig, D. E., and others, eds., Initial Reports of the Deep Sea Drilling Project: Washington, D.C., U.S. Government Printing Office, v. 87 (in press).

Carson, B., 1977, Tectonically induced deformation of deep-sea sediments off Washington and northern Oregon: Mechanical consolidation: Marine Geology, v. 24, p. 289–307.

Carson, B., Yuan, J. W., Myers, P. B., Jr., and Barnard, W. D., 1974, Initial deep-sea sediment deformation at the base of the Washington continental slope: A response to subduction: Geology, v. 2, p. 561–564.

Carson, B., and Bruns, T. R., 1980, Physical properties of sediments from the Japan trench margin and outer trench slope, Results from Deep Sea Drilling Project Legs 56 and 57, *in* Lee, M., and others, eds., Initial Reports of the Deep Sea Drilling Project: Washington, D.C., U.S. Government Printing Office, v. 56–57, pt. 2, p. 1187–1200.

Carson, B., von Huene, R., and Arthur, M., 1982, Small-scale deformation struc-

tures and physical properties related to convergence in Japan Trench slope sediments: Tectonics, v. 1, p. 277–302.

Chase, R. L., and Bunce, E. T., 1969, Underthrusting of the eastern margin of the Antilles by the floor of the western north Atlantic Ocean, and origin of the Barbados Ridge: Journal of Geophysical Research, v. 74, p. 1413–1420.

Connelly, W., 1978, Uyak Complex, Kodiak Islands, Alaska: A Cretaceous subduction complex: Geological Society of America Bulletin, v. 89, p. 755–769.

Cowan, D. S., 1983, Origin of "vein structure" in slope sediments on the inner slope of the mid-American trench off Guatemala, *in* von Huene, R., Aubuoin, J., and others, eds., Initial Reports of the Deep Sea Drilling Project: Washington, D.C., U.S. Government Printing Office, v. 67, p. 645–649.

Cowan, D. S., and Silling, R. M., 1978, A dynamic, scaled model of accretion at trenches and its implications for the tectonic evolution of subduction complexes: Journal of Geophysical Research, v. 83, p. 5389–5396.

Davis, D., Suppe, J., and Dahlen, F. A., 1983, Mechanics of fold and thrust belts and accretionary wedges: Journal of Geophysical Research, v. 88, p. 1153–1172.

Dehlinger, P., Couch, R. W., and Gemprele, M., 1968, Continental and oceanic structure from the Oregon coast westward across Juan de Fuca Ridge: Canadian Journal of Earth Sciences, v. 5, p. 1079–1090.

Folk, R. L., and Ward, W. C., 1957, Brazas River Bar, a study in the significance of grain-size parameters: Journal of Sedimentary Petrology, v. 27, p. 3–27.

Hafner, W., 1951, Stress distributions and faulting: Geological Society of America Bulletin, v. 62, p. 373–398.

Hubbert, M. K., 1951, Mechanical basis for certain familiar geologic structures: Geological Society of America Bulletin, v. 62, p. 355–372.

Karig, D. E., 1986, The framework of deformation in the Nankai Trough *in* Kagami, H., Karig, D. E., and others, eds., Initial Reports of the Deep Sea Drilling Project: Washington, D.C., U.S. Government Printing Office, v. 87 (in press).

Karig, D. E., and Sharman III, G. F., 1975, Accretion and subduction in trenches: Geological Society of America Bulletin, v. 86, p. 377–389.

Lundburg, N., and Moore, J. C., 1982, Structural features of the Middle America Trench slope off southern Mexico, *in* Moore, J. C., Watkins, J. S., and others, eds., Initial Results of the Deep Sea Drilling Project: Washington, D.C., U.S. Government Printing Office, v. 66, p. 793–814.

Maltman, A. J., 1977, Some microstructures of experimentally deformed argillaceous sediments: Tectonophysics, v. 39, p. 417–436.

Minster, J. B., and Jordan, T. H., 1978, Present day plate motions: Journal of Geophysical Research, v. 83, p. 5331–5354.

Molnar, P., and Sykes, L. R., 1969, Tectonics of the Caribbean and Middle America regions from focal mechanisms and seismicity: Geological Society of America Bulletin, v. 80, p. 1639–1684.

Moore, G. W., 1980, Slickensides in deep sea cores near the Japan trench, Deep Sea Drilling Project Leg 57, *in* Lee, M., and others, eds., Initial Reports of the Deep Sea Drilling Project: Washington, D.C., U.S. Government Printing Office, v. 56–57, pt. 2, p. 1107–1116.

Moore, J. C., 1973, Complex deformation of Cretaceous trench deposits Southwestern Alaska: Geological Society of America Bulletin, v. 84, p. 2005–2020.

Moore, J. C., and Geigle, J. E., 1974, Slaty cleavage: Incipient occurrences in the deep sea: Science, v. 183, no. 4124, p. 509–510.

Moore, J. C., and Karig, D. E., 1976, Sedimentology, structural geology, and tectonics of the Shikoku subduction zone, southwestern Japan: Geological Society of America Bulletin, v. 87, p. 1259–1268.

Morgenstern, N. R., and Tchalenko, J. S., 1967, Microscopic structures in Kaolin subjected to direct shear: Geotechnique, v. 17, p. 309–328.

Myers, P. V., Van Sciver, W. J., and Richards, A. F., 1974, Theory of nuclear transmission densitometry applied to sedimentology and geotechnology: Journal of Sedimentary Petrology, v. 44, p. 1010–1015.

Richards, A. F., Hirst, T. J., and Parks, J. M., 1974, Bulk density-water content relationship in marine silts and clays: Journal of Sedimentary Petrology, v. 44, p. 1004–1009.

Ritger, S. D., 1985, Origin of vein structures in the slope deposits of modern accretionary prisms: Geology, v. 13, p. 437–439.

Seely, D. R., 1977, The significance of landward vergence and oblique structural trends on trench inner slopes, *in* Talwani, M., and Pitman III, W. C., eds., Island Arcs, Deep Sea Trenches, and Back-Arc Basins: American Geophysical Union, Maurice Ewing Series 1, p. 187–198.

Seely, D. R., Vail, P. R., and Walton, G. G., 1974, Trench slope model, *in* Burk, C. A., and Drake, C. L., eds., The geology of Continental Margins: New York, Springer-Verlag, p. 249–260.

Shepard, L. E., and Bryant, W. R., 1983, Geotechnical properties of lower trench inner-slope sediments: Tectonophysics, v. 99, p. 279–312.

Shipboard Scientific Party, 1973, Site 175, *in* Kulm, L. D., von Huene, R., and others, eds., Initial Results of the Deep Sea Drilling Project: Washington, D.C., U.S. Government Printing Office, v. 18, p. 169–212.

Silver, E. A., 1972, Pleistocene tectonic accretion of the continental slope off Washington: Marine Geology, v. 13, p. 239–250.

Tchalenko, J. S., 1968, The evaluation of kink bands and the development of compression textures in sheared clays: Tectonophysics, v. 6, p. 159–174.

Trabant, P. K., Bryant, W. R., and Bouma, A. H., 1975, Consolidation characteristics of sediments from Leg 31 of the Deep Sea Drilling Project, *in* Karig, D. E., Ingle, J. C., Jr., and others, eds., Initial Reports of the Deep Sea Drilling Project: Washington, D.C., U.S. Government Printing Office, v. 31, p. 569–572.

Manuscript Accepted by the Society March 10, 1986

Geological Society of America
Memoir 166
1986

Deformation mechanism path diagrams for sediments undergoing lithification

R. J. Knipe
Department of Earth Sciences
The University
Leeds LS2 9JT, United Kingdom

ABSTRACT

The deformation mechanisms possible in sediments undergoing lithification and incorporation into accretionary wedges range from particulate flow, involving grain boundary sliding, to diffusion mass transfer, crystal plastic deformation, and fracture processes. A diagram illustrating these different deformation mechanisms in terms of the lithification state, the imposed strain rate, and the fluid pressure is introduced. Although at present qualitative, such diagrams do allow the rapid assessment of changes in the deformation processes that accompany lithification and aid the identification of the possible deformation mechanism paths associated with the production of preserved fabrics. The diagrams are particularly useful for illustrating the cyclic changes in fluid pressure, porosity, and strain rate that commonly accompany the evolution of fault rocks. The cyclic deformation mechanism path involved in the production of scaly fabrics associated with thrust faults in the Barbados accretionary wedge is used to illustrate the assessment of the time periods and strain rates associated with the different parts of the deformation mechanism path.

INTRODUCTION

The interpretation of sediment and rock microstructures, together with their geotechnical properties, is often complicated by the large range of environmental conditions and processes that have operated at some stage of the material's history. In addition, assessment of the deformation behavior of a sediment or rock is complicated by the fact that strength is not a simple function but is a time-dependent property, strongly influenced by the detailed history a sediment has experienced. This is particularly true of material in the top kilometer of a sediment pile where some of the most significant changes in lithification take place (Rieke and Chilingarian, 1974; Carson, 1977; Carson and Bruns, 1980; Karig, 1983, Shephard and Bryant, 1983, and Bray and Karig, 1985). Analyses of the wide range of deformation features recovered from this depth in Deep Sea Drilling Project (D.S.D.P.) cores from active margins (see papers by Arthur and others, 1980; Carson, 1982; Knipe, this volume; Lundberg and Moore, this volume; Moore and others, this volume; and Lucas and Moore, this volume) have already revealed some of the deformation processes under these conditions. In this paper I briefly re-

view the details of deformation mechanisms that may operate in sediments undergoing lithification and introduce some new diagrams (deformation mechanism path diagrams), which aid the assessment of deformation histories, together with the evolution of microstructure and geotechnical properties. This information is then incorporated into a discussion of the possible changes in the deformation processes and conditions associated with the generation of features recovered from D.S.D.P. cores. The paper serves as a basis and background to some of the more detailed microstructural studies reported in this volume.

DEFORMATION MECHANISMS

The range of deformation mechanisms that may operate in sediments and rocks include independent particulate flow, diffusional mass transfer, crystal plasticity, and cataclastic flow. Any of these mechanisms can give rise to ductile deformation, where the material remains coherent and continuous during straining. Each division includes a variety of separate mechanisms; these are outlined prior to the discussion of possible interactions between the processes in the context of active margin deformation.

Independent Particulate Flow

This intergranular mode of deformation, which can result in ductile flow on an aggregate scale, involves the sliding of grains past and over each other without any deformation of the particles and is controlled by shearing at grain boundaries or surfaces (Handin and others, 1963; Ashby and Verrall, 1977; Borradaile, 1981). The deformation by frictional grain boundary sliding is enhanced by low confining pressures and high fluid pressures and dominates the deformation of weak unlithified sediment (Kerr and Drew, 1968; Morrow and others, 1982; Maltman, 1984).

Deformation processes involving grain boundary sliding are some of the most difficult to identify in naturally deformed sediments and rocks. However, where no deformation of the individual grains has taken place, grain boundary sliding leading to independent particulate flow may offer the only possible mechanism of straining. (Borradaile, 1981).

Diffusional Mass Transfer (D.M.T.)

In this case, deformation is produced by the diffusion of material from sites of high stress to sites of low stress. Where the diffusion path is via a grain boundary fluid, the deformation is termed pressure solution. The deformation microstructures generated by this mechanism include evidence for the removal of material, for example the dissolution of fossils, and the deposition of material in pressure shadows (see reviews by McClay, 1977, and Rutter, 1983).

Crystal Plasticity

This is an intracrystalline deformation mechanism where strain is accommodated by the movement of defects (for example, dislocations) within crystals. The deformation is dominated by dislocation glide (slip confined to the glide planes) at low temperatures and by dislocation creep (involving the climb of dislocations out of their slip planes) at high temperatures and low strain rates (Nicholas and Poirier, 1976; White, 1976; Ashby and Verrall, 1977). The deformation microstructures developed during crystal plasticity include undulatory extinction, sub-grains, and dynamic recrystallization textures (Schmid, 1983).

Cataclastic Flow

Cataclastic flow involves a combination of grain boundary sliding, fracture (grain breakage), and volume changes. No attempt has been made here to review the details of the large number of fracture mechanisms that may be involved in cataclastic flow and faulting (see reviews by Mitchell, 1976; Sibson, 1977, 1983; Paterson, 1978; Logan, 1979; and Krantz, 1984).

Fracture processes are defined as those that induce a loss of cohesion and continuity of the specimen.

Where fracturing controls the grain boundary sliding, the deformation can be regarded as dependent particulate flow (see Borradaile, 1981). Note that elastic and/or plastic deformation of grains may pre-date the fracturing. The volume changes that may occur during cataclastic flow can be complex, with some pores being removed and others created. The volume changes experienced by individual pores need not be characteristic of the hand specimen scale volume changes. In partially cemented material, it is also possible for a volume reduction associated with a collapse of the sediment structure to take place during deformation (e.g., Bray and Karig, 1985), although a small volume increase associated with micro scale fracture sites, may occur before the overall collapse causes a volume reduction (see Knipe, this volume).

The exact contribution of each of the factors to a cataclastic flow event is a function of the sediment/rock characteristics (lithification state, porosity, permeability, composition, etc.), and imposed environmental conditions (fluid pressure, stress system, strain rate, etc.).

The flow diagram shown in Figure 1 reviews deformation behavior during cataclastic flow and emphasizes the potential cyclic changes in the relative importance of grain boundary sliding and fracture arising from different conditions. The diagram also highlights the role of fluid pressure and the difference between the initial deformation of lithified and unlithified material. A material is considered lithified when cohesion has increased by chemical (that is, cement growth) and/or mechanical (that is, compaction by grain rearrangement) processes so that intragranular deformation dominates (Maltman, 1984). In unlithified sediment, high or increasing fluid pressure enhances independent particulate flow and may induce failure and high strain rates by disaggregation, but in lithified material, high fluid pressures facilitate fracture, which may then induce independent particulate flow. Fluid pressure, porosity, and permeability are crucial interrelated factors in this situation, for an increase in the fluid pressure in a material with a low permeability may lead to a cushioning of deformation and a prevention of fracturing, (Lucas and Moore, this volume). The imposed strain-rate is separated from the fluid pressure in the diagram in order to emphasize the deformation arising from stress states when the fluid pressure is low. The strain rate will also influence the deformation behavior and increasing the strain rate will increase the likelihood of localized deformation and grain breakage.

DEFORMATION MECHANISM PATH DIAGRAMS

Analysis of deformation mechanisms in sediments undergoing accretion is complicated by rapid changes in the sediment properties through time. Lithification processes drastically change a sediment's response to a stress field. In addition, properties such as porosity, permeability, and lithification state are likely to change along with the strain rate and water pressure during a single deformation event. Changes in the strain rate and/or water

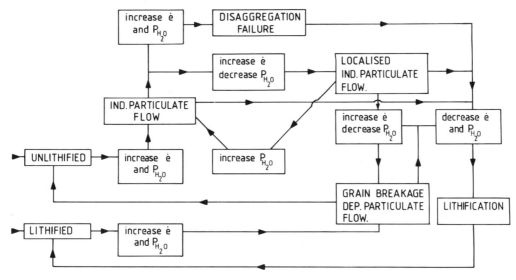

Figure 1. Flow diagram to illustrate deformation behavior during cataclastic flow. See text for detailed discussion.

pressure during a deformation event will induce the operation of a range of deformation mechanisms (each with different characteristic microstructural features). As an aid to the interpretation of the evolution of structures in sediments undergoing lithification, a diagram showing the possible distribution of deformation mechanism fields is shown in Figure 2. The axes chosen for the diagram are strain rate, lithification, and fluid pressure. For the purposes of this diagram, lithification increases as strength and cohesion of the aggregate increases due to compaction (by grain rearrangement) and cementation (growth of new grains that bind the aggregate). Increases in the lithification state induce an increase in strength and may be associated with decreases in porosity and permeability. In most cases, porosity may be used to quantify the lithification axis. Different sediments, which undergo lithification at different rates, will therefore move along the lithification axis at different rates. For example, cherts and limestones will move rapidly towards a lithified state compared to clays. Three lithification states can be separated: 1) unlithified states, where deformation by independent particulate flow is possible; 2) partially lithified states, where independent particulate flow is not possible without the deformation or fracturing of particles or the cement but the porosity is still significant; and 3) fully lithified states, where consolidation into a rock by compaction and cementation is essentially complete and the porosity low. It should be noted that in Figure 2 a loss of strength due to deformation-induced dissaggregation results in a reversal of the lithification process.

No absolute values have been placed on the diagram axes in order to allow its generalization to any sediment type, and although the relative position and orientations of the boundaries between deformation mechanism fields is correct, the exact location and orientation of boundaries will be different for sediments with different compositions and grain sizes. The diagram is meant only to provide a first-order attempt to assess the likely range of

processes and conditions that operate to produce final microstructures preserved in sediments and rocks and to aid the recognition of potential deformation histories. Future work combining microstructural observations of natural and experimental structures are needed before these diagrams can be fully quantified. In addition, the boundaries between volumes where one mechanism dominates are not necessarily fixed and are likely to "migrate" if deformation alters a feature (e.g. grain size) that controls the dominant mechanism.

As an introduction to these diagrams a brief background discussion on the location of the deformation mechanism fields is given, followed by a discussion on the use of these diagrams in the representation of deformation mechanism paths.

The exact location of the D.M.T. field, which dominates the low strain rate deformation of lithified material, will be controlled by composition and grain size. The D.M.T. field appears when material becomes lithified and expands as lithification proceeds and the strength of the material increases. At earlier stages of lithification, the dissolution of phases, although possible, is not likely to dominate over strain accommodation by independent particulate flow. At high strain rates, high lithification states, and low fluid pressures, the D.M.T. field is in contact with the crystal plastic field. At high fluid pressures and/or high strain rates the D.M.T. processes can give way to deformation by independent particulate flow, although transition into this latter field may be via a transient period of fracturing and disaggregation of the lithified material.

The exact size of the crystal plastic field will also depend on the composition and grain size of the material. This deformation mechanism field will be in contact with 1) the cataclastic flow and fracture field at high strain-rates and 2) the DMT field at low strain rates. The contact zone between the crystal plastic field or the D.M.T. field with either the cataclastic flow field or the inde-

R. J. Knipe

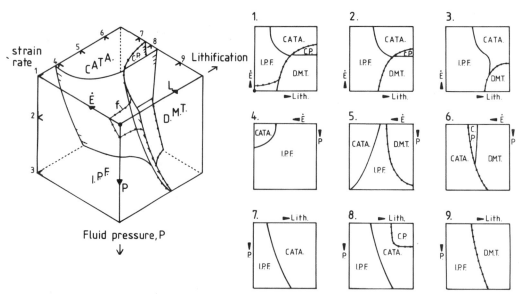

Figure 2. Generalized deformation mechanism path diagram showing the relative position of deformation mechanism fields on a strain rate (Ė), lithification (L), and fluid pressure (P) plot. These variables increase in magnitude in the directions of the arrow. The volumes on this diagram where deformation is dominated by cataclastic flow and fracturing (CATA.), independent particulate flow (I.P.F.), crystal plasticity (C.P.), and diffusion mass transfer (D.M.T.) are indicated. The surface (f) may be considered to represent a failure surface where deformation involves a loss of cohesion or continuity in the material. The distribution of deformation mechanisms fields in a number of slices [1-9] parallel to each pair of axes are also illustrated.

pendent particulate flow field can be considered to be part of a failure envelope. In unlithified sediments this failure may not involve any grain breakage but only a disaggration failure in the independent particulate flow field, induced by either stress (and thus a strain-rate) increase or a fluid pressure rise. The diagram also includes the approximate position of another transition from cataclastic flow, involving grain breakage to independent particulate flow where particles remain undeformed. The transition to independent particulate flow is enhanced by an increase in the fluid pressure or a decrease in the strain rate (Fig. 2).

The deformation mechanism diagram allows the rapid visualization and plotting of the potential changes in conditions and mechanisms that can take place during the production of a structural feature. That is, deformation mechanism paths may be plotted. The assessment of such paths is critical to the interpretation of preserved microstructures and geotechnical properties; Figure 2 emphasizes that the final microstructures sampled may contain elements generated during different parts of deformation history, and not just during the last stages of deformation. A few examples of the possible deformation mechanism paths involved in the generation of common structural features follow. These examples draw upon some of the microstructural studies presented in this volume.

Example 1

The microstructural analysis of vein structures found in

D.S.D.P. cores from the Japan Trench (Leg 57) by Knipe (this volume) outlines two possible models for the deformation history of these features. Both these models involve the disaggregation, displacement, and collapse of a partially lithified sediment, induced either by an increase in the fluid pressure (Model A) or by an increase in the stress without a high fluid pressure (Model B). These deformation histories can be plotted on the deformation mechanism path diagram (Fig. 3), which in addition to outlining the sequences involved also highlights the possible histories between these "end-member" paths where deformation mechanism paths involving a combination of increasing strain rate and high fluid pressures would plot. It is interesting to note that the porosity collapse that may be involved in the later stages of vein development (see Knipe this volume for details) may produce an increase in the final lithification state compared to the original (Fig. 3) although a transient dilational event is associated with the paths shown.

Example 2

A similar deformation mechanism path involving disaggregation displacement, and collapse can also be inferred from a fault zone from the Japan Trench described by Knipe (this volume). In this case, there is evidence that features produced by different deformation mechanism paths are preserved in the fault zone. Breccias indicative of fast strain rates are found near the hanging wall of the fault, while fabrics characteristic of slower

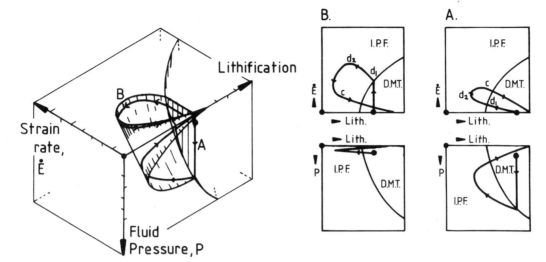

Figure 3. Deformation mechanism paths for vein structures preserved in D.S.D.P. cores. The two "end-member" paths (A and B) are shown in the block diagram and as seen in views either along the (P) fluid pressure axis or along the (E) strain rate axis. Model A involves an increase in the fluid pressure, while Model B illustrates an alternative deformation history where the fluid pressure does not increase. Both of the deformation mechanism paths include a strain rate increase after failure followed by a strain-rate decrease associated with the collapse of the deformation zone. Note in Model B a loss of fluid pressure following disaggregation may enhance hardening and collapse. The deformation mechanism path may involve a disaggregation d_1-displacement (d_2)-collapse (c) history. The surface linking these two paths contains the possible intermediate paths where a combination of the two "end-member" paths would plot.

strain rates are located in the fault zone near the footwall. These features are interpreted to indicate the preservation of features formed at different stages of the fault displacement history and at different slip rates. The more ductile deformation near the footwall may represent the slower, later stages of slip. A deformation mechanism path can be constructed for each part of the fault zone, which emphasizes the different histories experienced by different sections of the same fault (see Fig. 4 for details).

Example 3

The deformation mechanism path diagram is not limited to the analysis of structural features in partially lithified sediments, but is also a useful aid to the interpretation of deformation features generated in consolidated rocks. For example, Figure 5 outlines some possible deformation mechanism paths involved in the development of fault gouge. Each of the deformation mechanism paths shown is composed of cyclic changes in deformation mechanisms and conditions where there are also important changes in the details of each successive cycle. In the examples shown there is also a progressive delithification of the fault zone during deformation, which may eventually lead to the creation of a fine grained aggregate where independent particulate flow is possible. The examples shown outline some of the possible deformation mechanism paths involved in a progressive change from an initial discontinuous slip to more continuous displacement.

The three deformation mechanism paths illustrated have been chosen because they represent separate situations where fracturing during gouge development is dominated by different processes: A) fluid pressure changes, B) pre-failure crystal plasticity; and C) pre-failure elastic straining.

A) In the idealized sample of gouge development (Fig. 5a), when fluid pressure changes dominate the fracture process the repeated deformation cycles involve three stages: i) a strain rate increase following failure, ii) a decrease in the strain rate associated with the locking up of displacement surfaces because lithification increases as fluid pressure drops, and iii) increases in the fluid pressure leading to failure and the repetition of stage i. Stage iii may be preceded by fault sealing by the growth of a cement phase. This sequence of events has been discussed in detail by a number of authors, including Sibson (1977) and Stuart (1979).

B) Where fracture is controlled by the accumulation of plastic strain energy, the cyclic changes in the deformation mechanisms leading to the generation of a gouge differ from the last case and involve the following stages: i) a strain-rate increase following failure; ii) a decrease in strain-rate due to locking along displacement surfaces, and iii) work hardening and an increase in stress at locking sites, leading to failure and the repetition of stage i (Fig. 5b). Failure induced by the build-up of damage caused by crystal plastic deformation in material undergoing thrusting has recently been discussed by Knipe (1985).

C) Fracture processes preceded primarily by elastic strains are characteristic of high strain rate and low temperature defor-

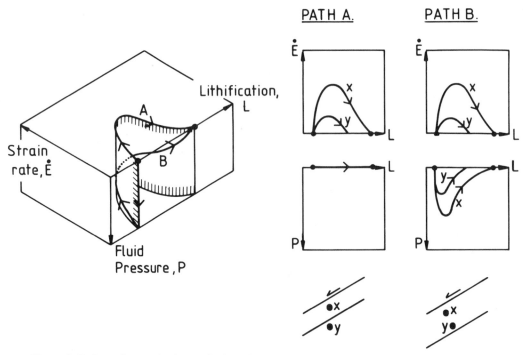

Figure 4. Deformation mechanism paths for a fault zone present in the Japan Trench. The diagram illustrates the surfaces on which the deformation mechanism paths lie for two points (X and Y) involved in the faulting. The sketches A and B locate the positions of these points in the fault zone. Point Y is only incorporated into the fault zone late in the history of displacement and thus experiences a different deformation mechanism path. That is, when point Y is experiencing its maximum strain-rate at time T_s, point X is already past its maximum strain-rate. The two surfaces are part of a family of surfaces along which points between X and Y would move. The surface L in this case represents the junction between lithified and unlithified material.

mations. In this case the deformation cycles involve i) an increase in the strain rate following fracture, ii) locking of slip surfaces and a decrease in the strain rate, and iii) a rapid build-up of stress, leading to fracture after elastic straining and a repeat of stage i (Fig. 5c).

It is emphasized that the examples chosen above are idealized cases—a natural gouge may include components of all of these deformation mechanism paths. One of the challenges to future fault rock analysis is the unravelling of the combination of the processes and conditions involved in producing specific gouges.

Example 4

An important aspect of the interpretation of microstructural features preserved in sediments and rocks is a consideration of the time and the strain rates associated with the generation of these features during the overall tectonic history. Such an assessment is critical because the microstructure preserved may contain elements that are pre-, syn-, or post-tectonic. An evaluation of the possible modification mechanisms of the early structures, either by later deformation processes or by post-tectonic processes, is particularly important. For example, in partially lithified sediments the continuation of the lithification processes may obscure

the early deformation features. The fourth example of a deformation mechanism path considered here is from the North Barbados Ridge complex; this is one of the few examples of a location where it is possible to outline both the time period involved in the different stages of the sediment history and the deformation mechanism path.

The work of Chase and Bunce (1969), Westbrook and others (1973), Speed and Larue (1982), and Westbrook (1982), together with the D.S.D.P. results from Leg 78A (Biju-Duval, Moore, and others, 1984; Moore, 1984) provide some exceptional geological constraints for estimating time markers in the deformation history. The geometry of the thrust faults associated with the accretion of sediments in this area and their displacements has been assessed by Moore (1984). By assuming a probable range of displacement rates on the faults, the active displacement time period can be estimated. This allows some insight into the possible time involved in the deformation mechanism paths associated with the fabrics located along these faults and a comparison of the histories of sediment on different faults.

Figure 6a shows the cross section presented in the tectonic synthesis of Moore (1984). Two tectonic slices (slice 1 and 2) can be identified; each has an internal array of imbricate faults. Using this geometry the total displacement on these faults is approxi-

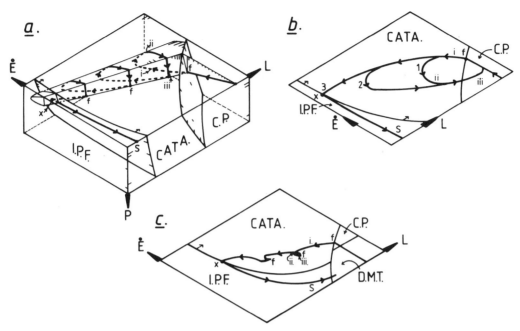

Figure 5. Examples of some possible deformation mechanism paths involved in cataclastic flow. a) illustrates the evolution of repeated cycles of deformation involving changes in fluid pressure. In this case the deformation mechanism path after failure at (f) moves along a surface that approximates to a cone. b) illustrates a situation where the cycles of deformation involve crystal plastic deformation before failure. c) shows one possible path that may arise from deformation where failure is preceded by rapid elastic deformation. Only a small number of cycles are shown in each case and the stages i–iii of each cycle are described in detail in the text. X marks the location where deformation by independent particulate flow may occur. The last part of the history (S) of each example shown represents the final decrease in the strain rate when displacement dies out and fault-sealing processes may take place. It is emphasized that many natural cataclastic rocks may involve a combination of the paths separated here.

mately 1.48 km. The fault array at the base of slice 1 accounts for a displacement of 220 m, and the fault (F2) at the base of slice 2 (located at sub-bottom depths of 263 m and 276 m in Hole 541) has a displacement of 1.26 km. The fault (F2.1) encountered at a sub-bottom depth of 172 m in Hole 541 within slice 2 has a displacement of 77 m, assuming a throw of approximately 20 m and an average dip of 15° (see Moore and others, 1984). Assuming that the convergence rate range of between 0.7 km/Ma (Moore and others, 1984) and 5.0 km/Ma (Molnar and Sykes, 1969) represents the possible displacement rate ranges, then the active displacement period on the fault at the base of slice 1 is between 4.4×10^4 and 3.2×10^5 yrs, and the displacement time on the faults within slice 2 is between 2.5×10^5 and 1.8×10^6 yrs.

The displacement period on fault F2.1 within slice 2 is then between 1.5×10^4 and 1.1×10^5 yrs. The faulting sequence in the section appears to have included propagation oceanward; that is, the displacement on the highest fault (F2.1) was earliest and displacement on the fault at the base of slice 1 was latest. Thus, for a sediment of early Miocene age (5.1 Ma) now located on the fault (2.2) at the base of slice 2, between 5 and 33% of its history has been involved in deformation during displacement on this fault. In addition, for a time period equal to approximately 20%

of the deformation period, the sediment has been undergoing lithification as part of the hanging wall of the fault at the base of slice 1. The history of a sediment of the same age located on-fault (F2.1) within slice 2 is different in that only between 0.3 and 2% of its history is associated with displacement, and for approximately 18 times this period it was involved in post-deformation processes such as continued lithification.

The type of deformation mechanism path experienced by the sediment located on the fault at the base of slice 2 can be identified from the microstructural study of scaly fabric characteristic of this zone by Moore and others (this volume). These authors have suggested that a sequence of failure-displacement and slip surface hardening is involved in the generation of this fabric. This sequence is similar to the disaggregation-displacement and collapse sequence thought to have operated during the development of veins and faults in partially lithified sediment (Knipe, this volume). A possible deformation mechanism path for the scaly fabric incorporating the time periods inferred from above is shown in Figure 6b and c. It is likely that during the displacement there was a large number of repeated cyclic events (Moore and others, this volume), each with a deformation mechanism path similar to the one illustrated.

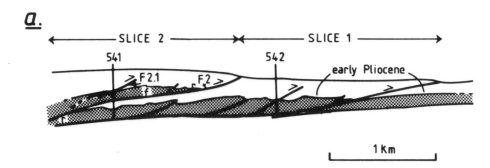

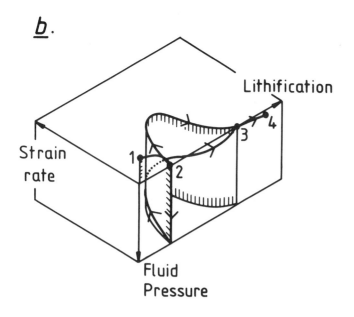

STAGE	Ḋ = 0·7km/Ma	Ḋ = 5·0km/Ma
1 - 2	$2·9 \times 10^6$ yrs.	$4·8 \times 10^5$ yrs.
2 ↔ 3	$1·8 \times 10^6$ yrs.	$2·5 \times 10^5$ yrs.
3 - 4	$3·6 \times 10^5$ yrs	$5·0 \times 10^4$ yrs.

DEF.	Ḋ = 0·7km/Ma	Ḋ = 5·0km/Ma
$\dot{\gamma}_{homog}$	$4·4 \times 10^{-13}$ /sec	$3·2 \times 10^{-12}$ /sec
T_{homog}	$1·8 \times 10^6$ yrs	$2·5 \times 10^5$ yrs
$\dot{\gamma}_{loc}$	$4·9 \times 10^{-12}$ /sec	$3·5 \times 10^{-11}$ /sec
T_{loc}	38 yr	5·3 yr

Figure 6. An example of a deformation mechanism path from the North Barbados Ridge, where it is possible to estimate the time period involved in different stages of sedimentary history. a) illustrates a geological cross-section (from Moore, 1984) with the tectonic slices and faults present marked. b) shows a possible deformation mechanism path for the scaly fabric developed at the base of slice 2 along fault F2. The stages involved include Stage 1-2, an increase in the fluid pressure leading to failure; Stage 2-3, a period of increasing and then decreasing strain rate, during which the porosity collapses by particulate flow; and Stage 3-4, during which post-deformation lithification takes place. c) lists the time periods involved in these stages for different displacement rates (D). Note that the time periods for Stage 2-3 listed are for the total deformation time on the fault zone, assuming homogeneous deformation (shear) in the fault zones. An estimate of the strain rates for homogeneous deformation ($\dot{\gamma}_{homog}$) and the associated time period (T_{homog}) as well as the strain rates ($\dot{\gamma}_{loc}$) and time periods (T_{loc}) associated with the creation of individual localized slip surfaces.

Given that the fault zone 2.2 is approximately 50 m thick (see Moore and others, 1984), it is also possible to estimate the strain rate in this zone. For a displacement rate of 0.7 mm/yr and assuming a homogeneous shear, the shear strain rate is 4.5×10^{-13} sec^{-1} while it is 3.15×10^{-12} sec^{-1} for a displacement rate of 5 mm/yr. If the deformation was, as is likely, heterogenous and composed of sequential movements on zones 100 μm wide and some 1 mm apart, the estimated strain rate is increased to between 4.9×10^{-12} sec^{-1} and 3.5×10^{-11} sec^{-1} for the dis-

placement rates used above. The time period for each deformation event would have been between ~5 and 38 years (see Fig. 6). Although both the time markers and the deformation mechanism path outlined above are at best only approximate, the analysis does provide an important framework for the interpretation of the sediment's history and thus its preserved microstructures.

The above calculations do not highlight the importance of the fault geometries in the evolution of sediment geotechnical properties and microstructures. The ramp-flat geometry characteristic of accretionary wedges has an important influence on the sediment burial history because the rate of burial is dependent upon the geometry of the ramps. Burial by a hanging wall ramp creates the fastest burial rate, since this has the largest wedge angle; burial by a hanging wall flat has the lowest. Changes in the burial rate will affect the rate of change of porosity, permeability, and consolidation processes. Such changes are likely to affect dewatering processes and lead to changes in water pressure and deformation behavior. For example, the movement of a hanging wall ramp over a sediment previously undergoing lithification and dewatering under a hanging wall flat will induce a more rapid increase in the load. This may promote changes in compaction, porosity, and permeability and possibly lead to a rapid increase in water pressure and/or dewatering. The geometry shown in Figure 6 for the fault at the base of slice 2 in the Barbados example indicates that the burial rate experienced by the sediment below F2 in Hole 541 decreased by a factor of between 4 and 5 during emplacement of slice 2, because of the change from burial by a hanging wall ramp to burial by a hanging wall flat. The influence of dewatering "bursts" initiated by changes in the burial rate during the emplacement of thrust sheets with complex geometries may be an additional factor in the creation of mud volcanoes described by Westbrook and Smith (1983).

CONCLUSIONS

The deformation mechanism path diagrams presented in this paper are a first-order attempt to assess the evolution of microstructures and geotechnical properties of sediments undergoing lithification. Future research integrating microstructural and experimental information is required before quantification of the diagrams is possible. However, the diagrams do provide a rapid visualization of possible deformation mechanism paths and they allow investigation of the changes in sediment properties during their history. It is hoped that future studies will be able to assign specific values of time, porosity, permeability, and depth to points on the deformation mechanism paths, which will then provide a further aid to the assessment of sediment histories and deformation behavior as well as aid the integration of geotechnical properties into structural analysis.

ACKNOWLEDGMENTS

The author acknowledges helpful discussions with Drs. Casey Moore, Neil Lundberg, Ed Beutner, Alex Maltman, Chyuen Wang, Darrell Cowen, and Jerry Leggett, as well as colleagues at Leeds. The work was part of National Science Foundation-sponsored research grants (Nos. OCE 8110394 and OCE 8315836) which are gratefully acknowledged.

REFERENCES CITED

Arthur, M. A., Carson, B., and von Huene, R., 1980, Initial tectonic deformation of hemipelagic sediments at the leading edge of the Japan convergent margin, *in* Langseth, M., Okada, H., and others, eds., Initial Reports of the Deep Sea Drilling Project: Washington, D.C., U.S. Government Printing Office, v. 56–57, p. 569–713.

Ashby, M. F., and Verrall, R. A., 1977, Micromechanisms of flow and fracture and their relevance to the rheology of the upper mantle: Philosophical Transactions of the Royal Society of London, Series A, v. 288, p. 59–95.

Biju-Duval, B., Moore, J. C., and others, 1984, Initial Reports of the Deep Sea Drilling Project: Washington, D.C., U.S. Government Printing Office, v. 78A, 621 p.

Borradaile, G. J., 1981, Particulate flow of rock and the formation of cleavage: Tectonophysics, v. 72, p. 305–321.

Bray, C. J., and Karig, D. E., 1985, Porosity of sediments in accretionary prisms and some implications for dewatering processes: Journal of Geophysical Research, v. 90, p. 768–778.

Carson, B., 1977, Tectonically induced deformation of deep-sea sediments off Washington and northern Oregon: Mechanical consolidation: Marine Geology, v. 24, p. 289–307.

Carson, B., and Bruns, T. R., 1980, Physical properties of sediments from the Japan Trench Margin and outer Trench Slope, Results from Deep Sea Drilling Project Legs 56-57, *in* Langseth, M., Okada, H., and others, eds., Initial reports of the Deep Sea Drilling Project: Washington, D.C., U.S. Government Printing Office, v. 56-57, p. 1187–1200.

Chase, R. L., and Bunce, E. T., 1969, Underthrusting of the eastern margin of the Antilles by the floor of the western North Atlantic Ocean, and the origin of the Barbados Ridge: Journal of Geophysical Research, v. 74, p. 1413–1420.

Handin, J., Hager, R. V., Friedman, M., and Feather, J. N., 1963, Experimental deformation of sedimentary rocks under confining pressure: Pore pressure effects: American Association of Petroleum Geologists Bulletin, v. 47, p. 717–755.

Karig, D. E., 1983, Deformation in the Forearc: Implications for mountain belts, *in* Hus̈, K., Mountain Building Processes: Academic Press, p. 59–71.

Kerr, P. F., and Drew, I. M., 1968, Quick-clay slides in the U.S.A.: Engineering Geology, v. 2, p. 215–238.

Knipe, R. J., 1985, Footwall geometry and the rheology of thrust sheets: Journal of Structural Geology, v. 7, p. 1–11.

Krantz, R. L., 1984, Microcracks in rocks: A review: Tectonophysics, v. 100, p. 449–480.

Logan, J. M., 1979, Brittle phenomena: Reviews in Geophysics and Space Physics, v. 17, p. 1121–1132.

McClay, K., 1977, Pressure solution and Coble creep in rocks: A review: Journal of the Geological Society of London, v. 134, p. 57–70.

Maltman, A. J., 1984, On the term "soft-sediment deformation": Journal of Structural Geology, v. 6, p. 589–593.

Morrow, C. A., Shi, L. Q., and Byerlee, J. D., 1982, Strain hardening and strength of clay-rich fault gouges: Journal of Geophysical Research, v. 87, p. 6771–6780.

Mitchell, J. K., 1976, Fundamentals of soil behavior: New York, John Wiley and Sons, Inc., 422 p.

Molnar, P., and Sykes, L. R., 1969, Tectonics of the Caribbean and Middle America regons from focal mechanism and seismicity: Geological Society of America Bulletin, v. 80, p. 1639–1684.

Moore, J. C., 1984, Tectonic synthesis, Deep Sea Drilling Project Leg 78A: Structural evolution of offscraped and underthrust sediment, Northern Barbados Ridge complex, *in* Biju-Duval, B., Moore, J. C., and others, eds., Initial Reports of the Deep Sea Drilling Project: Washington, D.C., U.S. Government Printing Office, v. 78, p. 601–621.

Nicholas, A., and Poirier, J. P., 1976, Crystalline plasticity and solid state flow in metamorphic rocks: New York, John Wiley and Sons, Inc., 444 p.

Paterson, M. S., 1978, Experimental Rock Deformation: The brittle field: Berlin, Springer-Verlag, 254 p.

Rieke, H. H., and Chilingarian, G. V., 1974, Compaction of Argillaceous Sediments: New York, Elsevier, 424 p.

Rutter, E. H., 1983, Pressure solution in nature, theory and experiment: Journal of the Geological Society of London, v. 140, p. 725–741.

Schmid, S. M., 1983, Microfabric studies as indicators of deformation mechanisms and flow laws operative during mountain building *in* Hsü, K., Mountain Building Processes: Academic Press, p. 95–110.

Shephard, L. E., and Bryant, W. R., 1983, Geotechnical properties of lower trench inner slope sediments: Tectonophysics, v. 99, p. 279–312.

Sibson, R. H., 1977, Fault rocks and fault mechanisms: Journal of the Geological Society of London, v. 133, p. 191–213.

—— , 1983, Continental fault structure and the shallow earthquake source: Journal of the Geological Society of London, v. 140, p. 741–768.

Sibson, R. H., McMoore, J., and Rankin, A. H., 1975, Seismic pumping—A hydrothermal fluid transport mechanism: Journal of the Geological Society of London, v. 131, p. 653–659.

Speed, R. C., and Larue, D. K., 1982, Barbados: Architecture and implications for accretion: Journal of Geophysical Research, v. 87, p. 3633–3643.

Stuart, W. D., 1979, Aging and strain softening model for episodic faulting: Tectonophysics, v. 52, p. 613–626.

Westbrook, G. K., 1982, The Barbados Ridge Complex: Tectonics of a mature forearc system, *in* Leggett, J. K., Trench-Forearc Geology, Geological Society of London Special Publication, p. 275–290.

Westbrook, G. K., Bott, M.P.H., and Peacock, J. H., 1973, Lesser Antilles subduction zone in the vicinity of Barbados: Nature Physical Science, v. 244, p. 118–120.

Westbrook, G. K., and Smith, M. J., 1983, Long decollements and mud volcanoes; Evidence from the Barbados Ridge Complex for the role of high pore-fluid pressure in the development of an accretionary complex: Geology, v. 11, p. 279–283.

White, S., 1976. The effects of strain on the microstructures, fabrics and deformation mechanisms in quartzites. Philosophical Transactions of the Royal Society of London, Series A, v. 238, p. 69–86.

MANUSCRIPT ACCEPTED BY THE SOCIETY MARCH 10, 1986.

Typeset by WESType Publishing Services, Inc., Boulder, Colorado
Printed in U.S.A. by Malloy Lithographing, Inc., Ann Arbor, Michigan